Everynight Life

A book in the series

Latin America Otherwise: Languages, Empires, Nations

Series editors: Walter D. Mignolo, Duke University

Irene Silverblatt, Duke University

Sonia Saldívar-Hull, University of California at Los Angeles

Everynight Life

Culture and Dance in Latin/o America

Celeste Fraser Delgado and José Esteban Muñoz, editors

Duke University Press Durham and London

1997

© 1997 Duke University Press

All rights reserved

Printed in the United States of America on acid-free paper ∞

Typeset in Palatino with Gill Sans display by Keystone Typesetting, Inc.

Library of Congress Cataloging-in-Publication Data

Everynight life : culture and dance in Latin / o America / edited by
Celeste Fraser Delgado and José Esteban Muñoz.

p. cm. — (Latin America otherwise)

Includes bibliographical references and index.

ISBN 0-8223-1926-8 (cloth : alk. paper). — ISBN 0-8223-1919-5
(pbk. : alk. paper)

1. Dance—Latin America—History. 2. Dance—Latin America—
Sociological aspects. 3. Dance—Political aspects—Latin America.

I. Delgado, Celeste Fraser. II. Muñoz, José Esteban. III. Series.

GV1626.E84   1997

792.8'098—dc20   96-43796   CIP

Para Ramón Torres

Seguimos trazando los pasos que tu bailaste en este mundo.

We are still tracing the steps you danced in this world.

Contents

About the Series

Latin America Otherwise: Languages, Empires, Nations is a critical series. It aims to explore the emergence and consequences of concepts used to define "Latin America" while at the same time exploring the broad interplay of political, economic, and cultural practices that have shaped Latin American worlds. Latin America, at the crossroads of competing imperial designs and local responses, has been construed as a geocultural and geopolitical entity since the nineteenth century. This series provides a starting point to redefine Latin America as a configuration of political, linguistic, cultural, and economic intersections that demand a continuous reappraisal of the role of the Americas in history, and of the ongoing process of globalization and the relocation of people and cultures that have characterized Latin America's experience. *Latin America Otherwise: Languages, Empires, Nations* is a forum that confronts established geocultural constructions, that rethinks area studies and disciplinary boundaries, that assesses convictions of the academy and of public policy, and that, correspondingly, demands that the practices through which we produce knowledge and understanding, about and from Latin America be subject to rigorous and critical scrutiny.

Everynight Life is a collection of critical pieces that makes us rethink "Latin America," disciplinary boundaries, and methodologies. The traditional "Latin America"—the essentialized entity of imperial origin—is replaced with a dynamic view *from* Latin America. "Latin America" becomes a field of geopolitical, cultural, and economic relations that span the globe and whose transformations in history continuously redefine the configuration of the Americas. Latin America is in Europe; Latin America is in the United States. *Everynight Life* is a foray into the "politics of location."

The contributors to this volume construct dialogues: between worldwide forces and regional configurations; between processes re-imagining (Latin) America and the local experiences that gave rise to them—at the North Carolina conference that attracted musicians, dancers, scholars, and students from Guatemala, Peru, the Caribbean, Miami, Cleveland, and other places in America; and above all between the colonial legacies that engendered the Latino/as communities in the United States, thereby creating conditions to manufacture "loci of enunciation." Contemporary imperial restructurations and the massive migrations they spawned force us to reconsider the European imagination of (Latin) America within these novel global configurations. Moreover, this volume presents us with inventive methodologies: the configurations of America are expressed through innovative dialectics confronting the text with dance and bodies in motion. *Everynight Life* makes enormous contributions to a revisioning of "Latin" America and opens up new avenues toward the future of (Latin) American cultural studies.

Everynight Life

In the 1977 film *Valentino,* Rudolf Nureyev dances the tango
with his partner (Christine Carlson) in a sequence for *The Four Horsemen of
the Apocalypse* (Rex Ingram, 1921). (*Courtesy of the Kobal Collection*)

Preface

Politics in Motion

Celeste Fraser Delgado

Best Bets

January 16–23

Dance: Oh boy! A conference at Duke and UNC, sponsored by the universities' joint program in Latin American Studies! Yawn, yawn. But wait—this is not just another gathering of overserious academics. This is a conference about dancing. Latin American dancing. Sure, there will be some sociopolitical analysis of the lambada, salsa and merengue— four conference sessions on Friday and Saturday, free of charge. But the lectures have titles like "I Came, I Saw, I Conga'd." And the conference opens Thursday (Jan. 24) at 8 with a performance by Los Pampas, an Argentine duo that taps and twirls expertly through indigenous Argentine dances (Nelson Music Room, East Duke Building, Duke, $8). And it finishes with a flourish Saturday (Jan. 26) at 8 with Feel the Rhythm!, where dance instructors will teach you to tango and do other Latin American dances until 9, when dancing begins to the authentic sounds of Los Tramperos del Norte and Combo Latino (American Legion Post #6, Legion Rd, Chapel Hill; $5).—Bob Moser

A "Best Bet." That's what the left-leaning newsweekly of North Carolina's Triangle declared the "Politics in Motion" conference that inspired this anthology. This heady pronouncement, reprinted above, replays the tensions that animate the essays collected here: between "lectures" and "twirls"; between "taps" and "yawns"; between the mind and the body—or, as summed up by the *Independent*, between "overserious[ness]" (read "academics") and "dance" (read "fun"). Bob Moser's mock surprise at the coupling of academia and excitement rests on the assurance that even such crowd pleasers as "the lambada, salsa and merengue" would require rescue from deadly dull "sociopolitical analysis" by a very lively sense of humor. Enter Gustavo Pérez Firmat's

"I Came, I Saw, I Conga'd." That conga, the dance, seems out of place in the space of the conqueror is as suggestive as it is amusing. This laughable linguistic overthrow—like the *Independent*'s conjunction "And" that links the daytime "sociopolitical analysis" to the nighttime performance of "indigenous Argentine dances" and the dance-until-dawn "Feel [of] the Rhythm!"—promises a collusion of dance, theory, and rebellion.

Everynight Life follows the conference "Politics in Motion" in exploring the historical and potential function of dance in social struggle in Latin/o America. Translating the motion of bodies into speech, the gestures of dance into a kind of political or theoretical grammar, we risk what contributor Mayra Santos Febres has called, in "Salsa as Translocation," "complicity in the process of taming culture." We trip over our tongues. What would it mean to comprehend the dance of consciousness? What do we gain in translating this consciousness into words? What do we lose? We could be dancing right now. Instead, we join our contributors in wielding rhythm and dance in Latin/o America—rumba, mambo, salsa, tango, samba, norteño—"as a theoretical device that presents alternative methods of analysis and cognition." From the varying perspectives of literary, cultural, dance, and performance studies, we take dance as a privileged site in the production of cultural identities, national boundaries, and subversive practice in Latin/o America.

In theorizing dance and culture, we cannot evade the implications of our own location. The peripheral relation of Latin to North America has profoundly influenced the material conditions that produced *Everynight Life,* as well as its point of view. Presented in English, sponsored by the Mello Foundation and two North American universities, published by a North American publisher, *Everynight Life* presents Latin dance from a decidedly northern perspective. This journey north provides one more gesture in the continuous movement of cultural contact and conflict initiated by the first encounters of the indigenous people with the European conquerors and the enslaved Africans transported to the New World. It is not surprising that as editors and organizers of this endeavor we "come from" Miami, currently considered by many to be the "capital" of contemporary Latin/o music and the hub for a new, transcontinental Latin/o elite. Nor is it surprising, given the bicultural approach to this project, that Celeste was born in Cleveland and José in Havana. The location of "Politics in Motion," the event, as the site of our professional existence may have more interesting implications.

Staged in North Carolina, an old plantation state that now has the fifth fastest-growing Hispanic population in the United States, the conference enacted the dynamics of culture contact that many of the theoretical sessions set out to explore. Mexican dance and music, such as norteño, had already found a permanent home in the cantinas of the northern counties where cucumber and tobacco farms employ large numbers of Mexican migrant and, increasingly, H-2 workers. The universities, hospitals, and high-tech enterprise of the Triangle attract a growing number of Latin American professionals, creating semi-permanent venues for salsa, merengue, and cumbia on special "Latin American" nights in local restaurants and hotels. The complex of economic crises and political persecution that contributes to this immigration of peoples and migration of cultural forms made available the services of the musicians, dancers, and dance instructors and to a certain extent determined the participation of many of the conference speakers and organizers.

We had a difficult time contracting Los Tramperos del Norte, because the bandleader works in the fields in Selma, North Carolina, where he lives without a telephone on the farm of his daytime employer and where the band plays norteño every weekend night in a Selma bar. Even before its importation to North Carolina, playing norteño meant playing the music of the cross-cultural experience of migrating workers, having evolved along the Mexico-Texas border during the 1930s. Originating from the dance music of the rural people of Mexico and migrants from Czechoslovakia and Hungary, norteño joins a tradition of duet singing and the use of the bajo sexto with the button accordion. Legend attributes the use of the accordion to the purchase of these instruments from pawn shops, abandoned there by the upper classes who fled the country during the Mexican Revolution. Called Los Tramperos or "the trappers" after their famed ability to trap listeners and convert them into dancers, this extremely talented group played to a tough crowd at American Legion Post #5 in Chapel Hill.[1]

While the promise of dance instruction at 8 P.M. had lured several hundred curious North Americans for whom the lambada had served as the most recent illusion in the U.S. media phantasmagoria of "hot!"

"sexy!" Latin dances, the cosmopolitan Latin American students and professionals living in the Triangle came expecting "authentic sounds" akin to those of the urbane international megaband Juan Luis Guerra and 4-40. The two Venezuelan dance instructors could not have prepared the unexpected crowd of four hundred eager would-be students of Latin dance for the quick regional norteño hop, even if they had known how. And no one cared. The salseros stood waiting on the sidelines. Younger North Americans swung back and forth. Older North Americans did a version of the polka. The friends of Los Tramperos danced norteño. A ninety-year-old North American woman whose children and grand-children had dropped her off at each conference event bent over her feet on the side, lacing her ballet slippers.

The freestyle response by those unfamiliar with the regional dance form norteño contrasted sharply with the steps executed to the interna-tional sound of Combo Latino, a seven-piece group based in Charlotte, North Carolina, with members from Cuba, Guatemala, and Peru. Con-fronted with an overwhelming turnout, the dance instructors hired by the conference committee enlisted dancing theoreticians, who jumped on top of the American Legion picnic tables to help convey a basic salsa step and merengue twirl and finally inspire the students to form a shaky conga line. The arrival of more practiced dancers later in the evening shook this lineup further, revealing an even more complicated process of the embodiment of identity. A survey of the vast dance floor at any given moment during a Combo Latino set revealed accomplished sambistas and salseros, cumbistas and merengueros, working through and against the predominant rhythm as their bodily memory dictated.

The generic noncoincidence of the musicians' rhythmic beats and the dancers' rhythmic movements mark out a loose approximation of na-tional or cosmopolitan identity manifest in a local dance idiom and syn-chronous with an underlying Latin American identity manifest in West African–inspired polyrhythms. The nonsynchronous rhythm of norteño jammed this Pan-Afro-Latin impulse, requiring dancers to acquire a re-gionally specific dance style in order to partake in the cultural practice of the dancing community or to ignore that community altogether in draw-ing movement from an unrelated idiom in their own repertoire. Had we been ready or willing to repeat this event over time with the same musi-cal groups and the same community of dancers, this community would likely have come to define itself by overlaying these rhythms and rhythmic movements once again, further hybridizing the forms to create something like an Afro-Latin norteño characteristic of the Triangle of North Carolina.

It is hard to imagine the social and political conditions that would forge a lasting community characterized by such a dance. While the euphoric moment of the conference did produce the conditions of possibility for an effervescent Afro-Latin norteño, we contend that this euphoria would have to include a sense of urgency—the necessity of survival—for a new dance form to cohere. Rather than develop a new form, the conference participants enacted the pedagogical role inherent within the rumba, mambo, salsa, and merengue. In shifting from speakers to dance instructors, the participants reenacted this pedagogy not only through didactic recitation but more profoundly through the performance of the historical crossings and double-crossings of continents and oceans contained within the collective rhythm and dance memory of Latino communities. The theoreticians/dance instructors participated in the fundamental rite of Latin rhythms: marking the ephemeral sites of Latin/o American history with the magnificence of socially significant motion and sound.

This undertaking would not have been possible without the help and active support of many people and institutions. Natalie Hartmann and Sharon Mújica played a key role in helping us organize the conference. Martha Nelson shared her expertise and helped us locate performers. Deborah Jakubs, Adam Versanyi, and Monica Rector enriched the conference with their critical contributions. Ariel Dorfman gave much-needed support at the initial stage of the proposal. We would also like to thank the Duke-UNC Joint Program in Latin American Studies, the Mellon Foundation, the Duke Museum of Art, and the Duke University departments of literature and film studies for their important material support. For good advice from beginning to end, we would like to thank Cathy N. Davidson. For astute suggestions on the manuscript we would like to thank our readers from Duke University Press—especially that reader most attuned to our omissions. We would like to thank our contributors for bearing with us—especially those who made helpful suggestions after participating in the conference. Our gratitude goes to Berta Jottar and Susan Searls, who devoted their time and energy to setting the details of the manuscript right. Most of all, we would like to thank Ken Wissoker for his unflagging persistence in assuring that we pursue this project through its many vicissitudes.

Notes

Please note that all translations in this volume are by the author (or the chapter's translator), unless otherwise noted.

1. We are indebted to folklorist Martha Nelson from the University of North Carolina at Chapel Hill for introducing us to Los Tramperos del Norte.

Rebellions of Everynight Life

Celeste Fraser Delgado and José Esteban Muñoz

Tonight, at the Palace of Happiness, Federico presents the Big Dance with Two Orchestras: Noro Morales, the famous Puerto Rican pianist, and Ricardo Rico with his Authentic Dominicans, each playing Merengues, Mambos, Boleros, and Cha cha cha.

Leaning out of the window of el Palacio de la Alegría (the Palace of Happiness) in Brooklyn, Federico Pagani—the famous promoter who created the legendary dance hall, the Palladium—exchanges a conspiratorial glance with a tuxedoed man in the street. Looking past tonight's menu of merengue, mambo, bolero, and cha cha cha, Pagani might be inviting his companion to join in the dance. Alternatively, Pagani might be calling his comrade to a meeting of the Puerto Rican Voter's Association, whose members gathered in the dance hall when the orchestras were silent. On the back of this photograph someone has written: "this is the place where the Hérnandez brothers held their dances and their political meetings." Associated with the Merchant Marines and the National Maritime Union, the Hérnandez brothers were active in the political struggles of the growing Puerto Rican community in New York in the 1940s and 1950s. The periodic transformation of the Palace of Happiness into a Puerto Rican voters' forum suggests the potential proximity of pleasure and political life. Tonight's *pasos* (dance steps) glide across the same surfaces as tomorrow's political debate. In the overlapping space of dance and debate, a shifting sense of community is configured and reconfigured—day after day, and night after night.[1]

Dance sets politics in motion, bringing people together in rhythmic affinity where identification takes the form of histories written on the body through gesture. The body dancing to Latin rhythms analyzes and articulates the conflicts that have crossed Latin/o American identity and history from the conquest of the continent to California's passage of the·racist Proposition 187. Whether forced into slave labor in the sugarcane fields, migrant labor in the apple groves and vineyards, or undocumented labor in sweatshops and restaurant dishrooms; whether lynched

Announcement of the "Gran Baile" ("Big Dance") at the Palacio de la Alegría (Palace of Happiness) on Tompkins Avenue in Brooklyn on November 11, 1955. (*Courtesy of the Justo A. Martí Photographic Collection, Centro de Estudios Puertorriqueños, Hunter College, CUNY*)

in the newly annexed territory of Texas, sterilized without consent in Puerto Rico or the Dominican Republic, or detained in immigration camps in Haiti and South Florida: Latin/o bodies serve as the site of a long history of racial, cultural, and economic conflict. Dance promises the potential reinscription of those bodies with alternate interpretations of that history. Magnificent against the monotonous repetition of every-day oppressions, dance incites rebellions of everynight life.

History as Choreo-Graphy

"The word rumba means magnificence," claims César Castillo in Oscar Hijuelos's Pulitzer prize–winning novel, *The Mambo Kings Play Songs of*

Love. Mambo king and music teacher César repeats for us a familiar history, whose "magnificence" can be heard in the drumming that connects not only the rumba and the mambo, but all Afro-Caribbean rhythms back through the cultural resistance of the enslaved peoples in the Americas to the religious practices of Western Africa. A frequent lack of specificity in the telling only makes that history more forceful in the living memory of Latinos today; the cultures of Africa survived the institutions of slavery and colonization and continue to survive, despite the institutions of capitalism and so-called development, in the sounding of the drums. In the times of our ancestors, the drums invoked the gods and the gods dwelled within the body for the duration of the dance. And they still do.

César's history lesson traces the contours of the history of the forced migration and enslavement of Africans in the Americas through the steps of the rumba and the mambo:

The slaves who first danced this were usually chained up at night by the ankle, so they were forced to limit their movements: when they danced their rumbas, it was with much movement of the hips and little movement of the feet. That's the authentic rumba from the nineteenth century, with drums and voices and melody lines that sound Spanish and African at the same time . . .

The mambo, now that's another dance. That came along in the 1940s, before you were all born. As a dance it's like the rumba, but with much more movement of the feet, as if the chains had been removed. That's why everybody looks crazy, like a jitterbug on fire, when they dance the mambo.[2]

Focusing on the triumph of motion over constraint, these two movements serve as compressed sites of two moments in the choreo-graphy—the bodily writing—of Latin/o American history.

The popular history contained in Latin music and dance has generated an extensive published history, whose most notable chroniclers include the musicologist Fernando Ortiz, anthropologist and author Lydia Cabrera, Brazilian scholar Muniz Sodre, and art historian Robert Farris Thompson. These historians provide valuable information about the origins and methods of retention of particular African and indigenous practices in the New World, as does the work of scholars emphasizing related African American traditions such as anthropologist and choreographer Katherine Dunham on the dances of Haiti and historian Katrina

Hazzard-Gordon on popular dance in the United States. Our object in this volume is not to trace genealogies, but to build upon the work of these scholars by analyzing at specific historical moments the work of these retentions in making possible oppositional histories. In isolating Latin/o dance from other African American dance forms we do not simply follow the legacy of colonial rule, rather we attempt to trace the ways in which these African traditions have been transformed and encoded as Latin/o through processes of migration and mass mediation. African-inspired rhythms ranging from tango to danzón to rumba and mambo have traveled across the continent, embodying static and interchangeable "Latin" or even "Spanish" identities in first-world music and film while paradoxically setting in motion processes of Pan-Latino identification.

Stasis and motion serve as emblems for the tension between hegemonic and choreo-graphic histories in the New World. British dancemaster Frank Borrows articulates this tension as a problem for Anglo and Anglo-American students and instructors of Latin dance, which he claims to resolve in his classic manual *Theory and Technique of Latin-American Dancing*. Borrows first published the book in 1948, at the height of the international rumba craze, then laid out its mission in a revised edition: "The methods of analysis in use for English Style dancing were not applicable and new methods of dealing with technique had to be devised." The method devised aimed not at keeping pace with a changing form, but with bringing the unruliness of improvisation under control: "the technique I then offered has come to be accepted as standard, almost in its entirety, and Latin-American dancing now has a recognized standard technique, as static as may possibly be expected for a living and still developing form."[3] Through a relentless process of Anglicization, Borrows sets out to standardize Latin dance to the point of stasis.

The static standard of Anglo-American "Latin dance" must expel what Fernando Ortiz has described as "the rapid and extremely complex movements of the African dance, in which feet, legs, hips, torsos, arms, hands, head, face, eyes, tongue, and finally all human organs take part in mimetic expressions that form steps, gestures, visages, and uncountable dance figures."[4] While the complexity of the rhythms elude Western systems of musical notation, the inscription of these rhythms on the dancing body in Afro-Caribbean dance evades any attempt at capture by classical

Drawing of a Cuban country dance by Pierre Toussaint Frédéric Mialhe from his book *Viage pintoresco alrededor de la isla de Cuba* (Havana: L. Marquier, 1848). (*Courtesy of the Cuban Exile Collection in the Richter Library of the University of Miami*)

Western dance notation. The complex articulation of each part of the body, from the limbs to the viscera, always in motion writes history otherwise, moving within and against the constraints of Western writing.

The intricate gesticulations of New World dance forms inscribe and are inscribed by three broad historical movements: (1) the reorganization of the world produced by conquest, colonization, and the institution of slavery; (2) the consolidation of capitalism and the building of nations characteristic of modernity; and (3) the transnationalization of global culture effected by the incessant flow of capital characteristic of postmodernity. These broad movements are not discrete stages nor do they form any kind of direct linear progression from one moment to the next. Rather, we take the polyrhythm as a metonym for history that allows for an understanding of the simultaneous sounding of incommensurate historiographies.[5]

While infinite, these historiographies—these contending modes of writing history—can be usefully conceptualized through the distinction

Gayatri Spivak has designated in her article "Time and Timing: Law and History" as the conflict between "Time" and "timing." Set to the clock of dominant interests, "Time" wrenches "timing," the chronological motion of "life and ground level history," into a law whose chronology produces hegemonic history. We understand "Time" as shifting to the rhythm of changing global hegemonies, but always presenting itself over and against the lived flux of timing as fixed and final. However, "timing," like the incessant rhythm of the clave, sounds over and through "Time" as "Law." As Muniz Sodre has observed, "rhythm as a way of structuring time is also a way of seeing and experiencing reality—it is constitutive of consciousness, not as an abstraction but as a physical force affecting all the organs of the body."[6] The bodily consciousness mobilized by the polymeter of Latin dance allows for the continual remembering (or rewriting) of the crossed rhythms of global history.

The process of signification in polyrhythmic music bears a striking resemblance to Stuart Hall's rendition of Derridean signification in his description of Caribbean identity: Hall "describe[s] this play of 'difference' within [Caribbean] identity" as containing the Derridean deferral of meaning in signification—a deferral or " 'doubleness' . . . most powerfully heard . . . 'playing' within the varieties of Caribbean musics."[7] Hall likens this "doubleness" to "differential points on a sliding scale," but we prefer a different metonymy. Rather than recurring to the Western musical priority of harmony, we would listen for the shifting layers of Latin American history as sounded out in polyrhythms and danced separately-but-simultaneously by distinct body parts.[8] The "endless repositioning" of the dancer in the *pasos* of the tango, samba, salsa, rumba, and mambo traces out new patterns of difference that can be taken up and recognized as new modes of identification—promising potential new avenues for the constant reformation of resistance. In our view, the dance of identity suggests neither being nor even becoming, but a body in motion that breaks into meaning to the polyrhythmic beat of history.[9]

Rhythm as Counter-Consciousness

Opinion diverges on the oppositional role played by dance in the history of the New World. Writing of the institution of slavery in the United

States, abolitionist and emancipated slave Frederick Douglass maintained that dancing allowed a respite from the grueling labor of slavery that diverted those enslaved from rebellion: "holidays were among the most effective means in the hands of the slaveholders of keeping down the spirit of insurrection among slaves . . . but for those [dances, frolics, holidays] the rigors of bondage would have become too severe for endurance and the slave would have been forced to a dangerous separation." In contrast to Douglass's view, Hazzard-Gordon draws from the Caribbean context to construe dance as a kind of prelude to or rehearsal for revolt: "ample evidence suggests that slave insurrections were either plotted at dances or scheduled to take place on occasions that involved dancing . . . The high pitch of emotions at these dances could serve as a pre-text for touching off a previously planned revolt. The links between dance and rebellion give these occasions a striking resemblance to war dances, or dances in which preparation for battle was the central theme." Rather than view dance as necessarily either a diversion from or an incitement to uprising, Hazzard-Gordon poses dance as a powerful instrument recognized by master and slave alike: "With the ability to curtail or encourage slave dance culture, the masters sought to turn occasions to their own use. When slaves made their own dances—and they often did—they accepted a terrible risk of harsh punishment."[10]

Enslaved people risked this punishment not only in dances of outright revolt. Dances such as the habanera, the danzón, and the rumba served as a crucible for forging a common cultural identity out of the diverse ethnic and linguistic groups yoked together in bondage. Hazzard-Gordon presents dance as a kind of lingua franca for peoples abducted from West Africa: "interethnic assimilation was more easily facilitated in dance than in other aspects of the African culture, such as language. Brought to the Americas in the motor-muscle memory of the various West African ethnic groups, the dance was characterized by segmentation and delineation of various body parts, including hips, torso, head, arms, hands and legs; the use of multiple meter as polyrhythmic sensitivity; angularity; multiple centers of movement; asymmetry as balance; percussive performance; mimetic performance; improvisation; and derision. These aesthetic and technical commonalities continued to be governing principles as dance moved from its sacred context to the numerous secular uses it acquired under slavery." Hazzard-Gordon's description touches upon

Three Kings Celebration in Havana, 1848. Drawing by Pierre Toussaint Frédéric Mialhe from his book *Viage pintoresco alrededor de la isla de Cuba* (Havana: L. Marquier, 1848). (*Courtesy of the Cuban Exile Collection in the Richter Library of the University of Miami*)

many of the aspects of dance that continue to play a role in resistive practices: the invocation of counterhistories through motor-muscle memory, the incorporation of incommensurate histories through polyrhythmic sensitivity, and the retention of these practices even as the dances retained by enslaved peoples moved from a sacred to a secular context.[11]

While sacred dance forms persist into the present in the practices of santería and candomblé, we are particularly interested in the retention of these practices in secular form, in what William Rowe and Vivian Schelling have called, in their landmark study *Memory and Modernity: Popular Culture in Latin America*, "decontextualization": the process by which "native practices break from a comprehensive complex of meanings but are still retained as practices."[12] These practices become available for the creation of new meanings; indeed these practices become the engine for re-articulating dance to changing historical conditions.

Dance vivifies the cultural memory of a common context of struggle[13] that bolsters a cultural identity itself forged through struggle and dance.

In her important article "Performing the Memory of Difference in Afro-Caribbean Dance," VeVe Clark details dance as a pedagogy of cultural memory. Cindy Patton summarizes Clark's argument as follows: "the perpetual stylization and restylization of dance by the dancer, the systematic (even if nonformal) teaching of dance forms, and the watching of dance create a structure in which participants and spectators produce cultural memory. Clark argues that interpretation and cultural meaning are embedded in the recognition of the 'memory of difference' from performance to performance. For subalterns, who lack cultural and historical capital, this 'memory of difference' (and the sense of dislocation/relocation which underlies diasporal cultures) sustains the trace of subaltern cultural products even if only in the hermeneutic circle of marginal interpreters at the edges of 'mainstreamed' forms."[14] The production of cultural memory as "cultural and historical capital" for subalterns obviates any facile dismissal of dance as diversion from more direct oppositional political pursuits. The diasporic dancing body becomes the vehicle for the articulation of culture under siege. Dance literally re-members cultural practices repressed over centuries of conflict.

If the cultural memory and oppositional history of Afro-Caribbean or Latin dance is only accessible to a "hermeneutic circle of marginal interpreters at the edge of 'mainstreamed' forms," the inaccessibility of those meanings to mainstream interpreters does not stem from a lack of initiation into subaltern rites of memory alone. The performance of those rites on the body eludes any understanding of history predicated on a rational, linear narrative preserved by the written word. The observation Patton makes of voguing, a contemporary U.S. subaltern dance form, we expand to Afro-Caribbean and Latin dancing as a whole: "If [Afro-Latin dance] cannot tell us from whence it came, that is because the *lieux de memoire* of [polyrhythmic dancing] is not in a time or place, but of the body."[15] Patton's inclusive, uncomprehending "us" is suggestive of the constraints on interpretation of the history performed through dance. As readers and writers of critical cultural analysis, we must shift our domain of investigation from chronology and geography to choreo-graphy.

Lieux de memoire, the place of memory, has two senses here: the body as the site of production of cultural memory and the body as the object of the history re-membered. The dancing body not only writes counterhistory, but the dance resists and reconfigures the subjugating history written on the enslaved or laboring body. History as choreo-graphy then eludes academic analysis on two accounts: the dancing body speaks a language irreducible to words and the dancing body enacts an opposition unassimilable to rational understandings of resistance as productive work.

Speaking specifically of samba, Rowe and Schelling consider secular dance "one of the means by which resistance to the reduction of the body to a productive machine was expressed." Indeed samba, like Afro-Latin dance in general "evoked not only the oppressive memory of slavery but also the present equally oppressive experience of exploitation tied to the process of primitive accumulation of capital" constituting a "counter-culture of play and leisure from which the petty-bourgeois values of work and respect for money and authority were excluded."[16] Even, or especially, when dances have been commercialized and/or fetishized as the embodiment of national culture, Latin social dance eludes usefulness and eschews exchange value through an insistence on improvisation in the production of cultural memory and on the human body as the place of the memory. As exiled Cuban novelist and cultural critic Antonio Benítez-Rojo asserts: "There is not much use to it. The improvisation can be taped by a record company, but the product is a recording, not the improvisation, which is linked indissolubly with a space and time that cannot be reproduced."[17] Improvisation links cultural memory to the here and now, where the meaning of the dance is continually renewed to the (poly)rhythms of history in force in the present. The dancing body not only assures survival of the cultural memory of the past, but the dances of resistance assure survival of the dancers in the present tense.

We might consider improvisation as the dancing body's response to what Paul Gilroy, in his groundbreaking study *The Black Atlantic: Modernity and Double Consciousness*, has called "lived crisis." Acknowledging dance as a strategy for negotiating lived crisis under slavery calls for a fundamental reconsideration of the categories of struggle proposed by Marxist analysis: "where lived crisis and systemic crisis come together, Marxism allocates priority to the latter while the memory of slavery insists on the priority of the former. Their convergence is also undercut by the simple fact that in the critical tradition of blacks in the West, social self creation through labour is not the core of emancipatory hopes. For the descendants of slaves work signifies only servitude, misery and subor-

U.S. tourism book depicts Afro-Cubans in Havana, 1899: "Negros are children of sun and fun." (*Courtesy of the Cuban Exile Collection in the Richter Library of the University of Miami*)

dination."[18] Frantz Fanon articulates the critical tradition referred to here in his chapter "The Negro and Recognition" in *Black Skins, White Masks*. Fanon launches a critique of the Hegelian coming-into-consciousness through recognition and identification as he challenges any notion of the reciprocity existing in the colonial master/slave dialectic: unlike the Hegelian master, the colonial master wants only work, not recognition.[19] The colonial master eradicates the need for recognition with his belief in the slave's incapacity for *cognition*—slaves work; slaves dance; slaves do not think. Hegel, in the guise of the colonial master, misrecognizes the slave's consciousness as articulated through the dancing body within and against the constraints of forced labor. More important for our analysis, orthodox Marxist analysis parlays that misrecognition into an emphasis on production, or work, as the condition for consciousness.

The slaves, however, do not require the master's recognition to mobilize their resistance. While the dismissal of the slave/worker/dancer's ability to think coincides with what Carolyn Cooper calls "zombification—that diabolical ownership of the enslaved in the material world"—enslaved people eluded "zombification" through "divine possession."

Rather than seeking recognition, "[p]ossessed of divinity, the believer dares to make that liberating leap from fact and history into myth and metaphor."[20] The secular form of divine possession, the other of the zombification of work, is dance. If production does not promise freedom, performance may. The locus of emancipatory hopes shifts from everyday to everynight life.

Barbara Harlow's important study of resistance through literary production, *Resistance Literature* (1987), offers us a makeshift critical apparatus with which to shift our consideration of dance as consciousness from the plantation system to the postcolonial frame of contemporary Latin/o American culture. Harlow explains the importance of poetry in different postcolonial struggles: "The role of poetry in the liberation struggle itself has thus been a crucial one, both as a force for mobilizing a collective response to occupation and domination and a repository for popular memory and consciousness." The point where the critical agenda of everynight life diverges from Harlow's understanding of cultural production centers once again around the issues of work and play. Her reading of the poetry of resistance is one that sets up resistance in a dichotomy with "pleasure": "Neither concerned with the contemporary theories of the 'pleasure of the text' nor invoking the Romantic tradition of 'recollection in tranquillity,' the poems of resistance, often composed on the battlefield or commemorating its casualties, the losses to the community, challenge instead the bourgeois institutions of power which often limit such luxuries to the economically privileged and leisured classes of a world readership."[21] Harlow's critical matrix is limited insofar as it cannot imagine resistance in dance or play, turning automatically to the image of the battlefield in a first-world romanticization of armed struggle. Lost in this critical logic are the emancipatory possibilities, the "bellicose joys" and pleasures that accompany practices of resistance through cultural performativity. While Harlow would dismiss "recollection in tranquillity" as an outmoded critical paradigm, we would not be so hasty to do so. Instead we would like to refigure tranquillity not so much as inactivity, but as listening to the historical and cultural body. This tranquillity thus leads to the "*re*-collection" of a cultural body that has fallen apart under hegemonic pressure. The enabling popular memory that is tapped into through cultural performativity is a broader one than the one Harlow invokes: the popular memory that the dancing body summons celebrates the identity-affirming pleasures of the (musical) text and the corresponding kinetic performance of dance, each carved out of the imperialist and hegemonic blocs of power that circumscribe bodies in motion.

We write this essay well past the moment of decolonization in Africa, the Caribbean, and Latin America, a moment when anti-imperialist armed struggles across the so-called third world are all but depleted. Are we then to understand that opportunities and occasions for resistance are also all but depleted? By employing a cultural studies approach to all levels of Latin/o American culture and dance, our contributors examine sites of struggle far from the battlefield and practices that cannot be understood within facile dichotomies as resistance or compliance, politics and culture, radical or conservative, or the West and the rest. Rather than prophesy grand movements of resistance and revolution, the essays collected here follow the intimate gestures of dance in an effort to understand the simultaneous constraint and production of political possibilities as these emerge from the constant choreo-graphy of power. Over and over again, our contributors find in dance a tension between the rules and rhythms that make movement meaningful and the moments of improvisation or subversion that render movement magnificent.

In "Headspin," Barbara Browning takes up what might be the most literal example of resistance through dance: capoeira. Browning recounts the competing histories of resistance played out through capoeira as a "strategic blending of fight and dance." Reputed to have served as a weapon in acts of resistance for embattled communities ranging from Africans escaping slavery to street youth clashing with police, capoeira exhibits the most literal instance of resistance through dance. However, Browning finds the chief principle of resistance in capoeira to reside not in the dance's affinity with martial arts but in "the subtle art of seeming to be in meaningless motion while actually reinforcing a circle of cultural and political race consciousness." Capoeira operates through "dissimulation," as the lethal spins and playful contortions that characterize the dance constitute opposition as "inversion." Where the fight in the dance speaks to literal-minded conceptions of political struggle, the dance in the fight—what Browning refers to as the "confusion of truth"—operates at a more profound level. Rather than take a limited view of resistance as direct opposition, the capoeira has the "ability to absorb rather than be displaced by other forms"—the ability to take on the forms of hegemonic histories and impart new meanings.

In "Hip Poetics," José Piedra finds the rumba—or, more precisely, the hip—the site for the displacement of hegemonic histories. Piedra outlines the strategies deployed through the rumba by "women of(f) color" in the Caribbean and in the United States. Spectacles of African or national culture in performances in Havana and spectacles of the exotic primitive for Anglo audiences in the United States, "women of(f) color" exert a poetics of motion that disrupts the spectacle through an "offensive display and defensive disguise." While the interpretation of this poetics by a politically more powerful, often white, predominantly male audience constrains these strategies, the hip always threatens to burst out of these constraints.

Syncopating Citizenship

This broad understanding of the concept of dances of resistance serves as a counterpoint to what Roberto González Echeverría has called "the voice of the masters" in his book-length study by that name, subtitled *Writing and Authority in Modern Latin American Literature.* González Echeverría considers the implications of the mutual development with modernity of Latin American literature "as a concept" and Latin America "as an entity": this mutual development depended upon a conception of Latin America as "a metaphoric field whose ground is nature." The grounding of "Latin America" in nature constituted a "rhetoric of power" that legitimated a particular vision of national identity and consequently legitimated the authority of a specific class. Modern Latin American literature, according to this analysis, gave voice to the masters, leaving later writers the task of disrupting that voice by revealing the ground in nature as a fiction. For González Echeverría the "rhetoric of power" holds a central place: "Remove the concept of culture and its corollary of national identity from the language of Latin American literature and that literature becomes nearly silent."[22]

Silence would seem to shut out other speakers in this articulation of "national identity" that assumes an equation of "the masters" and "the voice." To reinforce this point, González Echeverría quotes the Martinican Alfred Melon from his essay "Alrededor del Concepto": "It should be understood that when one talks about the discourse concerning national identity one refers predominantly to intellectuals and above all to writers. In any case, the problematic of national identity, like the one about national consciousness, worries almost exclusively intellectuals and political leaders, without the Indians and the blacks taking part in this reflection, which is why they don't feel directly involved . . . Until now the hegemony of the Creoles, half-breeds, and mulattos has been occasionally possible, but never that of Indians and blacks. In such circumstances, the discourse on national identity has for a long time played and continues to play an ideological function, which is to sustain the illusion of an already accomplished unity, concealing in that way inequities and marginalization of the disfavored classes."[23] Melon affirms the equation of "master" and "voice" when he defines the debate as a preoccupation of "intellectuals and above all writers" whose circle circumvents the participation of "Indians and blacks." Melon's analogy between "national identity" and "national consciousness" replicates this gesture of exclusion. To say that the "disfavored classes" neither speak nor write national identity is not to say that they are dumb: silenced by the masters with their rhetoric of power, but not inarticulate. Articulation is not uniquely a function of the domain of writing or speech; rather the definition of articulation derives from the "flexing of joints." If literature speaks the illusion of national unity, might dance not articulate the struggle that belies the illusion? We discover the political consciousness of those silenced by the dominant discourses of national identity in a place other than that of the "voice of the master" or the literature of the continent. We find politics in motion.

For the masters ground their voices not only in nature as landscape or national boundary, but also in nature construed as the bodies of those whose voices the masters have silenced. As Jane Desmond points out in "Embodying Difference: Issues in Dance and Cultural Studies": "it is no accident that both 'blacks' and 'Latins' are said to 'have rhythm.' This lumping together of 'race,' 'national origin,' and supposed genetic propensity for rhythmic movement rests on an implicit division between moving and thinking, mind and body. Even the upper classes of Latin America do not escape this stereotyping; since their 'Latinness' can be said to override their class distanciation from the realm of the supposedly 'naturally' expressive body." Linking "rhythmic movement" to nature negates dance as a conscious strategic practice. The naturalization of these strategies as an essential quality of the dancing masses allows the ruling class to nationalize the dances of resistance as they nationalized the Latin American landscape to create "the illusion of an accomplished unity."

With the formation of modern nations across the Americas, governing elites have undertaken precisely this process of naturalization/nationalization of dances such as tango, plena, samba, son, and merengue in an effort to incorporate new citizens into "national rhythms." However, the promotion of an official national identity through popular dance meets constant resistance and necessarily leaves out critical histories the movement of which the popular form of the dance contains. In "Medics, Crooks, and Tango Queens: The National Appropriation of a Gay Tango," Jorge Salessi details the appropriation of the tango as the sign of middle-class Argentine identity over and against the earlier associations of the dance with the popular and upper classes, each characterized by middle-class managers of the public welfare as sexual perverts. Tango as a musical and dance form developed at the turn of the century among the predominantly young male immigrants from Southern Europe. Through a thorough investigation of the archives of officials in the new fields of public health, criminology, and public education, Salessi investigates the process of making the tango a national dance in an effort to uncover the homosexual desire expelled in the process of nationalization. Salessi maintains that this desire continues to haunt the contours of the tango as national sign.

Efforts at setting strict musical borders across the Americas ignore the constant migration of peoples and musical forms across the hemisphere and, especially, across the Caribbean. As Juan Flores points out in his article " 'Bumbún' and the Beginnings of *Plena* Music," "son, calypso, merengue, and many other examples of the 'national popular' music of their respective countries were all inspired by the presence of musical elements introduced from other [Caribbean] islands." Flores's account of the origins of the plena reveals the transformation of the bomba through the introduction of new musical styles by emancipated slaves immigrating from the British colonies of St. Kitts, Nevins, Barbados, and Jamaica.[24]

A consideration of influences introduced from beyond national borders does not exhaust the heterogeneous social forces in conflict over and within the strains of national musics. The ascendance of the plena as the sound of Puerto Rican culture suggests the role of class and racial conflict in asserting national rhythms. By the 1930s, the working-class, African-inspired plena had displaced the refined, elite danza as a national music, a sign of a growing recognition of the African foundation of Puerto Rican national culture. While the history of the plena speaks to a hegemonic shift in the definition of national culture, the merengue in the Dominican Republic represents the musical redefinition of national culture through dictatorial fiat.

Like the plena, the merengue emerged with the introduction of extra-national musical influences among working-class Dominicans of African descent. The occupation of the Dominican Republic by Haiti early in the nineteenth century contributed to an official refusal to recognize any African presence in Dominican culture. Popularized in the early nineteenth century, the merengue was stylized and Europeanized for the upper classes by composer Juan Bautista Alfonseca at mid-century. In contrast to this refined form, the dictator Rafael Trujillo (1930–1961) promoted the popular dance and musical style as a sign of his own authoritarian populism and as a critique of the elites his rule unseated. Taking power six years after the U.S. occupation of the country, Trujillo promoted the production and dissemination of merengue by local musical groups and on nationalized radio stations as a symbol of defiance against the aggressor who had "imposed the fox-trot upon the society."[25]

Popular dance served as a particularly effective vehicle for control, allowing Trujillo to extend the symbol of his rule to the everyday and everynight life of his subjects—inscribing the terms of his rule onto the bodies of Dominican dancers. However, if the dictator could impose an alternative rhythm evocative of an "authentic," anti-imperialist culture in the service of his own regime, he could not ultimately dictate the use or, better still, "uselessness" of those rhythms. If the churning hips and shackled feet of rumba re-member the history of the African slave trade and the wild motion of the mambo evokes abolition, the merengue's sudden breaks into dizzying turns and the sheer speed of straight forward, straight back steps hints at the difficulty of maintaining control through popular cultural forms. The polyrhythmic layering of competing histories always challenges the nationalization of rhythms.

Transnational Latinidad

Modern technologies of radio and recording facilitated the dissemination of "national rhythms" such as the tango and the plena. The expanding reach of these technologies in conjunction with waves of migration across the Americas—particularly to the United States—produced the conditions for transnational soundings and hybrid musical identities. The invention of the jukebox and restrictions on the availability of mainstream music for radio play cleared the air for Tejano music to broadcast a counterhegemonic regional identity within the United States in the 1940s. The melding of Cuban rhythms with big-band sound gave rise to the Cuban-inspired mambo dance craze across mainstream USA in the 1950s. More accessible technologies of production and transnational distribution, coinciding with massive immigration to the United States from Puerto Rico, Cuba, and the Dominican Republic, produced the conditions for the emergence of salsa in the 1970s and the resurgence of merengue in the 1980s and beyond.

Despite the undifferentiated image of Latinidad as the exotic other to North-of-the-Border rationality and rule, transnational networks of distribution generalizing musical forms and transporting national rhythms across borders facilitated the production of alternative and strategic Pan-Latino identities. Marked in a time other than the rhythms of hegemonic nationalisms, music and dance serve to resist incorporation into any rhythm nation. A number of scholars, including Manuel Peña, José Limón, and Gloria Anzaldúa, have debated the ability of the insistent presence within the borders of the United States of Tejano or Tex-Mex music to contest the assimilation of Chicano identity into an anglicized national consciousness in the Southwest. In contrast to the mambo's role of entertaining Anglos, the emergence of salsa in the early 1970s—remarkably similar in rhythm and choreography to earlier styles such as the mambo and son—marked not a new musical form but a new social consciousness evident both among the diverse Latino populations gathered in urban centers in the northeastern United States and across the Latin American populations separated by national borders.

The history of the mambo, as told by Gustavo Pérez Firmat in his collection of essays on Cuban-American culture, *Life on the Hyphen*, reveals the role of mass media in accelerating and amplifying these musical migrations. As Pérez Firmat maintains, unlike the plena, the son, or the rumba, the mambo did not arise from a popular tradition, however multiple in origin; rather mambo represents the singular combination of big-band sound and Cuban rhythms by one man: *el rey de mambo*, Dámaso Pérez Prado. Moreover, if this combination makes mambo both Cuban and (U.S.) American, then Mexico City, the site of Pérez Prado's first mambo recordings, serves as the midwife. The mediation of the mambo through a Mexico City recording studio and the subsequent circulation of the genre via commercial networks and spaces serves as a contrast, but by no means contradiction, to the history of the rumba and the mambo as choreo-graphic instances of slavery and emancipation. Pérez Firmat fixes these dances as points of progressive commodification: "[t]he first rumbas were danced on the street; the first mambos were danced in dancehalls."[26] In "I Came, I Saw, I Conga'd," Pérez Firmat recognizes the critical role Cuban-American music has played within U.S. American culture. He views Cuban-American forms, rather than oppositional to any dominant culture, as "appositional": Cuban and U.S. elements enrich each other as Cuban Americans as each embraces its "opposite."

Where mambo latinized mainstream U.S. cultural forms, salsa emerged on the mainland of the United States as the vehicle for a bifurcated Latino identity radiating from the City of New York throughout the Americas. In "Salsa as Translocation," Mayra Santos Febres theorizes this process of Pan-Latin identification as the translocal mobilization of meaning across transnational networks. Working the breaks in the transnational production of music, like a good sonera, Santos Febres points out, the critic of salsa can envision a manner of working the constraints of late capitalism into a vehicle of transnational identification among local populations experiencing structurally similar forms of economic and cultural exploitation.

Puerto Rican poet and scholar Juan Carlos Quintero Herencia, in "Notes toward a Reading of Salsa," finds in salsa a resistant practice of interdicted nationality, claiming salsa as a Puerto Rican genre that evades all categorization as oppositional—aligned with one side or the other: "salsa does not presume stable poles to oppose; on the contrary, salsa plunders, corrodes, articulates, and superimposes without having the undergirding of any master text such as the conscience of one class foreclosed by another, without any zone of monolithic sociocultural production defining less industrious 'others' on the other side." Rather than a determinant mode of resistance, salsa is a mechanism for switching modes in anticipation of the shifts in political necessity, always poised to unleash a volley of improvisation—what salseros call a *soneo.* Salsa not only crosses borders, but corrodes them, convocating listeners not as citizens but as friends engaged in the "open conspiracy" of forging an "auditory 'free territory in the Americas.' "

The convocatory power of music and dance has special resonance for sexual minorities across the Americas. While the state power apparatus in countries like Argentina and Nicaragua clamp down on Latin American lesbians, gays, and transgender people with devastating force, drag queens and other transgender people are murdered on the streets of Bahia with horrific frequency. Cuba is currently one of the only Latin American nations beginning a public dialogue on heterosexism and homophobia. Yet those developments, manifest in Tomás Gutierrez Alea's *Strawberries and Chocolate,* are clouded by reports that, to some degree, human rights violations on the island still persist. Within these repressive zones, performances of queer nightlife, whether on the dance floor, in the streets, or on the stage, provide some of the only rebellions available.

We want to suggest that these performances possess queer-worldmaking capabilities. The most immediate example of queer resistance in everynight life is the U.S. 1968 Stonewall rebellion. Stonewall was a world-historical instance of nightlife resistance as Latina/o and black bar patrons openly rebelled against police harassment, commencing the international lesbian and gay rights movement. This collection is committed to a practice of Latin/o American studies animated by queer politics as well as feminist theory and critical discourses on ethnicity and race. Queer theories, as deployed in Jorge Salessi's examination of the tango as queer performance in Argentina at the turn of the last century and through the narratives of queer spectatorship provided by Augusto Puleo and David Román and Alberto Sandoval, make the case that queer politics play a central role in any understanding of the politics of everynight life.

In "Una verdadera crónica del Norte," Augusto Puleo combines a practice of queer spectatorship with a process of transnational identification to understand the ways in which the music and spectacle of contemporary salsa great la India reconceives of the discourse of interdicted nationality played out in older, patriarchal forms of salsa. Comparing la India to women blues artists and Puerto Rican feminist writers, Puleo finds in la India's self-presentation a feminist sensibility that at once corresponds to the feminized position of the island in relation to the United States and poses that feminization as the occasion for a refiguring of notions of Puerto Rican identity in feminist terms. By foregrounding sexuality as power, la India serves to forge a collective working-class identity through song.

In "Caught in the Web," David Román and Alberto Sandoval consider the fixing of notions of queer and Latino identities as those notions collide in the spectacle of the dancing body of Chita Rivera in her title role in *The Kiss of the Spider Woman, the Musical.* Rivera's body is the site upon which is written an allegory for AIDS in the form of tortured bodies of queers and revolutionaries in Argentina, and serves as the occasion for Román and Sandoval's critical engagement with the deadly representations of Latinos, queers, and people with AIDS in the United States. Watching Rivera together, Román and Sandoval find in critical collaboration a way to answer the question "what can *Kiss* offer Latino/a spectators with queer consciousness and AIDS awareness other than a vexed ethnic and queer identificatory process?"

In "Against Easy Listening," Josh Kun makes his consideration of Latinidad and blackness as "vexed ethnicities" a spatial practice, mapping the sites of the production of these ethnicities as "audiotopias." For Kun, the "extranational musical territory of the African diaspora and of the borderland between the United States and Mexico" provide the occasion for a demonstration of the ways in which "music acts as a network of connection among the geographies of the black Atlantic and of Latin/o America, unsettling the assumptions of territorially fixed notions of blackness and of *Latinidad.*"

In "Of Rhythms and Borders," film theorist Ana M. López traces the space of the audiotopia across the movement of dancing bodies. She examines the imbrication of contested nationalisms, genders, and sexualities both within and across national borders in her ambitious survey of the cinematic uses of Latin American music and dances in both Latin American and Hollywood cinema. Finishing with an analysis of *Danzón,* a film directed by a Mexican woman about the articulation of the sexuality of a working-class Mexican woman through the genteel Caribbean dance form danzón, López proposes a shift in the categories of analysis for nationalisms: "we can perhaps begin to think about a different rhythmic cartography, not tied to borders to be crossed or transgressed, but where spaces become lived-in and dancing places in which the body—reclaimed from its subservience to work—can be a locus of resistance and desire and enjoyed on that basis." The body dancing in the living present moves in syncopation to the rhythms of hegemonic identities.

The essays collected here aspire to perform the rite of embodying history in written form. We bring together just a few of the rhythms and dances that overlay the triangle of New World cultures in the modern and postmodern era: tango, samba, capoeira, candomblé, salsa, rumba, conga, mambo, Bolero, Broadway, and guaca roc. We do not intend to dismiss the strategic potential of indigenous American and other more regionally specific forms. Nor, in the isolation of New York and Los Angeles as sites of Latino musical migration, do we forget Miami, the critical crossroads for American cultures North and South, which we both still have occasion to call home. Rather, in this limited space, we take a small cluster of specific dances in the Americas as a model for understanding the interplay of national identity, cultural memory, conflict with central powers, and processes of transnational identification.

Each of these essays makes the foundational claim that whether in the capoeira circle or the "Desi-chain," communities of Latinos—across diverse sexual, gender, racial, geographical, and class coordinates—"create" themselves through the performative opportunities made possible by Latin/o American music and dance. Latino cultural identity is constantly making and remaking itself through a process of productive hybridization. Perhaps for this reason, so many of the essays that follow not only refer to processes of cultural formation, but do so by recounting personal histories of music and dance—by staging the performance of the contributors' own cultural identities. We conceive of the community of scholars enclosed by this space as forming a protective circle like that characteristic of Afro-syncretic dance—a circle we invite the reader to join. Through the course of the text, each of the contributors will at one time occupy the center of the circle to perform his or her own critical gesturings. We hope in the end to keep the circle open: to invite the dancers-critics outside to move forward in turn and multiply the moving center.

We may seem naïve in our wish to displace the opposition between grueling work for multinational capital and equally grueling work against our exploitation with the possibility of strategic engagement with multinational networks to produce alternate structures of community. We may seem foolish in our efforts to dance out resistance in everynight life. Or like the capoeiristas, rumbistas, mambo kings, tango queens, and salsa all-stars discussed here, we may simply play the fool as we bide our time, working the jams and breaks in the polyrhythms of history, as we dance our rebellion in everynight life.

Notes

1. Our thanks to Nélida Pérez and Pedro Juan Hérnandez, archivists at the Center for Puerto Rican Studies, for their help in locating this photograph and in identifying the Hérnandez brothers.

2. Oscar Hijuelos, *The Mambo Kings Play Songs of Love* (New York: Harper & Row, 1989), 279.

3. It is telling that Borrows's technique does not include the tango, whose popularity in the early decades of the twentieth century forced an opening into the standard techniques. African presence, rather than Latin origins, determines inclusion in Borrows's new regulations: in addition to rumba, samba, cha-cha-cha, merengue, and conga, Borrows's Latin American dancing includes North American Africanized forms such as the jitterbug, beat, jive, and rock (Frank Borrows, *Theory and Technique of Latin-American Dancing*, rev. ed. [London: Frederick Mueller], 1961, 1–11).

4. Quoted in Antonio Benítez-Rojo, *The Repeating Island: The Caribbean and the Postmodern Perspective*, trans. James E. Maraniss (Durham: Duke U P, 1992), 78.

5. We believe the metaphor of the polyrhythm allows for the formulation of the kind of "concept of cultural history as the constantly interpenetrating dynamic of traditions and social practices" called for by Juan Flores. Speaking in the context of Puerto Rican culture, Flores recommends not taking Afro-Caribbean culture as a static base, but instead "study[ing] how this basic strain of the popular culture is reconstituted, taking on new meanings and socio-cultural functions, in the varying contexts of national history" (Juan Flores, *Divided Borders: Essays on Puerto Rican Identity* [Houston: Arte Público, 1993], 9).

6. Quoted in William Rowe and Vivian Schelling, *Memory and Modernity: Popular Culture in Latin America* (London: Verso, 1991), 130.

7. Stuart Hall, "Cultural Identity and Cinematic Representation," in *Ex-Iles: Essays on Caribbean Cinema*, ed. Mbye Cham (Trenton: Africa World, 1992), 226.

8. For a more extensive examination of the "polyrhythms" of Caribbean history, see Benítez-Rojo, 1–29.

9. Hall, 228.

10. Frederick Douglass quoted in Katrina Hazzard-Gordon, *Jookin': The Rise of Social Dance Formations in African-American Culture* (Philadelphia: Temple U P, 1990), 28–29.

11. Hazzard-Gordon, 18.

12. Rowe and Schelling, 18.

13. We borrow this phrase from Chandra Talpade Mohanty, "Cartographies of Struggle: Third World Women and the Politics of Feminism," in *Third World Women and the Politics of Feminism,* ed. Chandra Talpade Mohanty, Ann Russo, and Lourdes Torres (Bloomington: U of Indiana P, 1991), 7.

14. Cindy Patton, "Embodying Subaltern Memory: Kinesthesia and the Problematics of Gender and Race," in *The Madonna Connection: Representational Politics, Subcultural Identities, and Cultural Theory,* ed. Cathy Schwichtenberg (Boulder: Westview, 1993), 89.

15. Patton, 98–99.

16. Rowe and Schelling, 128–130.

17. Benítez-Rojo, 19.

18. Paul Gilroy, *The Black Atlantic: Modernity and Double Consciousness* (Cambridge: Harvard U P, 1993), 40.

19. Frantz Fanon, *Black Skin, White Masks,* trans. Charles Lam Markmann (New York: Grove, 1967), 210–222.

20. Carolyn Cooper, " 'Something Ancestral Recaptured': Spirit Possession as Trope in Selected Feminist Fictions of the African Diaspora," in *Motherlands: Black Women's Writing from Africa, the Caribbean and South Asia,* ed. Shusheila Nasta (New Brunswick: Rutgers U P, 1992), 64.

21. Barbara Harlow, *Resistance Literature* (New York: Methuen, 1987), 16.

22. Roberto González Echeverría, *The Voice of the Masters: Writing and Authority in Modern Latin American Literature* (Austin: U of Texas P, 1985), 4, 8.

23. González Echeverría, 4.

24. Flores, 87–88.

25. Quoted in Alberto Pérez Perazzo, *Ritmo afrohispano antillano: 1865–1965* (Caracas: Publicaciones Almacenadoras, 1988), 143. For a more complete account of this history see Peter Manuel, *Popular Musics of the Non-Western World* (Oxford: Oxford U P, 1988), 42–46, and Deborah Pacini Hernandez, *Bachata: A Social History of a Dominican Popular Music* (Philadelphia: Temple U P, 1995).

26. Gustavo Pérez Firmat, *Life on the Hyphen: The Cuban-American Way* (Austin: U of Texas P, 1994), 84–85.

Embodying Difference

Issues in Dance and Cultural Studies

Jane C. Desmond

A man and a woman embrace. Each stands poised, contained. They look past each other, eyes focused on distant points in the space. Like mirror images, their legs strike out, first forward, then back. As one, they glide across the floor, bodies melded together at the hips, timing perfectly in unison. They stop expectantly. The woman jabs the balls of her feet sharply into the floor, each time swiveling her hips toward the leading foot. The man holds her lightly, steering her motion with the palm of his hand at her back. This is tango.

Most readers of this passage probably have some image of the tango in their minds, whether from dancing, watching others dance, or from seeing representations of the tango in Hollywood films. Most, if pressed, could even get up in their living rooms and demonstrate some recognizable if hyperbolic rendition of the tango. Few of us, however, have given more than passing thought to such an activity or have chosen to include it in our scholarly work. Dance remains a greatly undervalued and undertheorized arena of bodily discourse. Its practice and its scholarship are, with rare exception, marginalized within the academy.

But much is to be gained by opening up cultural studies to questions of kinesthetic semiotics and by placing dance research (and by extension, human movement studies) on the agenda of cultural studies. By enlarging our studies of bodily "texts" to include dance in all of its forms—among them social dance, theatrical performance, and ritualized movement—we can further our understandings of how social identities are signaled, formed, and negotiated through bodily movement. We can analyze how social identities are codified in performance styles and how the use of the body in dance is related to, duplicates, contests, amplifies, or exceeds norms of nondance bodily expression within specific historical contexts. We can trace historical and geographical changes in com-

John Gilbert and Mae Murray tango in *The Merry Widow* (1925).
(*Courtesy of the Kobal Collection*)

plex kinesthetic systems, and can study comparatively symbolic systems based on language, visual representation, and movement. We can move away from the bias for verbal texts and visual object-based investigations that currently form the core of ideological analysis in British and North American cultural studies.

Cultural studies remains largely text based or object based, with literary texts still predominating, followed by studies of film texts and art historical objects.[1] Even excursions into popular culture are concerned largely with verbal or visual cultural products, not kinesthetic actions. Much current work on rap music, for instance, focuses primarily on the spoken text or legal and economic aspects of the music industry. Even the now popular subfield of critical work on "the body" is focused more on representations of the body and/or its discursive policing than with its actions/movements as a "text" themselves.[2] In part this omission reflects the historical contours of disciplinary development within the academy.[3] In addition, the academy's aversion to the material body, and its fictive separation of mental and physical production, has rendered humanities scholarship that investigates the mute dancing body nearly invisible. That dancing—in a Euro-American context at least—is regarded as a pastime (social dancing) or as entertainment (Broadway shows), or when elevated to the status of an "artform" is often performed mainly by women (ballet) or by "folk" dancers or nonwhites (often dubbed "native" dances) are surely also contributing factors to the position of dance scholarship. However, these omissions signal reasons why such investigation is important. They mark clearly the continuing rhetorical association of bodily expressivity with nondominant groups.[4]

The rhetorical linkage of nondominant races, classes, gender, and nationalities with "the body," with physicality instead of mentality, has been well established in scholarship on race and gender.[5] But the implications of those linkages, their continuance or reworking within the context of daily bodily usage or within dance systems per se, have yet to be fully investigated. Nor have the complex effects of the commodification of movement styles, their migration, modification, quotation, adoption, or rejection as part of the larger production of social identities through physical enactment been rigorously theorized.

Such analysis will be responsive to many of the tools already developed in literary theory, film theory, Marxist analysis, and feminist scholarship, as well as ongoing theoretical debates about hierarchies based on racial, ethnic, and national identities. Bourdieu, for example, refers to the physical embodiment of social structures in his concept of "the habitus," though this idea has not been greatly elaborated.[6] But it will also require the acquisition or development of new tools as well—tools for the close analysis of movement and movement styles (already well developed in the dance field itself), just as such tools have been developed for detailed analyses of specific books and objects in literature and art history.

Dance scholarship, with a few notable exceptions, has until recently remained outside the influence of the poststructuralist shifts that have reshaped the humanities during the last twenty or so years. And conversely, cultural analysts have evidenced little interest in dance,[7] although literary, filmic, and art historical texts have garnered great attention. But there is evidence that this is changing, both within the dance field itself and with isolated excursions into dance by literary critics and philosophers in the recent past.[8]

Movement Style and Meaning

Of the many broad areas of movement investigation sketched out above, I specifically want to discuss dance as a performance of cultural identity and the shifting meanings involved in the transmission of dance styles from one group to another.

Like Bourdieu's concept of "taste," movement style is an important mode of distinction between social groups and is usually actively learned or passively absorbed in the home and community.[9] So ubiquitous, so "naturalized" as to be nearly unnoticed as a symbolic system, movement is a primary, not secondary, social "text": complex, polysemous, always already meaningful, yet continuously changing. Its articulation signals group affiliation and group differences, whether consciously performed or not. Movement serves as a marker for the production of gender, racial, ethnic, class, and national identities. It can also be read as a signal of sexual identity, age, and illness or health, as well as various other types of distinctions/descriptions that are applied to individuals or groups, such as "sexy." Given the amount of information that public display of movement provides, its scholarly isolation in the realms of technical studies in kinetics, aesthetics, sports medicine, and some cross-cultural communications studies is both remarkable and lamentable.

"Dance," whether social, theatrical, or ritually based, forms one subset of the larger field of movement study. And although we tend to think of dances, like the tango, lambada, or waltz, as distinctive aggregations of steps, every dance exists in a complex network of relationships to other dances and other nondance ways of using the body and can be analyzed along these two concurrent axes.[10] Its meaning is situated both in the context of other socially prescribed and socially meaningful ways of moving and in the context of the history of dance forms in specific societies.

When movement is codified as "dance," it may be learned informally in the home or community, like everyday codes of movement, or studied in special schools for social dance forms (like the Arthur Murray Studios) and for theatrical dance forms (like the School of American Ballet). In either case, formal or informal instruction, and quotidian or "dance" movement, the parameters of acceptable/intelligible movement within specific contexts are highly controlled, produced in a Foucauldian sense by specific discursive practices and productive limitations.

To get at what the "stakes" are in movement, to uncover the ideological work it entails, we can ask what movements are considered "appropriate" or even "necessary" within a specific historical and geographical context and by whom and for whom such necessities obtain. We can ask who dances, when and where, in what ways, with whom, and to what end? And just as important, who does *not* dance, in what ways, under what conditions, and why? Why are some dances, some ways of moving the body, considered forbidden for members of certain social classes, "races," sexes? By looking at dance we can see enacted on a broad scale, and in codified fashion, socially constituted and historically specific attitudes toward the body in general, toward specific social groups' usage of the body in particular, and about the relationships among variously marked bodies, as well as social attitudes toward the use of space and time.

Were we to complete a really detailed analysis of social dance and its gender implications, for example, it could provide us with a baseline from which to pursue further larger-scale questions. We might ask, for instance, how the concept of pleasure is played out in this kinesthetic realm. Who moves and who is moved? In what ways do the poses display one body more than another? What skills are demanded of each dancer, and what do they imply about desired attributes ascribed to men or to women? What would a "bad" rendition of a particular dance, like the tango for instance, consist of? an "un-Latin" or "un-American" version? an "improper" one?

These questions are useful for historical as well as contemporary analysis. For example, the waltz was regarded as too sexually dangerous for "respectable" women in Europe and North America when it was first introduced in the nineteenth century. The combination of intoxicating fast whirling and a "close" embrace was thought to be enough to make women take leave of their senses. Some advice books for women even claimed waltzing could lead to prostitution.[11]

Nineteenth-century dance manuals include drawings showing "proper" and "improper" ways to embrace while dancing, specifying the position of the head, arms, and upper body and the required distance to be maintained between male and female torsos. In manuals directed toward the middle and upper classes, bodies that pressed close, spines that relaxed, and clutching arms were all denigrated as signs of lower-class dance style. The postural and gestural maintenance of class distinction was a necessary skill to be learned, one that could even be represented with precision in "yes" and "no" illustrations of dancing couples.[12]

Such detailed bodily analysis of the linkage of gender and class provides another discursive field through which to understand the shifting constitution of class relations and gender attributes during the nineteenth century. Changing attitudes toward the body as evidenced in the "physical culture" movement, and changes in dress such as the introduction of "bloomers," as well as new patterns of leisure activities and their genderedness provide part of the wider context through which such dance activities gain their meaning. Similarly, the rapid industrialization and class realignments that took place during the latter half of the century, giving rise to new ideas about the division between leisure and work, between men and women, and toward time and physicality, are played out in the dance halls. As "dance," conventions of bodily activity represent a highly codified and highly mediated representation of social distinctions. Like other forms of art or of cultural practice, their relation to the economic "base" is not one of mere reflection, but rather one of dialogic constitution. Social relations are both enacted and produced through the body, and not merely inscribed upon it.

Appropriation/Transmission/Migration of Dance Styles

Obviously, ways of holding the body, gesturing, moving in relation to time, and using space (taking a lot, using a little, moving with large sweeping motions or small contained ones, and so forth) all differ radically across various social and cultural groups and through time. If dance styles and performance practices are both symptomatic and constitutive of social relations, then tracing the history of dance styles and their spread from one group or area to another, along with the changes that occur in this transmission, can help uncover shifting ideologies attached to bodily discourse.

The history of the tango, for example, traces the development of movement styles from the dockside neighborhoods of Buenos Aires to the salons of Paris before returning, newly "respectable," from across the Atlantic to the drawing rooms of the upper-class portions of the Argentine population during the first decades of the twentieth century. As Deborah Jakubs has noted, the taste of the upper classes for "a fundamentally taboo cultural form is a recurrent phenomenon,"[13] as evidenced by the passion for Harlem jazz exhibited by many wealthy white New Yorkers in the 1920s and 1930s.

A whole history of dance forms could be written in terms of such appropriations and reworkings occurring in both North and South America for at least the last two centuries and continuing today. Such practices and the discourse that surrounds them reveal the important part bodily discourse plays in the continuing social construction and negotiation of race, gender, class, and nationality, and their hierarchical arrangements. In most cases we will find that dance forms originating in lower-class or nondominant populations present a trajectory of "upward mobility" in which the dances are "refined," "polished," and often desexualized. Similarly, improvisatory forms become codified to be more easily transmitted across class and racial lines, especially when the forms themselves become commodified and sold through special brokers, or dance teachers.

In studying the transmission of a form, it is not only the pathway of that transmission but also the form's reinscription in a new community / social context and resultant change in its signification that are important to analyze. An analysis of appropriation must include not only the transmission pathway and the mediating effects of the media, immigration patterns, and the like, but also an analysis *at the level of the body* of what changes in the transmission. Often in the so-called desexualization of a form as it crosses class or racial boundaries we can see a clear change in body usage, especially (at least in Europe and North and South America) as it involves the usage of the pelvis (less percussive thrusting, undulation, or rotation, for instance), and in the specific configurations of male and female partnering. For example, the closeness of the embrace may be loosened or the opening of the legs may be lessened. In analyzing some of these changes we can see specifically what aspects of movement are tagged as too "sexy" or "Latin" or "low class" by the appropriating group.[14] Of course, the same meaning may not at all be attached to the original movements by dancers in the community that developed the style.

Looking back to the early years of this century in North America, for instance, the case of the professional dance team of Vernon and Irene Castle provides a good example.[15] The husband-and-wife duo became well-known among the middle and upper classes through their exhibition ballroom dancing and their popular movies. They were so popular that Irene Castle set the standard for fashion and hairstyle, appearing in magazines. Performing in elegant dance clubs and running their own dance school in New York City, they built their reputations on popularizing (among the middle and upper classes) social dances that originated in the lower classes, especially within the black population. They "toned-down," "tamed," and "whitened" such popular social dances as the turkey trot and the Charleston. These revisions tended to make the dances more upright, taking the bend out of the legs and bringing the buttocks and chest into vertical alignment. Such "brokering" of black cultural products by whites increased the circulation of money in the white community as white patrons paid white teachers to learn white versions of black dances.

But it would be a mistake to consider that such appropriations, while they seem to recuperate the potential contestatory power of cultural production by subordinate groups, do so monolithically. While to some extent markers of social "difference" can be reduced to "style" and re-positioned from a contestatory marginality to more mainstream fashionable practice, both the specific practices themselves and their meanings shift in the process. Indeed, even in those instances where the recuperation seems very "successful," there is some change in the dominant population's cultural production.

And, of course, appropriation does not always take the form of the hegemonic group's "borrowing" from subordinated groups. The borrowing and consequent refashioning goes both ways. To take just one example, the "cakewalk," a strutting couples dance performed by African Americans during the slavery era, is thought to have been based in a mimicry of European social dance forms, where coupled dancing was prevalent, as opposed to the separate-sex dance traditions of West Africa. The meanings of the movement lexicons change when transported into the adopting group. While the notion of "appropriation" may signal the transfer of source material from one group to another, it doesn't account for the changes in performance style and ideological meaning that accompany the transfer. Concepts of hybridity or syncretism more adequately describe the complex interactions among ideology, cultural forms, and power differentials that are manifest in such transfers.

Dialectics of Cultural Transmission

In their work on African American cultures in the Americas, Sidney Mintz and Richard Price have argued persuasively for this more dialectical conception of cultural transmission. They emphasize the strong influence that slavery, as an institution, exerted on both African- and European-derived cultural practices. They argue against a simplistic back-writing of history, which would unproblematically trace African American practices to origins in Africa. While they acknowledge that some specific practices as well as very large epistemological orientations toward causality and cosmology may have survived the violence of enslavement, they emphasize instead the particularity of African American cultures—their distinctiveness from African cultural institutions and practices.

New practices necessarily arose within the new historical context of slavery, which mixed Africans from many distinctive linguistic and social groups and resituated these "crowds" (their term) within the parameters of the subjugating relationship of slavery. New religious practices, male and female relationships, reworkings of kinship patterns and their meanings, as well as artistic practices arose from these new conditions of prohibitions and possibilities. And while the balance of power remained ultimately and overwhelmingly among the slave owners, this too was negotiated at the micropolitical scale and varied from country to country, region to region, and even plantation to plantation. White cultural practices, including notions of paternity, cooking, language, and so forth, were also reformed by the relationships of the plantation.

Mintz and Price state it succinctly: "the points of contact between persons of differing status, or different group membership, did not automatically determine the direction of flow of cultural materials according to the statuses of the participants . . ." Quoting C. Vann Woodward, they note that, "so far as their culture is concerned, all Americans are part Negro." And following Herskovits, they quote, "whether Negroes borrowed from whites or whites from Negroes, in this or any other aspect of culture, it must always be remembered that the borrowing was never achieved without resultant change in whatever was borrowed, and, in addition, without incorporating elements which originated in the new habitat that, as much as anything else, give the new form its distinctive quality." Mintz and Price go on to say that "borrowing" may not best express the reality at all—" 'creating' or 'remodeling' may make it clearer."[16]

I have quoted at length on this point because the emphasis in some cultural studies work on appropriation, which helpfully situates these exchanges in the unequal power economies in which they take place, also serves to dampen the transactional, relational aspects of the process. When tied with political assertions of cultural specificity (as in the liberal version of "multiculturalism" or in versions of "identity politics" on the Left), this can ultimately slide into what Paul Gilroy has termed "ethnic absolutism."[17]

Identity, Style, and the Politics of Aesthetics

Mintz and Price are right about the complexities of cultural transmission and exchange. But in counterpoint to that complexity (i.e., what "really" happens) is a more two-dimensional public discourse that marks some cultural products as X and others as Y, as "black" dance or "white" dance, for instance. Sometimes these designations are used in the service of celebrating a particular cultural heritage, and an emphasis on uniqueness is one way to do so. Within these ideologies of difference, the historical realities of cultural production and change are muted. Dance, as a discourse of the body, in fact may be especially vulnerable to interpretations in terms of essentialized identities associated with biological difference. These identities include race and gender and the sexualized associations attached to bodies marked in those terms, as well as national or ethnic identities when these are associated with racial notions, as they so often are.[18]

In the United States, the dominant structuring trope of racialized difference remains white/nonwhite. Within this horizon, black/white and Latin/white dyads of difference reinforce essentialized notions of cultural production. In reality, a much more complicated matrix of racial/cultural identities is played out with the specifics of the relationships among and between various groups shifting in response to changing events, demographics, economics, and so on. But while these dyads may be misleading and historically inaccurate, such distinctions function powerfully in popular discourse both within communities (serving as a positive marker of cultural identity) and across communities.

In cases where a cultural form migrates from a subordinate to a dominant group, the meanings attached to that adoption (and remodeling) are generated within the parameters of the current and historical relations between the two groups, and their constitution of each as "other" and as different in particular ways. For example, the linkage in North American white culture of blacks with sexuality, sensuality, and an alternately celebrated or denigrated presumably "natural" propensity for physical ability, expressivity, or bodily excess tinges the adoption of black dances. On one level, it allows middle- and upper-class whites to move in what are deemed slightly risqué ways, to, in a sense, perform a measure of "blackness" without paying the social penalty of "being" black. An analogue might be "slumming," a temporary excursion for pleasure across social dividing lines.

The submerged class dimension in this metaphor is an important one that is often missed when we concentrate solely on discussions of cultural transmission and modification across racial lines. For the process is ultimately more complicated than that. The meaning of moving in a style associated with "blacks" is different for various classes of whites, for various classes of blacks, and for people who affiliate with other categories of race, such as Asians. And such categories of "othering" vary significantly geographically, in the Caribbean, for instance, and in Latin America, where the strongly bipolar white/black discourse, which until recently at least has been a structuring trope for difference in the United States, is too simplistic.

Furthermore, in the process of "whitening" as the dance form migrates across social lines, it is no longer the same form in the community of origin. Rather, the dance retains traces of that origin, now refashioned both through changes in movement style and through its performance by different dancers in different contexts. While there is in all this a containment and subduing of the difference or particularity of the originating group, there is also a shift in the bodily lexicon of the dominant group. Rather than "black" movement styles or "white," a gray scale may give a more accurate metaphor. Even ballet, the most highly codified, highly funded, and perhaps most elite symbol of European-derived theatrical dance in the United States,[19] has undergone changes that some scholars associate with African American aesthetic values, including rhythmic syncopation and accented pelvic articulations. Brenda Dixon-Gottschild makes this argument specifically with regard to Balanchine's ballets when she proposes looking at an African American "blues aesthetic" as a Barthesian intertext for ballet.[20]

To take a contemporary example drawn from North American popular culture, we can consider the enormous influence that black rap music and its accompanying dance style, hip-hop, has had over the last few years. Hip-hop dance classes can now be found in predominantly white neighborhoods at the local aerobics studio. The dance style and the music are featured in the mass media in commercials and on MTV.

Such popular black groups as Public Enemy have developed a very percussive style. Their music videos emphasize the sharp, repeated thrusting of the pelvis as well as complex stepping or hopping patterns that clearly mark out and punctuate the beat of the music. Pelvic grinds, slow or fast circling, also feature prominently, often with the knees well bent and legs spread. Both women and men perform these movements.

In addition, in some videos the male dancers (and more rarely the female) grab their crotches and jerk them forward. In the upper body we see strong, isolated movements of the head, hands, and arms, often in complex counterpoint to the pumping movements of the lower body and legs. In the dance style we can see striking similarities to some forms of West African dance, where pelvic articulation features prominently along with polyrhythmic relationships between stepping patterns in the feet and concurrent arm gestures.

In dance traditions originating in Europe, both popular and theatrical, such as ballet, the torso tends toward quietude and verticality, and the pelvis rarely functions as an expressive bodily unit of its own. In a "white" version of hip-hop, represented by the enormously popular and financially successful group New Kids on the Block, we can see a similar toning down of the movement. The emphasis on vigorous, patterned stepping and hopping remains, as do the punctuating arm gestures, but the pelvic thrusting, rotating, and crotch grabbing are much attenuated, as is the explicit sexuality of some of the lyrics. Even the name of the group, while asserting a sort of cocky arrival, evokes more the "boy next door" image, kids rather than men, a far different image from the outlaw and outsider designation of Public Enemy.

In this "whitewashing" of the hip-hop style we can see several factors at work. Members of the hegemonic group reap economic success built on the exhibition of a black-derived movement and song style. They do so by transposing the sexuality of the original into a more acceptable form. In this case, the stereotypical image of the aggressively sexual, young black male is defused and transposed to an image of adolescent heartthrobs, suitable for consumption by white teenage girls and less threatening to white male sexuality. But at the same time, a sort of reverse sexualizing and aggressivity, deriving from the vigor of the tightly patterned movement as well as from the words of the songs, accrues to these "new kids" from a working-class background. Class and gender remain the submerged elements in this analysis of transmission and popularity. The explosion of rap into the middle-class youth market, facilitated by the mass-mediated commodification of rap music and its accompanying dance styles via radio, MTV, and national commercials and movies, has shifted the context of consumption and thus the meaning of participating as listener/viewers or dancers. What was once

45

a "black" music and dance style has now become more a marker of "youth" than only a marker of racial identification.[21] In addition, most rap singers are male, although there is a visible contingent of black female singers. Rap remains a male-dominated and to some extent male-identified form.

To talk about the circulation of rap music and associated dance styles from the lower classes of urban black populations to the predominantly white middle-class suburbs is to map one part of the trajectory and would result in a reading that emphasizes the appropriation theme again. But it would also ignore the change in the forms as they travel, their shifting meanings, now standing more for "youth" than just for "black" culture, as well as the complexities of class involved in the successful mass marketing of such a cultural product. For rap can be found in white working-class neighborhoods and in black middle-class neighborhoods too. And for each of these groups the meanings attached to this type of music and dance must be different. Detailed studies of patterns of consumption and of the particularities of movement style in each community would be necessary to really trace the changes and similarities associated with the style and its usage as social dividing lines are crossed.

As noted above, issues of class and of locality (urban/nonurban, for example) are often played out through changing movement lexicons. Sometimes this differential marking out comes not in the form of transmission and remodeling, as I have discussed above, but rather in a form of bodily bilingualism. To take one striking example from North America, we can consider the use of movement on the *Bill Cosby Show.* Cosby often inserts Afro-American movement markers into his otherwise white-identified, upper-middle-class professional demeanor. Slapping high fives or adding a street-style knee-dipping walk, Cosby signals "blackness" to his audience. Here, interestingly, class and racial identification collide, with North American middle-class body codes being derived from Anglo and northern European styles, and "black" body language being associated not with the black middle class but with the lower economic class. Cosby and his successful family represent a form of bodily bilingualism rather than hybrid movement forms. Each way of speaking with the body is used in specific instances, depending on whether class or racial codes are semantically overriding.

46

At an outdoor nightclub in Dakar, Senegal, I observed a different case of bilingualism a few years ago. To the music of a very popular band that played electronic music mixing Euro–North American and West African instruments, rhythms, and harmonies, the Africans on the dance floor, dressed in shirts, slacks, and dresses, executed a version of popular dancing similar to that seen in the United States. With vertical postures, each member of a couple stepped softly in place while bending the knees slightly and gesturing close to the body with relaxed arms. However, as the night went on and the dancers warmed up, traces of the Senegalese rural dance styles I had seen earlier in the week bled through. Knees bent more and opened wider, arms swung more forcefully, feet stepped more sharply, and hands grabbed garments to hold them slightly out from the body, as was done with more traditional dress. Here in the movement of social dance forms we saw the rural/urban tensions being acted out. The adoption of a more European-style verticality, for instance, formed part of a whole complex of behaviors, including dress, that differentiated the urban population from the rural. The urbanization-modernization-Westernization ideology was being carried on here, acted out as a bodily trope that gradually slipped away as the night went on.

"Hot and Sexy" Latin Dances

The emphasis on pelvic motion and syncopated rhythms that character-ize hip-hop is found, in a very different way, in "Latin" dances imported from South to North America. While the specific characterizations and stereotypes associated with "Latins" and with "blacks" in dominant public discourse in the United States vary, there is significant overlap.

In such cases, a discourse of racialism that ties nonwhites to the body and to sexuality expands to include Latin American populations of Euro-pean origin. Racial, cultural, and national identities are blurred, yielding a stereotype of "Latin" along the lines of Carmen Miranda crossed with Ricardo Montalban. The ascription of sexuality (or dangerous, poten-tially overwhelming sexuality) to subordinate classes and "races" or to groups of specific national origin (blacks, "Latins," and other such lumped-together terms to denote non-Anglo-European ancestry) yields such descriptions as "fiery," "hot," "sultry," "passionate." All of these terms have been used to describe the tango, for instance, or the lambada, or in marketing recent movies using those dances, such as *The Mambo Kings*.

In North America, it is no accident that both "blacks" and "Latins" are said to "have rhythm."[22] This lumping together of "race," "national origin," and supposed genetic propensity for rhythmic movement rests on an implicit division between moving and thinking, mind and body. Even the upper classes of Latin America do not escape this stereotyping, since their "Latinness" can be said to override their class distanciation from the realm of the supposedly "naturally" expressive body.

So what does it mean for an upper-middle-class Anglo suburban couple in Indiana to dance the tango, or samba, or lambada? On one level, by dancing "Latin" or "black" dance styles, the dominant class and/or racial group can experience a frisson of "illicit" sexuality in a safe, socially protected and proscribed way, one that is clearly delimited in time and space. Once the dance is over, the act of sexualizing oneself through a performance of a "hot" Latin style, of temporarily becoming or playing at being a "hot Latin" oneself, ceases. The dance then becomes a socially sanctioned way of expressing or experiencing sexuality, especially sexuality associated with subtle, sensuous rotations of the pelvis. But in doing so the meaning of the dance and of the act of dancing undergoes a change. It is no longer "Latin" but now "Anglo-Latin," and its meaning arises from and contributes to the larger dialectic between these two social and political entities and their current political and economic relations. Within the United States, these relations vary distinctly from region to region and city to city.[23]

The history of social dance in the United States is strongly marked by these periodic importations of styles from Latin America, and more recently by the popularization of styles developed within Latin American or Caribbean communities within the United States. But in almost every case the spread of the dance craze to the non-Latin population is represented and promoted in terms of the dance's sexual allure. Over time, these dances become more and more codified and stylized and often pass into the category of "sophisticated," marked as sensual rather than sexual. The tango, rumba, and samba all now fall into this category, as evidenced by their canonical inclusion in social dance classes and in national ballroom dance competitions. With this passing often comes a generational change in the avid performers as well: older dancers tend to perform the more "sophisticated" versions.

Sometimes the symbolism of the dance becomes detached even from its performance and permeates different nooks of popular culture. The Carmen Miranda figure, perhaps the most enduring and potent stereotype of the Latin bombshell, recently reappeared on the stage of the Brooklyn Academy of Music. Arto Lindsay, Brazilian pop musician, calls her "a foreigner reduced to the foreign."[24] His tribute to Miranda featured Brazilian performers such as Bebel Gilberto, Miranda's sister Aurora, and Laurie Anderson, pop icon of the U.S. avant-garde, in an attempt to rescue Miranda from her "every-Latina" stereotype.

Miranda's own story reveals the complexities of translation and transportation. A singer and a dancer, her bodily display was significant in her rise to stardom in North America, where her flirtatious charm ("Look at me and tell me if I don't have Brazil in every curve of my body") and style of florid excess made her the premier symbol of Latinness during her heyday. Showcased by Hollywood in films like *That Night in Rio* (1941), *Weekend in Havana* (1941), *Springtime in the Rockies* (1942), and Busby Berkeley's extravaganza *The Gang's All Here* (1943), by 1945 Miranda was the ninth-highest paid person in the United States.[25] Her Brazilianness was soon turned into a generic "Latin" stereotype.

What remained unnoticed in this U.S. translation was the source of her character and trademark costume (frilly dress with bare shoulders, oversized jewelry, and fruit-topped turban). To the Brazilian audience that first saw this costume when it debuted in the film musical *Banana da terra* in 1938, the stylization of the black *baiana* woman, often seen selling food on the streets of the northern city of Bahia and associated with the practice of the candomblé religion, would have been immediately apparent. As Julian Dibbell has noted, Miranda's "racial cross-dressing" occurred in a Brazilian climate of increasing racial fluidity,[26] but the origins and meanings attached to such recreations were lost on the middle-class U.S. populations who flocked to her movies and sambaed the night away. For most North Americans, Miranda came to symbolize "Latin" music and dance. Within Brazil, a different type of genericization took place. The samba, which developed in the African Brazilian community and which

Miranda helped popularize in the United States, soon spread to all sectors of the Brazilian population and came to be a marker of "Brazilian" culture.

Back home in Brazil, Miranda's increasing genericization did little to endear her to her Brazilian audiences. Eventually, years after her death in 1955, her image resurfaced in Brazil, reclaimed within the "tropical-ismo" movement within the arts. In the United States, her image recirculates in the male "drag queen" pantheon of characters, her manufactured sexual excess providing a ready-made performance persona. And it greets us in the supermarket in those little Chiquita banana stickers, each marked with a flirty Miranda figure.

The Miranda case points out several aspects of the transportation of music and dance styles. The importance of the mass media in facilitating such spread during the last fifty years has been exceptional. Such mediated images flatten the complexities of the dance style (as a social practice) into a "dance" (transported as a series of steps to music) removed from its context of origin and its community of performance. Such representations are a key factor in the reworking of the meanings of these movements as they travel. Further, the identities once attached to certain styles of moving (associated with "black" or "white" or "mestizo" populations in Brazil, for instance) become genericized in the transportation, standing now for an undifferentiated "Latinness," with original markers of class, racial identity, and national specificity all but erased.[27]

The effect of such generalization is often to reinforce U.S. stereotypes of Latin Americans as overly emotional, inefficient, unorganized, and pleasure seeking. The very same qualities that may be valued in the movement—characterized in the United States as sensuous, romantic, expressive, emotional, heterorotic, and passionate—reinforce these stereotypes even while they contribute to the perception of the dance in those same terms. (The unstated equation is that Latins are how they dance, and they dance how they are.) The fact that dancing is a bodily discourse only enhances the perception of these characteristics as "true," or truly expressive. The pleasure aspect of social dancing often obscures our awareness of it as a symbolic system, so that dances are often seen as "authentic," unmediated expressions of psychic or emotional interiority. They are often taken as evidence of a "character," sometimes of a "national character" and often of "racial character." This is where the non-verbal aspect of dance, and our general ignoring of movement as a meaningful system of communication, reinforce popular beliefs about the supposed transparency of expressivity.

Theatrical Dance

The preceding discussion has focused on aspects of identity, transmission, and perception relating to the performance of social dance forms. Similar issues arise when considering the more highly codified dance forms of the professional theatrical world. These forms are less likely to be disseminated through the mass media and rely more on the physical transportation or migration of performers, students, teachers, and choreographers from one locale to another, especially when national boundaries are involved. There are differences too in this category between professional performance forms that are more or less popular. For instance, the dynamics are slightly different in the categories of show dancing, like jazz or Broadway-style dance, than they are in the modern dance world. I want to close by giving two brief examples of the migration of dance styles across national boundaries, the first looking at ballet in China, the second at selected aspects of Latin American modern dance.

Even though we might be tempted to dismiss the importation of ballet to China as just one more example of Western cultural imperialism, the complexities of the transmission belie such a simple explanation. Ballet in China represents a striking case of a creolized form still very much emerging. It exhibits a combination of movements from the Soviet ballet tradition and the theatrical dance, folk dance, and operatic traditions of China.[28] In some cases, this mixture results in arresting moments where half the body looks "Chinese" in its lexicon of movement, and the other half looks "European."[29] In these cases, we might see the legs poised en pointe in arabesque, while the upper torso, arms, and head are molded into a dramatic pose drawn from the Chinese tradition, especially the Chinese opera, where dramatic pantomime plays a large role.

The Chinese example is particularly interesting because it represents a case in which the change in a form of cultural production occurred largely from the top down, that is, as a state-level government decision.

All the complexities of the migration of various forms from one community to the next at the local level, or even among regions or countries when facilitated by the mass media, are somewhat streamlined here, yet the particularities of the Chinese experience remain distinct. Chinese ballet is different from its counterparts in Europe and America not only at the level of movement vocabulary and syntax (i.e., which movements are done and the ways movement sequences are put together) but also in terms of choreographic method (where collective projects of choreography are not uncommon) and in terms of audience (ballet in China is conceived of as a popular entertainment). In addition, the narrative or storytelling aspect of ballet, which has dropped in prominence in European and American ballet forms since the mid-nineteenth century as more abstract styles have emerged, is a strong component of the Chinese repertory. Thus, far from representing merely the appropriation of a "Western" form, the Chinese ballet produces a whole complex of meanings as well as formalistic innovations specific to its function in China.

Gloria Strauss has written about the history of dance in China and has speculated on the reasons why ballet might have been actively imported by the state during the Cultural Revolution.[30] The arts were considered integral to the ideological functioning of the new China, and dance received a lot of attention at the state level. The choice to import Soviet ballet forms revealed more than the Soviet economic and political influence of the time. Strauss speculates that the government was actively seeking the creation of art forms that would make visible the need for rapid and radical change that the revolution called forth.

With the exception of the dramatic forms in the Chinese Opera, theatrical dance in China had fallen into a decline among the Han (the Chinese majority population) after the Sung period (A.D. 959–1278). A contributing factor in this decline, argues Strauss, may have been the widespread practice of foot binding, which severely reduced female movement, especially, but not exclusively, among the upper classes.[31] Acrobatic and folk dance forms survived, but they did not bring with them narrative traditions. (In addition, the folk forms were heavily marked with ethnic associations, and the government wanted to play down ethnic enmities while celebrating the nation as a whole.) The narrative possibilities of ballet may have been one factor in its adoption, as the leaders sought the creation of art that would reinforce the tenets of the revolution and appeal to the masses. Furthermore, it offered visions of action and strength, through a combination of Chinese acrobatic traditions (also found in the opera) with the leaps and turns of the ballet vocabulary. Strauss notes that "highly extended postures such as attitudes and arabesques and a variety of flying leaps such as *grand jeté en avant* are given great prominence" in Chinese choreography.[32] Similarly, the female dance vocabulary could be extended to showcase women who were as strong and active as men, literalizing the emphasis on equal legal rights for women that the government supported. In the well-known *Red Detachment of Women*, gun-toting ballerinas fight for the revolution while leaping across the stage in grands jetés. This in itself represents a shift from the earlier history of European ballet, through a particular emphasis on some of its characteristics along with a downplaying of others (for example, the soft, light movement style of female roles in the traditional nineteenth-century ballets such as *Swan Lake* that continued to be performed in the Soviet Union). But it would be misleading to posit a simple correspondence between the new status for women in the Cultural Revolution and the martial movements of ballerinas in these works. There is also a strong tradition of female warrior characters in Chinese opera, and historically popular entertainments often featured women dancing with swords. The gun-toting ballerina, while unusual in European or American ballets, becomes meaningful in *The Red Detachment of Women* through a complex nexus of old and new forms of both Chinese and non-Chinese origin.

In the more recent past, the ballet repertories have expanded. The dramatic, narrative ballet remains a staple, but it now exists side by side with nonnarrative ballets as well as modern dance works. Little of the U.S. modern dance repertory has been seen in China yet, although a few companies have toured and some teachers have done guest residencies. But some of the younger dancers copy poses found in dance magazines, making up their own versions of "modern dance."

In China, a state policy that would seem at first to foster imitation of industrialized nations' art forms instead results in new, hybrid forms. The wider geopolitical relations between China and the industrialized nations, whence certain cultural forms are originally borrowed, may ultimately form a horizon circumscribing the meanings that can possibly circulate with those forms. But it does not determine the use, ultimate shape, or socially constructed aesthetic valuation of the resultant hybrid.

Owing to a greater flow of professional dancers between countries in North and South America and to different governmental policies about the arts, the situation in Latin America is different. But here too we can see the process of hybridization and recontextualization, influenced but not determined by the dance institutions in the various countries, as well as international arts exchange and funding policies.[33] Without trying to generalize about the wide range of Latin American theatrical dance, let me close with brief examples that demonstrate something of the variety of forms and situations encompassed.[34]

When discussing contemporary dance in Latin America, one must cover a wide range, and while the U.S. tendency may be to think of Latin American dance in terms of the popular and well-known social dances, in fact a full range of traditional and contemporary styles coexist on the stage. The case of DanceBrazil is interesting. Although based in New York, this contemporary company is composed mainly of dancers born and trained in Brazil. Their repertory consists of what appear to be stagings of ritual ceremonies based on the Afro-Brazilian candomblé religion, traditional capoeira (a martial arts–dance form), the samba, and, to some extent, dance vocabulary derived from U.S. modern dance styles.

DanceBrazil foregrounds its "Brazilness." That in fact may be what it is selling to both its Euro-American and Latin American audiences in New York. In live and televised appearances, this is a company that "stages" tradition. A televised performance presented on U.S. public television in 1989 was particularly interesting. Shown as part of the *Alive from Off-Center* series, DanceBrazil was contextualized as part of a contemporary avant-garde showcase. Each week the series presents dance and performance works featuring (mainly U.S.) artists outside of the mainstream. Susan Stamberg, the announcer, introduces the night's offerings with brief comments about artists who are reinterpreting traditional dances through "modern sensibilities," evidence of cultural contact. In fact, the words "culture contact" float by on the screen. On the show with Dance-Brazil, interestingly, are a solo by Raul Trujillo, who reinterprets his American Indian heritage in "The Shaman," and a duet by the Japanese-born, United States–based duo of Eiko and Koma, whose excruciatingly slow movement underlines the sculptural qualities of their nearly nude bodies in what Stamberg terms a melding of Japanese Butoh and American avant-garde techniques.

It is interesting that of these three examples of "culture contact," only the Japanese piece is not based on religious rituals and "traditional" costuming. Japanese Butoh is a relatively recent stylistic development, and it may be that essentializing the Japanese through a discourse of traditionalism is more difficult in the United States due to Japan's new position as our primary economic competitor on the world financial scene. On the other hand, American Indians and Latin Americans may more easily be situated within such a traditionalizing/primitivizing discourse of preindustrialism.

Trujillo's piece, which was first, set the stage for the DanceBrazil piece that followed. In fact, both feature large circles drawn in the earth (literally, truckloads full of dirt dumped in the television studio). Trujillo dons traditional American Indian dress, complete with feathers, and enacts a ceremonial type of dance that concludes with his vanishing in a hazy light. By the time DanceBrazil appeared, their stage set of dark earth, white chalk circle, and flowing white curtains around the perimeter came as no surprise. We were already placed firmly in the "primitive" aesthetic, with people enacting magical ceremonies in village clearings on rich, dark earth.

The set effectively shuts the dancers and the "ceremony" off from any historical time or place. These rituals are presented as "timeless," but this "outside of time" quality refers to the past and somehow fails to index the present. If the dances cannot be contemporary, then neither, we are to assume, can the people who perform them. In an odd category of "avant-garde folklore," PBS has produced another hybrid form, one reflecting the dominance of the United States, with economic and political power played out in the staging decisions of a television series, the framing of its discourse, and the composition of its audience, self-selected connoisseurs of the "avant-garde."

This is not at all to imply that theatrical dance companies in or from Brazil always work in traditionally based styles. The Grupo Corpo of Brazil, which appeared in New York City during the fall of 1990, presented an evening of works nearly indistinguishable in movement vocabulary from that of many U.S. companies based in New York. Also during the same season in New York, Hercilia Lopez, director of the Venezuelan troupe Contradanza, and Luis Viana, founding member of the Venezuelan Acción Colectiva Dance Company, presented solo works. In both cases the movement vocabularies and presentation of these works showed strong affiliation with contemporary U.S. modern dance production. Of course, we could say that this merely reflects the dominance of U.S. modern dance on the worldwide dance scene, and indeed many of these performers have trained in the United States. But this would be to overlook the specific meanings that arise in the performance of such works in their home cities in Latin America, and in the United States where they are framed and marketed specifically as "Latin American" artists.

On the same program with Lopez and Viana, marketed as Latin night at Movement Research, Inc., in downtown New York City, was a piece by Arthur Aviles, a spectacular dancer with the New York–based Bill T. Jones Company, here presenting his own work. Titled "Maeva (A New York-Ricans Ensalada)," the piece features as the main character an irrepressible woman, squeezed into a too-small frilly gown, regaling the audience with a nonstop monologue in Spanish and English. Creating a whirlwind of energy with her breathless talking and exuberant posing, she recalls the larger-than-life Carmen Miranda, here both reasserted and caricatured at the same time. She introduces herself with a skein of fifty names, marking the maternity and paternity of past generations, and talks about her fifteen "childrens" as four other dancers crawl around and through her legs to the pulse of Tito Puente music. Periodically, someone offstage yells out "Spic!" but she continues, unflappable, picking up the monologue where she left off, addressing the audience directly, with "So, as I was telling you . . ." Dancers samba around her like backup singers as she jokes about lazy "caballeros." At times, the dancers climb on top of her, holding her down, but she always emerges, still talking and gesturing, claiming, in heavily accented English, "What do you mean you won't hire me, I don't have an accent!"

Although obvious and somewhat heavy-handed in its attempt at political critique, this piece is effective in its mix of Spanish and English, of abstract modern dance movements with the ethnically coded gestural language of the Latin caricature. It simultaneously genericizes and particularizes, placing the 1940s "every-Latina" stereotype in the contemporary struggle to find work and to create community within the heavily accented hybrid space of New York. Its placement on a program of "Latin dances" in a small loft downtown, part of the "avant-garde" circuit, also signaled the complex mix of identities being played out on that stage. Somewhere between Carmen Miranda and the successful avant-gardism of the Bill T. Jones Company, Aviles staged his own bilingual modern dance, articulating through its bodily enunciation the complexities of his own position and the permeability of movement lexicons always in transition.

Concluding Thoughts

I have argued throughout this piece for an emphasis on the continually changing relational constitution of cultural forms. Concepts of cultural resistance, appropriation, and cultural imperialism are important for the light they shed on the unequal distribution of power and goods that shape social relations. And indeed these inequities may form a kind of limit or substrata that ultimately determines the topography of cultural production. But an overemphasis on such concepts can obscure the more complex dialectics of cultural transmission. Such concepts can overemphasize formal properties that circulate or are "lost" in the process of moving from one group to another, thus resulting in an inattention to the contextual specificity of meanings attached to or arising from the usage of formal properties, and obscuring as well the hybridization of such forms.

I have also argued for increased attention to movement as a primary, not secondary, social text, one of immense importance and tremendous challenge. If we are to expand the humanities to now include "the body" as text, surely we should include in that new sense of textuality bodies in motion, of which dance represents one of the most highly codified, widespread, and intensely affective dimensions. And because so many of our most explosive and most tenacious categories of identity are mapped onto bodily difference, including race and gender but expanding through a continual slippage of categories to include ethnicity and nationality and even sexuality as well, we should not ignore the ways dance signals and enacts social identities in all their continually changing configurations.

But to do so will require special tools. Although I have been emphasizing the larger theoretical level of analysis of the transmission and hybridization of cultural production in this essay, extended treatment of specific cases, both historical and contemporary, is clearly necessary. Such research will allow us to test the validity of these frameworks and to provide the data necessary for detailed accounts of exchange, change, and circulation and the ways those are attached to the social production of identity. But if we are to talk about dancing in anything other than the broadest terms, we must be able to do close analysis of dance forms, just as we might of literary texts. While most scholars have spent years developing analytic skills for reading and understanding verbal forms of communication, rarely have we worked equally hard to develop an ability to analyze visual, rhythmic, or gestural forms. As cultural critics, we must become movement literate. Here is where skills drawn from the dance field become indispensable.

Systems of movement analysis developed in dance, such as Laban's Effort/Shape system, provide a good starting point. Effort/Shape methodologies employ abstract concepts of continuums in the use of the weight of the body (ranging from "strong" to "light"), in the body's attitude toward space (ranging from "direct" to "indirect"), and in the use of time (ranging from "quick" to "sustained"). In so doing, they can provide an analytical system as well as a language with which to speak about the body moving in time and space.[35]

Consider, for example, the pioneering work of Irmgard Bartenieff. In the 1960s and 1970s, she explored the efficacy of Effort/Shape for describing and comparing movement patterns in particular communities.[36] Such work provides one model for cross-cultural comparisons of movement lexicons. I think it can also provide a model of the changes that take place in movement style among populations undergoing cultural contact of either a voluntary (immigration, for example) or involuntary (colonial occupation or slavery) sort. We could, for example, relate this to Homi Bhabha's work on mimicry, although he does not develop this line of argument directly himself.[37] Bhabha discusses the slippage that occurs when colonial behaviors, such as military ritual, are performed (always, he says, "imperfectly" or "overly perfectly") by the colonized. When combined with a detailed system of movement analysis, his concept of mimicry could provide us with a useful way to chart some of the changes that occur in the semantics of movement as a result of cultural contact and/or domination. The key in cases such as he refers to would be to look closely at what constitutes "imperfection" or "over-perfection" in movement performance.

Although the Effort/Shape system does not code movements in terms of gender or cultural affinities, all analytical systems reflect the contours of their historical etiology and of their objects of analysis. The Effort/Shape system, for example, developed out of Rudolph von Laban's analysis of twentieth-century European movement patterns. Given the demands of cross-cultural and intracultural research, no one system will be sufficient. To keep our broader levels of analysis anchored in the materiality and kinesthesia of the dancing body, we need to generate more tools for close readings, and more sophisticated methodologies for shuttling back and forth between the micro (physical) and macro (historical, ideological) levels of movement investigation. The difficulty of this research will repay us well, expanding understanding of the ways the body serves both as a ground for the inscription of meaning, a tool for its enactment, and a medium for its continual creation and recreation.

Notes

I thank the organizers Celeste Fraser Delgado and José Muñoz for inviting me to speak at the conference "Politics in Motion: Dance and Culture in Latin America." My thanks also to Jennifer Wicke, Cathy Davidson, Bryan Wolf, and Jane Gaines for their helpful critiques on this material, and especially to Virginia Dominguez for sharing her thinking on cultural processes with me and for bringing the Mintz and Price material to my attention.

1. The debates about what "cultural studies" is, should, and should not be have intensified during the last ten years as the term has gained greater circulation and as its practitioners have gained increasing institutional power in the academy. I use this term in the sense of a group of self-nominated scholars who affiliate themselves and their work with such a term. Implicit in its usage is usually a concept of critique, antidisciplinarity, and the importance of investigating the linkages between social/economic/political power and cultural production. See Richard Johnson, "What Is Cultural Studies Anyway?" *Social Text* 16 (Winter 1986–1987): 38–80, and the collec-

tion *Cultural Studies* edited by Lawrence Grossberg, Cary Nelson, and Paula Treichler (New York: Routledge, 1992) for discussions about the scope of cultural studies.

2. For example, see Thomas Laqueur's *Making Sex: Body and Gender from the Greeks to Freud* (Cambridge: Harvard U P, 1990), and Emily Martin's *The Woman in the Body: A Cultural Analysis of Reproduction* (Boston: Beacon Press, 1987).

3. The humanities disciplines' emphasis on words is exemplified in the histories of the disciplines. The prestige of literature is followed by that of art history, which discusses art historical objects. Usually the making of those objects is segregated into a separate "art" department. Funding asymmetries reflect the different valuations placed on the act of making "art" versus the act of writing about art. Music history and theory has attained a higher status in the academy than dance history, due in part to its more extensive written history, in terms of both criticism and the musical scores that stand in for live performance and permit extensive, reflective study. Dramatic literature holds an analogous position, thanks to its written texts and extensive critical history. Until recently, dance has remained the most ephemeral of the arts, its "texts" existing primarily in the moment of viewing and leaving little in the way of material residue. This is one reason its historical and theoretical analysis represents a relatively tiny body of work. (I am always reminded of the attitude toward dance scholarship when I go to the library and search for books that are invariably filed in the section bounded by "games and cards" and "magic tricks and the circus.") Although some movement analysis systems do and have existed, they are often schematic at best or, if very complex like Labanotation, very difficult to read except by those specifically trained as professional notators and reconstructors. In any event, only a very small portion of dance practice is notated in any way. The field remains predominantly a "corporeal" tradition, passed on from person to person in both formal and informal settings. Video has mitigated this problem to some extent, but all video records are partial, showing usually one visual angle and recording only one specific performance of a dance.

4. Here I am referring specifically to the post-Enlightenment scholarly tradition developing from European sources.

5. See, for example, articles in Henry Louis Gates Jr., ed., *"Race," Writing and Difference* (Chicago: U of Chicago P, 1986).

6. See Pierre Bourdieu, *Outline of a Theory of Practice*, trans. Richard Nice (New York: Cambridge U P, 1977).

7. Interestingly, as Janet Wolff has noted, metaphors of dance figure prominently in the work of several literary critics. However, this metaphoric invocation contrasts sharply and provocatively with a distinctive absence of interest in the material and social practice of dance (personal communication with Wolff).

8. Within the dance field, an excellent work by Susan Foster, *Reading Dancing: Bodies and Subjects in Contemporary American Dance* (Berkeley: U of California P, 1986), marks the first full-length study situated within a structuralist/poststructuralist position, and increasingly articles and new books evidence a familiarity and willingness to engage ideological issues. See, for example, Mark Franko, *Dance as Text: Ideologies of the*

Baroque Body (Cambridge: Cambridge U P, 1993). The important conference "Choreographing History" at the University of California, Riverside, in February 1992 brought together dance scholars and nondance scholars who write about bodily discourse. Among those participating were Randy Martin, Susan Manning, Thomas Laqueur, Elaine Scarry, Norman Bryson, Peggy Phelan, and Lena Hammergren. And critical journals like *Discourse* have recently published articles on dance. This still remains the exception rather than the rule, but does indicate a growing conversation between dance scholarship and cultural studies.

9. Pierre Bourdieu, *Distinction: A Social Critique of the Judgement of Taste,* trans. Richard Nice (Cambridge: Harvard UP, 1984).

10. This is not to imply that the division between "dance" and "nondance" is always clear, nor that it is always of primary importance in formulating research. Such a designation is subject to change historically and geographically. What may be particularly useful to note is which movements and spatial sites are associated with "dancing" when that concept is used and which are not. By asking what constitutes "dance" within a particular context, we can find out more about the values associated with dance, whether as entertainment, social activity, ritual, or "art." For example, debates over "pornography" include arguments over what constitutes "lewd" movement with no "redeeming" artistic value. By recontextualizing such movements as dance or by relocating them to a so-called legitimate theatrical venue, an argument could be made that such movements are artistic and therefore not subject to censure. The shifting dividing line between dance and nondance activities and the moments of such an invocation are part of a political history of bodies and movement.

11. I thank Cathy Davidson for bringing the information about advice books to my attention.

12. On women and dance halls in the nineteenth century, see Kathy Peiss, *Cheap Amusements: Working Women and Leisure in Turn of the Century New York* (Philadelphia: Temple U P, 1986), especially "Dance Madness," 88–114.

13. Deborah Jakubs, "The History of the Tango," talk delivered at the conference "Politics in Motion: Dance and Culture in Latin America," Duke University, Durham, NC, January 1991.

14. In asking what an "un-Latin" rendition of a particular dance would be, for instance, we can begin to identify the movement parameters deemed necessary to identify it as such both within and outside of "Latin" communities.

15. See Lewis Erenberg, *Steppin' Out: New York Nightlife 1890–1930* (Westport, CT: Greenwood, 1981).

16. Sidney W. Mintz and Richard Price, *An Anthropological Approach to the Afro-American Past.* ISHI Occasional Papers in Social Change 2 (Philadelphia: Institute for the Study of Human Issues, 1976), 16, 43–44.

17. See Paul Gilroy, "Ethnic Absolutism," in *Cultural Studies,* ed. Lawrence Grossberg, Cary Nelson, and Paula Treichler (New York: Routledge, 1992), 187–198, whose argument focuses on the need to reconceive black culture in terms of an Atlantic diaspora. He argues that "much of the precious political, cultural, and intellectual legacy

claimed by Afro-American intellectuals is in fact only partly their 'ethnic' property. There are other claims to it which can be based on the structure of the Atlantic diaspora itself." My argument similarly calls for a historical examination of the movement of people and their cultural products, although drawing on Mintz and Price I have accented the difficulty in applying concepts of absolutism to Euro-American and African American populations that have developed in intense relationship to each other.

18. In the United States, for example, see the rise of the category "Hispanic" as a racial identity in federal census forms during the last two decades. Country of origin and language are ignored in this categorization.

19. With rare exceptions, African American dancers were not welcome in U.S. ballet companies until recently. Even today their numbers remain small, for reasons related to class as well as race. Early arguments against their participation were based on racialist assumptions that their bodily configurations were incompatible with the aesthetics of line for the European form. The Dance Theater of Harlem, pioneered by former Balanchine dancer Arthur Mitchell, has not only provided a forum for African American dancers to perform the traditional "white" ballets, but has also developed a number of ballets based on African American themes or African-style movement resources.

20. Brenda Dixon-Gottschild, "Some Thoughts on Choreographing History," talk delivered at the conference "Choreographing History," University of California at Riverside, February 1992.

21. This is not to imply that patterns of consumption are the same within, for example, predominantly black urban communities, as they are in predominantly white suburban communities.

22. Remember that the character Ricky Ricardo, Lucy's husband on the *I Love Lucy* show, was a bandleader. Even all these years after the show, his character still represents the longest-running and best-known Cuban character on American television. See Gustavo Pérez Firmat, in this volume.

23. Due to the mass media, dance styles, like music styles, can migrate separately from the groups of people who develop them. With New York's large Latin American and Caribbean populations, dancing the lambada is likely to mean something different in Scarsdale than in suburban Indiana, where the ratio of Latin Americans to Anglo-Americans is much lower and less a source of friction than in the New York metropolitan area.

24. Julian Dibbell, "Notes on Carmen: Carmen Miranda, Seriously," *Village Voice* 36.44 (29 October 1991): 43–45.

25. Dibbell, 44.

26. Dibbell, 43.

27. Jazz dance, like jazz music, represents an analogous creolized form of cultural production in the United States, with body usage and rhythmic elements drawn heavily from African American and Euro-American sources. Now no longer identifiable as "black" or "white," jazz has, like the case of the Brazilian samba, become

"nationalized" or genericized into an American product, often regarded as quintessentially so in other countries. Its history both in the United States and abroad, however, is deeply imbricated with issues of racial identification. In the early decades of this century, for example, during the rise of modernism with its reliance on "the primitive," the Parisian passion for jazz coincided with an appetite for African American performers like Josephine Baker, known for her "banana dance" in a skimpy bikini of those fruits. The national versus racial identification of jazz is a tension that still exists today.

28. These comments are based primarily on personal observations in a number of state training schools in China during 1990.

29. The European reference is schematic at best, meant to imply the ballet tradition as it developed in Europe and the former Soviet Union and then was transplanted to the United States, where it has since taken on its own particularity.

30. Gloria Strauss, "Dance and Ideology in China, Past and Present: A Study of Ballet in the People's Republic," in *Dance Research Annual 8. Asian and Pacific Dance:* Selected Papers from the CORD-SEM Conference, ed. Adrienne L. Kaeppler, Judy Van Zile, and Carl Wolz (New York: CORD, 1974) 19–54.

31. Strauss notes that this explanation is certainly not fully adequate. Bound feet would not prevent women from performing kneeling dances, for instance, nor would the practice have any influence on male dancing. However, she notes that the binding practice was very widespread, especially in areas where the Han population predominated. Some estimates argue that in areas like Tinghsien, more than 99 percent of all females born before 1890 had bound feet. The most severe practices were reserved for upper-class women. Although both the Manchus and reformers after the 1911 revolution tried to outlaw the tradition, foot binding was not fully extinguished until after 1940. See Strauss, "Dance and Ideology in China, Past and Present," 28–30.

32. Strauss, "Dance and Ideology in China, Past and Present," 43.

33. Whereas the transmission and transportation of social dance forms is effected by mass media marketing and population migrations, in the professional art world, although population demographics have some influence, equally important are the internal politics of each country (multiculturalism as a current funding paradigm in the United States, for example), and the circuit of exchange set up among departments of state in various countries, as well as the international avant-garde circuit. A study of State Department funding of leading artists and companies would reveal an interesting profile of what is promoted as "U.S. art," for example.

34. Live performances cited: DanceBrazil at the Alliance Française Theater, New York City, December 1991; Grupo Corpo at the Joyce Theater, New York City, November 1991; Hercilia Lopez, Luis Viana, and Arthur Aviles at Ethnic Arts Theater, December 1991.

35. Cynthia Novak's ethnographic study of contact improvisation practitioners is exemplary in its use of movement analysis as a basis for group investigation. See her *Sharing the Dance: Contact Improvisation and American Culture* (Madison: U of Wisconsin P, 1990), especially chap. 5. Also outstanding is Sally Ness's study of contemporary

Philippine dance, *Body, Movement, and Culture: Kinesthetic and Visual Symbolism in a Philippine Community* (Philadelphia: U of Pennsylvania P, 1992).

36. Irmgard Bartenieff, *Body Movement: Coping with the Environment* (New York: Gordon and Breach Science Publishers, 1980).

37. Homi Bhabha, "Of Mimicry and Man: the Ambivalence of Colonial Discourse," *October* 28 (Spring 1984): 125–133.

Headspin

Capoeira's Ironic Inversions

Barbara Browning

A few years ago I had a friend named Wilson dos Santos. He'd written a screenplay about himself called *Capoeirista in New York*. It was mostly a true story, embellished with some high-powered fight scenes. Wilson dreamed of doing for capoeira, the Afro-Brazilian dance and martial art, what Bruce Lee did for kung fu. When he was a scrappy, restless kid, a beach urchin in Bahia, he got into some scuffles. There's a thin keloid "remembrance" of the tip of a knife near his nipple, another on his arm. But once he made up his mind to get to the United States and make it as a performer, he gave up all that and began to think of himself as a dancer. He stayed here for a few years, disappeared to Los Angeles, and ended up in Las Vegas doing acrobatics on a casino stage. Wilson had two looks: in one, when his face would fill up with a childlike uncontrollable exuberance, his smile was all teeth, and he was liable to go bounding off in a series of flips; the other was when he'd slip on his dark glasses, plug into his Walkman, and tuck into his stride. He had a small brown body like a clenched fist.

Capoeirista in New York—that was me too, and I played the part: my friends and I used to stride through the park leonine and muscular, feeling the mechanism of our bodies walking and the material presence of the sun on our shoulders. The first capoeiristas in New York were Jelon Vieira and Loremil Machado, and they arrived in 1975. Old friends, they had utterly different personalities, and their games showed it. Jelon is massive, solid as a rock, and his capoeira is stonily intimidating. It's only when he cracks a shy smile that you get a glimpse at his tremendously tender part. Loremil had a small, agile body of incomparable finesse and almost unbearable charm. He was constantly goofing, his game loaded with humor. He never "fought" a match, but played with the pure joy of a child discovering the freedom of motion. It was only rarely that you glimpsed his real strength: the flexible but accurate, piercing arrow of Oxossi. Jelon has taught many Americans to play capoeira, and has inspired in all of them a quiet, profound respect. Loremil's effect on people was different: mad, aching, passionate love.

I knew Loremil for ten years, and I suppose I loved him as achingly as I'll ever love anybody. But all of his friends and students, however much time they spent with him, say he taught them this: how to throw themselves headlong into the pleasure of having a body. When he passed away a few months ago, forty years old, as childlike and innocent as ever, I think this is what hurt us most: the thought of his having to leave behind a body that he enjoyed so intensely. But maybe that last maneuver was just the ultimate acrobatic stunt—a cartwheel into a world of truly free motion.

Capoeira is a game, a fight, and a dance, composed of kicks, acrobatics, and traditional Kongo dance movements. One doesn't speak of "dancing" or "fighting" capoeira, but rather of "playing" (*jogar capoeira*).[1] Or one can eliminate the substantive and use the simple verb *vadiar* (to bum around). And yet capoeiristas universally take the game very seriously. Most, when asked to define it in a word, call it an art.[2] In New York I once saw a capoeirista wearing a button that said "Doing strange things in the name of art." And it's true, they will go to extremes.

While some people will tell you there are two basic styles of capoeira,[3] there are in fact as many as there are great capoeiristas. But certain generalizations apply. Capoeira is always played in a *roda*, the same circle formation that delimits all traditional Afro-Brazilian dance. Two players enter the roda at a time and their focus remains on each other, while they may pivot either clockwise or counterclockwise throughout the game. Motion is generally circular. Kicks and sweeps are more often than not arched or spinning, and they loop together in a series of near misses. The idea is to keep one's eyes fixed on one's opponent. At times this necessitates having eyes in the back of one's head. But the relative placement of body parts or facial features seems to be constantly ridiculed anyway. The capoeirista spends a good deal of time inverted, with hands planted firmly like feet on the ground, feet slapping happily like palms in the air. The upside-down face, like those magical cartoons from our childhood where the hair became a beard and the creased forehead a smirking, lipless mouth, grins at your attempts to fix it. And still, those eyes are on you.

How do I reconcile this silly picture with what I want to communicate of capoeira's elegance and even gravity? The game can be humorous, but it is not self-ridiculing—at least not simply so. This is partly because of the obvious physical prowess involved, but even more because of the understanding of the role of capoeira in popular histories.

As with all diasporic forms, a linear history of capoeira is far from satisfactory. The popular histories that circulate most commonly seem to pit forces of influence against each other in a struggle for control of the game: African versus European or Asian values and gestural vocabularies; ruffianism versus links to the military police; tradition versus corruption; chaos versus discipline. Depending on one's perspective these influences may seem to be playing out a struggle between good and evil. But capoeira, whatever one's style or perspective, always ironizes the notion of Manichean extremes. Just when you think you've determined who are the good and the bad, it all suddenly strikes you as rather an aesthetic issue, except that you can't tell anymore what is ugly and what is beautiful. And an upside-down mug is grinning at you, plug-ugly, gorgeous.

Generally nobody "wins" a game of capoeira—although in recent years there have sprung up various tournaments and other events—but that's all part of the story. There are take-downs, and certainly the ability to apply them effectively adds to one's prestige as a capoeirista. But gratuitous, unprovoked violence or even humorless humiliation of one's opponent (or partner?) is never admired. The question is at what point provocation occurs. In a tight, "inside" game (*jogo de dentro*), when the players are interweaving spinning kicks, the agility and precision of one opens a precise space for the elegant partnering of the other. But there may be a moment imperceptible to a spectator when somehow synchronicity shatters and there are in fact two opposing forces. Someone provoked. Someone sprung malice, which was always inherent in the moves.

However they have developed, the question of where these moves originated is one that inspires impassioned arguments from most capoeiristas. Capoeira is decidedly an Afro-Brazilian art, but which half of that term should be weighted? The simplest narrative in circulation is something like this: Prior to their captivity and enslavement in Brazil, the people, predominantly men, of the Kongo/Angola region practiced certain kicking games for sport and recreation. In Brazil, the games were prohibited for all too obvious reasons. But the Kongo people continued practicing their games in seclusion. The roda was formed as a protective circle, and the choreographic elements—as well as music—were added to disguise the fight as a dance. Repression of the practice continued even after abolition. The players invented a special rhythm, *cavalaria,* an imitation of the sound of approaching horses' hooves, to warn each other of police surveillance, and on that cue the capoeira became an "innocent" samba. In other words, capoeiristas generally acknowledge that a martial arts technique and choreographic and rhythmic vocabularies were brought from Africa. But the strategic blending of fight and dance occurred in Brazil, under specific pressures. And while that strategy appears to have been directed against forces outside of the roda de capoeira, it became the fundamental strategy within the game. Dance—as seduction, illusion, deception—became dangerous, and kicks became elements of choreography. The Portuguese tolerated the roda de capoeira because it was merely dance—perceived as motion without purpose or effect, other than aesthetic. And within the circles, Africans in Brazil trained like fighters in the art of dissimulation: how to grin upside down.

This story is typical of those recounted in the capoeira community, although there are variations placing greater or lesser emphasis on tradition or change, on Africanness or Brazilianness. Ethnographic narratives of origin also vary, although the most powerful arguments come from scholars who view themselves as advocates of African diasporic culture. Righteously countering centuries of European dismissal of sophisticated African traditions, scholars like Robert Farris Thompson, Kenneth Dossar, and Gerhard Kubik[4] have given a strong case for the ever-fresh inscription of Kongo cosmology in capoeira's designs. I find these arguments powerful not simply because of their convincing "evidence," but because of their commitment to the principles of resistance that are at the heart of capoeira.

More politicized capoeiristas in Brazil also tend to emphasize African sources. If the seeds of the game existed in Angola but the intention or strategy developed in Brazil, then it would appear that capoeira must be acknowledged as an authentically Afro-Brazilian form. But when black nationalist Brazilians regard capoeira as an African form, their argument is strong. If one recognizes that Bahia, the capital of capoeira and Afro-

Brazilian culture generally, resembles much more closely a West African port city than it resembles any other point in Latin America, the gap of the Atlantic begins to seem quite incidental. The historical fact of forced migration is not forgettable, but the racial and cultural constituency of Bahia is overwhelmingly African. The dance forms that developed there were influenced by Europeans and indigenous Brazilians, but they developed in a culturally African metropolis.

Gestural vocabularies, of all cultural productions, are perhaps the most difficult to trace genealogically, so frequently arguments regarding the history of capoeira rest rather on linguistic etymologies. The etymological debate has been characterized by one historian as "a linguistic version of antiquarian disputes over empirical details in history."[5] There is something oddly literal-minded about this line of research, considering that capoeira's own strategy is founded on irony: saying one thing and meaning another. Capoeira, like samba, is an alternative language to the dominant one. Gerhard Kubik[6] suggests a Bantu derivation of the term, and given the general acceptance of the largely Kongo-Angolan roots of the game, it's surprising this argument hasn't gained greater currency. But etymological hypotheses are also narratives, and they have political significance.

In contemporary usage, the word "capoeira" refers most often to the game, but there are two other meanings in standard Brazilian Portuguese: the bush, and the chicken coop. This latter meaning derives from the Portuguese word "capao," which means rooster and is related to the English "capon." Some suggest that the game resembled a chicken fight, the scrambling of two birds in a cage. Whether the term would have been applied in this way by Portuguese observing the practice or ironically by capoeiristas themselves is not clear. Another suggestion is that the chicken coop label was attached metonymically rather than metaphorically: it was the blacks taking fowl to sell at the markets who practiced the game in public plazas, transferring the name of their merchandise to their pastime.

Capoeira as bush or wild space is said to derive from Tupi roots (caa: forest, puera: extinct). Again, the etymology may be "true" or "false"— although its accuracy is less interesting than the association of a term for wildness with the indigenous Brazilian. As I have argued elsewhere,[7] the figure of the "Indian" or *caboclo* absorbs wilderness from both Portuguese and African imaginations in Brazil. While no explicit connection is indicated between indigenous games or dances and capoeira, the caboclo figure bears certain similarities to the capoeirista. The caboclo functions generally in Afro-Brazilian culture as an emblem of the refusal to be or remain a captive. One popular conception of capoeira is that it was developed as a means of self-defense for slaves hoping to escape to independent black communities in the backlands of the agricultural states. These communities, *quilombos,* have been documented as remarkably developed urban centers with organized political and market systems.[8] The best known was called Palmares, in the interior of the state of Alagoas. Capoeiristas insist that it was the art of capoeira that defended Palmares against repeated attempts to dismantle it and return its residents to captivity.

The efficiency of capoeira in defending a community against mounted, armed invasions is questionable, and this part of the story may well have been inflated over the years.[9] Brazilian director Carlos Diegues's 1984 film *Quilombo* shows highly romanticized scenes of young boys practicing cartwheels in training for the defense of their society. But to return to the etymological significance of the bush, the wild place, the caboclo's terrain: one fact should be mentioned. Capoeira is an urban phenomenon. It has always flourished in high-density areas: Salvador, Bahia, possibly Palmares, even New York City. The Urban Bush. The notion of its wildness, even the animality of its motion, doesn't mean it came organically from an uncivilized, non-Europeanized space. It was constructed specifically to counter European pressures.

Most capoeiristas and historians are in agreement on most of the details of this account of capoeira's origin. But its consequent developments are contested. The roda de capoeira ostensibly began as a protective circle enclosing the capoeiristas who were in training—in the process of an organized transmission of techniques of resistance. But capoeira's bright image as a system of righteous defense becomes confused in the eighteenth century with boundless, undirected or uncontrolled violence. In the major cities, gangs known as *maltas,* largely composed of mixed-race, impoverished free men, we are told,[10] used capoeira technique in general looting and gang fighting. Under such circumstances, they dispensed with the roda, as well as the dance.

This is the beginning of capoeira's association with ruffianism, an association that has continued to have currency, to varying degrees, over the years. But the idea of breaking out of boundaries, of getting out of control, is not only figured in the broken circle, the shattered roda where dance explodes into class unrest and violence. Ostensibly, racial borders as well were being broken. The so-called mulato capoeirista is a figure moving between categories. He exists at the anxious point of contact between blacks and whites. And while that point of contact was sexualized in the body of the mulata sambista, it is made violent in that of the capoeirista. In fact (as is the case with the crack sambistas as well), while they may be narrated as embodying the mixture of races, capoeiristas are, in the majority, black. But in the period immediately preceding and following slavery's abolition in 1888, they absorbed some of the racial fears of a society in transition.

The music stopped—at least in the soundtrack of the romanticized, cinematic version of the story. But there is something suspect in the suggestion that the intention of capoeira had essentially changed. Was it a black dance when contained within the roda, when it expressed self-irony, restricted to black-on-black aggression? Even on the quilombos, the roda de capoeira as a training ground for defense seems ultimately unthreatening to white authority because it is isolated. The quilombos were remarkably successful, but basically self-contained. This may be what allows for their romanticization in retrospect: Palmares has come to represent a never-never land where racial injustice didn't have to be dealt with as long as there was minimal contact with white society.

During the "ruffian" stage, it's said that capoeira was still occasionally played in the "old style": as a dance, a game, a diversion. But this qualitative difference may not have been so much a change in style or form as a change in perspective and context. Capoeira, however dissimulating, has always held violent potential. It has also long maintained an ambiguous relationship to white authority. In the early nineteenth century, at the start of Dom Joao VI's monarchy, the first official police force was instituted in Brazil, and the head of the Royal Guard, a Major Vidigal, is supposed to have been a powerful capoeirista. He is also supposed to have been charged with keeping the ruffian capoeira contingent in line.

Capoeiristas were absorbed into the order during the brief war with Paraguay in 1865. They were forcibly recruited and are said to have fought valiantly. A number of traditional capoeira song lyrics refer to this event. The capoeiristas returned to the cities of Salvador and Rio with renewed prestige, although the situation was short-lived. When the roda, the circle of control, could not be maintained, capoeira was again perceived as a threat. The penal code of 1890 legislated corporal punishment or forced exile for the practitioners of capoeira. Even early in this century, according to the great fighter Master Bimba: "the police persecuted a capoeirista like you chase after a damn dog. Just imagine, one of the punishments they gave capoeiristas that were caught playing was to tie one wrist to a horse's tail, and the other to another horse. The two horses were sent running toward the police station. We even used to make a joke, that it was better to play near the police station, because there were many cases of death. The individual couldn't support being pulled at high velocity along the ground and died before arriving at his destination."[11] But it was Bimba, in fact, who initiated certain changes so that, in time, capoeira began to be tolerated as a game—under certain circumstances. It was more or less institutionalized. And you still find in Brazil the popular conception that street capoeira is for troublemakers, and the only respectable place for the game is in the capoeira "academies."

If the joke was that it was better to play near the police station, the academicization of capoeira in some ways realized that approximation. The academy became the controlled space. It was a structure of containment—not a protective circle like the roda. And yet ostensibly the academy serves the function of an educational space. Politicized black parents today send their children to capoeira academies to learn about their cultural heritage.

As an initiate in the U.S. "academy," I am always particularly interested in notions of pedagogy in the Afro-Brazilian context. The "alternative" pedagogical institution may appear to be a simple ironic response to dominant, repressive, or exclusionary institutions: the capoeira academy in opposition to the police academy, or the samba school in opposition to an educational system that denies the cultural validity of one's African heritage. But it isn't that simple. The phrase "escola de samba" is popularly held to derive from the schoolyard location of the first group's early rehearsals. That metonymic explanation doesn't preclude irony, but the Rio samba schools can't really be held up as shining examples of antihegemonic, popular education.[12] The capoeira academies also reiterate, sometimes, a rigid, linear pedagogical technique that seems purchased wholesale from the police academy. Still, there are valuable lessons of African history and aesthetics. I take all this to heart as an educator who attempts to transmit non-Western culture through historically Eurocentric institutions.[13] Certainly the way we read, teach, and write about culture is as important as the particular manifestations we're considering. The capoeira academies demand that we rethink inclusion and exclusion, cultural containment and liberatory pedagogy.

When Bimba instituted his academy, he modified not only the vocabulary of capoeira, but also its mode of transmission. Bimba was born Manoel dos Reis Machado about a decade after abolition. His nickname, which means "little boy's dick," was given at birth by the midwife who delivered him. As a child he studied capoeira with an African shipper who worked in the bay. But in 1932 he founded a school for a practice he called "a luta regional baiana" (Bahian regional wrestling). What he called this activity is a matter of particular interest to those who subsequently took issue with Bimba's teachings. The game he developed came to be called "capoeira regional," and is now usually regarded as one of the two principal styles of capoeira—and certainly the most popular. In distinction, another style, which is generally regarded as more "traditional," became specified as "capoeira angola."

Today the angoleiros, or practitioners of the "old" style, sometimes argue that "regional" isn't even capoeira. They point to the name Bimba first gave it as evidence. This position has been reinforced by the Brazilian ethnographic community, which, as usual, is unimpressed by the apparent absorption of non-African influences into Afro-Brazilian forms. In a 1975 work on capoeira, Edison Carneiro reduces regional to a dismissive paragraph: "The capoeirista Bimba, a virtuoso on the berimbau [the main instrument of capoeira music], became well-known when, in the 1930s, he created a school for the training of athletes in the so-called Bahian regional wrestling, a mixture of capoeira with ju-jitsu, boxing and tag. Popular, folkloric capoeira, the legacy of Angola, has little, almost nothing to do with Bimba's school."[14] The young capoeiristas today who opt for an orthodox angola style are disinclined to acknowledge regional as having anything to do with capoeira. And they keep pointing to that name—a luta regional baiana—as evidence.

But this preoccupation with nomenclature again strikes me as mis-guided considering that capoeira's foundation is one of dissimulation. Capoeira has always been a fight. Calling it a game or a dance has never detracted from the fact that Africans in Brazil developed it with the potential to disarm whites, whether through literal blows or through the subtle art of seeming to be in meaningless motion while actually rein-forcing a circle of cultural and political race consciousness.

In fact, the angola-regional division is much less clear-cut than it may seem. Following the terminology of a contemporary master, John Lowell Lewis has identified a third, synthetic rubric: capoeira atual, or "current, up-to-date" capoeira.[15] As I have said, capoeira styles vary greatly from one master to the next. If the whole premise of the game is not to block one's opponent but rather to take his movement in and invert it, then it's easy to see how apparently differing styles can be absorbed and modi-fied by each other. It gets even more complicated. Lewis suggests that in recent years, the increased interest in capoeira angola in Brazil might have been spurred by the enthusiasm of black American players, who studied the regional style at home and then went to Brazil to find an expression of African roots culture. Their "discovery" of the funkier version may have influenced Brazilian players' perspectives on angola.[16] Lewis suggests that regional expressed a drive for "modernization," while capoeira atual might be seen as a postmodern expression. This observation highlights several interesting features of contemporary ca-poeira: its temporal alinearity (such that what's oldest appears most up-to-date); its entanglement in global cultural exchange (such that Ameri-can players may have encouraged Brazilians to reject extrinsic influences that have "contaminated" regional); and its indecipherable self-irony (such that it's impossible to say if capoeira atual is angola goofing on regional, or vice versa). But then again, all these riddles—temporal, cross-cultural, self-ironic—are what we have been reading as central to capoeira from its very origins.

If capoeira was repressed during the historical period when its expres-sion of racial tension became too clear, Bimba in a sense was deploying a very orthodox capoeira strategy in remasking the game not as an "An-golan" art, but as a regional, Bahian one. The new name smacked of local political savvy—call it not only Brazilian, but Bahian. It doesn't sound like African nationalism or black consciousness, unless one suggests, as I suggested earlier, that many cultural developments in Bahia, seen from an African nationalist perspective, are African.

But Bimba's reforms went further than the name. Carneiro is accurate in saying that he added moves from Asian martial arts as well as American boxing to capoeira's vocabulary. One of Bimba's students has argued:

Mestre Bimba was accused of introducing into Capoeira movements from other martial arts. He laughed at this criticism but on several occasions admitted he had used attacks and defenses from boxing and jujitsu. One who did not know anything about Capoeira could easily have taken these statements literally.

However, I believe that Mestre Bimba only adopted this stance to bring the prestige of foreign arts to Capoeira in order to attract more students.[17]

When the angoleiros dismiss these modifications on style as being "not real capoeira," they are arguing for something more important than the maintenance of a tradition. If capoeira is regarded as historical evidence of black resistance, they want to show that African forms are in themselves valid, durable, and effective weapons. This is doubtless true. But if part of the genius of African religion in Brazil is syncretism, its ability to absorb or account for Catholic or other systems, part of capoeira's genius has also been its ability to absorb rather than be displaced by other forms. It is a survival tactic consistent with the premise of the game.

Locating what is "really" African in Brazilian culture is not, or should not be, a simple project of mapping surface continuities. Much more interesting is the continuity of strategies for cultural survival. Of course, this argument itself is a tricky maneuver. It's what allows Bimba—and his student—to give two accounts of the sources of capoeira regional. Bimba "laughed at" the charges of foreign influences. He also "admitted" drawing on American and Asian techniques. His student tells us not to take the statements (which ones?) literally, because they were strategic—and the strategy is recognizable to anyone who is familiar with the strategy of the game. In other words, the apparent contradiction is resolved by the fact that the very strategy of appropriating extrinsic movements is intrinsic to capoeira. The larger argument is that the very strategy of appropriating extrinsic *culture* is intrinsic to African culture. There is obviously a downside to this line of reasoning: one loses sight of the abundant clear and stunning manifestations of powerful traditions that mark themselves as African not only in evasive strategy, but in outright, dignified cultural and political reference. A proud angoleiro who calls his game by its African name makes a powerful statement. Centrifugal and centripetal forces act upon each other. Neither tells the truer story: they are both necessary and perhaps complementary strategies.

Bimba was a jet black Brazilian. The majority of his students were white. Some were members of the same police force that in his youth rounded up outlaw capoeiristas. Bimba's style of teaching was based on a notion of discipline. The rigorous control of his academy so impressed local political figures that he was invited to make presentations at the governor's palace in Bahia and, in 1953, before the then-president of the Republic, Getulio Vargas. After this demonstration, Vargas announced: "Capoeira is the only true national sport."[18] The path was open for official acceptance, and this had as much to do with Bimba's disciplinary example as it did with his athletic prowess. Bimba's teaching method entailed a classification of movements and the training of "sequences"— choreographed exchanges between partners. The sequences are symmetrical: kicks and ducks are trained equally on each side. The first partner executes a series of kicks with the second responding with the "correct" defenses, and then offensive and defensive roles are switched.

Politicized angoleiros generally seem much more critical of Bimba's bringing white moves into the roda than they are of his bringing in white students. But it is even rarer to hear an angoleiro complain about Bimba's methodology—his introduction of a linear, sequential mode of instruction into a quintessentially circular form. This may be because they recognize that different organizational principles may be helpful or even necessary for political mobilization. The protective roda has been a charged space for cultural transmission and creativity. But determined linearity has its advantages for activism. Bimba's relation to the political authorities was complex: even as he was embraced by them, he depicted himself as a rogue. And even those who reject regional as a style seem to respect his personal resistance.

In Bimba's academy, individual progress was marked by the *formatura,* or graduation ceremony. The students would demonstrate their skills in pairs, until the moment of the "orator's" speech. This was an advanced and particularly articulate student who would be called on to recount some of capoeira's history as well as the accomplishments of the master.

A small medal and a silk scarf were handed to the "godmother" accompanying each student. A blue scarf signified completion of the course. The scarf, according to Bimba, was a reminder of the old-time rogue capoeiristas who wore silk around their throats to thwart the razor's cut. Then all students would have to execute correctly a series of moves and finally prove himself in the game by completing a match without "dirtying his clothes"—a euphemism for falling on one's ass.

Many academies today operate on a "cord" system resembling the belt system of Asian martial arts. The cord is strung around the waist, or through the belt-loops of the *abada,* a pair of regulation white pants. But different groups have designated different color codes, some based on the colors of the Brazilian flag, some based on the colors associated with the *orixas.* Formaturas—full graduations that constitute something like teacher accreditation—are much less common today than *batizados,* or baptisms, which simply mark intermediate stages of progress. At most batizados, the students are given nicknames (*nomes de guerra*—literally, war names) according to some personal peculiarity. They then get the baptismal dunking: a patronizing match with a superior player, concluding with a supremely humiliating sweep. The batizado is of course a clever turn on Catholic ceremony. The dunking is not in water, but in earth, and the affected part is more likely the ass than the head. But in a more serious vein, the player is ceremonially brought to that liminal place that divides the sacred and the profane, the immortal and the mortal: the ground. Bimba instituted academic training, but now many angoleiros subscribe to the ceremonial marking of progress toward a goal. And perhaps the marking of individual progress is just part of a larger acceptance of the benefit of marking progress toward communal goals. Of course, as usual, one moves forward by getting closer to the ground of one's ancestral past.

There is another great figure in capoeira's modern history who is usually discussed in counterdistinction to Mestre Bimba, and he is the old-time angoleiro Mestre Vicente Ferreira Pastinha. Whereas Bimba was a large, bolt-upright, barrel-chested man, Pastinha was short and slight. At the end of his life he was blind and stooped, and in the late photographs he seems to be swallowed up by his baggy clothing and the mashed-up old hat on his head. His big dim useless eyes had an expression of exquisite tenderness, despite a curious half-smile. An elderly priestess from the candomblé, the dominant African religion practiced in Bahia, told me: "Ha! Everybody thinks Pastinha was such a sweet little guy. I knew him and he was a woman-user and a dirty son of a bitch like the rest of them." That may be, though it doesn't mean I don't love the idea of him. A woman friend and I were looking at one of his last snapshots: fragile, bent over playing capoeira music, the stick of the berimbau pressing into his tiny thigh. His miniature feet seem lost in their oversized sandals; the cuffs of his trousers are rolled up to show two rickety little ankles. "But look at his dick!" said my friend. There it is in the folds of cloth, unmistakable: the dick of the trickster Exu, divine engorged rod of mischief.

Angola speaks softly and carries a big stick. The style of the game is much less apparently aggressive than regional. The angoleiro wreaks havoc not through his powerful athleticism, as does the regionalista, but through the subtle art of *malicia,* which doesn't translate as malice, really, so much as street smarts or cunning. It is the art of irony, trickster Exu's domain, and the roda is the circle within which all words have doubled meanings. Even no means yes.

Pastinha's teachings are passed on by angoleiros with reverence. But in contrast to Bimba's directives, Pastinha's aphorisms, inscribed in a little book he wrote and recorded on an LP, sound like riddles. He went around planting these seeds of confusion. Bira Almeida opens his book on capoeira with one:

Once I asked the wise Mestre Vicente Ferreira Pastinha—
what is Capoeira, Mestre? "Capoeira is whatever the mouth eats."[19]

Almeida goes on to describe Pastinha's extinguished eyes, his soft voice, his tattered little world, and confesses, with hushed respect, "I did not understand his answer." No kidding.

Most everything Pastinha said is lyrical and indecipherable. But his ambiguity isn't without significance. It's strategic lyricism. Much of Pastinha's philosophy is embedded in the lyrics of capoeira songs that he sang. Most capoeira standards are ancient, passed on by generations of nameless players. But the great masters mark themselves by self-referentiality into songs, or by creating images so powerful that a particular lyric is indelibly associated with them. Capoeira songs generally express the ambiguity of the game, and the most obvious example is this simple call-and-response pattern: "Oi sim sim sim, Oi nao nao nao" (Oh yes yes yes, oh no no no). This is the basic tension of the game—not a struggle between positive and negative forces, but rather the exploration of what is negative, painful, or malicious within the ostensibly positive, whole, and benignant.

The no in the yes, the big in the little, the earth in the sky, the fight in the dance—these are the riddles Pastinha passed on, with a characteristic grand humility.

Ie, God is great.
Ie, God is great and I am little.
All that I have, God gave me.
All that I have, God gave me.
But in the roda de capoeira—
Ha ha!
I am a great little man.[20]

The roda is the circle in which such ironies can take place. All Afro-Brazilian dance—religious, secular, or martial—is circumscribed there. The circle of candomblé dance is the space where human bodies incorporate divine energy. The roda de samba lifts humanity, secular energy, to a higher level; in capoeira, the roda contains bodies all too aware of their earthly nature. Capoeira is not contrary to the spiritual realm. And while the priestess may have expressed her disdain for their lot, many capoeiristas feel a profound link to the principles of the candomblé, and particularly to the idea of ancestor spirits. But capoeira developed as a way of dealing with very immediate, material historical and political pressures. If the roda is viewed as a cosmographic emblem, a little map of the world of hard knocks, within that sign the capoeirista acknowledges his or her potential for action.

When capoeiristas pause in a game to pace—always counterclockwise—around the inner limits of the roda, this is called taking a walk around the world. But the circle is not the only sign in capoeira readable as earth. Robert Farris Thompson has analyzed in detail and with grace the variety of Kongo-derived cosmograms in the New World.[21] The emblem of Bimba's capoeira school, while it may appear to be a mixture of Judeo-Christian and military emblems, is in fact part of the Kongo inscriptive tradition in Brazil known as *pontos riscados:* There is a circle, but there is also a cross, which in this context must be recognized as a crucifix, but also as a cosmological sign of the Kongo tradition. Thompson cites Wyatt MacGaffey on the Kongo sign of the cross: "One line represents the boundary; the other is ambivalently both the path leading across the boundary, as to the cemetery; and the vertical path of power linking 'the above' with 'the below.' This relationship, in turn, is polyvalent, since it refers to God and man, God and the dead, and the living and the dead."[22] And while Bimba's school may be read by some angoleiros as having broken the roda, the protective circle of African consciousness in capoeira, its emblem rather shows a circle made up of discontinuity. And precisely when it would seem that Western influence—the crucifix—interrupts the circle, that sign of the cross may rather be a mark of continuity with African strategies of defense.

The sign of the cross is sometimes embodied in the players. Before entering the game, capoeiristas generally squat before the berimbau and cross themselves—but they also touch the ground, indicating the probability of a Kongo, not just Christian, reference. And at a certain point in an angola game, one player may pause and extend his arms, seemingly creating the image of the crucified Christ. The head hangs slightly, the hands appear limp, and the gesture is one of not only apparent vulnerability, but of submission. But this gesture is in fact a challenge. The other player will demonstrate, at a distance, his wiliest moves, and then approach the one who called the challenge. What follows may seem to a spectator a strange, subtle dance of exquisite gentleness, two men delicately pressing their heads to each other's shoulder, arm draped sensitively over arm, thigh just barely pressed against thigh. But then the second man, the challenged one, will spring his malice, and most likely will be surprised back with kick or sweep. This is treachery, but it doesn't mean the sensitive dance was false. All gestures of submission and openness in capoeira can be read as such, but they all contain the potential of violence.

The cross of the body is also set askew in the *au*, or cartwheel, one of the most important moves of the game. The au literally inverts the sign of the cross. Demonstrating the ambivalence of "the above" and "the below" noted by MacGaffey above, in fact the au sets "up" and "down" spinning.[23] If God is in heaven, then all is right with the world. But if nothing is right in the world, and hierarchies, human or divine, are set off balance, then men will invert themselves until they can make sense of it all. The cross, of course, is not only significant in Christian and Kongo symbology. It is also the sign of the crossroads, playground of Exu, a Yoruba figure. The crossroads mark the place where everything becomes relative—including good and bad. It is appropriate that it should also mark the collision of belief systems of the cultures that comprise African Brazil.

In a world of ironic inversions, which way is up? Perhaps the most beautiful *ladainha,* or extended, plaintive solo lyric of capoeira, was sung by Mestre Pastinha:

Already I'm fed up
With life here on the earth.
Oh mama, I'm going to the moon,
I talked to my wife about it.
She answered me,
We'll go if God wills it.
We'll make a little ranch there,
all full of greens.
Tomorrow at seven o'clock,
we'll have our breakfast.
I really can't abide
people who tell unbelievable stories.
Eh, the moon comes to the earth.
Eh, the earth goes to the moon.
All this is just talk,
now let's get to work . . .

Upside down, the sky is the ground beneath your feet, and the only heaven is the earth to which you are bound. It's an unbelievable story, but true. The plaintiveness of the ladainha is that that upside-down world is a better one than this one. It is a world where there will always be food to put on the table. But the song stops itself: all this lyricism is just talk. And the call to get to "work" is a call to action—a call to begin the game, to come back through the game to the ground of significance, of political reality, and of the fight.

That doesn't mean the music has to stop, nor the dance. The fight is in the dance, and the music itself, even this kind of lyricism, can be a weapon and can be pointedly, politically significant. The berimbau is a hauntingly beautiful instrument. It consists of a curved wooden bow strung with a single wire chord and with a resonating gourd attached at the base. The gourd pressed against his belly, the player strikes the chord with a small stick while simultaneously varying the pitch by manipulating a small stone or coin near the base of the instrument. Effectively two notes are achieved, although variations in pressure allow for a much wider spectrum of sounds. The sound emitted is an eery twang. There is something deeply sad and mysterious about berimbau music. It is said to be an instrument of communication with the dead. There are various rhythms played for capoeira, and in this century they have been classified and categorized ad infinitum by different masters.[24] But unlike most of the highly sophisticated rhythmic patterns of African Brazil, capoeira music doesn't dictate stepping on a certain beat. Rather, the music dictates the emotional tenor of the game and its intent. The moves themselves move in and out of synchrony with the berimbau.

The rhythm isn't the only thing hard to pin down about the berimbau's sound. Pitch too is neither here nor there. Lewis describes this accurately:

For some time I assumed that the interval between stopped and unstopped strings on the berimbau was in fact a whole tone, but upon closer listening, and comparing several bows, I realized that the interval was usually somewhat less than a whole step but more than a half-step. In Western musical terms this kind of pitch is sometimes called a "quarter tone" or (more generally) a "micro-tone," and the effect in this case is that the interval can be heard (by Western ears) either as a major second (whole step) or a minor second (half-step). In practice this means that berimbau music can be used to accompany songs in various modes or scales, with either a major or minor feel, but always with a slight dissonance.[25]

Lewis suggests that this indeterminacy might be a way of explaining the "call" of the berimbau—that quality that seems to summon a listener to participate in its musicality. As in my own earlier discussion of "bent" rhythms in the samba, the "micro-tone" explanation, enlightening as it is, is probably not quite as satisfying as the acknowledgment of *axe,* or spiritual energy.

A capoeira song says, "the berimbau is an instrument / that plays on just one string. / It plays angola in C-major. / But I've come to believe, old pal, / berimbau is the greatest / comrade." The simplicity of the berimbau is misleading. Pastinha said: "A lot of people say that it's an instrument—berimbau berimbau berimbau, it's music, it's an instrument. Berimbau, then, is music, it's a musical instrument—it's also an offensive instrument. Because on the occasion of happiness, it's an instrument—we use it as an instrument. And in the hour of pain, it stops being an instrument and becomes a hand weapon." The use of the thick wooden bow as a weapon is not taught in capoeira academies. But if the wood is in hand and the occasion for violence arises, it is not difficult to imagine what uses other than musical might be made of the berimbau.

In capoeira, apparent musicality always contains violent potential, and all aggression is transformed into dance. This is why the simple opposition of categories seems to me clearly unsatisfactory. Regional and angola styles strike me rather as in dialogue with one another and speaking, finally, the same double-talk, whether or not you call it "up-to-date." And while most scholars of the art have come down on one side of the fence (with Lewis an exception), the majority of capoeiristas, at least until very recently, did not necessarily ally themselves with one camp—including "atual." How do you make rigid alliances in a world where you must trust everyone but can't trust anyone?

My first capoeira master in Bahia was certainly among those who refused to define his game restrictively. Mestre Boa Gente (which means "Good People") was the baddest good people I may ever have met. I wouldn't trust him as far as I could throw him, although he's weightless and wiry so I could probably throw him pretty far if I could just get my hands on him. Mestre Boa Gente is more than just a master of capoeira. He is also a broadcaster, bar owner, local hero in the Valley of Pebbles, and a general *gato esperto* (a smart cat). Boa has one academy at the old Red Cross Club in the middle of town and another at his house in the Valley. The Vale das Pedrinhas, Valley of Pebbles, is a notorious Bahia slum. Boa Gente runs a makeshift bar there, a shack by his house where you can get a beer or a shot of rum, buy an individual cigarette, a cake of soap, chewing gum, a sanitary napkin, or a little slab of guava paste. Boa has also installed a microphone and an old turntable and wired them up to a network of speakers throughout the Valley. The system operates at 300 watts, every day, reaching the Valley's 30,000 inhabitants. Boa plays samba and rhythm and blues, tells truths and lies about life, politics, and art.

I used to take class at the Red Cross Club three days a week. We were a mixed lot: mixed race, mixed gender, mostly domestic and service workers, myself being the only gringa. Women train increasingly in the academies, although this is really quite a recent phenomenon. While Bahia is acknowledged as the cradle of capoeira, it lags behind in drawing women into the game.[26] Academies in Rio, São Paulo, and Brasilia receive more women students, and capoeira classes in the United States, often held in dance studios, commonly have a 50-50 gender ratio. There is a female "mestra," Edna Lima, teaching out of New York. But the only women of somewhat legendary status in capoeira lore seem to be a few common-law wives of the old masters, and somebody called Maria Doze-Homens (Twelve-man Maria), whom nobody has ever identified for me. But Boa told me he felt women had an advantage in capoeira: in a machista culture, women had already been forced to learn about seduction as a weapon; men had to study it. I learned a great deal about it myself in Brazil. If I hadn't I would have been knocked flat on my *bunda* even more often than I was. But capoeira also taught me athleticism. We trained hard in the sweltering heat, for hours at a time. Women were exempted from nothing. Sometimes, trembling through a thirtieth push-up, I'd look at Boa Gente's little, sinewy body, popping up and down effortlessly as he rested just on the tips of his fingers and toes. Women have a different center of gravity, and it is difficult for many of us to remain for long upside down. Boa insisted this was no excuse; the important thing was being able to see the world upside down.

That means more than one thing. Certainly it means being able to see the irony in life. It also means offering another perspective on social inequity—from the underside—and in this sense women clearly have much to say in the roda. And, as Dossar has argued,[27] it means looking into that upside-down world that is the world of the dead. This last significance perhaps seems incongruous in the context of so much irony, humor, and play. But the play can be dead serious, and the world of the dead can seem altogether lively when we understand it as animated with ancestral lessons.

I used to have some friends who gave free capoeira classes in the evenings to kids in a dilapidated public school in Bahia. They would often ask guest speakers to come in and tell the kids about the history of Africans in Brazil. One night at the end of class the wife of one of the teachers came in to talk about the quilombos and capoeira's historical association with black resistance. We were seated in a circle, sweaty from our workout, listening intently to this eloquent, dignified woman. She had traveled to Nigeria as an emissary from one of the carnaval groups, and on this evening she was wearing an elaborate head tie she'd received there. As the usually wriggly kids sat somber and rapt, one by one the little wooden blocks that made up the floor began to—pop. When the first one went, several kids jumped. There was a pause, and then—pop—pop—pop. The place was going off like popcorn. A bunch of us scrambled toward the door, thinking the building was collapsing; others were too surprised to move. Once we managed to scoot everybody out into the courtyard, the popping subsided.

Afterwards, the speaker's husband, who was a geologist, told the class the popping had been the result of an unusually rapid drop in temperature. But he told the adults in private that he had gone back to examine the structure and could find no explanation. A candomblé priestess was called in, who winced and shook her head as soon as she got a wiff of all the riled-up ancestor spirits in that room. It took a heavy herb bath to get things calmed down. Apparently a righteous woman's words and all those trembling, eager, hot, hungry, muscled little bodies were too potent a combination.

But the dead can communicate as much calm and restraint as impatience and explosivity. If it is the act of physical inversion that brings one closest to the other side, then it is true that it is the angoleiro who is in closest contact with his ancestors. Angola play is deliberate, earthbound—and often inverted. Some upside-down moves occur in regional play as well, but the pace of the game usually demands that you right yourself as quickly as possible. The au, for example, is only occasionally prolonged for effect, but is more often a swift escape maneuver. It goes spinning by like a pinwheel. In angola play, the au is slow, meaningful, and *fechado* (closed). It's crooked, contracted, pretzeled in on itself, knees bent, feet flexed. Unlike the Olympic-style, perfectly symmetrical cartwheel of capoeira regional, the angoleiro's *au fechado* is gorgeously ugly, elegantly awkward. Closing the body means leaving it in a position of readiness and protection.

In the candomblé, one refers to a ritually protected initiate as having a *corpo fechado*—a closed body. The trace of this operation is a raised scar on the shoulder. The healing of a ritual wound marks a doubled closure: of the individual into her body and into her community. In the same way, the angoleiro who closes his body in the *au fechado* appears to make himself vulnerable by pulling the rug out from under himself, and yet the subsequent contraction heals him not only of his vulnerability to attack, but into the body of racial memory and the world of his ancestors.

I rarely went on my free days to train at my master's second academy, in the Valley of Pebbles. But one night I went there with Jorge, one of Boa's older students. He was a certain type of capoeirista ("atual" doesn't do his style justice): graceful, deliberate, taciturn. He used to do a slow-motion cartwheel, bending his arms as he went over so that his head rested for an instant, delicately, on the ground. It was heart-breaking.

The night we went to the Valley, there was a strange electric crackling in the air, and little colored paper flags and Christmas tree lights strung up around the crossroads. The Valley is one of those unsettling, magical places in the world where you can't quite tell if the atmosphere is carnivalesque or under siege. It's both. It's dark, and firecrackers explode sporadically. Unkempt children play in little clumps in the streets. Skinny women with plucked eyebrows, ratty, straightened hair, and torn cotton dresses stand in the shadows with their arms crossed. One man goes running by, scared; another leans against a pole and pees. And over this dim scenario blasts the ecstatic, scratchy, reassuring voice of Boa Gente. He was in the studio when we arrived. He greeted us, tuned off the record he was playing, and announced that coming up was an exclusive interview with me, Barbara Browning, a famous journalist from the famous American magazine-newspaper *The New York Time*. I'm neither famous nor a journalist, connected to neither *Time* nor the *Times*, but Boa can't resist a good interview. Jorge, "Dr. Jorge," he claimed, was a famous dentist who would come back later to give the people of the Valley some tips on oral hygiene. Jorge, who worked in fact as a "boy" in an office building, looked mortified. Lucky for him, he never had to give his interview on oral hygiene. But I did get a good on-air grilling on poverty and multinational corporate politics. Finally Boa pointed at the sad little gang of underfed kids clustered around the studio door. He asked me if, as a famous journalist, I felt that the American public heard enough about hungry Brazilian children. Sweating, I answered quite solemnly that, as a famous journalist, I felt Americans didn't hear enough about that. Boa put a record on and gave me a hug and a drink.

Boa Gente tells truths and lies. I'd like to say that I believe that he does not suffer from lapses of honesty. Rather, these small falsehoods are a demonstration of the rigor that Boa exercises in regard to truth. When I met him, I thought I had encountered the incarnation of a Nietzschean principle. Nietzsche wrote that the truth needs to confront opposition from time to time and be able to fight. We need to pit truth against falsehood, or it will grow tiresome, powerless, and insipid—and we with it. This is Boa's game. I gave him a Portuguese translation of *Beyond Good and Evil* for his birthday and inscribed it:

To Master Boa Gente, who taught me
that beauty can be a weapon, and
strength can be an art.

How could you classify capoeira as a dance or a fight? One seldom strikes a blow to hit—more often to demonstrate the beauty of the movement and to harmonize it with the movements of the other. And the most powerful players are those who incapacitate their opponents by doing some stunning trick of pure gorgeousness: a flip, a slow, twisting cartwheel, a headspin, or just a graceful *ginga,* the swaying dance step that comes between blows. A capoeirista can have such a pretty ginga, arms twisting in impossible beautiful waves, that it confuses.

It was my first master who taught me the philosophical implications of the beauty and illusion of capoeira. That's why I came to syncretize, in my mind, Boa Gente with Nietzsche—and, of course, Exu. In the Catholic context, the candomblé entity Exu has defied syncretism. His pairing with the devil is misleading. Exu is more playful than evil. Jorge Amado says he is "just a deity in constant motion, friend of fracas, of confusion, but, in his heart of hearts, an excellent person. In a way he is the No where only Yes exists."[28]

Exu, Boa, Friedrich: they make up a trinity. They are the No in the Yes, the Falsehood in Truth, the big mix-up, the good laugh. It's an inverted trinity, just as the sign of the cross is inverted in the roda.

Many of capoeira's maneuvers are inversions, whether literal or ironic, physical or linguistic. One of the most basic blows is called the *bencao*, which means blessing or benediction. But instead of giving a good word or extending a pious hand, the capoeirista "blesses" with the sole of his foot, shooting it forward toward the other player's chest. The move is at least physically perfectly straightforward. But the response to it is usually an exaggerated pantomime of getting clobbered: part of the defense actually might be to fake getting hit, although that rarely happens. The one receiving the blow may even issue an ear-piercing shriek, snapping back his head in mock deflection of the kick. Sometimes that kind of defense is more dramatic, more satisfying than the blow itself.

Capoeira defensive moves are not so much blocks or even counterattacks as they are ironic negations of the offense.[29] The basic defensive position is called, in fact, the *negativa*. The player squats, one crooked leg extended, and leans forward and across that leg, pressing the side of his head toward the ground. To the uninitiated, it feels like an almost impossibly uncomfortable, impractical, and vulnerable position. But it is the ground zero from which a vast number of deep maneuvers can be deployed.

The low-to-the-ground moves are the ones most often used in capoeira angola. They don't look efficient—who would think to bend over and look through his legs in order to fight? But they are wily and sly. Many moves are named after animals, such as the stingray tail, an unexpected backlash, or the monkey, a lopsided back flip. The apparent impracticality of these acts has to be understood within the context of creating irony. To regard the animal references as evidence of the "natural" origins of capoeira seems to me a limited idea. Rather, these references seem to be in part ironic responses to projections on black culture in Brazil of stereotypes of innocence. A 1980 ethnography cited an Angolan informant who suggested that capoeira had developed from an ancient

Angolan ritual called "the dance of the zebra," in which young men imitated a mating ritual of zebras, fighting to win first choice of the young, marriageable women.[30] This document was quickly absorbed by some members of the capoeira angola contingent who began circulating the story. It is not unreasonable to suggest that some of the maneuvers of capoeira were inspired by animal motion. But I have also heard of a dubious older angoleiro who, on hearing this story, shook his head: "The only 'dance of the zebra' I ever saw was in the zoo, and it was two zebras fucking."

That kind of cynicism isn't a self-wounding rejection of Africa. And maybe a romanticized version of Africa has to exist on a certain level in capoeira history. But when it is ridiculed, it is also an affirmation of the developments of black culture in urban Brazil. Regional moves are self-ironizing as well. Bimba himself had a trick of "modernizing" capoeira while simultaneously making fun of modern technologies and of Western influences. He developed a sock to the head that set the ears ringing and called it the "telephone." That joke strikes me as remarkably reminiscent of the Nigerian "naïve" (read ironic!) novelist Amos Tutuola, who introduces a character with a "voice like a telephone" in the middle of the wildest, deepest, most "African" bush, residence of ancestral spirits.[31] Another of Bimba's head-banging techniques was a knockout punch called "godeme," his phonetic transcription of the "God damn it" gasped by an American marine who got busted in his challenge to the master. If people complained he was incorporating boxing techniques, he Brazilianized those blows and made them capoeira.

A friend sighed to me recently, watching a rapid-fire, exquisitely executed regional game, "capoeira has really developed into a sophisticated art over the last twenty years." It's true that some regionalistas are remarkable athletes. Their speed, flexibility, precision, and strength seem in perfect harmony. But though I defend the validity of their modifications on the game—they continue cannibalizing gymnastics, kick boxing, ballet, and, in the '80s, break dancing (a form that some have speculated was at least partly derived from or inspired by capoeira)[32]—it is still an old-fashioned, flat-footed, earthbound game of angola that brings tears to my eyes. Capoeira angola's wit is defter and more stunning than any feat of athleticism. I'm certainly not alone. The most sought-after master in New York today is Joao Grande—Big John—an old-guard angoleiro of Bahia, former student of Pastinha.

It isn't just a question of wit. Nor is it just that an angoleiro's play is funky with wisdom that's been fermenting for centuries. Young, politicized angoleiros have a point. It is important to reaffirm—constantly—the history of capoeira as an art of resistance. Hotdog regionalistas can spin so fast they sometimes lose sight of the past, and the present. The postmodern cultural critic must acknowledge that he or she too is a product of the times. We're sometimes giddy with the new language available to us for expressing our enthusiasms for cultural cross-fertilization. But in rejecting a restrictive, static notion of cultural authenticity, we risk losing some of the political potential of rootedness, of respect for deep funk, of the eloquence of an old man's body in motion.

Beyond the issue of tradition and modification, capoeira also raises the more general problem of "playing" politics. The black consciousness movement in Brazil has been hampered by conflicting strategies. But both traditionalist and syncretic enclaves might appear, to American eyes, to fall prey to an overly aestheticized idea of activism. It's true of the class struggle as well. Every political rally in Brazil degenerates (explodes?) into music minutes after its inception. Every body is in motion— But is it progressive motion, or simply a circular dance that expends energy without changing the world? That's the familiar question asked of carnaval. To an outsider, capoeira may appear particularly ineffective as a martial art, since so much of its energy is expended on dance—on motion for the sake of pleasure.

But the capoeiristas say that in life, as in capoeira, you have to keep doing the ginga, dancing between the blows. Maybe it's true. The political and economic situation in Brazil has been so bad for so long sometimes it seems inevitable that this people will get disheartened. What hope would be left if there weren't that distant, exciting rumble of the samba and the scratchy voice of Boa Gente on the air? I wish, in fact, his voice could carry across the water and make us feel watched over here in New York. I miss Loremil terribly. I feel as though, when he went skyrocketing out of here, he burst a hole in the electrified firmament. It's 3 A.M. in another city that is part war zone, part ecstatic celebration.

Headspin

I imagine Boa Gente could be on the air now, live from the Valley of Pebbles. And he could be saying the words of Nietzsche's Zarathustra:

Lift up your hearts, my brethren, high,
higher! And do not forget your legs!
Lift up also your legs, ye good dancers
—and better still if ye stand also on
your heads!

Notes

1. The English verb "to play" can be translated three ways in Portuguese: *brincar* (intransitive) = to play freely, like a child; *jogar* (transitive) = to play a sport or game; or *tocar* (transitive) = to play a musical instrument. Capoeira may appear to be a physical game or sport, but, as John Lowell Lewis has pointed out, all three kinds of play are demanded of the capoeirista, who must be an athlete, musician in his own accompaniment, and—at the highest levels—a master of childish imagination. See Lewis, *Ring of Liberation: Deceptive Discourse in Brazilian Capoeira* (Chicago: U of Chicago P, 1992), 2.

2. See, for example, Bira Almeida, *Capoeira, a Brazilian Art Form* (Palo Alto: Sun Wave, 1981).

3. I discuss below the distinction between angola and regional styles, as well as the counterarguments to their division.

4. See Robert Farris Thompson, *Capoeira* (New York: The Capoeira Foundation, 1988); Kenneth Dossar, "Capoeira Angola: Dancing between Two Worlds," *Afro-Hispanic Review* 11.1–3 (1992): 5–10; and Gerhard Kubik, "Angolan Traits in Black Music, Games and Dances of Brazil: A Study of African Cultural Extensions Overseas," *Estudos de Antropologia Cultural* 10 (Lisbon, 1979): 7–55.

5. Thomas H. Holloway, "'A Healthy Terror': Police Repression of Capoeiras in Nineteenth-Century Rio de Janeiro," *Hispanic American Historical Review* 69 (1989): 643. Waldeloir Rego (*Capoeira angola* [Salvador: Editora Itapua, 1968], 17–29), gives a fairly extensive account of the debate, which is summarized and modified in Lewis, 42–44. See also Almeida, 17–20.

6. Kubik, 29.

7. See my *Samba: Resistance in Motion* (Bloomington: Indiana U P, 1995), which contains a version of this essay.

8. See Decio Freitas, *Palmares, a guerra dos escravos* (Rio de Janeiro: 1982).

9. Lewis, 38, expresses skepticism about this historical narrative, while acknowledging its cultural significance.

10. See Almeida and Rego.

11. Raimundo Cesar Alves de Almeida, *Bimba: Perfil do mestre* (Salvador: UFBA, 1982), 13–14.

12. Alma Guillermoprieto recounts a disturbing history of political and financial manipulation and corruption at the leadership level of the samba schools in Rio. See *Samba* (New York: Knopf, 1990).

13. John Guillory's considerations of multiculturalism and canon formation are most instructive on this point. He warns that limiting the discussion to what is included in or excluded from the canon can obfuscate the greater question of pedagogy: "To have drawn up a new syllabus is not yet to have begun teaching, nor is it yet to have begun reflection upon the institutional form of the school" ("Canon, Syllabus, List: A Note on the Pedagogic Imaginary," *Transition* 52 [1992]: 54).

14. Edison Carneiro, *Capoeira* (Rio de Janeiro: Ministerio da Educacao e Cultura, 1975), 14.

15. See Lewis, 62.

16. Lewis, 64.

17. Bira Almeida, 115n.

18. Raimundo Almeida, 18.

19. Bira Almeida, 1.

20. Mestre Vicente Ferreira Pastinha, *Capoeira Angola.*

21. Robert Farris Thompson, *Flash of the Spirit: African and Afro-American Art and Philosophy* (New York: Vintage, 1984), 113–16.

22. Thompson, 108.

23. Kenneth Dossar explicitly links the au to Kongo games that act out a "dance between two worlds," that of the living and the dead, by inverting the body ("Capoeira Angola: An Ancestral Connection?" *American Visions* 3.4 [1988]: 38–42).

24. For a sample of the wide variety, see Bira Almeida.

25. Lewis, 159.

26. Lewis, 73, discusses the gender barrier—although perhaps he exaggerates it (not acknowledging, for example, Edna Lima's work, which I mention below).

27. Dossar, "Capoeira Angola: Dancing between Two Worlds," 5.

28. Jorge Amado, *Bahia de todos os santos* (Rio de Janeiro: Record, 1980).

29. Lewis, 98, writes that the taxonomy of "attacks" and "defense moves" is never clear. Many moves "can function either as attacks or defenses, or even as both at the same time!"

30. Jair Moura, "Capoeiragem—Arte e malandragem," *Cadernos de Cultura* 2 (Salvador, 1980): 15–16.

31. Amos Tutuola, *The Palm-Wine Drinkard* (New York: Grove Press, 1984), 35.

32. Dossar, "Capoeira Angola: An Ancestral Connection?" 38–42.

Hip Poetics

José Piedra

Although no one ever could be keener than little Nina [a señorita from Argentina], on quite a number of very eligible men who did the rumba, when they proposed it to her, she left them flat.
—Noel Coward, *Coward at Las Vegas*[1]

Mind over Hip

Ⅲ "Hip . . . the projecting part of each side of the body formed by the side of the pelvis and the upper part of the femur and the flesh covering them; haunch . . . Slang, familiar with the latest ideas, styles, developments, etc.; informed; sophisticated, knowledgeable."[2] I suspect that this slang application of the word "hip," which dictionaries admit is of unknown origin, arose from an African American out of the firmament of U.S. fads about the time of the flower children of the sixties. The fad has survived as an instant antidote to what is in vogue, across the board and not just across the hip. Brains rather than brawn, up-to-dateness and sophistication keep mind over the hip. And yet I believe that there is a more direct and problematic source for the quality of being hip: an attitude that clearly relates to the mindlessly physical, rather than to the mindful or clever aspects of the exchange between individual and group. In fact, being hip may have had, once upon a time, a close relationship with the anatomical part, and women of(f) color may have been involved in issuing this shaking motion, if not always in the shaping of the ensuing notion.

Would it be racist, sexist, and classist to say that being hip has always had something to do with a hip-hugging, bawdy attitude and body language, and that women of(f) color have been their mind shapers and shakers? Am I thus sitting on an ethnically or musically prejudiced divide, between those who are dark, rhythmic, and hip(ped) and those who are not? Or is acting hip and being hip(ped) once and for all to be a catchy phrase for anyone loving to show off differences? What is the

Hip party fun in Puerto Rican New York in the 1950s. (*Courtesy of the Justo A. Martí Photographic Collection, Centro de Estudios Puertorriqueños, Hunter College, City University of New York*

difference, anyway, between acting hip and the fact of being hip(ped) when you are marked to service someone else's love and show? Is it not true that in the capitalist, industrialized, and Westernized world the hip, as an act or as a fact, is being systematically erased as if it were a disposable body part, while the indelibly hip(ped) is being exploited as a love token and a sideshow? Are the fads and the vogues fighting for our bodies inadvertently promoting pockets of rebellion, too often dismissed as bawdiness and nonsense? Could not the "practice" of the hip be more than an offense—a defense for all those whom society invests with such bigoted extremes as, on the one hand, invisibility, riches of ends, and body beyond moderation and, on the other hand, visibility, poverty of means, and mind below standards?

The hip, of course, has been raised, bared, rocked, and rolled before in a few campaigns of dissent—not just those headed by women of(f) color. In fact the rumba, a neo-African song and dance performance pivoting the hip, was once spectacular and survives under other rhythmic disguises, while its literary rendering retains enthusiastic endorsers, even though they are preponderantly buried in the folkloric side of culture, the wrong side of the tracks, or beyond the United States' southern borders. And yet the critical reaction to the hip from academic circles remains virtually nonexistent. This is not a surprising situation for either the subject of the hip or for African cultural contributions to the marketplace of written ideas. Furthermore, we would be hard-pressed to avoid targeting women as models for theatrical abuse (show of love and love of show), not to mention for the literary folklorization and academic neglect that usually ensue. It would also be difficult to defend the covert advantages of such an overtly offending practice for the very women who are enrolled, often out of desperation, in such voyeuristic and exhibitionist stages. Finally, it would be even more difficult to defend the language of the hip as a form of poetics: a questionably ethical and superficial means of compliance aimed at yielding a profound and aesthetic message of defiance.

As is often the case, wording might confuse or be unfair to issues that are best expressed through body language. And I suspect that such a confusion or unfairness actually serves a good purpose in the theater of the hip. Most of us find it difficult to attack what we cannot fully translate into words; we tend rather to dismiss such items, thus inadvertently protecting them by pushing them onto, or beyond, the margins of discourse. Theatrical agents and the public also take advantage of such a discursive marginalization of gestures; they can avoid full (written-down) responsibility for a vaudeville-like act fraught with bad ethos and worse taste. The situation also helps the actors of the hip, as well as the reactors to it— among both of whom I count myself. I assume that the actors, and in turn the reactors, learn the art of accepting at face value, or of neglecting the ethical and aesthetic consequences, of their "irresponsible" acts in order to face what is for them a greater responsibility: meeting face-to-face their desperate lives' needs. When our survival is at stake, who cares about bad ethos and worse taste? Who are we to condemn a profession based on the display of body and disguise of mind that feeds so many?

Hopefully, we can at least learn a couple of potential lessons in ethics and aesthetics from the show-and-tell and hide-and-seek strategies, neither of which are treated here as amusing children's games. Instead, they symbolize patterns of offensive display and defensive disguise that constitute the dead-serious grammatical core of these women's body language. In other words, we can learn the strategic advantage of hiding, with full awareness and with little illusion, one's own sour academic words deep within a bittersweet pop show. We can also learn to seek to relieve theatrically the hysterical frustrations of one's world through a historic love dance of the hip that a few strategically perform for our pleasure and for their own desperate expression and survival. Such a hiding of the worse upon seeking the better as a form of bluff is an acceptable part of "professional" conduct, a practice that aids one's progress in art as well as in life. The bluff should be acceptable even for those who cultivate it by strutting their hips nearly in the buff.

If I am right, in supplying a poetics of the hip the rumba is a hermeneutic queen, for it has a long and comprehensive tradition as the source for tunes and lyrics that turn a meaningless body part into a signifying bodily attitude, compliance into defiance. Thus the hip is well equipped as a feisty source of poetics. The rumba shoots from it, even when absent from its definition or from its performance; after all, the rumba can also be lodged, as it were, in the hip of one's mind. I wish to defend the rumba's hip poetics as a form of feminist posturing of African origin that is applicable to marginals beyond the inner circle of women of(f) color hailing from the Americas. For such women the hip remains a poignantly dubious token or icon of femininity that is activated mostly in somebody else's offense and their own defense. In short, the rumba that I intend to address cannot be judged by its superficial values alone, including its seemingly obligatory sexual, racial, and class components, or, for that matter, the icon or token of the hip, or any other part of the dancer's being.

Moreover, the act to which these women, or parts thereof, commit themselves, must be set, not only within the context of their economic need and survival pressures, but also within the larger context of diminishing possibilities for their discursive participation in their own culture. In this, the industrialized, capitalist, and Western bloc of cultures does not have an exclusive hold on the curtailing of women's participation. And yet the neo-African heritage of the Americas, not necessarily known for its feminist campaigns, offers unsuspected possibilities deep within mythological structures that accommodate matriarchal and patriarchal branches and attitudes. The Pan-African mythology in question, how-ever hybrid and altered it must be by the time it is applied to the New World heritage of colonialism and slavery, gives us inhabitants of the Spanish-speaking Americas a concentrated opportunity to search for a woman's voice within her image and beyond her figure. These women react to their colonial and enslaved encasement by defensively hiding their cultural participation behind a likely offensive show of skins and a pretended love of moving hips. The hiding effort, which is shared by most colonized and enslaved people, be they from the light or from the dark populations vying for survival in the Americas, becomes an even more crucial issue among the women from either of these groups. These women are condemned to seek through desperate measures a part of the already scant cultural choices of participation available to the colonially less fortunate. Paradoxically, we have already noted that the rumba's "show-offs" hardly seem to qualify as "hiding" activities. To which we should add, if there is any accompanying "seeking" activity, it is a less than discreet form of seduction organized theatrically for a fee. Ostensi-bly both of these activities are performed at the beckoning of the mating call and the drum beat for which the rumba is known. In fact we have already begun to suspect that such choreographed gestures of the hip likely have a hidden meaning that seeks a place not just on the margins, but also within the traditionally male-dominated discourse of words. Most importantly, the rumba demands a critical appreciation that be-longs as much or more to women and to marginals than to mainstream men. Is the rumba the saving grace or the damning agent of the hip?

I have chosen to center my discussion on the sacred and secular history of the rumba as a neo-African performative and discursive strategy that peaks in the Caribbean during the 1930s with the so-called *negrista* move-ment. I will draw most of my examples from the images of a few women whose life and/or literature fit the Afro-Latin mold of the rumba. This sung and danced discourse was born and raised among them, and it is to them that we most owe a critical clarification of the denigration of the rumba as a theatrical routine. The women in question do not necessarily get in the first, the last, or any word; they are more often than not talked about—perhaps a natural continuation of being ogled and otherwise ex-ploited as stage "presences" by Self-nominated theatrical "essences" and even by critical "eminences" who speak in the name of Others.

I will capitalize the words Self and Other to indicate that I am not referring to any given individuals, but to notions of persons at opposing ends of colonial structures, respectively representing the colonizer and the colonized. Let us keep in mind that such positions are indeed not only arbitrary but also reversible, through revolutionary processes that allow or accept marginals to wield their own power as a central grammatical core of communication. This is so even when that grammar, as in the case of the rumba, is one based on metalinguistic gestures. Indeed the exchange between the roles of Self and Other is most convincing at the level of gestures. For instance, rumba performers are routinely both externalized and internalized, objectified and subjectified, by the talkers and the oglers, be they their impresarios, their public, or other critical exploiters. Most likely, in the end, the dividing line between objects and subjects, as well as that between what is external and what is internal, blurs as their mutual dependence is well established. As we will see, this is particularly so in a rumba style of exchange.

Let me anticipate that my critical treatment takes to heart the fact that in the world of the rumba, life and literature, reality and magic, ethics and aesthetics, low and high culture, the nude and the clothed tend to become one, or such is the illusion of the impresarios, performers, and public who share this world. On such a "stage," the important "thing" is the proper theatrical end and not the means, however untheatrical and improper they might be. After all, we become what we share in the rumbalike stages of the world and of the word, no matter where we are standing in regard to its staging, or whether we are or are not showing or moving any hip.

Rumba's Hip

Mmaa atopagyengyen na ekum mmarima.
[Women's violent shakings of the hips kill
(that is, give them power over men).]
—Akan proverb[3]

Rumba, in a dictionary definition catering to users from the United States, ignores the hip. It is, in the best of instances, "a dance Cuban

The spectacle of the hip: Ruth Fernández at the Teatro Puerto Rico. (*Courtesy of the Justo A. Martí Photographic Collection, Centro de Estudios Puertorriqueños, Hunter College, City University of New York*

Negro in origin and complex in rhythm . . . an imitation or adaptation of this dance in the U.S."[4] I sense that what is moving in a "complex rhythm" is mostly hips, jutting through words dressed with the pretense of neutrality and neuterness. At any rate, in few and vague words, the rumba becomes a misunderstood and/or dismissible form of expression "blacker than the norm" and from "south of the border." It appears to be a model for another type of rumba place north of the border and in the mythically official and white Western world. The implicit reversal of the traditional traffic of influences (west to Africa and north to south) or any concession to the complexity of the form would not be taken as compliments, but as the habitual model makers claiming no responsibility for somebody else's impossible model of rhythm, one that can hardly be translated into intelligible words (or civilized hips).

Practically any dictionary definition or discursive application of the rumba is relatively colored by race, tainted by ethnicity, blushed by sexism, and reeking with classism. Naturally such a situation tends to be discreetly upheld by absences, omissions, and disclaimers within what we all, Selves and Others alike, accept as Self-proclaimed official discourse—whether authoritative dictionary or academic criticism. In fact, in interviews of a number of the United States' approved mainstream critics of literature, they are more likely than not to claim no understanding of (read "no need for") the rumba. Maybe a few of the older ones have heard of it, admit a casual acquaintance, and have even tried it on a dare; fewer yet would claim it as their own. The rumba is not, after all, a ready literary category, they might argue—Who has ever heard, much less understood, rumba lyrics? It should probably be left as a misunderstood expression of hip-hop Otherness seething in the midst of relatively imperturbable intellectual Selfhood, in both its "Cuban Negro" home and abroad.

Neglect or its equivalents, whether intentional and malicious or not, remains a double-edged sword. Through its practice some Self-proclaimed mainstreamers attempt to erase their Others, and/or their Others' differences, as marginal variants of an alien(ating) model. Meanwhile, these Others preserve their own identities and differences as hidden icons or exaggerated tokens of bodily parts. Think, to that effect, of the kind of bodily determinism pivoting on the hip, the routine attempt at erasing, and exceptional persistence of, this part of the body among mainstream tastemakers of the United States. Their own people are consistently semantically dehipped into neutral or neuter carriers of Self-authorization; their Others are cosmetically hipped for the sake of love and show, that is, for the (pro)creative entertainment of Selves pretending to be acting like or reacting to Others, but only in their behalf and in their company.

Finally, the rumba or any similar hip exchange is not without danger to both parties, actors and reactors. According to the Akan saying quoted above, the hip emerges as an offensively overt "killer" of women and a covert "killing" part, one that can either turn against oneself or against others. Moreover, the Akan and larger African contribution to theatrical poses of the hip suggests an attitude not so radically different from that assumed by other individuals in similar situations the world over. In its stead, the neo-African hip poetics emphasizes a keen awareness of the rumba performer's show of love and love of show as an attitude that is more hard to sell than heartfelt. It also takes the ensuing responsibility that pitches mind over body to its ultimate, if often deadly, consequences—as announced by the double jeopardy of an Akan woman's killing/killer hips. Thus it would be important to view the rumba in terms of the compensatory empowerment of, as well as the dangers to, givers and takers bipartisanly engaged in a biased show of love and love of show. The compensatory empowerment derives from a critical viewing of these performers' act that is not just strictly based on love and show, but that takes into consideration the strategies emerging from the mixing and matching of these ingredients: "show-and-tell" with "hide-and-seek."

Hip's Balance

Danza
que bailaron los esclavos
parche y ritmo
en su elemental rueda de gallo.
[Dance performed by slaves,
hiding and rhythm
in their elementary cocky circles.]
—Virginia Brindis de Salas[5]

Hot Voodoo . . . I want to take a vacation from my conscience.
—Marlene Dietrich[6]

Allow me a basic description of the choreography of a "protoclassical" rumba as the first step in our approach to the literary rumba's poetics of hip equality. The description, I might add, is based on some personal experience. Thus I do not intend a depersonalized, scientific, and ethnographic approach, but a personalized, literary, and graphic rendering. In my attempt to translate gestures into words, I intend to stress angles of the dance that offer critical lessons for the definition of hip poetics. Any similarities between this description and so many other dances of Afro-Latin feeling and soul is not purely coincidental, as the protoclassical rumba could be their likely source or act as their eagerly mothering umbrella.

The rumba is at heart a dance teasingly patterned as a take-off on the me-Tarzan-you-Jane model of dialogue and is expressed in gestures that isolate different parts of the body as if they were independently mechanical parts of a Self-revealing, congenially assertive, and Other-confronting move. Shoulders and hips, rib cage and back, stomach and chest serve as counterpoints thrown into a unifying (w)hole seemingly ruled by rhythmic breathing alone. The stomach abruptly caves in, accenting the side movement of the hips; the chest softly reels; and the shoulders and back rotate forward in a compensatory movement. Arms and legs bend loosely as they follow the lead of the shoulders and hips in keeping alternately the stress of the rhythm and the cadence of the melody. In spirit, this is the "get down" movement that has been popularized by African Americans to general audiences in the United States. Meanwhile, the face is impassive, except for the eyes, kept low or in a high intense stare to disguise or to display the need of engaging in dialogue.

The woman's role is, voyeuristically speaking, the center of attention: she hardly moves her feet, concentrating on contortions and shuffling within a small square of a space, a floor tile, according to Cuban standards. Conversely, the man's role prescribes exhibitionist acrobatics performed while circling endlessly around the woman in what is called *rueda de gallo* (cock's or cocky circles).[7] Periodically, he will come charging at her, without ever touching. Then he retreats in a form of danced collapse or defeat, a formal "break"—which could be considered an exaggerated version of the "get down" movement.[8] Eventually the woman fakes giving in to the empty power of the man's gesturing, chiefly throwing in a kerchief as a phallus substitute. Other times, the woman dances with the kerchief and throws it menacingly or coquettishly to the man.

The traditional rumba dialogue between women and men, or those who "impersonate" such roles, marks the choreography of the dance as a well-balanced power play. Even though women appear to have the losing role, the grammar of the dance dictates the symbolic exchange—gift or violation—at best only of a woman's parts, not of her whole sense of Self, Sex, and Text (capitalized to indicate that each category is a category of discourse rather than just an existential source of identity). This is represented choreographically by a woman's isolating a particular part of her body, as well as the fact that such a movement does not actually change the whole position of the person, not even as she "gets down" or "breaks." She remains paradoxically in her place, still tall or low, and as much as possible within the square root of her symbolic floor space. She might lead men to believe that her body is a shaky and snaky monument to the hurts of love and the pleasures of show, a sample of life and art that is contented or condemned to remain firm on her modest pedestal.

In the end, the man's movements become the signified to the woman's signifier, or better yet, a variant of the model's part. In spite of the improvisational virtuosity reserved for male rumba performers, women overtly set the grammatical pattern of the dance and covertly that of song, including the manipulation of their partner's "triumph" and the choreography of their own joint defeat as a "get down" or "break." Even though, according to popular belief, hers is the show of love and his is the love of show, the rumba itself triumphs over such differences. The roles of the woman and the man or, for that matter, those of the virgin and the whore, the macho and the weakling, collapse into a unity of shaking, perhaps a shaky unity. Such a gender-bending, aesthetic/ethic-stretching, Other/Self exchange of moves at once serves to warm and warn men and women who are hip to the rumba about keeping pace with an egalitarian form of poetics.

Of(f) Color

Inga na ngai na respect.
[Dance with me with respect.][9]
—Popular Lingala song from Zaire

Mi hija es un marimacho. Anda de la ceca a la meca. Pero ella es una mujer libre y puede hacer de su cuerpo lo que le dé la real gana.
[My daughter is a butch. She goes all over the place. But she is a free woman and can do with her body as she pleases.]
—from Adalberto Ortiz, *Jujuyngo*[10]

No sé entenderé por primera vez su sentido en la hermenéutica de sus nalgas, repicando alegremente por entre los tamores del Congo.
[I don't know whether I'll figure her out right by the hermeneutics of her buttocks, happily bouncing amidst the Congo drums.]
—from Rosario Ferré, "Maquinolandera"[11]

My epigraphs shuffle the dangers of marketing a woman's side-to-side moves as a questionable notion of identity and doubtfully progressive motion toward freedom. I have deliberately chosen examples that, in theory, do not necessarily reflect the rumba as a specific and complex rhythm, but that endorse it as a practice—a generic strategy combining the right balance of offense with defense of ethics and aesthetics that we have come to associate with the rumba. However, the first thing that these quotations question is that revelation of the bodily kind does not necessarily translate into assertion of the mindful type, nor does shaking the body necessarily help shape either the mind or the conscience. In all of these instances, it is the male protagonist who tends to minimize his role as a suitor, guardian, or judge embarked on the mission of justifying the woman trapped in his text. This is particularly the case in works by women writers. In her short story, Rosario Ferré depicts a man diluted, practically neutralized and neutered, but still active as the narrative presence who conjures up a woman's "haunch" as a potent hermeneutic device.

The use of women or their parts as hermeneutic devices ostensibly validates them within male-dominated configurations. However, there is considerable resistance to such a system of validation. For instance, the Lingala/French proverb speaks about a woman who does not equate dancing with giving herself to a man. The quotation from the Ecuadoran novel addresses a father's equating his daughter's body moves "de la ceca a la meca" (all over the place) with a form of manly impersonation that attempts to erase the father figure. The quotation from the Puerto Rican short story puzzles over a woman's bodily challenges to men, (ad)dressing it as a potentially shared hermeneutic problem.

Critics who strive to guarantee the equality of genders in matters of ethics and aesthetics should count the rumba on their side. In our effort to guarantee, we could follow in the footsteps of the three types of women of(f) color" alluded to, respectively from Zaire, Ecuador, and Puerto Rico, who do not appear afraid of exhibiting their bodies or of challenging their moves, notions, and motions (even insofar as it concerns gender definition) as "part and parcel" of their identity. Shouldn't we trust them enough to aid them with our critical intervention, particularly because at least one of the quotations is about a woman by a woman, both of whom, to my mind, are aware of the joys and the perils of the womanly hip?

Let us also take into consideration the impending threat from the "outside" to the balance of these women's acts of offense/defense. The male marketing of third-world women, whether as commercial goods or even as bad ethos, worse taste, corruption, and pornography, takes its lead from tactics that are all too familiar in the capitalist, industrialized, and Westernized world. The female product is presumed to be always passively waiting, so that the right and duty of the males in charge consist in producing the proper market conditions to suit the product and its consumption. Such conditions include wrapping or unwrapping the product as befits its salability, shaking it, and shaping it at will.

The trading and betraying males in question might find, among the very circle of their human commodities, that females' attempts to shake and shape themselves into their own picture are indeed lax in aesthetics and lacking in ethics, but are above all deprived of market sense and marketing savvy. Who has ever heard of commodities attempting to impose their own moves, tastes, and prices?

The women in question are taking some incredible chances as symbolically wrapped and physically unwrapped, destined-to-become-perishable products. The stage life of these women's identities is as relative as their shelf life. The traditional question of a woman's being damaged by the loss of her virginity, which is, paradoxically, a requirement for womanhood, serves as a model for a more progressive form of damage: to unveil herself, which is, paradoxically, a step toward Self-assertion and the minimum requirement for gaining a sense of Self, Sex, and Text.

Self, Sex, and Text refer not to specific entities, but to their idea, independent of their being absorbed by a dominant identity, gender, or notion of the text. However, I am fully aware that in the marketplace of(f) course, intercourse, and discourse it is hard to avoid at least the ghost of male domination. Such a domination might persist even when a marginal critic like me attempts to counteract it and reclaim as his or hers the models of expression, by literally capitalizing (on) mainstream notions of Self, Sex, and Text.

For women, the perils of literary commodification do not end there. As a married Zairian woman in a free moment visits a "man's place," the bar from the song in the first epigraph to this section, she becomes a male partner's target as well as his commodity. That is why she has to ask for "respect"—in a French aside within a Lingala song. Respect is equivalent to appreciation, a matter of price. Freedom becomes a gesture of manliness for the Ecuadoran woman in Ortiz's novel—a man defining and justifying his daughter's freedom, or should I say the free use of her body as a commodity. The daughter has little to say about the appreciation of her male-impersonated marketing strategy. And finally, as the Puerto Rican woman moves past men, in Rosario Ferré's short story, she becomes the target of wonder (object of desire, marketable commodity): men attempt to "figure her out" by *reading* her body in transit. Reading is, for critics, the ultimate form of appraisal and marketing of their own selfish, sexual, and textual sense of identity. I might be about to launch into my own triple transgression of the traditional rules of the marketplace, whether I speak as a woman, her unpaternalistic and liberating father, or her critical and sensitive lover and/or confidant. If this is so, I beg your pardon, but I must take the risk in order to attempt to go beneath the skin and beyond the teasing of a woman's hip *poetics*.

Navel of the Rumba

[R]umba immortal que dice que un amante dolido y maltratado y vengativo puso una inscripción en la tumba de su amada . . . que es una copia de la rumba: *No la llores, enterrador, no la llores, que fue la gran bandolera, enterrador, no la llores.*
[Immortal rumba about a rejected lover who seeks revenge by composing this epitaph on his sweetheart's tomb . . . which are the lyrics of the rumba: *Don't weep for her, gravedigger/Don't weep, please/She's not my wife, she is a whore/You dig, gravedigger?/If you do, don't weep.*]
—"Requiem Rumba" in *Tres tristes tigres* (*Three Trapped Tigers*)[12]

In spite of my attempt to widen the circles of the hip, in the United States when we think of the rumba we probably still zero in on the shake-it-or-leave-it dance of voluptuous seminaked women of(f) color who would send even the mildest feminine audience into convulsions and its performers to the equivalent of an aesthetic, ethical, cultural, and political death. It would also evoke the most racist of Latin American clichés abroad: our quasi-African being-through-hips, a prejudiced perception that is far from being confined to female victims south of the border and west of Africa. Furthermore, critics who respect differences could easily dismiss the rumba as a dance of rampant racism, sexism, and classism; perhaps worse: a self-demeaning selling of an Other's identity as a performer of contortionist and conformist acts. In fact, for its players, dancers, singers, and fervent spectators, the rumba remains a state of both body and mind, a deadly serious badge of the marginal, or better yet the seminal, Selfhood—not enough, but a definite start. Of course, Sex and Text are as much a part of it as they would be in the rest of anybody's life. At least in my native Cuba, a *rumbera* is not simply a person who exists through her hips and duties to men but also through her own mind and rights. The rumba hips, exaggerated, voyeuristic, exhibitionist, deified, and prostituted as they might appear to be, might also be a signifier of both acceptance of our bodies and defiance of foreign impositions, and even further: a substitute for the silenced or muffled voice, and not just for women or through women.

And yet the rumba's very strategy at once seemingly exploits and deploys a woman's presumed debt to a male-dominated theatrical setting, whose impresarios seems to be educated in the north-of-the-border, squarely Western techniques of womanly confinement. Without the rumba, women in such settings have a scant choice: to succumb unconsciously to the act or to do it while taking a kind of "vacation from . . . the conscience"—an option previously offered by Marlene Dietrich's lyrics. In the case of the rumba, as with so many other "marginal" forms of expression, it provides a skill for survival that is available to practically anyone who is willing to engage in a willful, if not necessarily willing, sacrifice of ethics and aesthetics. Once survival is guaranteed, the song and dance skills could also furnish a relative measure of political and cultural gain, perhaps even an unsuspecting form of power beyond the power to seduce. In spite of placing an individual and/or community in an act of bad taste and worse faith, the rumba and its equivalents could put someone on the map, geopolitically and discursively, perhaps just the "media" map. This form of forced participation in the international marketplace is something that is tacitly admitted by even the most succinct definitions of the rumba as model for a U.S. fad.

After considering the alternatives, I am willing to endorse bad taste and worse faith for the sake of political and cultural gain as a fair exchange. The ensuing shortcomings can always be attributable to being conditioned by desperation. In my conditional endorsement I take into consideration that the rumba performer not become an unconscious candidate for the time and space warp, or an accidental casualty in the gender, race, and class war. Thus the rumba is not, per se, a solution to feminist calls for liberation; it remains a choice and a challenge for certain women who pay dearly for it and, in turn, make us pay dearly for their act—perhaps inadvertently. In this, the rumba provides a partial form of liberation and also a form of revenge that shakes and undresses the motives of those who watch to pay for the shaking and the undressing.

Ultimately what the rumba contributes to the deadly challenging course, intercourse, and discourse of the marginal is a tradition of awareness tucked away in a poetics of desperation that is capable of generating a subversive hip poetics both at the national and international level. It is not surprising that the rumba has to attract the attention of its nonbelievers toward a relatively deep message of the soul. It is precisely such a delusive, concentric form of signifying, which we have termed offensive display and defensive disguise, that guarantees the preservation of the legacy of the original Kongo *tumba* as a Cuban rumba. The voyage of the hip on the vessel of gestures and of words departs from a Kongo form of dispersed sung and danced identity to land on a very specific and rich Cuban application. *Tumba* and *rumba* coexist in the Spanish vocabulary as sister words and notions; at least this is so in the musical vocabulary, in which *tumba* remains an instrument, a group, an occasion, and/or a source for the rumba. In fact *tumba* also suggests the Spanish verb *tumbar,* meaning "to throw down," "to conquer," "to bed," "to inseminate," "to kill." The neo-African voyage of the rumba can be a reckless one, or one ending in a wreck.

There is more to the rumba's hip poetics than already meets the ogling eye of its public or the reluctant academic eye. The word itself continues to be a rich source of suggestions for those who care to engage in the reconstruction of its etymological voyage to the New World. Elaborating on the research of Cuban scholar Fernando Ortiz, we can say that the word, song, and dance of the rumba strip down to the Bantu roots *ntu* and *mba,* roughly "talent" and/in "motion," which play both with and against the grain of European cognates, such as *tumba, tomb* and *rumbo, rhumb*—not to mention, by prejudicial homonymy, *ron, rum,* and the English-only *rump.*[13] In such a guise the sacred African sources are theatrically displayed with what, to a Eurocentric audience, might appear to be Self-demeaning gestures. Meanwhile, the rumba strategically disguises its subversive message.

Last but not least in my etymological reconstruction of the rumba, I should corroborate my linguistic intuitions and historical projection of the rumba with a non-Cuban perspective, that of German scholar Janheinz Jahn. He praises Ortiz's rich etymology of the word *rumba* and the richer history of the song and dance, and adds yet another layer. Jahn proposes as the core of the dance a navel-touching step originally known as the "rumba-sounding" word *nkúmba,* which simply means "navel."[14] The navel, in this sense, can be either an embodiment of life, a strategic button in line with creation and procreation, or a sight/site "to kill for," with both passion and poison. I marvel at the choice of the nongendered body part to signal a movement of union between two or more beings. However, by virtue of built-in gender and other societal prejudices, the woman expressing her freedom through a belly-dancing and/or hip-bulging discourse accompanied by the appropriate throaty noises and/or pregnant silences is accused of being a whore or taken for granted for her macho-style daring.

Hispanic and Bantu, chiefly Cuban and Kongo, sources combine with other cultural sources to enrich the rumba and give it applications making the full cycle from joy to sorrow, from conception to death, from machismo (hypermaleness) to hebrismo (hyperfemaleness), from feminism to masculinism, and finally from yet another bleeding bout of liberalism to a new test of healing radicalism. So what, if in order to survive, thrive, or avenge, the hidden code and their codifiers have to peel off some clothes, show off some skin, or blur some boundaries? In the end the rumba might also peel off some layers of prejudice, all for the sake of a strategy centered on the *pronouncement* of the hip. Such a pronouncement is superficially physical and profoundly hermeneutic in nature; it also has proven to be a lasting form of poetics.

A most recent incarnation of the strategic sacrificial pronouncement of the rumba's hip and of its subversive redemption is given to us by Rosario Ferré. This woman's "Maquinolandera" is a "rumba" as well as a story about four female singer-dancers (including Celia Cruz as Queen Mother of the Rumba), backed up by an equal number of male musicians. The story is told by a man who is a prisoner in "Las tumbas" and who actually composed "Maquinolandera," the song to dance by.[15] The rumba multiplies into seemingly paradoxical, if not necessarily viciously circular, forms of signifying, which are both deadly (tumba) and joyful (rumba) in their implications against a male-dominated discourse. After all, a woman writes (a rumba and a tumba) about a man in prison, from whose musical rumba and tumba he fantasizes about the rumba and tumba performed by some rather free-spirited women beyond, or practically sitting on the edge of, his walls. This was previously made evident in the epigraph from Cabrera Infante's *Tres tristes tigres,* in which the novelized "rumba" on a famous musical rumba, the "Requiem Rumba," written, as it were, as a concentric and ominous evocation of a tumba, is evoked by a male envoy of the pen and the lens, a photojournalist who also doubles as Señor Códac and Mr. Kodak.

The concentric signification of the rumba always entails a deadly tug-of-war between offensive display and defensive disguise, life and death, meeting and mating, creation and procreation. The war is conditionally waged in the male (en)trails of a woman's course, discourse, and intercourse. As such, the rumba is not just a haven and a trench for extraordinary forms of conduct paired against the ethical and aesthetic guidelines of the master code. It is also a threatening trip that takes real guts either to tread or to tend. The rumba's seemingly excessive displays of humanity are nothing compared to the hidden release that seals the fate not just of a single teasing performer, but of an entire society's strip. In fact, such a rhetorical and real defiance of death adds yet another to the many "deadly" layers of interpretation in the tradition of the rumba.

The word "rumba" deserves more clarification than I am capable of giving. However, let us be warned that if there is considerable critical resistance to African interpretations of worthy and worldly ideas, this is only worsened by the challenge of African interpretation to words in common usage in European languages. "Rumba" is no exception. Too often it is the case that Eurocentered critics, even bona fide, well-meaning etymologists, simply content themselves with suspecting that certain European-sounding words are not strictly of European origin—a fact usually marked in dictionaries and encyclopedias by a question mark in brackets—as we saw in the slang definition of "hip." Even though in the case of "rumba" the "probability" of an African origin is undeniable and often acknowledged, it is in itself no great improvement over the prejudiced denial of a source. The situation can be best understood if we say that a word used in the United States is probably of European origin.

The individuals engaged in etymological skepticism toward African-derived words are often the very ones who advance the contiguity of meaning in European homonyms as a form of enriching (peaking in intuitive links and the subversive act of punning), and use them to proclaim the historical progression of Western languages. They might be prepared to deprive African languages of this form of linguistic richness, mostly arguing that such languages do not privilege writing and thus, presumably, have no certainty (read "recorded progress") in linguistic history. The argument ignores the fact that homonyms are chiefly "oral" in their construct and that the oral connection of words is at least as meaningful, enriching, intuitive, subversive, and historically progressive as European writing. Furthermore, African languages have written and other forms of visual, gestural, and oral records, including fortunate and unfortunate contacts with European or Euro-accepted written languages virtually since time immemorial.[16]

Finally, a word such as "rumba" is etymologically enriched by the different meanings that it can acquire according to its being placed in different contexts as well as being given different accents and tones. This is the case within and without the hybrid convergence of its African and European sources onto a song and dance of the hip: through flesh, mind, identity, gender, class, and rhythm. The homonymous haven/trench strategy at hand extends from the naming of neo-African signs and signifying grammars to the objects and discourses themselves that they name or render "grammatical." A woman might strategically choose, or be forced to choose, lascivious moves to disguise her powerful moods, the selling of the most superficial aspects of her womanhood for the sake of overt, but profound, gains in the market and theater covertly dominated by manhood (or the master model that presumes to represent it). Her sung and danced language might by homonymous to lyrics of sacrificial virginity and steps of tormented whorishness. But other meanings are kept hidden under veils that hide Salomeic undertones geared to the headhunting of encroaching maleness.

The Hip in the United States

Negra rumbera no bailes más
la danza negra de los bananos . . .
[Black rumba dancer, don't dance ever again
the black dance of the bananas . . .]
—Carmen Cordero, in "Negra rumbera"[17]

In spite of its Afro-Caribbean success and its worldwide source and appeal, the roots of the rumba remain vaguely African in its Caribbean-ness and Anglo-American in its commercial success. In transit between these three sites, the rumba changed its tune and its tone to accommodate the perils of exile. By the time the word and notion, show and emotion of the tumba arrived in Cuba (via Haiti) to become the "rumba," the maternal lineage of the sacred ritual in question had become mostly a secular performance barely hidden in a paternalistic show of women's skin, rhythm, and sin. It made its debut as a Creole performance in the dance halls of the Cuban proletariat and soon became a permanent fixture attached to the fancy balls of the bourgeoisie in the region of Cuba closest to Haiti. As the rumba moved westward toward the island's capital, it began to live two lives as an unofficial hymn and movement of a whole range of women, from solid society "virgins" who would disguise themselves as members of the proletariat to itinerant "whores" who would earn their living as career women of the night. The former became adept at dancing the *rumba de salón,* and the latter assumed the role of *mulatas de rumba* or *de rumbo*—epithets that, from either the salon or the whorehouse, jointly evoke images of "women of the song and dance routine," "women of the street," "free women," "women of direction," and/or "women of destiny."

As a song and dance medium in its current commercial form, the rumba was first "performed" as an export product in the Cuban pavilion of the 1932 Chicago World's Fair, and only then became accepted on the home front—where it had been periodically forbidden as too daring (for whom, I wonder?).[18] Since then it could be considered a significant Cuban contribution to a world market in which women have been compelled to trade a piece of body for a piece of bread, peace of mind, and a slim pick at the power structures. The fact is that since that fateful Chicago performance, a series of Latin American "rumba" performers have become commercially successful on the stages of the world. Many still are. The success of these performers partly confirms, and yet greatly problematizes, the "hippy" Afro-Latina stereotype. These examples range from Carmen Miranda to Celia Cruz; both have been unequivocally successful in the commerce not only of teasing Self, faking Sex, and parodying Text, and having Others pay for this, but also of provoking and deserving less obvious ideas, prices, and prizes loosely wrapped in the rumba.

Miranda, in exile in Hollywood, received cinematic kudos as she flew on the Disney-generic samba-rumba beat, ruffed wings, elevator shoes, fruit-laden headgear, and hip load down to Rio, Havana, and any other hot spot, while Chiquita bananas (the Miranda-associated label) are still fed to paying customers far away from the sweaty plantation.[19] Celia Cruz, in exile in New York, received Yale University kudos as ambassador of Cuban art to the world. Her now aged loose hips and still young, tight, throaty voice have claimed Cruz a doctorate *honoris causa* as the "Reina rumba" (Queen of the rumba) of academically hip nostalgia.[20] Her living heritage, such as Gloria Estefan, is doing well, thank you, after marketing the conga, sister of the rumba, as an Afro-Latin rhythm serving and eroticizing the world. After becoming the United States' mouthpiece for Cuban sounds, gestures, signs, and sighs, transformed in exile into the Miami Sound Machine, Estefan has taken for her sisters and brothers, as well as for herself, a bite of the international pop music pie. Miranda, Cruz, and Estefan head a list of so many other mostly anonymous or enigmatic but at times also commercially (if seldom ideologically) successful "heroines" who begin, and possibly end, their lives as "martyrs" of a desperate language of convulsive bits, beats, and bites. Their songs and dances, hips, hops, and hypes appear to swallow more than they project.

The moves and voices of too many heroines emerge as economically successful sound machinations from the martyrdom of their own flesh

and national, social, sexual, and racial differences—even though they re-
tain a certain classless appeal. They depend on being sold in foreign, or at
least alien(ating) markets. This is also true of non-Caribbean divas in the
United States who have profited from rumbalike stagings of expression. I
am thinking of Josephine Baker, who triumphal(ly) survived her war-
tired international audiences at the Lido of Paris and other entertainment
forums, from which she threw the skin of the bananas to reveal her own.
From there she went on to become the centerpiece for such rumba poems
as that by Cuban poet Carmen Cordero, which served as my epigraph.
Early in her career, Baker was honored by Nancy Cunard in her pioneering *Negro Anthology* of 1934; Cunard also lamented la Baker's becoming a
black beauty co-opted by the white French.[21] This anthology reviews la
Baker's latest sketch, titled "Josephine est blanche"—that is, "Josephine
is (and belongs to the) white"—and presents her to the reading public
through a demurer/paler-than-life photograph.[22] Even though only her
face is showing, I sense in her look the seductive pose of a decoy that
has readied itself for its white hunter with plenty of rosy Pan-Cake on
the face and hip poetics below the belt. And yet, la Baker's memory is
still fierce with speaking hips, as testified by homages for her forgiving
African American admirers who praise her for her "rainbow tribe" of
adopted children and her European admirers who praise her for her
work in the anti-Nazi resistance. For this she won the Légion d'honneur
while also making a theatrical career out of lack of *honneur* to a *légion*
(étrangère) of fans. Indeed she danced a banana-republic type of rumba
while unpeeling the body a fruit at a time.[23] Who is monkeying with
whom in this song and dance act?

In the tragically heroic rumbera category in the United States, I can
also think of Madonna, the material girl who in the near past has been
known to throw relatively "barbaric" bits and pieces of Afro-Hispanic
ghetto salsa and religion to her wild audiences. She has donned the
mantilla of interracial and intercultural religion as a Salomeic rumba veil
in the video *Like a Prayer*, ostensibly set in an Afro-Hispanic ghetto.
Through a masturbatory fantasy full of male bravado and syrupy female
hip appeal, she meets the Afro-Latin effigy and flesh of Saint Martin of
Porres, to no avail for either. The female whore meets the male virgin in
the former's fantasy (produced and acted by herself) and nothing really

changes, except the echo of interracial and interethnic, and intermusical, fantasy. The music and the strategy backing up her song and her dance resound with a beat that would be at home in a rock-and-roll rental property owned by the rumba. She is still "unrepentant" in her Afro-Latin impersonation, male parodies, musical and gestural take-offs, all of which she combined for her recent *Interview* cover: black net theatrical stockings, cut-off satin-striped men's "tuxedo" pants held at the crotch by one of her own hands, rumba- (flamenco and/or Caribbean) style bolero jacket (complete with oversized polka dots, ruffles, and midriff showing, as underlined by the other hand), topped by a Pan-Cake–white face fakely stressing her own paleness, killer lashes, straight black wig, and vaudeville/minstrel bowler hat barely shading an eager mouthing of a silent scream and confrontational pleasure.[24]

These are but a few of the women who have played a rumba role to the hilt and over the edge. In fact, we could say that salsa and samba, cumbia and bomba, beguine and merengue, conga and rock and roll, not to mention tango and break dancing and, of late, the lambada and the electric slide, are the symbolic survivors (or martyrs?) of the worldwide rumba heyday of half a century or so ago. Every one of these hip moves includes the "get down" movement complete with a balancing act played tricksterlike on an uneven length of leg—the penile third leg in absentia? Singularly or jointly they provide a most "spectacular" pop podium of human rights disguised as woman's private rites of passage. I am suggesting that in each of these overtly male-dominated dance crazes there is a covert female voice and subversive human message to be had, and that rumba leads as a strategic critical model.

The task remaining is to exploit the critical lesson of the rumba's critically evasive and sexually invasive strategy of performance: the "outing" of the body—ethically and aesthetically risqué labels, for example— as a prelude to a mindful, if sacrificial, form of empowerment. This is a strategy, mind you, that we might not want to privilege at the end of the twentieth century, or perhaps at any other time, but one that has its historical place, at least when there are fewer choices than we have today. The strategy that I propose should be placed within the ample Afro-Latin context of Others engaged in a Self-search, one that sets in its proper perspective the subversive compromise between offensive display and defensive disguise. While the body is barbarically stripped of its presumed civilization, the stripteaser is calling to consciousness that the paying audience is at least as barbaric as the performer. Those of us who pay to receive, or simply put up with, the banana strippers, may very well be setting ourselves up to slip on a woman's peels.

If Man's Hips, Then Woman's Rumba

Sale ya del vientre del tambor la selva.
Ya la piel del toro muge en el tambor.
Y contra el silencio de sus ruidos roncos
la negra desnuda parece una voz.
[By now the jungle has burst from the drumming womb.
By now the hide of the bull bellows from the drum.
And against the silence of her throaty noises
the naked black woman appears to be a voice.]
—Manuel del Cabral, "Aire negro" (An air of blackness)

      Coronada de palmas
como una diosa recién llegada,
ella trae la palabra inédita,
el anca fuerte,
la voz, el diente,
la mañana y el salto.

      Chorro de sangre joven
bajo un pedazo de piel
y el pie incansable para la pista profunda del tambor!

[Crowned with palms
like a newly arrived goddess,
she brings the unpublished word,
the unknown gesture,
the strong haunches,
voice, teeth of
morning and its leap.

   Gush of young blood
beneath fresh chunk of skin,
never wearying feet for the deep music of bongó!]
—Nicolás Guillén, "Mujer nueva" (New woman)[25]

Culipandeando la Reina avanza,
y de sus inmensa grupa resbalan
meneos cachondos que el gongo cuaja
en ríos de azúcar y de melaza.
Prieto trapiche de sensual zafra,
el caderamen, masa con masa,
exprime ritmos, suda que sangra
y la molienda culmina en danza.
[Ass-expanding the Queen advances,
and from her immense rump slide the
lax tremors that the bongo crystallize
into rivers of sugar and molasses.
Black mill in season of sensuous yield,
the hip machinery, masse en masse
squeezes out rhythms, sweats blood,
and the milling action climaxes in dance.]
—Luis Palés Mato, "Majestad negra" (Black majesty)

Through the rumba, a woman's skin and hips (or their substitutes) remain superficial gestures of a deeper set of signs, as bawdy and mindless a means to as bodily and mindful an end as the act might appear to her harshest critics. I have tried so far to find a kinder and, I hope, more reasonable approach to this troubling state of affairs. The unavoidable individual circumstances and (inter)national politics of the skin with which I have burdened the hips, as well as the rest of the body and mind that is shaped and shaken to perform the rumba, represent a feminist strategy born of desperation. It is a forced and/or forceful love of show and show of love that provides its user with the power to express his or her Self, Sex, and Text, however shockingly. In fact, as I have shown, for the women involved in the poetics of the rumba, there is little choice but to become forcibly exploitative of the weakening circumstances and lack of political muscle to which they have been traditionally forced in life as well as in art. If only their body is deemed to be a productive machine of abundance, then "let them" work with it, or at least, "let them" go against the grain of discursive prejudices that penalize a woman for showing both superficial and profound aspects of her femininity.

Faced with the predicament of living, as it were, by the skin of the hip, as well as by other presumed icons and tokens of femininity, the rumba dancers are bound to rise above either their shocking cover-ups or exposures. This is so whether these women are covered or inscribed in their own or somebody else's layers of symbols (a nun's habit, a woman's business suit, virgin's veils, whore's ruffles, holy books, or master codes) or shaken free from any symbolic covering but their own naked and bulging signifying body surfaces. This will to love and to show and its corollary of empowerment is at the root of the "admission" (rather than submission) of women as cosigners of discourse. Unfortunately the "dean of admissions" remains a traditionally male role, and admission thus reveals a submissive side: submitting to a test of competitiveness. In order to improve the terms of admission, the submissive quality of the test of competitiveness has to be recognized by the men in power as an artificial construct, reminiscent of the paternalistic freedom of staging granted to Others by an alien(ating) Self-serving ego and Self-evasive impresarial Self. It matters little whether the desperate test takers undertake a striptease or a travesty for a pass or a passing grade. I am referring to the prohibitively male testing ("selfing," "sexing," and "texting") that binds in a common frustrating show of alienation individuals as dissimilar as a virginal saint or a whorish star. At the very least, the men that so far have been in charge of the deanship should admit to placing themselves in a neutral and neuter position of policing admission. In other words, such men must stop pretending that the rules of admission enforce themselves, and that they serve such rules as mere vehicles of a judgment, the more vague and Self-effacing the more powerful. The literature emerging from the poetics of the rumba offers some hope for male awareness of corruption and the eventual correction of their own foibles in their Self-styled and Self-effacing politics of female admission.

The three major male poets of Caribbean negrismo, Manuel del Cabral, Luis Palés Matos, and Nicolás Guillén, at work on rumba poems during the 1930s, seem to agree on their approach to a poetics of the hip.

Their works suggest the possibility of a woman's liberation through the unveiling of body form and formal veiling of the message pronounced by such poetics, even when they do not systematically either announce it as a feminist posture or denounce its machista exploitation. Let us also be aware that, as in our previous consideration of the rumba as a popular expression of song and dance, appearances actually serve as a haven and a trench for the strategic defense and offense of a woman involved in the rumba's show of love and love of show.

The negrista poems that serve as epigraphs for this section indeed initiate us into worse dangers for a woman than accepting "admission" of equality for males. I am referring to the male playing and/or silencing of a woman's instruments, not only skin and hips (as tokens of the body and of movement, respectively), but also voice and rhythm (as icons and expressions of the soul), which often merge in one and the same "organ" of communication. Chief among such slippery organs are two musical instruments: the *sesribó* and the *bongó,* both of which stand for "(ear) drum" or "(jingle) bell," "home (drum)" or "(sacrificial) vessel," which are silently or stridently "played" with a stick (phallic inscription) or with a visual image/gesture, cosmetic massage or cosmic message (vaginal inscription).[26] Either way, the woman's tune and tone played by men is virtually a form of forced friction of signification (or lack thereof) on its surfaces. But who is or is not playing what and for whom?

These poets' "muses" own the instruments of the rumba, chief among which are the muses' own bodies and, in turn, the poets' own. Consider, for instance, del Cabral addressing a woman: "tu cuerpo mismo el bongó [your body as the very bongo drum],"[27] perhaps realizing that he is "playing" the woman's very body, rather than some intermediary tune, tone, and instrument that belong to her. In turn, his conscience and his poem, perhaps his very sense of Self, Sex, and Text, are being played/ plagued by women. Del Cabral and his generation of Caribbean negrista poets indeed set an important precedent of which they might not have been aware: not just setting up but *becoming* the very stages for the rumba's performance. Ultimately their poems are stagings of a woman's space as a curse and a course, a curt, cursive, recursive, discursive, and intercursive poetic site that they share.

The unheralded male/female drama of rumba cooperation is to my mind the best-kept secret of Afro-Latin coliberation proposed by Caribbean negrismo and beyond. Upon closer historical scrutiny, the rumba emerges as a strategy of assimilation/confrontation against colonial hegemony that dates back to pre-European Africa. As usual in the transatlantic African renaissance brought about by slaves, cultural syncretism under the aegis of the colonial master code predominates over any single ethnic origin. However, in spite of the many godly figures (*Orishas, Potencias,* or Powers), animals, and objects that uphold the rumba's principle of communication (all of which contribute to the grand strategy for assimilation and confrontation), we also have a central anticolonialist source/force: Sikán. It is one, mind you, that refuses to be held under the aegis of the colonial master code. Under her stellar but elusive tutelage a whole entourage performs it partly hidden feminism of(f) color. I will deal first with the godly heritage of the rumba queen and later with the three tragic women powers-behind-the-scenes who are her sisters in the surprisingly unified performance of neo-African mythology in the Americas. Sikán, as the ultimate model for the transatlantic rumba queen, was likely a product of the mythology of the Old Calabar and, more precisely, the Cross River Delta region, which was once a crucial point of contact between Bantu, Semi-Bantu, Sudanese, and Ewe-Fon linguistic groups of cultural influences. This geographically apt and ethnically rich area soon became a point of embarkation for New World slaves and is today part of southern Nigeria. Across the river, the Ejagham (known in Cuba as the Efó) developed an unusual strategy against the invasion of the Efik (known in Cuba as the Efí).[28] The Ejagham (or Efó) mounted what seems at first glance a passive resistance toward the belligerent Efik (or Efí) by accepting their superior force and even adopting their language.

Meanwhile the Efó were literally and symbolically swallowing mythologically their Efik invaders. The Efó, after all, claimed to have hidden the voice of the Efik tradition, incarnated in Africa and in Cuba as Ekwe or Ekué (the Leopard Lord). Under such singular colonial circumstances, the voice of Ekué is orchestrated as a secret language and Sikán is Ekué's guardian.[29] In fact, Sikán could be said not just to guard but even to assimilate, perhaps even engender, adapt, or adopt Ekué. This is so at least at the linguistic level: Sikán is better known as Sikanue, or Sikanekua, further gender-neutralizing or feminizing the notion of cultural seed/ voice implied by the traditionally male emblem of cultural power: Ekué.

This Ekué inhabits a woman, a goddess, or her avatars. The issue to contest through a mythological review of the African tradition is whether the inhabiting act implies for women an intervention or, worse yet, a violation. The male representative of culture is often revealed to Sikán as an amphibian appendage (represented musically by a percussion stick) that she can neither readily identify or ever reveal, name, play, or play with. In fact she does, biting, so to speak, the apple if not always her tongue, while offering it to her brothers and sisters. But her sacrifice remains both offensive and defensive, and thus still a debatable issue in the search for egalitarian policy in neo-African ethics as well as aesthetics. The rumba offers us perhaps the only egalitarian, or at least compensatory, hope.

The rumba is a singularly apt medium for the orchestration of a strategy of offensive display and defensive disguise that derives from Sikán's exchange with Ekué. Through this type of performance and the like, a woman sacrifices her own skin (but only through that of a scapegoat) for the sake of the community.[30] This performance leads to the breaking of the sacred vessel of language, ranging from the tearing of a woman's own clothes or substitute "hide" stretched over the surface of the drum to the altering or silencing of her voice and/or that of her offspring.

If I continue to view as ethically problematic the sacrifice of woman and of one of her instruments of expression for the sake of a social structure that is, at least officially, dominated by men (in fact, traditionally her instrument is played by a man or not played at all), I also consider that in the mythological exchange between the two, the man is condemned to create and procreate through the woman. His voice is forced to be lodged in a part of her: skin, hip, vagina, womb. More importantly, he has to impersonate her. If sometimes she has no choice but to go along with either his creation, procreation, violation, or impersonation, she also has a power not only of rejection but of initiation. He is at least as much hers as she is his. That is a neo-African alternative in which the linguistic play of signifiers and signifieds changes my attitude toward the Western obsession with male domination of signification. However, let us view the evolution of Sikán from a strategic figure of desperate sacrifice to one of cautiously optimistic feminism and beyond, to a transgendered perspective in the poetics and politics of the hip.

To my knowledge, Sikán is never mentioned by that name in literary texts, at least not in "high-culture" written texts, except as an ethnographic borrowing from a decontextualized African heritage—as in the case with Cabrera Infante's apparently out-of-place treatment of the legend, which will be discussed later on. And yet her performance and presence invades the womanly script and, in turn, the manly script ostensibly superseding, personalizing, or impersonating that of the woman. This aspect of her personality is embodied by the "unmentionable" or "escapable" linguistic and traditional seed of neo-African cultures: Yewá, the deadly Self-effacing (as well as Sex- and Text-effacing) beauty. Her name is sometimes vulgarized in Cuba as Yegua, "she-horse," or "she-pony," and by extension Mula-ta, "mule," "mulatta," or "mulah." All of these representations of Sikán as the auto-effacing Yewá appear frequently in the rumba-inspired texts.[31]

Sikán, in her many deceptions, whether lively or deadly representations, is the literary keeper of the secret and thus must remain a nameless or alternatively named goddess whose presence is mostly felt through "vibrations" and "shadows" of musical and cosmic instruments and, above all, through the performance and presence of rumba Stars. She breaks herself "in the wild" or breaks out "into the wild" rather than breaking the code in the text; and since her skin and her voice, her image and her being are one and the same, she is capable of extraordinarily subtle metatextual revolutions as well as passionate bursts of signification.

Sikán becomes a constant presence-in-absence, in oral legends and rituals, particularly of the Abakuá black-pride society. There her place is most significantly elusive. The Abakuá is an "all-male" society centered on the idea of woman: Sikán, the goddess of(f) color par excellence, is evoked as part of the discourse of tradition, "played" and "downplayed," and impersonated by a man through musical instruments, clothing, and voice. Even the Anaforuana grammar of the group, which is ostensibly written by men on men's bodies, floors, and walls, is arguably based on erasable womanly shapes and echoes.[32] Indeed the Anaforuana observes the combined superficial Self-exhibiting and deeper Self-effacing attitudes that are practically a trademark of the participation of marginal groups in mainstream discourse—as observed, for instance, in African American slang. I would argue that in such groups women and their symbology constitute a hidden code within another code.

Anaforuana plays tongue-in-cheek with "traditional" Afro-Latin stereotypes of womanhood, potentially generalizable to other "marginal" groups: curves, globes, bays and inlets, sighs, screeches, nonsense, and silent gestures, which are as suggestive as they are determined to signify the power of womanhood, phoenixlike from the still-hot ashes of male-born prejudices. The female grammarian/grammatical principle is both a play of images and a voice-in-residence, pretending to be the echo of exile, a blank of blanks. That is, in the Anaforuana and in the whole of Abakuá society, woman is ever present when we draw or pronounce the signs, look or speak them below the surfaces and between the lips, not to mention between the lines, rather than as part and parcel of male-contaminated and -manipulated discourse.

The woman's covert sense of her overt presence is essential to the rumba strategy of offensive display and defensive disguise. Hers is the crucial flaw and flow of knowledge that men regret and covet so much, conventionally demeaned as curiosity, indiscretion, nest- and children-making. To have her whole part by part is common enough. From such a sieve of a screen, she demands our critical unearthing of her voice and image, as well as her soul, in defensive disguise from her body's display. Some men are compelled to "play" the woman. Thus, in male-dominated societies womanhood emerges from a realistic trap as a manipulated effigy to a theatrical haven from which she faces an impersonating audience imbued with hymeneal envy as well as vaginal urges. This is precisely the theatrical haven that the rumba transforms into a pubic and public trench. Because of the danger of a purely staged manly fulfillment of womanhood, the rite of the rumba advocates a performance and presence of women's rights that should be sensed rather than felt, filled, or otherwise fulfilled—that is enough reason for her not to be named or otherwise rendered obvious, readily intelligible, or easily had other than as a scornful stripper on the other side of the lights. Even the man who impersonates her cannot claim to be her, by logic, seed, or deed.[33]

Others take Sikán's place as potentially feminist figures seemingly engaged in a male-supervised and socially beneficial martyrdom. They are three goddesses (or predominantly female Powers)—Yemayá, Oshún, and Oya—who share a superficial sexual dependency on their male partners. The male partner is capable of the most extreme acts of machismo or of impersonating its parallel role of hebrismo. Besides the three goddesses, Sikán is also named and embodied by a triumvirate of deified animals and another of ritual vessels. On the one hand, there are the frogs, birds, and snakes that represent women's offensive and defensive mutations, as well as a pair of totemized animals that serve to enact the offensive and defensive strategies represented by the triumvirate: the crocodile, official emblem for female secret societies of defense, and the mule, which has become the unofficial emblem for the female yielding to the male, particularly to the white male. On the other hand, there are the ritual vessels: sieve/net, clay pot, and gourd, all of which are full of unsuspected holes, echoes, bulging slopes, downs, and breaks. Jointly the goddesses, the animals, and the vessels inform both the superficial traits and the deeper meanings of Afro-Latin womanhood.

In the realm of the rumba, women superficially hyperact, and thus subversively claim for themselves and counteract demeaning traits that have been traditionally assigned to, revoked from, and theatrically imposed on them by a predominantly male-run establishment. It is in fact mostly the men who attempt to feel from the hip, while women, in the worst of circumstances, are thinking from the hip and, in the best, shooting from it to the tune and tone of the rumba. Furthermore, part of these women's strategy seems to be to accept a traditional marriage, symbolic or real, with men, manly attributes, and manipulated objects as well as their institutions, which are fraught with extreme, capricious, and paradoxical compromises as well as dutiful revenge. Deep down, rumberas are not loose, lost, geared by lust—whether to (pro)create or to procrastinate for a while or forever the act of fulfilling themselves through man and child. They have found a stage in the night, for a night engagement as stars of their own, commercially contaminated destiny. Self-validation takes many forms, including baring and flashing the body, stuffing it into barely appropriate and flashing costumes, and bearing the brunt and the flak from audiences that represent a range from extreme machismo to extreme feminism. The act in question might become justifiable as an emergency measure. This is a form of offensive display worth its value in the goal of defensive disguise.

We could stretch the symbolism of these goddesses, animals, and vessels of womanhood to the evolution of women's rights through three generations, attitudes, and formulations: (1) Yemayá is the grandmother who strives for justice and security within the confines of the rules of a husband, home, and society: she is the frog or any other amphibian that seems just to sit until it is time to jump and flee a predator, to assault prey, to attack or run for no apparent reason; she is also the sieve and the net that, although meant for house chores and fishing, are also perfectly capable of catching, drying up, or releasing the unexpected. (2) Oshún is the mother who seeks truthfulness toward and balance with a partner and a love; she is also a bird that is preyed upon for its beauty, movement, and song but also feeds on the eyes and the rest of the body and mind of the ogling hunter and, at times, on the debris of the world; she is also the *múcura* or clay pot and the porcelain or iron *sarabanda* that doubles as an everyday jar/cooking pot, festive soup tureen/ancestral urn, or medicine/deadly chest. (3) Oya is the daughter who finds fulfillment and revelation through her (love of her) own identity and (tradition of) voice; she is also the snake of lascivious coils equally ready to mate or to swallow; she is also the gourd that once dry serves as a ladle, a child's toy, or a musical instrument—the *güiro,* maraca, or gourd rattle, which are not just devices to entertain/console men and children.[34] To these young women's instruments we add the snake of temptation, seduction, and venom, which doubles as the unassailably slippery stripper of the forest: outgrowing her skin, as well as any sense of space or time imposed upon her.

In the end, from any of its syncretic ethnic angles and representations, the rebellious womanly spirit is sacrificed every time it is evoked and/or impersonated by the believers and performers of a pointedly deceiving song and dance of Sex and Self whose Text is pending a critical reading. Whatever sacrifice is incurred, it represents a martyrdom from which a whole language will subversively emerge, bit by bit, as a subterfuge against the grain of the master-coded charmer, not just a charming mistress's trump card.

Balancing a Hip of Tradition

Reventó la selva, desde tu cintura
hasta el paraíso de tu mordedura.
Tu canción de curvas canta más que tú:
sabe los secretos que te dió el vodú.

Negra que sin ropa, tienes lo de aquel
que siendo secreto se quedó en tu piel.
[The jungle burst, from your waist
to the paradise of your biting mouth.
Your song of curves sings more than you:
it knows the secrets offered by Vodun.
Black woman without clothes, you own
the secret that was left on your skin.]
—Manuel del Cabral, "Tropico suelto"
(Loose tropics)[35]

Beneath the covers the eyes of the initiated widened. They felt intruded upon by a strange malaise. Strange things were going on behind their backs, in a corner of the sanctuary . . . RRRRrrrruuuu . . . RRRRrrrruuuu . . . RRRRrrrruuuu . . . Sounded like the croaking of a frog, a file against a mule's hoofs, the hissing of a snake—, the plaintive noise of a twisted leather strap . . . A drum, a reptile, some evil spirit, someone's complaint? . . . It was Ecue . . . !
—Alejo Carpentier, *¡Ecue-Yamba-O!*[36]

I have chosen four literary examples from seemingly independent sources to illustrate the rumba's critical strategy. All of them are based on approximations of the sacrifice and heritage of Sikán. They are Guillermo Cabrera Infante's near-ethnographic account in a chapter called "Seseribó" (Sikán's "silent" rumba drum) from his novel *Tres tristes tigres*—which is a more complete version than Carpentier's earlier description in *¡Ecue-Yamba-O!* (whose opening lines appear in the epigraph); Lydia Cabrera's story "Suandende," from her collection *Cuentos negros de Cuba* (Black tales from Cuba), which was originally published in French for a Parisian audience used to the Afro-Latin endeavors of Josephine Baker and other rumba divas of(f) color; Rosario Ferré's short story "La muñeca menor" (The smallest doll), from her collection *Papeles de Pandora* (Pandora's papers), written in white letters on off-color screens; and the Xhosa oral legend transcribed and translated into written English by A. C. Jordan in *Talk That Talk: An Anthology of African-American Storytelling.*

The first example is by Cabrera Infante. His account, emerging within "Seseribó," appears to be his own drummed-up legend that he has actually inherited from the silent or screeched female secret of the all-male Abakuá.[37] The legend informs the life and art of la Estrella, the Afro-Latin diva protagonist. "Seseribó" is significantly preceded and followed by several chapters all of which are called "I heard her sing." In fact the author, disguised as protagonist, reveals that he has actually not understood "her," that is, Estrella, the rumbera star of the Tropicana nightclub, even though he is willing to try to break her code.

From a shaky podium built as a pedestal for Sikán, Estrella/Cabrera Infante suggests that we listen in order to consume and, in turn, subsume the hidden message on the sacrificial skin of the text. Stardom and destiny run deep below the stripped surfaces of the male shooting of the film (the author dictating his script through the protagonist Codác, a cameraman-of-the-vedettes who is illiterate in several languages) or his own authorized female-riding, male writing. Cabrera Infante's proclaimed transactional grammar (between the sexes or races as well as below the belts and beneath the masks) is composed of offensive signifiers and defensive signifieds, violated images and critical violators, at once representing a raped culture and the rapist interveners. In short, this book consciously fails to be written, linguistically speaking, at prick's length. I think Sikán's poetics of the rumba has a lot to do with *Tres tristes tigres*'s balancing the male and female viewpoints even within a theatrical stage of language chiefly ruled by an authorial and a narrative male's impresarial voice.

In order to underline the balancing act implicit in the novel's Sikán episode, while reproducing Cabrera Infante's own version of the legend, I will interject in brackets some of my own comments. I hope that my critical co-optation/impersonation of Cabrera Infante's words, and in turn those of his Sikán, will help us to listen more closely while uncovering a feminist message that, under the "original" textual circumstances, seems otherwise to be paradoxically either missing or worn inside-out.

Ekué [the male-dominant tradition] was sacred and lived in a sacred river [the symbolic serpent of existence]. One day Sikán [future goddess of the rumba] came to the river. The name of Sikán perhaps meant curious woman once or just woman. Sikán, just like a woman, was not only curious [I'd say, mentally and physically aggressive] but indiscreet [I'd say, determined to break her silence, challenge the will to know, exercise her power].

Sikán came to the river and heard the sacred sound which only a few men of Efó [her Ejagham cultural group] were permitted to hear. Sikán returned to the river and listened again and this time she also saw. She saw Ekué and heard Ekué and told all about Ekué with her gourd [a seed-filled maracalike instrument that, like the sacred bells and drums, represents the hymen and womb of identity as well as practical and private generation, which are counterparts to the penis and the more abstract and showy line of male-centered tradition] (which she used to drink water with) and she caught up with Ekué, who wasn't made for running. [In fact the gourd was an appendage attached to most men, which she had ceremoniously detached to serve her purposes—we have here a parallel to the Freudian situation of penis envy, with the big difference being that the castration solution becomes a pragmatic one: it relieves society of its stiffly male-dominated biases. The woman, having found the penis, throws away the man attached to it.] Sikán brought Ekué back to the village in her gourd of drinking water. Her father believed her now.

When the few men of Efó (their names must not be repeated) came to the river to talk to Ekué, they didn't find him. The trees told them that he had been chased and followed, that Sikán had caught him and taken him to Efí in the gourd of water. This was a crime. But to let Ekué talk without stopping up the ears of profane listeners and to tell his secrets and to be a woman (but who else could have done such a thing?) was more than a crime. It was sacrilege.

Sikán paid with her skin for her blasphemy. She was skinned alive and died [other versions have an animal skin taking her place as a symbolic scapegoat]. Ekué died too, some say of shame at letting himself be caught by a woman or of mortification when traveling in the gourd [in other versions he lives on trapped in Sikán's gourd]. Others say he died of suffocation in the pursuit—he certainly wasn't made for running. But his secret was not lost nor was the custom of reunion [cultural or sexual] nor the happiness of knowing that he existed. With his [not her] skin they clad the Ekué that speaks no more in the rites for initiates and is magic [the power of tradition is no longer obviously represented by the penis]. The skin of Sikán has neither nails nor ties and has no voice, because she is still suffering the punishment for not holding her tongue [nonetheless, she is free to show or rather to whisper and screech, rather than overtly speak meaning—a strategic option for both males and females involved in passive resistance and aggressive if mute signification]. She wears four plumes with the four oldest powers of her four corners. As she is a woman she had to be beautifully adorned, with flowers and necklaces and cowries. But over her drumhead she wears the tongue of a cock as a sign of eternal silence [only a grammatical or linguistic, not a graphic silence]. Nobody touches it and it is unable to talk by itself. It is a secret and taboo and it is called seseribó.[38]

Cabrera Infante—and other literary writers like him—finds himself in a woman's world of words unjustly reported by men, including himself. He becomes an ill-fitting, pseudo-ethnographic tool of Sikán's legend; his pages, as it were, serve as her drummed-up skin. The same can be said of male "ethnographers," ranging from Salvador Bueno through Samuel Feijóo to Sosa Rodríguez, who have collected the greater number of variants of this Afro-Cuban woman's text and sex without attempting to derive a feminist interpretation.[39] Not surprisingly, other ethnographic as well as literary interpretations, particularly those by women, are more subtle in their allusions to the legends and more determined to find feminist undertones. Furthermore, in such cases only a minimum of Sikán's skin and name but a maximum of offensive display and defensive disguise inform the covert attitudinal intent and the overt intentional lassitude of her rumba.

The crucial example of the latter group of Sikán champions is Lydia Cabrera, who gives us Sikán piecemeal, mostly distilled from the impersonating opinions of male informants. After all, they are the only members of the "all-male" Abakuá sect, a situation that she complements by her own (transvestite?) incursions into this society.[40] Her main literary version of the "myth of Sikán" is most apropos for the present scope: the story "Suandende," in which, once more, Sikán's figure is given to us indirectly, as shared by the female protagonist with a man, in this case the narrative viewpoint of the husband, who is a jealous bird trapper. The Sikán-like wife, who remains anonymous, is a daring woman with enough savvy and beauty to transform herself into a bird decoy for Suandende, a shy *tinajero* (maker of clay pots to carry and/or preserve liquids or solids). When the married woman, who lives deep in the bush (the Monte and the Muntu of her people's Afro-Latin memory), meets Suandende by the river, she is not afraid of the potential for danger. In fact Suandende makes the woman's eyes shine with the eagerness of a

The neo-hip: Carnaval Miami
1992 on Calle Ocho. (*Courtesy of the
Kiwanis Club of Little Havana*)

queen about to flee from her jeweled throne: "Y la mujer, haciendo brillar sus joyas de agua, rotas [And the woman, showing off her jewels of water, broken]."[41] Her jewels of water are material sparks signifying for her a trap, instantly and symbolically broken. From such a setup she will break away and mend her conscience, not to mention finding her own will and ways to seek and give pleasure—which the husband fails to give her and Suandende helps her find as a mirage image of herself in the water. Indeed, the main home jobs of these men are to serve their women, each in their own way, in what they think of as their male-centered household. Their professional occupations in the outside world are also related to the women. Each of them ruffles his feathers in a contest of male display of prowess dominated by a woman's secret power. The contest takes the shape of a professional competition between a jealous trapping husband and a free-spirited, sensitive man (updatable to the busy executive-yuppie and the solicitous lover-confidant, respectively).

The macho pleasure seeker tends to think that he is always on top of the woman whom he has presumably selected to please him, but who is on top of whom? The pleasure seeker likely gives as much or more of himself as he receives from her. He is also at least as thin-skinned as the woman whom he pretends to have undressed down to the skin, or indeed the one he has ordered skinned (as in the case of Sikán). According to the legends at the source of the rumba, he falls into her velvet glove, as a wriggling amphibian appendage or adulterated sound (Sikán holding the Ekué, king fish and song king of Calabar tradition, and suffering the consequences). Eventually she flows through the flaws of his catcher's mitt (the star fooling the Kodak or Códac that pretends to capture tradition in male-dominated images and echoes of a Kongo tradition, and suffers the consequences). In fact the hip poetics of the rumba emerges from legends in which material and symbolic goods, as well as pleasure and knowledge, can only be carried and preserved in a sieve made from visual or musical instruments. Among them there is the gourd or a calabash, a perforated drum or the purposely broken clay pot that Suandende is known for. As we have seen, this form of cultural participation is less precarious than would seem to be the case on the surface in spite of the apparent dangers of offensive display and defensive disguise, showing off the body to save the mind. Furthermore, it undermines and counteracts the other option implicit in abiding by the hip poetics of the rumba: exposing oneself to the theatrical stage or the camera angle.

Suandende himself acts as a sieve or clay container not just for the pleasure and knowledge of his female companion but also in respect to himself. The hands, everybody's significant organ of pleasure, particularly ostensibly selfish ones, are the ultimate sieve. Through them, the harshest mark or the softest face moons in and out. Cabrera places the hand gesture in parentheses upon describing Suandende's professional demeanor: "de oficio tinajero. (Ocultó la cara entre las manos y la miraba por las juntas de los dedos) [a clay pot maker by profession. (He hid his face behind his hands and looked at her through the cracks between his fingers)]."[42] Still, this woman expresses herself through the auto-willed pleasure and knowledge she has with a sensitive male no less "masculine," and indeed wiser, for his coquettish peekaboo.

The third of our examples of approach to the Sikán tradition also comes from a woman, Rosario Ferré, and is likely the most subtle and diluted of all that I am considering. Perhaps even more interesting to me is the possibility that Ferré's allusion to the tradition of Sikán is purely coincidental or, better yet, so much a part of the Afro-Latin subconscious that it is impossible to detect anything but its essence, hard to acknowledge its sources, much harder to reveal its secret message. If this is so, Ferré, a woman who by birthright has an Afro-Latin cultural heritage, becomes a most effective handler of the strategy of offensive display and defensive disguise—perhaps in spite of her own conscience.

In Ferré's "La muñeca menor" (The smallest doll) a woman sits by the river while her powerless life passes before her eyes. However, deep in her memory and in her flesh is the day she ventured into the stream that unavoidably leads to the far-off sea. There she meets her destiny in the ugly but telling presence of a *chágara,* a mysterious double that begins to inhabit her with defensive ethics or an offensive aesthetics. As her leg swells out of shape, as have those of so many other tricksters of African ancestry, her body becomes her critical text, no longer that of a passive beauty in a faded world of wealth and privilege, but at best a flawed beauty of intense partial powers. Her ugly leg is her questioning tail and unfolding tale. She is pricked by the chágara, and the chágara becomes a zoomorphic impersonation of her prick(ly) identity—her virginity without showing her swollen member to her chosen mate. Only two generations of doctors making house calls know for sure. She sublimates her creation, procreation, and procrastination as a fulfilled woman, making dolls rather than mating men, keeping house, and making nests. She resists turning her skills as a dollmaker (her crafty imaging of womanhood) into a business, refusing marriage, gestation and digestion, consumption and assumption into a male-dominated world. When the youngest of her nieces is about to be married by the son of the doctor who has been fondling her leg for profit—in fact paying for his son's medical career— the lady artiste makes a honey-filled doll to ensure her avenging heritage. At the end of the story, the aunt lives through ants and to her animalistic rites of passage. Chief among them is the riverborn chágara of tradition that comes out of the jeweled Eyes/I's of her adopted niece.

Finally, as my fourth example, I have chosen a rare surviving African model with important repercussions in the Caribbean, in which Sikán practically appears with her own name as a martyr of males with feminist revenge in mind. I am referring in particular to an oral tradition that has been transcribed into English from sources deep in South Africa's Xhosa country and deep within the black country and black subconscious of Cuban culture. The African tradition is embodied by the tale of "Sikhamba-nge-nyanga" (She-who-walks-by-moonlight), which, once again, does not present a flashy dancer but a sleight-of-hand that is an equally effective trick in gaining power. Like so many other women whose hip strategies we have reviewed, the hipness and hippiness of this protagonist is more of the mind and attitude than of the body and lassitude. In the case of Sikhamba, she might have actually repressed even her song-and-dance routine to ensure her ability to ambush the traditionally male-dominated taboos. However, our Sikhamba, like so many other more adamant and more seemingly vulnerable rumba heroines, still reflects a woman's concern about subversive revelation. She is a woman condemned by society to the subtlest of exhibitions of her body—from which Lydia Cabrera possibly derived her Afro-Cuban tale "Susudamba no se muestra de día" (Susudamba does not show herself by day).[43] Susudamba's reticence to show off her beauty amounts to an incredible conceit; her lack of show is just as daring a form of experiment as some other women's excess of show. The extreme levels of traumatic exhibition of lack thereof with which Sikán and her sisters become associated is always attributed to an infringement of woman's position regarding knowledge. In other words, the setting has been prejudicially exemplified as a performance of woman's "natural" intuitive curiosity against the limits imposed by man's "supernatural" learning capacity—a prejudice that Christians bestow upon the figure Eve. In fact, the name Sikán itself suggests both a Bantu and Semi-Bantu allusion to the essence of womanhood, that is, the implicit female breaking of the male boundaries—as playfully suggested by Cabrera Infante himself and routinely performed in the rumba's choreographed "get down" step and moment of "break."

In the Sikán tradition in general, and in the Xhosa legend in particular, a model woman agrees to break the taboo and bear the punishment for her bodily beauty, for the sake of her people, men and women, by only showing herself at night. However, she is not totally resigned to be a fleeting star of the night; even in the song that punctuates the legend, a chorus of women-birds signals her path to a symbolic victory as queen of signification. The doves, in fact, are a woman's saving grammar of half-gestures and glimpses of voice within the bird-rich text controlled by men's rule of polygamy and sense of textual order. The seemingly fleeting grammar of birds translates Sikhamba's strong disguised will and discreet downplay of beauty (the same could have been said about other avenging animals, from the most unsuspecting amphibians on their pads to the more obvious snakes in paradise). As such, Sikán's rumbaesque message, which brings to conscience a woman's sacrifice and warning about a woman's death, transcends her own symbolic sacrifice and death, as a form of flight just as problematic as a rumbera's song and dance:

Asingo mahotyazan' okubethwa,
Size kubika Sikhamba-ngenyanga;
ube kukha ngomcephe, watshona,
Waba kukha ngompanda, watsona,
Waba kukha ngengubo, yatshona,
Waba kukha ngeqhiya, yashona,
Waba kukha ngezandla, watshona.
[We are not doves that may be killed,
For we come to tell of Sikhamba-ngenyanga;
She dipped the ladle, and it sank,
She dipped the pot, and it sank,
She dipped the mantle, and it sank,
She dipped the head cover, and it sank,
She dipped her hands, and she sank.][44]

The doves sing of Sikhamba's will to sacrifice and her death as her ethical and aesthetic way: her way, that is, to go deeper into her own conscience and image, piercing the essence of skin-deep meanings, thin surfaces, is the tragically amphibian choice of an earthly and watery milieu (traditionally divided between men's and women's realms)—or the snake in the garden's ominous tempting of traditional fate. Sikhamba's beauty of body and mind had a price, for which she paid with extraordinary punishment—ranging from nightstalking to death by way of drowning in her own image—but she is also the prize and pride of a hidden tradition and the symbolic death of a woman's physical bonds and borrowed image. Sikhamba upholds this change by coming back again from the deep to suckle her progeny (offspring and followers); her beauty is more than an evanescent and fruitless show of skin, it is functional and it is lasting.

Hip Poetics

The Lust Hip

Viviana Angola remece bruscamente las caderas:
Goringoró-goró-goró-goró
[Viviana Angola shakes her hips brusquely:
I dare you to mess with my "jingle bells"]
—Lydia Cabrera, "El mono se perdió el fruto de su trabajo"
("How the Monkey Lost the Fruit of His Labor")[45]

In Lydia Cabrera's story "El mono se perdió el fruto de su trabajo" ("How the Monkey Lost the Fruit of His Labor") a woman, married to a weakling, lifts her skirt as a sign of power, daring an invading troupe of one hundred theatrically male monkeys to touch her bells, or is it her balls? They are subdued by the superficially touch-freely, yet profoundly untouchable, sight: "without ever knowing what was hidden, what was so fascinating, what tinkled and twinkled under the skirts of Viviana Angola."[46] Thus she ends a food war between men and monkeys, ostensibly giving victory indirectly to the former and directly to herself.

A close examination of the Kikongo-Cuban phrase Viviana sings and of the gesture that it informs leaves them open to question. The two-word phrase ("Goringoró-goró-goró-goró") is made of the names for a show of will (to go along or to refuse) and for the bells (sounds of silence) that represent them, as well as other variants from both sides of the Atlantic. The instruments in question are either played with a stick or left silent, so to speak, at the end of a stick. The words in question are also metaphorically connected with the notion of a woman's strategy of revelation, evasion, acceptance, and refusal. On both African sides of the Atlantic, the very words in question are even employed as names of taboo women and sites, on the order of "she who does not want" (to be named, to be heard, and to be had) or a "mountain that one does not want to climb" (or, perhaps, a mountain that does not want itself to be climbed).[47] Even without the benefit of our tentative etymological and ethnopoetical adventure from Cuba back to the Kongo, it is difficult not to interpret the strip dance of Cabrera's protagonist as an empowering gesture of daring toward society in general and males in particular. The women in question become stars of the hip and/or hip stars—through the shaking rump of the rumba or through their less than shaky rhumb.

Notes

1. My thanks to Anthony Appiah for bringing the lyrics of Coward's song to my attention.

2. *Random House Dictionary of the English Language,* unabridged ed. (New York, 1967), s.v. "hip."

3. I am thankful to Anthony Appiah for this Akan proverb, and to Lady Appiah for providing a translation.

4. *Random House Dictionary of the English Language,* s.v. "rumba."

5. Virginia Brindis de Salas, "Tango numero dos," in *Pregon de Marimorena* (Montevideo: Sociedad Cultural Editora Indo-Americana 1953), 50; my translation. The poet deals with the tango as if it were a rumba, that is, as a discursive unit of gestures and sounds that disguises a woman's neo-African cultural identity in a sung and danced routine available to the Spanish New World theater of cultural events. Not just in this poem, but also throughout the book, hip is queen. In fact the African core of this poem is the yumba, that is, the rumba under an Afro-Uruguayan disguise. See also the brief discussion of the African roots of the tango, in the introduction to the book, 11–12.

6. From the 1932 film *Blonde Venus,* directed by Josef von Sternberg.

7. Present in the entire Afro-conscious area of Spanish Americas, also known as the "magic circle." For a Cuban example see "Tale of Moons," my annotated translation of Alejo Carpentier's "Histoire de lunes," in *Latin American Literary Review* 8 (1980): 67–68.

8. I discuss the hermeneutical implications of such a break in "Through Blues," in *Do the Americas Have a Common Literature?*, ed. Gustavo Pérez Firmat (Durham: Duke U P, 1990), 107–129.

9. My thanks to Jonathan Ngate and Elizabeth Mudimbe-Boyi for supplying me with the line of the Lingala/French song and its translation, as well as for our discussions of the subject.

10. Adalberto Ortiz, *Juyungo* (1943; Barcelona: Seix Barral, 1976), 138; in English as *Juyungo,* trans. Susan F. Hill and Jonathan Tittler (Washington: Three Continents, 1982), 104. I have slightly modified, adding a more sexually stressed reading, Susan F. Hill and Jonathan Tittler's exemplary translation.

11. Rosario Ferré, *Papeles de Pandora* (Mexico: J. Mortiz, 1976), 206.

12. The character Códac, self-styled commentator and photographer of the stars, glosses the famous (in Cuba) "Requiem Rumba," in Guillermo Cabrera Infante, *Tres tristes tigres* (Barcelona: Seix Barral, 1968), 81; in English as *Three Trapped Tigers,* trans. Donald Gardner and Suzanne Jill Levine, in collaboration with Cabrera Infante (1971; New York: Harper & Row, 1985), 79. Page numbers will refer either to the original publication or to the pocketbook reprint of the translation, depending on whether I use the title in Spanish or in English.

13. See Fernando Ortiz, *Glosario de afronegrismos* (Havana: Siglo Veinte, 1924), 405–411. I have verified Ortiz's etymological research against the following classical works on Kongo culture: K. E. Laman, *Dictionnaire Kikongo-Français* (1936; reproduction

Ridgewood: Gregg, 1985); Janheinz Jahn, *Muntu: The New African Culture*, trans. Marjorie Greene (New York: Grove Weidenfeld, 1961); and several of Fernando Ortiz's works, particularly "Los cabildos afrocubanos" (1921), posthumously reprinted in the collection of his essays *Ensayos etnograficos*, ed. Miguel Barnet and Angel L. Fernandez (Havana: Editorial de Ciencias Sociales, 1984). The first part of the word *rumba,* in its original form of *(n)tumba,* embraces the many variants of *ntu*—"individual," "source," "appendage," "head," "end," "goal," and "life-death transaction" (see Laman, 799–800)—all of which are related to the crucial Bantu notion of "ntu," or principle of linguistic/existential classification of knowledge (i.e., the knowable "being" of the life forces), which Jahn registers and summarizes from his own and other scholars' studies (see Jahn, "NTU. African Philosophy," 96–120). Ortiz, 13, defines the *ntú,* pronounced in Cuba as *talento, talent,* to be a leader both politically and theatrically. The ending of the word *rumba, mba,* is an equally important notion of motion: "movement," "change," "continuity," "break," "(r)evolution," and "rebellion," all of which are related to the crucial discourse of song and dance (i.e., "force" of being, which one gets to live or perform). The discourse of *mba* renders public, records, inscribes, and politicizes the *ntu. Mba* is also related to deadly actions, most concretely to a quick, lethal bite, burning, or a fall, particularly the action of a poisonous snake, the *mbá-koko (kanza* or *Naja melanoleuca),* which "sings like a cock." Finally the word *mba* also signifies the natural or borrowed vessel for such a dramatic action, from the very sign of uncertainty to the word for testicle (see the variants of the notion of "Nba" in Laman, 516). The compounded word *ntumba* itself appears to be classical Kikongo, with the paradoxical connotation of consecration-desecration, truth-lie, virgin–"spoiled" woman (sickness of the breast), horned butterfly or field rat, opening (in door) and closure (by nail), the highest–the lowest and the actions that go with or reverse them. It also qualifies a man's docility (see the variants of "Ntumba" in Laman, 801). Some of these paradoxical connotations in Kikongo are resolved by choice of pronunciation. The etymological parallelism is found in Cuban American Oscar Hijuelos's prizewinning novel *The Mambo Kings Play Songs of Love* (New York: Harper & Row, 1989), 105. I am grateful to Gustavo Pérez Firmat for pointing out this play on words in Hijuelos's work.

14. Jahn, 81. For a concise narrative description of the evolution of the rumba as a navel-touching dance, see Alejo Carpentier, *La música en Cuba* (Mexico: Fondo de Cultura Economica, 1972), 65–71.

15. Ferré, 204–223. The composer of the song "Maquinolandera" was Ismael Miranda. See Angie (née Maria de los Angeles) Névarez, "Subversión, transformación, y rescritura: Acercamiento a la obra narrativa y poética de Rosario Ferré," master's thesis, Emory U, 1989, 39.

16. The possibilities for homonymous coincidences are enhanced by the very fact that the original African languages were mostly agraphic in nature and in many cases susceptible to accents and structurally tonal. The enhancement works at two levels: it provides more homonymal possibilities, and it hinders the ability to uncover the full potential of the hidden meanings.

17. Carmen Cordero, "Negra rumbera," in *Poesía afroantiallana y negrista: Puerto Rico—Republica Dominicana—Cuba*, ed. Jorge Luis Morales (Rio Piedras: Editorial Universitaria, U Puerto Rico, 1981), 428. Cordero is addressing Josephine Baker about the African American's role as the banana stripper (my translation).

18. See Fernando Ortiz, *Los instrumentos de la música afrocubana* 4 (Havana: Direccion de Cultura del Ministerio de Educacion, 1952–1955), 196, summarized in Jahn, 84.

19. For the political implications of Carmen Miranda's image, see Cynthia Enloe, "Carmen Miranda on My Mind: International Politics of the Banana," in *Making Feminist Sense of International Politics: Bananas, Beaches, and Bases* (Berkeley: U of California P, 1989), 124–150.

20. Yale commencement ceremony, 1989. *Reina rumba* is also the subtitle of Umberto Valverde's biography *Celia Cruz* (Mexico: Editorial Universo, 1982), appropriately prologued with a letter written by Guillermo Cabrera Infante to the author. Cabrera Infante finds uncanny coincidences between Valverde's work and Jahn's in their appraisal of the rumba as a significant center of the Afro-Caribbean (and by implication Afro-Hispanic) *son*. See my discussion of the *son* as a man-centered philosophical seed of the Caribbean, as opposed to the woman-centered rumba, in "Through Blues."

21. See Nancy Cunard, ed., *Negro, an Anthology* (New York: F. Unger, 1970), 328–329.

22. See Cunard, 329.

23. The latest of the opuses written on Baker's peeling skin is Phyllis Rose, *Jazz Cleopatra: Josephine Baker in Her Time* (New York: Doubleday, 1989).

24. See *Interview*, June 1990, cover and 116–127.

25. Nicolás Guillén, "Mujer Nueva," in *Obra poetica* 1, ed. Angel Augier (Havana: Editorial de Arte y Literatura, 1974), 120. This translation, or I should say adaptation, is by Langston Hughes and Ben Frederic Carruthers and was part of a collection of Guillén's poems published under the title *Cuba Libre* (Los Angeles: Anderson & Ritchie, 1948). The most significant change from the original is the translation of *tambor* (drum) as the *bongó* of "bongó drum" we have come to associate with a woman's instrument of resistance, which is part of the ritual death of Sikán.

26. For an ethnographic description of the *seseribó* (also *sese, sesé, eribó*) and the *bongó* (also *(e)bongo, (n)gongo, (n)gogo,* and *(n)gogó),* see Enrique Sosa Rodríguez, *Los ñañigos* (Havana: Casa de las Americas, 1982), esp. 177–179. Refer also to *mbok* and *bogw,* 91–95 and 171, respectively. Furthermore, consult variants of the Kikongo *ngodi, ngori, ngongi,* and *ngongo* in Laman, 689–692. Finally, in Kongo-Cuban the word and particle *go* signifies "silence" and signals a ritual break or interruption in the liturgy; its derivative *gon* means *afirmación* (affirmation), as pointed out by Lydia Cabrera, *Vocabulario congo: El Bantu que se habla en Cuba* (Miami: Ediciones CR, 1984), 147. This latter usage further defines the earlier wider-angled interpretation by Ortiz. See the entry "Bongo" in his *Glosario de afronegrismos*, 63–64, which includes overtones of "dressing," "treasure," "property," "vessel," thus enriching the interpretation of this sacred instrument as a means of communication for a woman's voice.

27. del Cabral, "Colasa con rumba," in *Obra poética completa,* 115.

28. See Sosa Rodríguez, 43, 114.

29. As is, or slightly modified, Ekué becomes the family name of the male protagonist as well as a woman-centered myth in two Cuban novels, Alejo Carpentier's *¡Ecue-Yamba-O!* (1933) in *Obras completas* 1 (Mexico: Siglo Veintiuno, 1983), 21–193, and Guillermo Cabrera Infante's *Tres tristes tigres*. The most traditional women's counterpart for the Leopard Societies is the Crocodile Societies of Africa and possibly of the Americas.

30. See the English version of the rite, taken from Fernando Ortiz's ethnographic accounts, in Jahn, 69–78.

31. The image of the mule appears not only in literary texts that are, according to Jahn quoting Ortiz, "in rumba rhythm," but also in the most demeaning aspects of the rumba dance itself. Jahn shares Ortiz's indignation in describing the choreography of " 'Herrar la mula,' 'shoeing the hinny' [in which the] female dancer, on all fours, represents the she-ass, the male dancer represents the smith who is shoeing her 'hooves.' " This "degenerate" form of the rumba was "created for the entertainment and exploitation of foreign tourists" (see Jahn, 85).

32. The classical sources for the Anaforuana are three books by Lydia Cabrera: her study of the society, *La sociedad secreta Abakuá narrado por viejos adeptos* (Miami: Ediciones CR, 1970); of the Ñañigo (Abakuá language in letters), a Spanish dictionary entitled *La lengua sagrada de los ñañigos* (Miami: Ediciones CR, 1988); and her dictionary of ideograms, *Anaforuana: Ritual y símbolos de la iniciación en la sociedad secreta Abakuá* (Madrid: Ediciones Erre, 1975).

33. An Abakuá man dresses as a woman or invites a postmenopausal woman to "perform" the role of Sikán (see Sosa Rodríguez, 157–159). At times, such a man also sings in falsetto voice (see Sosa Rodríguez, 229).

34. For a most comprehensive view of Oshún and Yemayá, see Lydia Cabrera, *Yemayá y Ochun: Kariocha, Iyalorichas y Olorichas* (Eastchester, NY: E. Torres, 1980). For Oyá, see Judith Gleason, *Oya: In Praise of the Goddess* (Boston: Shambhala, 1987).

35. Del Cabral, "Tropico suelto," in *Obra poética completa*, 216.

36. The title of this novel approximately translates as *Praise Be the Keeper of Tradition!*

37. See Cabrera Infante, 237, 446.

38. Cabrera Infante, 85–86.

39. Refer to the ethnographic works by Alvaro de la Iglesia, Salvador Bueno, and, above all, Samuel Feijóo, whose *El negro en la literatura folklórica cubana* (Havana: Editorial Letras Cubanas, 1980) contains perhaps the most quoted version of the myth of Sikán: the legend of "Siquillángama," 171–174. However, the state-of-the-art ethnographic renderings are by Sosa Rodríguez and to my mind the best literary renderings are by Lydia Cabrera, who also shares Sosa Rodríguez's ethnographic work, indeed serves as his mentor and source.

40. See n. 34.

41. Cabrera, *Cuentos negros de Cuba*, 133.

42. Cabrera, *Cuentos negros de Cuba*, 132.

43. Lydia Cabrera, *Por qué . . . : Cuentos negros de Cuba*, 2d ed. (Madrid: Ramos, 1972), 219.

44. A.C. Jordan, "Sikhamba-Nge-Nyanga," in *Talk That Talk: An Anthology of African American Storytelling*, ed. Linda Goss and Marian E. Barnes (New York: Simon and Schuster, 1989), 242.

45. A woman addresses, in Kikongo-Cuban dialect, some male monkeys. I thank Georgina Dopico for suggesting this text to me. See Cabrera, *Por qué* . . . , 217, and her "How the Monkey Lost the Fruit of His Labor," trans. Mary Caldwell and Suzanne Jill Levine, in *Other Fires: Short Fiction by Latin American Women*, ed. Alberto Manguel (New York: C. N. Potter, 1986), 204.

46. Cabrera, "How the Monkey Lost the Fruit of His Labor," 219.

47. See "Ngòngo" and "Ngöngo," in Laman, 692. Notice that *ngòngo* also refers to the spine of a book, thus stressing the gap between the sound-making mechanism of marginal voices and their graphic mainstreaming. That is, it relates the superficial validation of intuitions as bookbound knowledge, or even worse: through bookbinding power. This forced game of validation provides a common ground to the examples of this last section and so many others throughout this essay.

Medics, Crooks, and Tango Queens

The National Appropriation of a Gay Tango

Jorge Salessi   Translated by Celeste Fraser Delgado

Del Buen Retiro a la Alameda
los gustos locos me vengo a hacer.
Muchachos míos ténganlo tieso
que con la mano gusto os daré.
[From Buen Retiro to the Alameda
My crazy tastes I've come to try.
Hold it stiff my fine young boys
With my hand I'll make you sigh.]
—Luis D., "Autobiografía," in his "Autobiography: A Professional
Sexual Invert," *Archives of Psychiatry and Criminology*, 1903

The tango syncretized Latin American, African, and European musical and cultural elements that mingled in an underworld of Buenos Aires at the turn of the century. Between 1880 and 1900 in the margins of the new Argentine metropolis flourished a rich subculture that created and circulated new meanings and pleasures by means of a dance of desire, marked by a highly syncopated music in four-four time and anonymous lyrics drawing from the words, idioms, tales, and characters of *lunfardo*. I suggest that in the history of this subculture there is a forgotten, or erased, memory of the sexuality of Buenos Aires. I venture that the original tango, repeatedly described by the historians of Argentine music as a simulation or a choreographic representation of sexual intercourse, is a cultural expression with significant homoerotic and homosexual connotations that today are deeply embedded in the imagined national identity of the large Argentine middle class.[2]

The history of the original tango, as performed just before the twentieth century, acquires a special relevance and coherence if considered in the broader context of the Argentine discourse of sexuality, a discourse that emerges and proliferates precisely at the end of the nineteenth and beginning of the twentieth century, when the "respectable" society still viewed the tango as a forbidden music form and a forbidden dance.

In attempting to reconstruct this greater context, while pursuing my original object of investigation, the history of the Argentine discourse of sexuality, I could not avoid the history of the tango. As we shall see, the two histories intersect in the brothel—a paradigmatic space of Buenos Aires at the turn of the century—when and where each one enriches or, using an image quite appropriate to the age, contaminates the other.

During this period in Argentina a discursive practice began to proliferate realizing the same "incorporation of the perversions and a new specification of individuals" described by Foucault in his *History of Sexuality*.[3] The Argentine discourse of sexuality, produced and disseminated by an Argentine fin de siècle class of positivist professionals subservient to the hegemonic class, enacted the regulation, control, and containment of the new social classes and cultural groups that emerged with immigration.

In the bourgeois project launched by the Argentine liberal elite in 1880, immigration played a key role in the country's modernization. But the class in power imagined this immigration to affect agricultural labor only and to have no impact upon the country's political life. Political activity at this time was restricted to a limited group of electors and elected members of the patrician landowning class that kept a close grip on power by means fair or, more often, foul. However, between 1890 and 1900, the new social formations generated by immigration presented a powerful challenge to the prerogatives of the hegemonic class.

Although smaller in numbers than the immigration reaching the United States earlier in the century, relative to the native population the immigration to Argentina was proportionately far larger. Most of these immigrants, unable to become small-farm owners due to the latifundio structure of land tenure, established themselves in one of two coastal cities, Buenos Aires or Rosario, and worked in the growing urban industries and commercial ventures. By the 1900s the suburban and white, preferably Anglo-Saxon, immigration that had been imagined by the Argentine ideologues of the mid-nineteenth century had became an immigration of large and visible groups of foreigners, mainly Italians and Spaniards, many of them young males without traditional family ties and often from the poorest areas of their home countries. Out of this

immigration grew a new Argentine middle class that forced the redefinition and rearrangement of the previous class structure. At the same time,
the concentration of most workers in Buenos Aires during the first decade of the twentieth century allowed a new Argentine labor movement
to develop and challenge the hegemony of the class in power. By the
1900s Buenos Aires had become a city of immigrants, farmers become
urban dwellers and laborers, in many cases seasoned in the class struggles of the old country. Thus the immigration that was meant to provide
the labor necessary for the integration of Argentina into the Eurocentric
blueprint of "progress," "modernization," and "internationalism" was
now a foreign force living within national borders and capable of striking against and paralyzing the meat and grain exporting economy that
kept enriching the landowning class. An Argentine sexual science seeking to define strict border controls around the definitions of sex and
gender, class and nationality, was an urgent response to this threat.

Implemented to control the new social formations of Buenos Aires,
this sexual science gave rise to a taxonomy of categories of sexual deviance, such as "pederasty," "the third sex," "sapphism," "sexual inversion," "uranism," and "homosexuality."[4] These categories establish unexpected relations and create connotations and meanings that resonate
between texts, articulating and illuminating shifting concepts of sexuality and the history of the tango. Intertwined with the discourses
of sexuality, involving medical, criminological, and pedagogical works
fraught with arbitrary and irrational connotations, is the undocumented
history of the marginal, subversive, literally *forbidden* world into which
the tango was born.

The Argentine Discourse of Sexuality

Foucault explains that between the eighteenth and nineteenth centuries
a discourse on sex proliferated from distinct foci, "sex became a 'police'
matter . . . [a] policing of sex: that is, not the rigor of a taboo, but the
necessity of regulating sex through useful and public discourses." Foucault adds, "One could mention many other centers which in the eighteenth or nineteenth century began to produce discourses on sex. First
there was medicine . . . ; next psychiatry . . . ; penal justice, too."[5] In

Argentina at the end of the last century these also were the centers from which a sexual science was produced and irradiated. In the works of Adolfo Bátiz, a subcommissioner of the police of Buenos Aires; José Ramos Mejía, a physician and founder of Argentine psychiatry; and Eusebio Gómez, a respected criminologist of the same historical moment, we shall see three instances of the Argentine discourse of sexuality that, between 1890 and 1914, when immigration unsettled virtually all of the cultural, social, and economic structures of Buenos Aires, implanted and disseminated a construction of homosexuality. This construction, along with its incoherences and contradicting definitions, was used in turn to characterize, specify, and control a heterogeneous culture in which the clear demarcations and apparently distinct categories that had ordered the old colonial city became blurred. The taxonomic elaboration of homosexuality provided the key categories of a medical, legal, and sociological analysis that focused on the acts and pleasures of a heterogeneous population, a language of secret codes, a fashion of dress, a forbidden dance and style of music that after being appropriated, *hygienicized,* became the mythic constructs at the core of the cultural identity of the mainstream Argentine middle class.

Bátiz, Ramos Mejía, and Gómez, in addition to being prime representatives of the policing, psychiatric, and criminological systems referred to by Foucault, are also examples of an important scientific and cultural movement that we have only begun to study in recent years. Hugo Vezzetti, in his history of *La locura en la Argentina* (Madness in Argentina), in which he traces the professional career of J. M. Ramos Mejía in particular,[6] describes a "professional class," of which Bátiz, Gómez, and Ramos Mejía form part, and explains that these psychiatrists and hygienists at the turn of the century constituted themselves into "a psychiatric and criminological bureaucracy that grew and became specialized within the institutions of the State, in the poorhouses, university professorships, and professional societies. Thus [this professional class] encountered a privileged opportunity for social ascendance in their service of the demands of power." These professionals occupied key positions in the state power structure, manipulating a network of influence from which no aspect of the public or private life of the inhabitants of the country seemed to escape. Vezzetti notes that these men served as "state officials of public health who integrated themselves into a techno-political func-

tion" in order to formulate "from the fields of public hygiene and psychiatric medicine to criminology certain attempts to medicalize the conduct
of the citizenry—attempts converging with juridical, penal, and pedagogical dispositions and practices."[7]

Hygiene in Argentina in the last decades of the nineteenth century
sought to contain the effects of immigration that were conceived of as
potentially "contaminating" the nation from outside. This same hygiene[8]
in the first decades of the twentieth century became, first, an Argentine
criminology, and finally an Argentine brand of nationalist education—an
Argentine psychology and national pedagogy—which after 1900 was
devoted to the formation of new Argentine citizens: the children of immigrants.[9] Furthermore, as Vezzetti explains, this development "seeks to
reorder the space of power accentuating the exercise of an intervention
that is not merely on the order of punishment and exclusion, but also
seeks to constitute a *moral subject* as the basic axis of the social subject . . .
a process that makes readily visible the convergence of political and
juridical tactics with the function of models of health and sanity, and
converts the psychiatrist at once into a modern incarnation of the moralist and a paradigm of the ruler."[10]

With the collaboration between the policing, psychiatric, and medico-
legal systems, a new Argentine criminology emerged, a criminology
that, preoccupied with the new sins of the modern metropolis, focused
upon the open expressions of social unrest and the demands of the nascent social classes and labor unions. Vezzetti points out that the police,
medical, and legal professionals "made brothers through the received
teachings of Ramos Mejía and through the common business of criminology, render the theory of degeneration as an instrument with a very
circumscribed use, directed at this socially marginal zone." In this zone,
"petty criminals"—women and men who refused to adopt the "respectable" and "healthy" way of life proposed by the hegemonic bourgeois
class as a synonym for nationality—cohabited with seamstresses, laun-
dresses, wayfaring laborers, servants, and transient immigrants, unemployed or recently arrived. Vezzetti explains that "degeneration became
easily identified with immigration" insofar as "this extensive zone of
wanton marginality rapidly became the principal enemy" of the new
professional class of functionaries. Ideologically this new functionary,
the criminologist and modern pedagogue, is the old "hygienic function-

ary . . . [as] their projects—and often their interests—intersect with the elite that controls economic and political resources."[11] Let's now see how these police, psychiatrists, criminologists and pedagogues define the marginal world of the immigrant and the tango.[12]

In his study *Buenos Aires, la rivera y los prostíbulos en 1880* (Buenos Aires, the riverbank and the brothels in 1880), Adolfo Bátiz, the policeman, not only recommends and promotes a *national,* state-regulated prostitution of women, he also reveals a persistent preoccupation with identifying another kind of prostitution: a "pederasty" represented as hidden, liminal, foreign, and threatening to the hygiene proposed as synonymous with security and nationality. J. M. Ramos Mejía, the psychiatrist, in 1898 published a sociological study entitled *Las multitudes argentinas* (The Argentine multitudes), in which he promotes a nationalist education as necessary for the reform of the "sexual invert's sensibility," which he believes to be disseminated throughout all the new social strata created by immigration.[13] Eusebio Gómez, the criminologist, in 1908 published *La mala vida en Buenos Aires* (The profligate life in Buenos Aires). Gómez's text modernizes both the "pederasty" of Bátiz's work and the "sexual inversion" introduced by Ramos Mejía. His trope becomes a criminalized "homosexuality" that has acquired an element of danger. Opposed to the fostering of prostitution promoted by Bátiz, the criminologist establishes the homology prostitution = criminality = homosexuality, alleging that "prostitution is nothing other than the equivalent or derivative of criminality." Within this criminalized prostitution Gómez identifies a "group of numerous homosexuals living in Buenos Aires, who have formed their own branch of prostitution."[14] Prostitution, promoted by Bátiz and regulated by Ramos Mejía in 1892 as president of the National Department of Hygiene, was originally conceived to "educate" an immigrant population made up of an overwhelming majority of adult males in heterosexual practices. When infiltrated by homosexuals, prostitution subverts its purpose. Thus during the first decade of the twentieth century the new strategy, promoted by Ramos Mejía (then president of the National Council of Education), would emphasize an Argentine brand of nationalist education.

The importance given homosexuality in these texts is evidence of both the changing sexual practices in the new metropolis of Argentina and a textual construction used to control a marginal population and curb political and social unrest. We can ascertain that the documents reflect indisputable evidence that at the end of the century in Buenos Aires an urban homosexual subculture acquired a new, sometimes glaring, visibility. Donna Guy writes, "*Higienistas* knew that Buenos Aires had a significant homosexual population and that male prostitutes were found not only among street walkers soliciting sex but also within the supposedly all-female bordellos."[15] A homosexual anxiety emerges in these texts in an instance of "homosexual panic," as studied by Eve Kosofsky Sedgwick: the homophobia "important not only for persecutory regulation of a nascent minority population of distinctly homosexual men but also for the regulation of the male homosocial bonds that structure all culture—at any rate all public or heterosexual culture."[16] In Gómez's text, for example, male-male sexual practices seem to take on unusual proportions when the criminologist writes, "The men pay [male prostitutes] because every day the nucleus of perverts grows in proportions that we will not mention for fear that we will be viewed as exaggerating."[17] This *exaggeration* is the homosexual panic fostered and deployed to reorganize and reinforce oscillating cultural structures. In the historical period that interests us, in Buenos Aires, the incorporation of women into the paid workforce, the visibility of a new urban homosexual subculture, and a growing prostitution of male transvestites signal deep changes in the sex/gender system and gender structure of the economy.[18]

In a study written in 1904 at the request of President Roca, *El estado de las clases obreras argentinas* (The state of the Argentine working classes), Juan Bialet-Massé anxiously notes: "The woman, among us, now participates with the man in professions and offices that until now were reserved by custom for men; the free institutions of the nation in no way serve as an obstacle and one might believe that, given the flight they have taken, women will end up as in the United States, exercising all professions and offices . . . In some cities, the industries already find employing cheap women's labor more advantageous." Claiming that "women's work must not be allowed unless fate absolutely demands it" (overlooking the unpaid work they traditionally performed at home), Bialet-Massé warns that women working for a salary become "that thing which we call the *third sex,* that has in London alone more than 300,000 representatives and in Europe more than 3,000,000. That has appeared in the United States as an invader, and that happily does not yet have among us more than a few affiliated individuals."[19] The woman characterized as "that thing" (*eso*)—a neuter or androgyne because she threatens the system of roles and hierarchies implicit in the division of labor between the "masculine" man and the "feminine" woman—is the *urning,* the "uranist," described also as the "third sex," the "intermediate sex," or *sexuelle zwischenstufe* by Karl Ulrichs and Magnus Hirschfeld between 1860 and 1879. Furthermore, in Bialet-Massé's text the characterization of the woman who "participates with the man in professions and offices that until now were reserved by custom for men" is represented as the precursor of a homosexuality described as an "invader." In the terminology of the Argentine hygienists of the time the term "invasion" is synonymous with "infection," and the two words are used interchangeably.[20] Here then the homosexual panic, "important for the regulation of . . . all public or heterosexual culture," is represented as the threat of an "invasion" or "infection" by women who are, furthermore, "affiliated" with the new labor unions. In the same text—a preliminary study for the project of the first Argentine workers' law seeking to palliate and control the new Argentine labor movement that between 1890 and 1910 challenged the hegemony of the patrician class—we see the Catholic Church called upon to exercise its influence in order to halt a new movement of women working in industry and commerce organizing in workers' groups and union actions. Bialet-Massé describes a group of women who "nearly two years ago had convened a demonstration and a collective strike, but a Priest told them in a sermon that the Catholic Church does not accept these proceedings or their consequences, and they quit, submitting themselves to their particular servitude." Women exploited by the new industrialists who "f[ou]nd employing cheap women's labor more advantageous" labored under a "particular servitude" despite surpassing men in efficiency. Bialet-Massé himself affirms that "doing the same work and better, [she is exploited] under the pretext that a woman cannot earn as much as a man."[21] "Third sex" or "pederasty," these representations of a homosexuality are the product of a very specific historical context. Let us further explore how sexual desires were constructed and distributed among the new cultural groups and social classes of modern Argentina.

In the introduction to his book *Buenos Aires, la rivera y los prostíbulos en 1880,* subtitled "A contribution to social studies," Adolfo Bátiz claims that he is compelled to write by the city's desire: "lust, and now lust and pederasty . . ."[22] "Lust" and "pederasty" are thus inscribed in the beginning of the text as the poles of an axis around which rotates a dense constellation of meanings. On the surface Bátiz's text promotes an officially regulated prostitution of women meant to contain the dissemination of polymorphous sexualities. In the first chapter, entitled "Prostitution—Social Sanitation," after alleging that "prostitution is an evil as necessary as life itself," the police officer explains that his form of "social sanitation," his writing, is "meant to mark the velocity of this wheel that for various reasons moves capriciously and without center, this is what all well-intentioned men like myself desire: that prostitution does not proceed so capriciously and at whim, without any guide to tell the various agents where the truth lies."[23] Capturing and reorganizing into a wheel-like system peripheral sexualities disseminated "capriciously" and "at whim," this "contribution to social studies" from whose center radiates a "truth" about sexuality, is what Foucault calls the "policing of sex, not the rigor of a prohibition but the necessity of regulating sex through useful and public discourses." But there is still another level of meaning.

In the second chapter Bátiz begins a description of the city of his childhood: "In the early years I explored the southern part of the city . . . to enter into [the southern neighborhood of] *la Boca* meant to enter into lust, especially when we entered some brothel, always ruled by Italians and women of the Italianate underworld." Thus in the symbolic pole of the south the policeman inscribes the "lust" of a foreign prostitution of females represented as "Italian" and "of the Italianate underworld." Here we should remember that between 1890 and 1914, with momentary exceptions, Italians constituted a visible majority of immigrants in Buenos Aires. Bátiz goes on to describe his childhood walks to the north: "Another day, I took the Paseo 9 de Julio from the *Casa Rosada* all the way to the docks of *Las Catalinas.* I had a special antipathy toward the gardens

of the Paseo 9 de Julio because they were the refuge of the passive pederasts who met around the statue of Mazzini, the revolutionary and man
of Italic liberties." In the north then, the other symbolic pole, "pederasty"
is inscribed also, as we will see, as Italian. Running from the south to
the north, from "lust" to "pederasty," the arcade forms a material metaphor that organizes the constellation foreigners-traffickers-criminals-
homosexuals, while articulating two distinct forms of prostitution. In the
same paragraph Bátiz says: "I found the arcade equally or almost as
frightful; I walked through expecting some thief [*lunfardo*] to thrust his
hands into my pockets and rob me; foreigners of the lowest sort convened here, the majority Italians and cosmopolitan rogues who arrived
in the country to make money through any means, however low." Here,
as in the majority of these texts, "cosmopolitan" signifies the international and frightening indefinition of nationalities and languages, sexualities, genders, and social classes. Parallel to the river the arcade is the
gathering place of "foreigners of the lowest sort," "lunfardos," and "cosmopolitan rogues." The enclosed and open space of the arcade serves
both as a physical site and a symbolic locus of multiple articulations and
contacts: between the lust of the south and the pederasty of the north,
between nationalities and social classes, between the underworld of
petty criminals "below" and the world of "decent" people "above," between the *inside* of the *national order* of the city and the *outside* of the
invasion from the east. Here, as in Bialet-Massé's text, we see the contradictions and tensions of the Argentine nationalism promoted by the liberal elite of the times: following a Western or Eurocentric blueprint of
modernization, progress, and internationalism but rejecting what is perceived as the "cosmopolitan" confusion of a sex/gender system of "third
sex" women and "passive pederast" men.[24]

While the arcade on one hand separates and articulates "lust" and
"pederasty," providing the gathering place for traffickers and criminals,
on the other hand it serves as border between a "foreign" and a "national" prostitution. In the west, the symbolic interior of the new nation,
"along Paraguay Street or along Córdoba . . . until Maipú," Bátiz describes "the *humble* brothels of the indigenous colored (*chinas*) *criollas* of
pure race, of the Indian type, living only one or two to a house, without
the shrieking organ found in the houses of the Neapolitan ruffian."[25] The
"shrieking organ," also known in the history of Argentine popular music

as the "little street organ" (*organillo callejero*) is the musical instrument that popularized the original tango. The mobile street organ disseminated the immigrant music, its airy tunes erasing the barriers between public and private spaces. Rubén Pesce explains that the street organ "was the first mechanical instrument that could carry the tango through the streets and in this way introduce the music, through balconies and windows, into the houses that didn't want to listen."[26] The association of the sonorous "shrieking organ" with prostitution in the "houses of the Neapolitan ruffian" underlines the characterization of a "humble" national prostitution practiced by women of "pure race," the *chinas criollas* imagined and represented as submissive, modest, and discreet. In contrast with this "national" prostitution, Bátiz describes the *invasion* by that other prostitution, the "foreigners, the Polish, Hungarians, Australians, French, Tunisians, Belgians, Turks, Egyptians, Swedish, Persians, Circassians, Britons, Russians, and other nationalities from all of Europe. They live in ultra-luxurious houses." This is the city within the city, the internal invasion, "luxurious," draining the forces of an "immense Buenos Aires where since 1880 gold poured out by the handful to be snatched up by traffickers"; and these foreign "traffickers" are represented as having marked homosexual tendencies.[27]

Eusebio Gómez, the criminologist, upon establishing the same difference between a national prostitution and a foreign prostitution, alleges that "we discover in the first certain traces of nobility of which the other is incapable. The passion for true love . . . is very general in the Criolla prostitute, over and above the passion for accumulating money demonstrated by the imported whore." Gómez concludes his characterization of these foreign women by affirming that "these women feel for men a profound distaste and they dedicate themselves to a sapphic love."[28]

Parallel to this invasion by women characterized as foreigners, traffickers, and lesbians is an invasion by men, Jewish and Italian, characterized as "pederasts" or "sexual inverts," subversives, anarchists, and socialists threatening the hygiene and security of the state.

Bátiz, the police officer on the hunt for peripheral sexualities, weaves throughout his text an ambivalent image of the modern metropolis, simultaneously represented as Buenos Aires and Rome. Apparently concerned about the proliferation of heterosexual prostitution in Buenos

Aires, Bátiz alleges that "prostitution has taken on an alarming character because it is increasing beyond the normal and logical to such a level that we are on the edge of Roman decadence"[29]—the stereotypical decadence of the Imperial Rome of Edward Gibbon. In the following phrase, however, now constructing a stereotype of an atavistic Italian sexuality, Bátiz identifies in contemporary Rome "the existence in public life of an agency for procuring models for passive pederasts, located in Corso Humberto I [*sic*]" (*BA*, 76). Imperial Rome is thus conflated with the Rome of the fin de siècle, diachronically and synchronically (re)presented as the capital of homosexuality. A few pages before the end of the book Bátiz repeats his warning: "We must insist on the existence of the house of Rome, to which we referred as providing models for passive pederasts and of which much has appeared in the daily press," reaffirming again that "we are, and it is truly bitter, living in decadent Rome" (*BA*, 86). The "house" of this other prostitution, the agency that provides hired sex to the "passive pederasts," is the image that, appearing at the beginning and the end of the text, functions as a rhetorical device, conveying and relating two levels of meaning: (1) the necessary promotion of a "national" prostitution of "humble" women of "pure race," by which sexuality can be regulated and specified by the sexual science, implemented as a prophylactic measure against (2) an invasion or infection by a foreign "homosexuality" hidden in the interstices of the city, draining its forces and threatening national security.

Elaborating his characterization of an Italian homosexuality, Bátiz adds to it the connotation of an Italian anarchism infiltrating the nation. Where he first mentions "the house of Rome," the police officer calls it an "agency," a business office and means by which an Italian homosexuality is propagated abroad. After identifying the Roman origin of homosexuality, Bátiz warns the reader "that there exists an international traffic in models" (*BA*, 79). Then within the text the "Roman models" are represented emigrating from Rome to Buenos Aires, to reappear hidden in the "refuge of the passive pederasts who gather around the statue of Mazzini, the *revolutionary* and *man of Italic liberties*." These are the sexual "liberties" of "decadent" Rome, and Mazzini, the nineteenth-century Italian *carbonaro*, the "conspirator" who fought for the unification of Italy, the founder of *Giovine Italia*, international secret societies of young men who believed in a world republican federation, becomes identified as the symbolic "revolutionary" leader around whom cluster in conspiracy these anarchists of sexuality. Here my reading becomes clear in examining a broader context.

In his book *Nationalism and Sexuality,* George Mosse studies the bourgeois phobias that germinate in large modern cities, explaining that "conspiracies were supposedly the rule in the big cities, linking those hostile to society to their immoral environment. Immorality and conspiracy were closely associated throughout the nineteenth century."[30] Bátiz's association of the "immoral" and the "conspirator" gathered around the monument that identifies them is no coincidence. Carl Solberg examines the emergence of Argentine nationalism at the turn of the century, pointing out that in 1897, when the Italian community of Buenos Aires solicited parliamentary authorization to place a monument to Garibaldi in a city square, "the proposal offended the national pride of a large minority of congressmen who insisted that statues help form a people's character and that monuments to foreign heroes were clearly out of place when immigration already threatened the Argentine 'national soul.' "[31] In Bátiz's text we see the same official conception that statuary may promote or threaten national character and security. Alluding to the monument to Mazzini, Bátiz writes, "Today the conditions of hygiene and security have improved somewhat and we believe that around the fountain of Lola Mora, located in the garden, no pederasts prowl" (*BA,* 26–27). The fountain of Lola Mora, a birth of Venus notable for its sensual representation of a female nude—now discreetly located in a quiet and little-traveled place in the Costanera Sur—has a rich history of public scandals and transport from one part of the city to another, alternately promoting and subverting the "moral" or "social hygiene" of different historical moments. On the other hand, the monument to Mazzini up to the present day has apparently disappeared from the urban radius of the city of Buenos Aires.[32]

Here we should recall that between 1880 and 1910 an official politics of urban design developed, copying very closely Baron Haussmann's project for the new capital of the French Second Empire and transforming Buenos Aires into the "Paris of the Plata." Susan Buck-Morss, in her study of Benjamin's "Passagen-Werk," cites the German critic's description of an ideology that can be read in the surface of the city, explaining that "the urban 'perspectives' which Haussman created from wide boulevards, lined with uniform building facades that seemed to stretch to infinity and punctuated by national monuments, were intended to give the fragmented city an appearance of coherence. In fact, the plan, 'based on a politics of imperial centralization, was a totalitarian aesthetics, in that it caused the repression of every individual part, every autonomous development of the city.' "[33] Buck-Morss's description of the new capital works surprisingly well for a very characteristic perimeter of Buenos Aires built between 1885 and 1915, moving from the Plaza de Mayo to the Plaza del Congreso Nacional, from there along Callao Street to the Gardens of Palermo—the *porteño*[34] version of the "Bois de Boulogne"—following along the Avenida del Libertador to the monument of San Martín and from Retiro, along Florida Street to the Plaza de Mayo through avenues and boulevards flanked with symmetrical lines of uniform façades, the national monuments both connecting and articulating the physical perimeter, and the official aesthetics and ideology of the liberal elite of fin de siècle Buenos Aires. Citing Ramos Mejía's *Las multitudes argentinas*, Vezzetti explains that in the hygienist's text, for example, "Buenos Aires is already marked as the 'crucible of the future where the bronze is cast, perhaps somewhat too quickly, for the grand statue of the new race to come.' " The ideology cast in the bronze of this capital-statue is that of a "democracy that could become a sickness if it escapes the control of a central and, overall, unified authority whose geographical representation is the city of Buenos Aires."[35] In the physical and symbolic space of this city, ideological diversity—aesthetic, cultural, musical, or sexual—is marginal and subversive.

In Bátiz's text, the Italian sexual anarchists are also construed as dangerous "models" who, hidden in the shadows of the new metropolis, proselytize very effectively among the nation's "new youth." Describing the authorities' difficulties in repressing the dissemination of a polymorphous sexuality, Bátiz writes that the police are as yet "incapable of persecuting a scandalous new Argentine youth; some of them, already known in Buenos Aires, travel to Naples or Rome seeking models" (*BA*, 86), the models that—according to Bátiz—offer their services to a "scandalous new Argentine youth" of "passive pederasts." Thus the policeman of sexuality, after describing the immigration of models in traffic from Rome to Buenos Aires and now gathered around the statue of Mazzini, completes his investigation of an *inverted* traffic by noting the young Argentines who travel to Italy in search of models. The movement described by his text is drawn as a labile but growing "vicious circle" of sexual anarchists migrating between Italy and Argentina.

Here we should recall that at the turn of the century Italians represented a majority of the immigrant population of Buenos Aires and, as Tulio Halperín Donghi explains, starting from 1890 this immigrant population developed a new labor movement whose main organizers and militants were foreigners. Now to what Halperín Donghi calls "open and virulent xenophobia" and "xenophobic motives, so liberally evoked to justify the repression of the workers' movement and social protest,"[36] we might add a consistent and persistent homophobia—a homosexual panic whose origins and future reach we have just begun to assess.

This plot not only involves "sapphic" women from "all of Europe" and Italian "pederasts," but also Jewish men, represented as "feminine" and "sexually inverted," who threaten the security of the state. Mosse explains that the myth of a homosexual conspiracy parallels the myth of an international Jewish conspiracy. At the end of the century Jews and homosexuals were perceived as a "state within a state."[37] As we have already seen, the foreign women who worked in the brothels, in addition to being represented as lesbians, were characterized as Jewish. Let us now examine the sexual-textual construction of the Jewish man.

La bolsa (The stock exchange), a novel by Julián Martel, cited by Bátiz, published one year after the great Argentine economic crisis of 1890, is a good example of a type of "realist" fiction that describes "reality" while in fact helping to construct a social reality.[38] Showing its identification with the same "realist" canon to which Bátiz's book belongs, *La bolsa* is also subtitled "A social study." In it, Dr. Glow, a character who represents the new Criollo bourgeoisie created by immigration, introduces the Baron Mackser, the "speculator," with the warning: "The Baron Mackser is the advance general of an Israeli army deployed against the Americas in order to conquer it with money, the powerful arm against which all of our Aryan arms are impotent . . . The Jews, hidden in the shadow, advance step by step, buying the press and by extension the public opinion, the university professorships, the magisterial positions, the Government." Establishing an alliance between the Jews and a fin de siècle socialism, the same character adds: "And their triumph will be even more secure if they decide to take advantage of the socialist element as a fighting force to direct it in the frightful socialist revolution that approaches." Conforming to the same stereotype of the conspirator described by Mosse, this Jewish man is "feminine." The detail of the "objective," "scientific" narrator of Martel's novel—a faithful copy of the narrator of the clinical histories of the psychiatrists, hygienists, and criminologists that create a sense of veracity through narrative detail—describes the conspirator as "a pale, blonde, lymphatic man of medium stature, in whose unpleasant feminine face one can observe the expression of a hypocritical humility that the long custom of servility has made the stamp of the Jewish race."[39] Halperín Donghi has also remarked upon the novel's virulent anti-Semitism, assigning it particular significance given, in contrast to the Italian population, the small number of Jewish immigrants living in Buenos Aires in 1891.[40] Martel's characterization of Jewish men is further elaborated by Ramos Mejía.

In his book *Los simuladores del talento* (The simulators of talent), a text first published in the *Archivos de Psiquiatría y Criminología* in 1904 as an article entitled "La fauna de la miseria" (The fauna of misery), Ramos Mejía makes his own contribution to this notion of "hygiene" and "nationality" that coincides with the foundational moment of the modern Argentine republic. He describes a "Jew named Moses," the stereotypical usurer, alleging that "a rare association of features makes him an interesting example of the fauna in which the most opposed tendencies, united by a diabolical and gratuitous alliance, produce a physiognomy possessed by few in the large family . . . ; a bizarre result of the combination of the economic man and the *sexual invert*." After two insistent pages in which the author exposes his fear of women—a misogyny that emerges throughout most of his writings—Ramos Mejía concludes by "enlisting [Jewish men] in the extensive perversity of the sexual inverts."[41]

The texts of these representatives of a turn-of-the-century Argentine medico-legal bureaucracy are saturated with a clear homophobia, intermingled with hideous expressions of anti-Semitism, misogyny, and xenophobia. And this has broad and lasting implications in a critical history of Argentine culture. The writings of this Argentine technocracy have been crucial in the creation of guiding fictions of twentieth-century Argentina. If the nineteenth-century writings of D. F. Sarmiento and J. B. Alberdi established some of the master narratives of the Argentine "imagined community" before immigration, the texts we have briefly examined here created many of the guiding fictions of the modern nation. Vezzetti observes how many of these works purport "to investigate the keys for an interpretation of society and history. Within this frame, a sociological work or historiography like that of Ramos Mejía has a special relevance in the conformation of certain long-lasting models of analysis. In my opinion Ramos Mejía is the main ideologue of that entire generation of "functionaries of public medicine that integrated themselves into a technopolitical function" in order to formulate "from public hygiene to psychiatric medicine to criminology certain attempts to medicalize the conduct of the citizenry—attempts converging with juridical, penal, and pedagogical dispositions and practices" that perpetuated him in power while creating the "modern incarnation of the moralist and the paradigm of the ruler" of twentieth-century Argentina.[42]

The History of the Tango

Of all of the "imaginary dynasty of evils destined to pass on for generations,"[43] why should the figure of the "pederast," the "sexual invert," the "uranist," the "sapphist," or the "homosexual" serve as the paradigm of the virus, the infection, the invasion, and subversion of the new Argentine nation? Or as Eve Kosofsky Sedgwick asks rhetorically, "Is men's desire for other men the great preservative of the masculinist hierarchies of Western culture, or is it among the most potent of threats against them?"[44] In the case of Argentina the homosexual panic disseminated by the texts we have examined is a reaction to the demographic, cultural, and socioeconomic circumstances that created a new culture in fin de siècle Buenos Aires: a new *inverted* culture[45] that rose out of a prostitution that subverted the same principles prostitution was intended to reinforce.

In the process of creation of the new cultural formations of turn-of-the-century Buenos Aires, the brothel, like Bátiz's arcade, is a paradigmatic space of the Buenos Aires of the period. Here we have to pause to reconstruct a historical context of the prostitution of the times. In the "Preliminary Study" that serves as an introduction to Horacio Salas's book *El tango* (The tango), published in 1980, Alberto Sábato writes: "Toward the end of the century, Buenos Aires was a gigantic multitude of single men . . . in wine shops and brothels a social life developed from this mass of longshoremen and pimps, of masons and electoral committee bullies, of criollo and foreign musicians, of butchers and procurers."[46] These are the men who originally danced the tango. In the same book, Horacio Salas writes that the tango "at first was danced separately like the *candombes;* later the dancers came together and transformed the dance into one for partners intertwined, preferably men; thus it passed into the brothels."[47] In his first work in prose, Jorge Luis Borges revealed himself as an impassioned student of the male knife fighters and showoffs (*compadritos*) of the age. In *Evaristo Carriego* (1930), Borges evaluates the various conflicting versions of the original circumstances of the tango: "Despite the divergences that I have enumerated and that would be easy to increase by interrogating inhabitants of the cities of La Plata and Rosario, my informants concur on one essential fact: the tango originated in the brothels. (The same goes for the date of this origin, which no one places much before the eighties or later than 1890)." A few lines further on, Borges adds: "we do not lack other confirmations: the lasciviousness of the figures, the connotation evident in certain titles such as *El Choclo* [the Corn Cob, penis in *lunfardo*], *El Fierrazo* [the Iron Hit, the act of sexual intercourse in *lunfardo*], the circumstance that I could observe as a small boy in Palermo and years later in the Chacarita and Boedo neighborhoods, where men would dance in couples on the street corners."[48] José Gobello describes the movement of the body dancing the tango and stresses the "lascivious figures" noted by Borges: "The tango is a lascivious dance. The positioning, without ceasing to be dorsal, like the Flamenco, descends downward until it becomes pelvic. The movements are characteristically ambling . . . the overall representation is an erotic stimulation."[49] Andrés Chinarro, in a book on the tango published more than thirty years after Borges's, confirms the opinions of earlier commentators, adding that "with the exception of these 'houses' [brothels], the tango was danced only in the streets and exclusively by male couples. No evidence exists of the participation of homosexuals, even though uranists and the like-inclined must have attended."[50]

Danced in the brothels or on the city streetcorners by pairs of men, "uranists" or the "like-inclined," cutting "lascivious figures" or making an "overall representation of an erotic simulation," in the so-called age of forbidden music, the tango has significant homosexual and homoerotic connotations. It is for this reason that, in my opinion, the history of tango is an unsettled and unsettling history that has titillated the fantasy of innumerable authors. This sexuality and this (homo)eroticism are characteristic of the worlds of prostitution and immigration of the Buenos Aires of the age.

Prostitution in Buenos Aires at the fin de siècle is the *agency* of new cultural codes generated in establishments that, although intended to secure the "hygiene" of the last decades of the nineteenth century, promoted *inversions* that threatened the very hygiene they were meant to protect.

At the beginning of massive immigration, the *higienistas*, anxious about the dissemination of peripheral sexualities in a city with an overwhelming majority of foreign adult males, legalized and regulated a prostitution meant to promote, validate, and reinforce the ideology of the patriarchal bourgeois class in the process of modernization: permitting and promoting a double standard while training a "masculine" bourgeois man, purchaser and possessor of the "feminine" woman.[51]

In the *Primer censo de la república argentina* (First census of the Argentine republic), taken in 1869 and released in 1872, at the onset of immigration, the predominance of male immigrants arriving in Buenos Aires alone or without family is evident. The census records the total number of resident foreigners at 78,046; women make up 23,572 and men 54,474,[52] and this discrepancy grows proportionately with immigration. In the *Segundo censo de la república argentina* (Second census of the Argentine republic) in 1895 we read the analysis of the statistical figures: "as can be seen, it is the foreign population that constitutes the difference favoring men . . . that foreign immigration is verifiably made up of two-thirds men explains the difference."[53] Studying statistics from 1914, Carl Solberg notes that of all "males of age 20 and over, 77.2 per cent (in 1914) were foreign born. Thus nearly four fifths of Buenos Aires' male adults were foreigners."[54]

To the demographic imbalance evident in the Buenos Aires censuses of 1869, 1895, and 1914 must be added, between 1900 and 1914, a great number of single men, age twenty or older, who did not appear in the statistics. These were the immigrants who, when unable to become owners due to the latifundio structure of ownership of the land, passed through or lived temporarily in Buenos Aires, between harvests or between renting plots of land for agricultural purposes. Manuel Bejarano, comparing the number of people in 1910 working in agriculture during the entire year (82,368 men and 30,202 women) with the number of people employed in agriculture during the harvest months (226,328 men and 11,647 women), writes: "just the mention of these figures is sufficient to demonstrate without further commentary that family units represented a very low percentage, and that the majority of workers migrated to rural areas without their women and children, or was constituted by people who had none as of yet." Bejarano adds that toward 1910 "increasingly there existed a great mass of nomadic men without ties of any kind."[55] Furthermore, to these nomadic men must be added a great number of "swallow workers" (*trabajadores golondrinas*) who, thanks to large reductions in the transatlantic fares of the times, passed through Buenos Aires on their way to the interior of the country, where they worked temporarily for six months or a year bringing in harvests, passing once again through Buenos Aires before returning to their countries of origin. Most of these men arrived alone or in groups with other men and did not have families. When they did have them, these families often remained in Europe waiting for the man to return or to establish himself in the new country. All these men who escaped the statistics by entering, passing through, or establishing themselves temporarily in the city of Buenos Aires during the first decade of the twentieth century swelled the numbers of the demographic disproportion that is evident in the censuses.

Prostitution designed to control the sexuality of this population, in addition to being conceived of officially as "hygienic" and "educational," was also considered and promoted as a source of employment. In the *Primer censo,* in the analysis of the statistics and under the subtitle "Prostitution"—which, among twenty-three subtitles, suggestively comes third, following "The Professions of Men" and "The Professions of Women"— we read: "We can assure that, where authorities exist who prosecute prostitution, at the same time that they diminish a source of employment for the masses, they neglect or fail to understand the process of the masses' education."[56] Thus at the end of the century Buenos Aires became an internationally recognized center of prostitution. But this prostitution, conceived of in 1869 as a "source of employment and education for the masses," did not produce the expected results.

In 1908, Eusebio Gómez, the criminologist, writes that "regulated prostitution has not produced in practice the results foreseen at its institution," and for this failure he blames the "homosexual relations organized within the system of heterosexual prostitution."[57] Francisco de Veyga, a criminologist and favorite disciple of Ramos Mejía, professor since 1900 in the lectureship of legal medicine in the School of Medicine at the University of Buenos Aires and a specialist in the simultaneous study of "sexual inversion" and the marginality of the *lunfardo* world, writes in 1904: "The world of sissies, furthermore, is so intimately allied with that of petty thieves [*lunfardos*] and of prostitution that one might well say that the sissy world forms part of both." In a cutting generalization with which Veyga identifies as homosexual the entire underworld of the *lunfardo* (and the mythical core of the cultural identity and language of the inhabitant of today's Buenos Aires), he concludes categorically: "the *lunfardo* is a pederast by nature."[58] In 1903, in the clinical history of "Aurora," a homosexual transvestite who works as a homosexual prostitute, Veyga explains that s/he "had been very far, certainly, from supposing that in Buenos Aires there existed a whole 'confraternity' dedicated to this business . . . but very soon he found out that the means of living he had encountered was not his privilege alone and that on the contrary he had to confront numerous competitors already savvy in the practice of the office."[59] This is the prostitution that, intended to promote "hygiene" and "education" among a large population of single adult males, subverted its purpose by becoming the *agency* of a new culture of "masculine" women and "feminine" men, an *inversion* that emerges constantly in the histories of tango.

In his *Historia del tango* (History of tango), for example, Blas Matamoro writes that "the order of the evil city also has a mother, a manly lady who reigns over the dance houses and brothels."[60] This mother of prostitution *inverts*, for example, the concept of "the family." Vezzetti explains that during this period "the institution of the family, conceived as a matrix and miniature of the desired society, does not exist or it does so only in a weak form . . . and this absence of the family in the urban panorama extends to women: Buenos Aires is a city of men." Vezzetti describes the subversive family of the "brothel [that] circumscribes with its heavy iconography of sin an anti-family in which instinct, money, and vice become a peculiar combination."[61] E. Goldar adds that this mother "would seek out among her pupils a special girl with whom to fall in love."[62]

If the mother of the brothel and the tango is "masculine" and "inclined to a homosexual love," in the pimp and the showoff (*compadrito*) we see representations of men who capture the attention of historians and who are consistently described by them as "feminine." José S. Tallón writes that these men "imitate the rich and dress and deck themselves out with the exaggerated narcissism of women, evidently sexual and suspect."[63] Matamoro confirms the image used by Tallón, writing that the clothing of this type of men "was colored, brilliant and baroque like that of a woman, and it was not difficult to see him with his face whitened with powder and eyes darkened with kohl." Matamoro describes the women who work in the brothel, "on the other hand, uniformed in a kind of work suit, [who] sported button-up leggings, jack-knife in the garter, when not wearing riding pants and an open shirt."[64] Tallón also describes a "masculine" woman: "in her shady work she was brave as a dagger thrower, hence her name. Usually she used her poniard, but when she had to venture alone into the night to far-off places or to handle 'difficult' business—we just have to think of the resentment of the less distinguished ruffians, lax and good-for-nothing but nonetheless dangerous—she used to set out in high boots that reach almost to the knee and in the right boot she would hide her dagger or her bayonet saber." Accompanying this image of women are domestic men who exude an undulating sexuality used to characterize the Other. Describing the life of "The Civic," a renowned pimp of the age, Tallón writes: "they use the Criollo hip-swaying walk that originated with high heels, they made it look silly, and sissy-like. In the same way, they gave to the choreography of the tango their own style of erotic exaggerations. Everything about 'The Civic,' as with others the same or like him, was erotic. Sexuality was in him a passionate and exclusive vocation. He was a lover and porno-maniac."[65]

The "inversion" of these men and women is also reflected in the division of labor. While the woman works "at night in far-off places," Matamoro explains that the life of the man "was completely domestic, since he always stayed in his room until sundown when he went to supervise the work of some prostitute, grab a bite with friends, and dance tangos in the anteparlor of the brothel. Here the *cofradía* [confraternity] brought together single men."[66] In a tongue-in-cheek manner Matamoro, describing a *cofradía* of men dancing the tango alone in the anteparlor of the brothel, uses the same word used for self-identification by the homosexual subculture in Buenos Aires at the turn of the century.[67] Referring to an "inversion" of the roles of men and women of the world of tango, Matamoro adds that "behind the flashy possessive role, the relationship [of the pimp] with the prostitute maintained a strange structure . . . Here the possessive role, through the imposition of a division of labor, corresponded to the woman. The man played the passive and in a certain way feminine role."[68]

The tango brothel in the age of forbidden music, the *agency* of this new culture, is a site as paradigmatic as the opera, the theater, or the circus in fin de siècle Buenos Aires. In the brothel, a foundational transfer of models and semantic codes takes place among all the social formations of the Buenos Aires of the age. Here Peter Stallybrass and Allon White's reference to the marketplace is especially apt.[69] In the space of the brothel—where, in Sábato's words, "a social life developed from this mass of longshoremen . . . pimps, . . . masons, . . . electoral committee bullies, . . . criollo and foreign musicians, . . . butchers and procurers"—categories usually kept separate and opposed become enriched and confused: the center and the periphery; the urban and the suburban; the "masculine" and the "feminine"; the "active" and the "passive"; the outside of the street and the inside of the house; the foreign and the national; the new and the old; commerce and festivity; the codes and semantic models of "above" and the codes and semantic models of "below." Canonized in the salons of Europe and the United States, the dance and music prohibited in the "respectable" society of Buenos Aires until approximately 1910 will migrate from the lower to the upper classes when adopted by the hegemonic class as one of the principal national dances. In the same way the *lunfardo,* once the language of the tango, and the tango's "cosmopolitan," "trafficking" underworld in Bátiz's arcade, as well as the *"lunfardo"* type whom Veyga characterizes as a "pederast by nature," is today the most cherished mythical character of *porteño* culture, as well as the everyday language used to express the greatest idiosyncrasies of the mainstream Argentine middle class. The transference and displacement of semantic matter that takes place in the space of the brothel works in many directions. "In wine shops and brothels" men compete with each other in the creation of the most intricate filigrees of the tango, acquiring thus "their own style of erotic exaggerations." At the same time, as these men "imitate the rich and dress and bedeck themselves," they keep "the Criollo hip-swaying walk" that will be copied by the *patota*, the groups of "bad boys of good families," the sons of the new oligarchy that, as Fernando Assunçao explains, mingle in the brothel with "knifewomen in garters, strumpets and whores, tigresses of the brothel, Criollas, dark-skinned girls, Central European women, Italian, Galician and some French women . . . just like the dashing and valiant men of the underworld: pimps, licensed and licentious soldiers, daredevils sucked in by their fame among low women and born delinquents, of all origins, varieties, and flavors."[70] In the brothel mingle every nationality as well as every economic, social, and cultural group and subgroup of the Buenos Aires of the 1900s. Matamoro writes that "the great public is formed by the plebe who goes out in search of sexual release for a few pennies; these are the johns and the *compadritos*, the working people."[71] Women and men of all social classes, origins, varieties, and flavors: this is the new "great public" studied by Ramos Mejía in *Las multitudes argentinas*.

Ramos Mejía finds, as one of the models of phrenology, the *"guarango"* (the uncouth) to be the "type" most representative of the new society. According to the Argentine psychiatrist, the *guarango* (the masculine ending in Spanish makes clear he is described as a male) is as much the immigrant as the son of the immigrant who has ascended on the social scale or the Criollo who does not belong to the patrician class but to the lower classes. The doctor writes: "When you look at the *guarango*, even if he is a doctor, lawyer, engineer, or reporter, you smell, from however far away, his malodor." In these words, the "hygienist" describes a professional middle class of lawyers, engineers, or reporters. Describing the industrialist or nouveau riche bourgeois above the professional class, the doctor alleges that "the *canalla* [riffraff] is the *guarango* who has climbed the ladder well dressed and with money." Beneath these classes Ramos Mejía describes a transition from the middle to the lower classes, writing that "the bumpkin is the most grotesque species of *guarango* . . . from which, influenced by the environment, issues the urban braggart." Monied bourgeois or middle-class professional, braggart or bumpkin, according to this founder of Argentine psychiatry and sociology, "the *guarango* represents one of those vertebrates that sociologists of the future will seek with curiosity in years to come in order to establish the succession of types in our evolution. He is an invert of the arts and resembles the inverts of the sexual instinct who reveal their dubious potency through an irritable manifestation of their appetites. He needs brilliant color, shrill music, like the erotic stimulus of the intense scents of the body; he likes bizarre and tasteless combinations of things, like the invert of warped attitudes and dark procedures, to satisfy the special idiosyncrasies of his sensibility . . . what ideas a *guarango* has in terms of taste and art, only an invert can imagine."[72]

Foucault notes that in 1870 texts such as Karl Westphal's article "Contrary Sensations"—read and quoted by Ramos Mejía—the notion of homosexuality was categorized "not so much as a type of sexual relations with a certain quality of sexual sensibility, determined as an inverted manner within itself of the masculine and the feminine. Homosexuality appeared as one of the figures of sexuality when the practice of sodomy was reduced to a kind of interior androgyny, a hermaphroditism of the soul."[73] In Ramos Mejía's analysis, the "passive pederast" portrayed by Bátiz, like the sodomite of Foucault, has "evolved," becoming a "vertebrate" in the "chain of successive types" of the Argentine male. The homosexual as "species," whose main characteristic is the "interior androgyny," in the doctor's texts corresponds to the new "taste"—a new concept of (popular) "art," a new "sensibility" and an aesthetic in the world of tango—characterized throughout the histories of the popular Argentine culture of the turn of the century as *inverted* because it was this new sensibility that, revitalizing the culture, reelaborated and (con)founded old, rigid, and anachronistic social and cultural models.

Here we see an essential function of the new science of sex in Argentina that at the turn of the century constructed "homosexuality," a category used to analyze, characterize, and specify—in order to integrate—all of the new social classes issuing from the new "Argentine multitudes." Erasing differences, the definition and classification of *guarangos* homogenized this same multitude into a "national" identity in formation, giving it a negative value sign that, in turn, was used to (re)define, by contrast, a new oligarchy. Stallybrass and White explain that "the bourgeois subject continuously defined and re-defined itself through the exclusion of what it marked as 'low'—as dirty, repulsive, noisy, contaminating. Yet that very act of exclusion was constitutive of its identity. The low was internalized under the sign of negation and disgust."[74] Sedgwick likewise explains the phenomenon as it applies to homosexuality: "The historical shifting, and precisely the arbitrary and self-contradictory nature of the way *homosexuality* (along with its predecessor terms) has been defined in relation to the rest of the male homosocial spectrum has been an exceedingly potent and embattled locus of power over the entire range of male bonds, and perhaps especially over those that define themselves, not as homosexuals, but as against the homosexual."[75] Through their science of sex, the new Argentine oligarchy incorporated a concept of *homosexuality* with which they at once defined themselves and the great *national* middle class of Argentina.

The Argentine doctor concludes his foundational analysis of modern Argentina by affirming that this *guarango* "in multitude will be terrible if the national system of education cannot modify him."[76] In order to "modify him," in 1908 the national government named José María Ramos Mejía president of the National Council of Education. The hygienist of the nineteenth century—now transformed into the pedagogue of the twentieth—would oversee the launch of a "new" and aggressive project of "social hygiene" implemented in a nationalist program of education. Carl Solberg writes, "the issue of nationalistic education began to captivate the attention of Argentine intellectuals in 1908 when the government appointed José María Ramos Mejía," adding that "one of Argentina's most bitter xenophobes, Ramos Mejía used his position with single-minded determination to attack cultural heterogeneity."[77] One of the clear targets of this national campaign was the "new aesthetics" and the "sensibility" of the popular culture of the tango.

Referring to the tango in 1910, Manuel Gálvez, one of the intellectuals enrolled in the Argentine nationalist campaign,[78] describes the "repugnant and hybrid music" as one of the "lamentable symbols of our denationalization."[79] After 1910 the process of *nationalization* of the tango is clear. Beginning in this first decade of the twentieth century the tango underwent profound and significant changes. Carlos Jáuregui, referring to police ordinances that "at the beginning of the twentieth century" started to regulate public dances, cites the edict on "Public Dances, article 3, part A, punishing the 'Director, Manager or person in charge of a public dance, owner or person in charge of a locale where dance between male couples is allowed.' "[80] Eduardo Stilman explains: "The improvised character of the dance and the legendary ability of the dancers of the first epoch began to fade away as the tango left behind the atmosphere of the brothel to overtake a wider public . . . Moreover, a severe prohibition hindered the expressive possibilities of the talented: A little sign that said: 'Cutting Forbidden.' "[81] "Cutting" or "posing" is a break in the motion of the dancing couple, who skip a note and remain motionless, the leading partner leaning backwards from his waist up, leaving the couple with their hips in a perfect fit. In his poetry Evaristo Carriego left an eloquent image of the same prohibition. In a poem published in 1908, describing what must have been a working-class Argentine wedding, Carriego's lyrical narrator notes:

El tío de la novia, que se ha creído
obligado a fijarse si el baile toma
buen carácter, afirma, medio ofendido
que no se admiten cortes, ni aún en broma
la casa será pobre, nadie lo niega:
todo lo que se quiere, pero decente
[The bride's uncle, who thinks he is
obliged to make certain the dance maintained
good character, he affirms, half-offended
that they would not allow cutting, not even in jest
the house may be poor, that no one could deny:
whatever you want, but decent].[82]

With the changes in the choreography that eliminated the "lasciviousness" of "cutting" came changes in the lyrics. Stilman, like other historians, explains that "the primitive tango, danced in the brothels, depended upon *lunfardo* couplets, spontaneous rhymes—often obscene—that popular ingenuity added to the music . . . The tone was—except on rare occasions—festive, trivial" and "full of pleasure until the professional lyricist came along to, among other things, make the lyrics bitter."[83] With the recording studios arose the individual author for the tango lyrics. As Foucault explains, "The author is the principle of thrift in the proliferation of meaning . . . He is a certain functional principle by which, in our culture, one limits, excludes, and chooses; in short, by which one impedes the free circulation, the free manipulation, the free composition, decomposition, and recomposition."[84]

Cátulo Castillo, well-known composer of tangos, in 1935 described another change, purporting that it reflected the variation in the use of musical instruments: "[The] tango was gay, playful, much more agile than the one we hear now; but when the influences of music schools and the desire to complement the instruments in use obliged the masters to turn to other instruments, the tango began to lose the old cutting edge [*corte*] transforming it into the sentimental dance we know now."[85] Jorge Luis Borges also noted with nostalgia in 1935 that "the old tango, as a musical form, could transmit directly this bellicose gaiety" that became lost to "certain composers of today [who] seek out that brave tone . . . but whose works, with lyric and music studiously antiquated, are exercises in nostalgia, essentially mournful cries for that which is lost and gone."[86]

Considered from the present moment, in the context of this history of the tango, is not this sense of loss, this yearning for a "legendary skill," this "mournful cry for that which is lost and gone" a nostalgia for homosexual desire lost in the sanitization of a forbidden dance?

Notes

1. [*Lunfardo* translates simultaneously as "thief," as the "idiom of the tango," and more generally as the "slang of Buenos Aires." The shift in the meaning of the term from a criminalized to a generalized middle-class space parallels the movement of the meaning of the tango as described in Salessi's argument. To preserve this migration of meanings, I will leave both the term "lunfardo" itself and some of the terms current in lunfardo in—lunfardo. *Trans.*]

2. I draw here on Benedict Anderson's study of the nation as "an imagined political community . . . It is imagined because the members of even the smallest nation will never know most of the fellow members, meet them, or even hear of them, yet in the minds of each lives the image of their communion" (*Imagined Communities* 2d ed. [London: Verso, 1991], 6).

3. Michel Foucault, *History of Sexuality: An Introduction* (New York: Vintage, 1990), 1:42–43.

4. In a forthcoming article I examine the history, incoherencies, and contradictions of this taxonomic elaboration, an Argentine version of what Eve Kosofsky Sedgwick describes as a "turn-of-the-century crisis of homo/heterosexual definitions" in *Be-*

tween Men: English Literature and Male Homosocial Desire (New York: Columbia U P, 1985), 226. The importance of this history notwithstanding, its investigation here would take us too far from the theme of this article.

5. Foucault, *History of Sexuality*, 24–25, 30.

6. Despite its neglecting to point out the centrality of the various definitions of homosexuality in his analysis, I believe that Hugo Vezzetti's book marks a very important path for the future of a new critical history of Argentine society and culture. Here I wish to thank Sylvia Molloy, and not only for acquainting me with this book. It was she, in 1987, when I hinted to her that the issue of prostitution in fin de siècle Buenos Aires interested me, who advised me and suggested that I read the works of J. M. Ramos Mejía, thus giving a definite impulse to my present work.

7. Hugo Vezzetti, *La locura en la argentina* (Buenos Aires: Paidós, 1985), 20, 12.

8. Here the concept of hygiene proposed by Mary Douglas has particular relevance, for example when she refers to "people obsessed by the fear of dangerous impurities entering their system. They treat their body as if it were a beleaguered town, every ingress and exit guarded for spies and traitors." Douglas, referring to a minority that reacts like the hegemonic class of Argentina at the turn of the century, also explains that "the model of the exits and entrances of the human body is a doubly apt symbolic focus of fears of the minority standing in the larger society . . . The sociological counterpart of this anxiety is a care to protect the political and cultural unity of a minority group." Noting the importance of sexuality in this conception of hygiene that seeks to preserve the hierarchy of social stratification, Douglas adds, "Since place in the hierarchy of purity is biologically transmitted, sexual behavior is important for preserving the purity of caste. For this reason, in higher castes, boundary pollution focuses particularly on sexuality" (*Purity and Danger: An Analysis of the Concepts of Purity and Taboo* [London: ARK, 1989], 123, 124, 125).

9. In a forthcoming article on the construction of homosexuality in turn-of-the-century Argentina, I begin to examine the significance of the Argentine nationalist education of the times in terms of gender indoctrination and "sexual education." For a specific study of Argentine nationalism in the first decades of the twentieth century, see the article by Carlos Altamirano and Beatriz Sarlo, "La Argentina del centenario," *Hispamérica* 25–26 (1980): 35–48. For a more broad discussion on how the nineteenth-century romances create what Benedict Anderson calls "imagined communities," see Doris Sommer's book *Foundational Fictions: The National Romances of Latin America* (Berkeley: U of California P, 1991), as well as Sommer's article "Foundational Fictions: When History Was Romance in Latin America," *Salmagundi* 82–83 (Spring–Summer 1989): 111–141. See also Samuel Baily, *Movimiento obrero, nacionalismo y política argentina* (Buenos Aires: Hispamérica, 1985), and Marysa Navarro Gerassi, *Los nacionalistas* (Buenos Aires: J. Alvarez, 1967).

10. Vezzetti, 13–14; emphasis in original.

11. Vezzetti, 163, 167, 166, 37. The best example of this "functionary" is Ramos Mejía: founder and first director of the Public Assistance of Buenos Aires in 1882; president of the Department of National Hygiene and regulator of prostitution in 1892 (hygienist);

founding editor of the *Archives of Psychiatry and Criminology* from 1902 to 1914, as well as teacher and mentor of José Ingenieros and Francisco de Veyga, two central figures of the new Argentine legal medicine of the times (criminologist); and president in 1908 of the powerful National Council of Education (pedagogue).

12. Vezzetti, describing variations on a conception of an "insanity" that becomes increasingly difficult to define, points out that, "with criminology, toward the end of the century, madness acquires a new quality: danger, and thus it can no longer be described within a psychiatric paradigm . . . but [the new conception of madness] points toward a *latent* madness, not *manifest* . . . The criminologist is a psychiatrist who displaces the center of study and intervention from the interior of the asylum to the urban social space, particularly to the *margin:* the criminologist's domain is the *'profligate life'* " (21; my emphasis).

13. Bátiz's book is a memoir of Buenos Aires from 1880 to 1908. While the edition I use here does not have a publication date, in the prologue Andrés Chinarro explains that the first edition "dates in 1908, [but] the author undoubtedly must have begun the work several years earlier, as can be deduced from the dates cited in the text" (*Las multitudes argentinas* [Buenos Aires: Felix Lajouane, (1898)], 7).

14. Eusebio Gómez, *La mala vida en Buenos Aires* (Buenos Aires: Roldan, 1908), 122, 181–182.

15. Donna Guy, *Sex and Danger in Buenos Aires: Prostitution, Family and Nation in Argentina* (Lincoln: U of Nebraska P, 1991), 86.

16. Eve Kosofsky Sedgwick, *Epistemology of the Closet* (Berkeley: U of California P, 1990), 184. Here Sedgwick's discussion of homosexual panic is crucial for my argument. See especially *Between Men*, 83–96, and *Epistemology*, 19–20 and 182–212. Since in this essay I do not treat in depth the taxonomic elaboration at work in the texts considered here, I should clarify that my use of the expression "homosexual panic" as applied to Argentine texts of the turn of the century—as with the legal use of the concept in U.S. courts of justice at the end of the twentieth century—should be understood in the context "of an analysis based on systemwide skepticism about the positivist taxonomic neutrality of psychiatry, about the classificatory coherence (e.g., concerning 'individual responsibility') of the law" (Sedgwick, *Epistemology*, 21).

17. Gómez, 182.

18. The special preoccupation with "sexual deviation," to which is added the proliferation of definitions of "perversion," reflects an especially fluid social system. As George Chauncey Jr. points out, referring to the same historical period, "While the changing focus of medical inquiry into sexual deviance reflected a broad shift in conceptualization, each stage in that inquiry can be analyzed as a response to particular changes and challenges to the Victorian sex/gender system such as the women's movement, the growing visibility of urban gay male subcultures, and the changing gender structure of the economy" ("From Sexual Inversion to Homosexuality: Medicine and the Changing Conceptualization of Sexual Deviance," *Salmagundi* 58–59 [Fall 1982—Winter 1983]: 116). Marjorie Garber writes, "The presence of the transvestite, in a text, in a culture, signals a category crisis elsewhere" ("The Occidental Tourist," in

Nationalisms and Sexualities, ed. Andrew Parker, Mary Russo, Doris Sommer, and Patricia Yaeger [New York: Routledge, 1992], 125).

19. Juan Bialet-Massé, *El estado de las clases obreras argentinas a comienzo de siglo* (Córdoba; Universidad Nacional de Córdoba, 1968), 424–426.

20. See, for example, "Cholera—A Report from the Office of Sanitation," *Annals of the National Department of Hygiene* 8 (Buenos Aires, 1895): 85–116, and "Sanitary Maritime Defense against the Exotic Illnesses of Travellers," *Annals* 7 (Buenos Aires, 1898): 307–324.

21. Bialet-Massé, 151, 425.

22. Adolfo Bátiz, *Buenos Aires, la rivera y los prostíbulos en 1880* (Buenos Aires: Aga Taura, nd), 12; ellipses in original.

23. Bátiz, *Buenos Aires,* 15–16.

24. Bátiz, *Buenos Aires,* 24–26.

25. Bátiz, *Buenos Aires,* 29.

26. Rubén Pesce, *La historia del tango,* vol. 3 *La guardia vieja* (Buenos Aires: Corregidor, 1977), 315.

27. Bátiz, *Buenos Aires,* 315, 44, 38; emphasis mine.

28. Gómez, 132, 134. Taking up the title of Gómez's book, Ernesto Goldar further elaborates the criminologist's text in a volume edited as a collection of *Historia popular* (Popular history) entitled *La mala vida* (The profligate life) (Buenos Aires: Centro Editor, 1971). Describing the same "enormous quantity of prostitutes [now also characterized as] of Jewish ancestry," Goldar notes especially the "unnatural sexual relations that the Criolla prostitute only rarely accepts," and concludes: "The inclination toward homosexual love derived from a profound distaste felt for men is more frequent among the foreign prostitutes" (19). The turn-of-the-century notion that "organized prostitution was increasingly linked to Jewish immigrants residing in the city" (18) has been well established by Donna Guy in her book *Sex and Danger in Buenos Aires.* The date of publication of Goldar's book (1971) does not correspond to the historical moment that concerns us, but I use it to demonstrate how over time Argentine stereotypes charged with irrational and arbitrary connotations have been constructed, revalidated, and popularized.

29. Bátiz, *Buenos Aires,* 79. Hereafter *Buenos Aires, la rivera y los prostíbulos en 1880* is abbreviated as *BA.*

30. George Mosse, *Nationalism and Sexuality: Middle-Class Morality and Sexual Norms in Modern Europe* (Madison: U of Wisconsin P, 1988), 138.

31. Carl Solberg, *Immigration and Nationalism: Argentina and Chile 1890–1914* (Austin: U of Texas P, 1970), 138.

32. Together with the monument to Mazzini, the name of the former neighborhood of Villa Mazzini (today called Villa Urquiza) has also disappeared. The monument and Plaza Mazzini represent a very special symbolic space in which coincided the urban homosexual subculture and the labor movement of Buenos Aires. In *The Sexual Inverts,* a play by José Gonzáles Castillo first presented in Buenos Aires in 1914, there are two clear allusions to male-male sexual activity in the Plaza Mazzini; see *Los invertidos* (Buenos Aires: Argentores, 1957), 30. The same plaza is also the central scene of

popular celebrations and struggles of the Argentine labor movement at the beginning of the twentieth century. In the 2 May 1904 *La Prensa* article about an urban battle between the federal police and a group of protesters celebrating International Labor Day, for example, the journalist describes "the column that went from Córdoba to the avenida Rosales and turned there to go toward the statue of Mazzini, situated in the plaza of the same name. At this point, crowding around on the esplanade in between the double line of trees, waited great masses of people."

33. Susan Buck-Morss, *The Dialectic of Seeing: Walter Benjamin and the Arcades Project* (Cambridge: MIT P, 1989), 89–90.

34. *Porteño* is an adjective applied to people and things characteristic of the "port" city of Buenos Aires.

35. Vezzetti, 106, 104.

36. Tulio Halperín Donghi, *El espejo de la historia*, 222.

37. Mosse, 138.

38. As Carroll Smith-Rosenberg would say, this is a good example of "the dialectic between language as social mirror and language as social agent" (*Disorderly Conduct: Visions of Gender in Victorian America* [New York: Knopf, 1985], 45).

39. Julián Martel, *La bolsa* (Buenos Aires: Plus Ultra, 1975), 145, 149, 72.

40. Halperín Donghi, 221.

41. José María Ramos Mejía, *Los simuladores del talento* (Buenos Aires: Felix Lajouane, 1904), 234, 235–236; emphasis in the original text.

42. Vezzetti, 181, 12, 14.

43. Foucault, *History of Sexuality*, 53.

44. Sedgwick, *Between Men*, 93.

45. Here I use the concept of inversion that Barbara Babcock explains: " 'symbolic inversion' may be broadly defined as any act of expressive behavior which inverts, contradicts, abrogates, or in some fashion presents an alternative to commonly held cultural codes, values, and norms be they linguistic, literary, artistic, religious, social, or political" (*The Reversible World: Symbolic Inversion in Art and Society* [Ithaca: Cornell U P, 1978], 14).

46. Alberto Sábato, "Estudio preliminar," in *El tango*, ed. Horacio Salas (Buenos Aires: Planeta, 1986), 15.

47. Horacio Salas, ed. *El tango* (Buenos Aires: Planeta, 1986), 26.

48. Jorge Luis Borges, *Evaristo Carriego* (Buenos Aires: Emece, 1985), 110; emphasis in original.

49. José Gobello, *Crónica general del tango* (Buenos Aires: Fraterna, 1980), 27.

50. Andrés Chinarro, *El tango y su rebeldía* (Buenos Aires: Continental, 1965), 27.

51. Vern and Bonnie Bullough explain that "the primary function of prostitution has been to uphold the double standard, since without prostitution the double standard could have been preserved only through slavery, homosexuality, and rape" (*Women and Prostitution* [Buffalo: Prometheus, 1987], 296. Susan Buck-Morss, referring to prostitution at the end of the century, notes: "the prostitute is the ur-form of the wage laborer, selling herself in order to survive" (186–187).

52. *Primer censo de la república argentina* (Buenos Aires: Imprenta del Porvenir, 1872), 52.

53. *Segundo censo de la república argentina* (Buenos Aires: Imprenta del Porvenir, 1873), xxxv.

54. Solberg, 96–97.

55. Manuel Bejarano, "Inmigración y estructuras tradicionale en Buenos Aires (1854–1930)," in *Los fragmentos del poder,* ed. Tulio Halperín Donghi (Buenos Aires: Sudamericana, 1987), 123, 138.

56. *Primer censo de la república argentina,* vlviii.

57. Gómez, 126.

58. Francisco de Veyga, "El sentido moral y la conducta de los invertidos," *Archivos de Psiquiatría Criminología* 3 (Buenos Aires, 1904): 29, 28.

59. Francisco de Veyga, "La inversíon sexual adquirida," *Archivos de Criminología y Psiquiatría* 2 (Buenos Aires, 1903): 198.

60. Blas Matamoro, *Historia del tango* (Buenos Aires: Centro Editor, 1971), 53.

61. Vezzetti, 203.

62. Goldar, 33.

63. José S. Tallón, *El tango en sus etapas de música prohibida* (Buenos Aires: Instituto Amigos del Libro, 1964), 37.

64. Matamoro, 50.

65. Tallón, 38–39. As George Mosse explains, "lack of control over their passions characterized all outsiders . . . the insane, homosexuals, and habitual criminals shared this lack of control at the very roots of society" (134).

66. Matamoro, 51; my emphasis.

67. The evidence is in a letter published by Gómez. Apparently making few corrections, Gómez transcribes "the following letter directed to us by Mysotis, a congenital invert, a young man of the class we will call 'aristocratic' " (184). Responding to a request for information that the criminologist sends him, Mysotis writes, "Your requiring me to send you the details of my life, in the compromising form of a letter, is ridiculous . . . I am like this because I was born like this. Anyway, this is the way I should behave because beauty has no sex. I do not do anything extraordinary; I like men and for that reason I am frank with them. I treat them with exquisite *savoir faire,* as one of the members of the *cofradía* (who writes the social column for a certain newspaper) said . . . *Au revoir,* Mysotis" (185; my emphasis). Further on, the criminologist adds that "the homosexuals of Buenos Aires have a particularity worth noting: the tendency to associate, forming a kind of sect, which they designate with the picturesque name of '*cofradía*' " (191). See also, José Gonzalez Castillo, *Los invertidos* (Buenos Aires: Argentores, 1957), 30.

68. Matamoro, 51.

69. They note that the marketplace "is a place where limit, centre and boundary are confirmed and yet also put in jeopardy" (Peter Stallybrass and Allon White, *The Politics & Poetics of Transgression* [Ithaca: Cornell U P, 1986], 28).

70. Fernando Assunçao, *El tango y sus circunstancias* (Buenos Aires: Ateneo, 1984), 101.

71. Matamoro, 32.

72. Ramos Mejía, *Las multitudes argentinas,* 219, 221, 218, 274, 57.

73. Foucault, *History of Sexuality,* 43.

74. Stallybrass and White, 191.

75. Sedgwick, *Epistemology,* 185. While this essay does not study the contradictions and incoherences in the definition of "homosexuality" that, for example, in the work of Francisco de Veyga is simultaneously a "congenital sexual inversion" and an "acquired sexual inversion," the "historical changes" to which Sedgwick refers correspond to those of "homosexuality" or "sodomy" in the work of E. Gómez, which as we have seen is also "pederasty" in Bátiz's text, the "third sex" in Bialet-Massé's, and "sexual inversion" in Ramos Mejía's. We might add as well the definitions of "passive uranism," "impulsive uranism," "homosexuality," "spermatophagia," and so on that appear mixed in with other definitions throughout the contemporaneous texts we have considered here.

76. Ramos Mejía, *Las multitudes argentinas,* 220, 145.

77. Solberg, 145.

78. In a forthcoming article I start to examine this nationalist campaign of education launched from the national army and the public schools after 1900. The dissemination of homosexual panic was a key element of this nationalist campaign.

79. Manuel Gálvez, *El diario de Gabriel Quiroga: Opiniones sobre la vida argentina* (Buenos Aires: Moen, 1910), 54.

80. Carlos Jáuregui, *La homosexualidad en la Argentina* (Buenos Aires: Tarso, 1987), 164.

81. Eduardo Stilman, *Historia del tango* (Buenos Aires: Brújala, 1965), 31.

82. Evaristo Carriego, *Misas herejes: La canción del barrio* (Buenos Aires: Rosso, 1927), 161.

83. Stilman, 41.

84. Michel Foucault, "What Is an Author?" in *Textual Strategies,* ed. Josué V. Harari (Ithaca: Cornell U P, 1979), 159.

85. Cátulo Castillo, *Danzas Argentinas* (Buenos Aires: Ediciones Peuser, 1947), 45; my emphasis.

86. Borges, 113.

Salsa as Translocation

Mayra Santos Febres

al son que me tocan bailo
con sabor boricua
[I dance to the son they play for me
with Puerto Rican flavor]
—Marvin Santiago

From 1971 to 1975, the period when salsa evolved and boomed as a recognizable genre, I was a child, and in my house salsa was forbidden music. Música de arrabaleros, de tráfaras, de negros sin arrepentir.[1] My mother and father, very much interested in bringing up a "negrita fina y acepillá,"[2] probably the first chocolate-toned wife of a senator in the history of Puerto Rico, crammed my ears with Walt Disney songs that I could not understand or with traditional Spanish children's songs I understood even less. In their parties they played old boleros from Tito Puente, Rafael Hernández, Sylvia Rexach, of course some pachangas "decentes"—the old ones imported from Cuba BC (that is, BEFORE CASTRO), where musicians in rumberas sang about a white-washed blackness for tourists and gamblers in prerevolutionary Havana. In the Catholic nuns' school for girls I attended (with the help of all my aunts and uncles who chipped in for the monthly payments), salsa was more than forbidden music, it was demonic, sinful; it could turn any decent girl into a worthless hip-swinging tramp.

It was not until I escaped tight parental guidance and entered the university that I became aware of the ubiquity of salsa. El Gran Combo, Ismael Miranda, Rubén Blades, and Willie Rosario were being heard everywhere, providing metaphors, images, and comprehensive models of expression to most of my classmates. Yet its presence was not regarded as such; nobody talked about what salsa meant, what it represented, or how it expressed a popular idiosyncrasy and attitude toward life. Newspapers and journals were devoid of any discussion about the salsa phenomenon. Even though this cultural artifact was and still is so important in the lives of the Hispanic Caribbean majority, it has, with very few

New York City, 1971, *donde se cocinó la salsa.*
(Video capture from *Nuestra cosa/Our Latin Thing* [Jerry Massuci, 1971])

exceptions, remained untouched by intellectuals of all classes and ideologies after more than ten years of vigorous and growing presence
throughout our America.

Of course, this thematic exclusion from academic and/or journalistic
writing and discussion is quite deliberate and conscious. The fact that
salsa is not discussed in official settings reveals a great deal about those
who control spaces of intellectual exchange, that is, those who have
decided that salsa does not offer anything worth discussing. There are
numerous ways to explain such an attitude, starting with classism, racism, and Eurocentrism among Caribbean intellectuals. All of these prejudices arise because this musical phenomenon presents serious threats to
conventional analytical approaches. It also shakes the foundation of classificatory systems that depend on the differentiation between "national,"
"ethnic," and "popular" music.

Salsa is a participatory musical genre; it resists the binarisms of audi-
ence/artists, performers/consumers, founder/follower, subject/object.
It privileges both continuity and rupture, order and hazard, sequence

and simultaneity. Dancers, singers, and musicians inhabit parallel levels of participation. Each of those levels interacts violently as its inhabitants improvise to prove their mastery over the language in which the improvisation takes place. Therefore the phenomenon of salsa opens a space for codified violence, a violation of form and content that occurs within a very structured time-space: between the chorus that frames the *soneo,* the beat or *clave* that frames instrumental jams/*descargas,* and the basic salsa steps that frame the twists and turns of the dancing couple. Body, voice, and musical instruments all inhabit this space and, at the same time, they push its limits.

Salsa, however, also inhabits the world of multinational communications. This other world of salsa forces a separation between performers and audience and thus alters the participatory nature of the genre. It turns musicians and dancers into consumers. It also imposes controls on the improvisational element of the genre. Nowadays, improvisation has to conform to the rules of market economy: it has to generate profits. If approached in a conventional manner, this contradictory coexistence of salsa in both market and participatory "economies" raises questions about its "authenticity." But this approach leaves too much to be desired. I am not interested in discussing salsa's authenticity as much as its absolute "impurity." In other words, what I find most interesting about salsa are the ways this cultural product takes advantage of an international market economy, the ways this economy transforms salsa's inner structures, and finally, the ways salsa relies on two mutually excluding modes of access (direct participation and indirect consumption) and how this access is navigated by salsa musicians, artists, and a vast Latino community. I am not denying the existence of outside control, but as a good salsera I am privileging the jams, twists, turns, and soneos that occur within the structured choruses and motions of multinational capitalism.

Yet salsa inhabits still another world, the existential world of many Caribbeans who struggle to make sense of the world in a postcolonial way. Therefore, I am also interested in what the phenomenon of salsa means for Afro-Boricuas[3] like me who learned how to dance salsa while learning how to read Becquer's *Rimas y leyendas* (Rhymes and legends); for Afro-Boricuas like me who started buying Latin American literature at the same time that they purchased their first Rubén Blades LP; para curitas como yo[4] who later found out that the phenomenon of salsa, the boom of Latin American narrative, and the increase of foreign investment and military intervention in our region all coincided in time together. What epistemology did people like me learn from the consumption of these cultural products? Can I bring it to the surface? Can it be applied to understand our role in the multinational industry of Academia, this institution that assures and expands a market for particular merchandise (including "ours") and yet enforces particular ways of consuming it? Am I complicitous in the process of taming culture, making it "understood," arresting its motion and violence? Am I effectively deskilling its participants by placing another set of controls over them? Or can I translate that way of making culture into the language of theory in order to participate at another level in the fierce resistance to complete assimilation and commodification? Am I just hopelessly off-key? Well, even if I am, I would like to try to explore salsa as a theoretical device that presents alternative methods of analysis and cognition. I would like for the participants, or the consumers, to read this essay as a soneo, as an improvisation that intends to translate, not so much the content, but rather the form of making salsa to the regions of cultural analysis. *Bueno, aquí voy.*[5]

Since the beginning of the salsa phenomenon, many "serious" musicians and "ethnomusicologists" have denied any high artistic value to salsa because it does not have a particular rhythm or musical structure. For orthodox Cuban musicians, salsa is but a faulty variation of *son cubano,* while others name Cortijo and Ismael Rivera as the pioneers of the genre. But that very problem presents salsa as a new "form of making music" in which many rhythms coexist and fuse. Boricua sociologist Angel Quintero argues:

Las combinaciones de la salsa son nuevas y diferentes porque no se dirigen a, o intentan la formación de nuevas estructuras o tipos . . . los buenos compositores de salsa combinan y se mueven libre y espontáneamente entre diversos tipos tradicionales (plena, guaracha, cumbia, samba, bolero, guajira, chachachá y diversos tipos de bomba, aguinaldo y seis entre otros) de acuerdo a la sonoridad que quieran producir para el sentimiento o mensaje que intenten comunicar. Y es, precisamente la experimentación en esa libre combinación de formas una de las características fundamentales que identifican, a mi juicio, este movimiento, esta nueva "manera de hacer música." [Salsa's musical combinations are new and different because they are not aimed at creating new structures or types of music . . . good composers combine and move freely between different traditional types of music (plena, guaracha, cumbia, samba, bolero, guajira, chachachá, and diverse types of bomba, aguinaldo, seis, and others) in order to produce a particular sonority, and according to the feeling and message they want to communicate. And precisely this experimentation with a free combination of forms is one of the fundamental characteristics that identify, in my opinion, this movement, this "new way of making music."][6]

The impossibility of attaching fixed boundaries to the musical form points at that very fusion and confusion of musical traditions that is at the core of salsa production. Quintero connects this element of salsa to a process of national identification. He argues that "las innovaciones afincadas en la tradición revelan las potencialidades de reprentatividad nacional de una cultura popular que a su vez desafía (en su creatividad innovadora irreverente) los cánones de la cultura 'oficial' [these innovations based on tradition reveal the potentialities of national representation within a popular culture that defies (with its irreverent and innovative creativity) the canons of 'official' culture]." I am not entirely comfortable with his reduction of identity to a purely national enterprise, as gloriously irreverent as Quintero might describe it to be. New York City was *el caldero donde se cocinó la salsa,*[7] and the first *salseros en propieda*[8] were Boricuas from Hell's Kitchen and the South Bronx. However, "puertorricanness" is not the dominant signifier in salsa. Pueblo, that is, peopleness is. This identity coexists with national ones, in the form of the soneo. It mixes traditions, moves freely among them, chooses elements to highlight particular messages and feelings in a pragmatic way. It does not search for the formation of any structures of power, but attempts to mark out new spaces for improvisation, for those acts of violence inherent in questioning, pushing against, and threatening the limits of any structure. Therefore, the task of constructing a community of salseros must include the rescue of a tradition that is larger than national and broader than ethnic. This enterprise could be understood as multinational.

That is why salsa spread so fast throughout the Caribbean (i.e., the archipelago and the Caribbean coasts of Central and South America), and I suspect it is also one of the reasons why salsa can work so well

New York City, 1971, the cauldron where salsa was cooked.
(Video capture from *Nuestra cosa/Our Latin Thing* [Jerry Massuci, 1971])

within the multinational music industry. However, this music does not espouse the values and aspirations of the bourgeois nation-state, especially when the state works and benefits from its connections with a multinational market economy. On the contrary, salsa espouses the values of the street, of that space that creates an alternative criminalized market economy and that lies outside the margins of power of the bourgeois nation-state. Bourgeois morality, "informed consent," unwavering confidence in order and discipline are nowhere to be found, giving way to pragmatism and a profound mistrust in structures of indirect representation. In this sense, it is more fitting that salsa be considered a "translocal" phenomenon rather than a multinational one. It cuts across national boundaries to create a community of urban locations linked by transportation, communication technologies, and the international market economy.

Even at the level of its marketing, salsa is the quintessential "translocal" cultural production. The word "salsa" was imported from Venezuela, the monopoly that marketed it (Fania Records, created by Dominican Johnny Pacheco and Italian American Jewish lawyer Jerry Massuci) was located in New York, and its most famous stars—Willie Colón, Ismael Miranda, Roberto Roena, Richy Rey, and Bobby Cruz—were Puerto Ricans, either from the island or from el barrio. Venezuelan expert César Rondón argues in his *Libro de la salsa* that one of the features that distinguishes this music from other Latin genres is its referentiality to "el barrio."[9] But this barrio is not only in New York, but in Caracas, Santurce, Medellín, Santo Domingo, and in every Caribbean industrial center. The performers identified openly with it and testified to such a form of life. Immediately the space of the street, urbanism, the tradition of *guapería*, and crime became principal characteristics that distinguished salsa from its Latin predecessors.

Since 1954, when Cortijo y su Combo appeared on Puerto Rican television on the program *La taberna india*, Caribbean popular music became identified with violence. Cortijo's bombas and plenas represented a threat to the dominant groups because the music was no longer coming from or trying to arrive at a rural arcadia, nor did it have in mind the romanticization of its surroundings in order to please the oligarchic groups. Its ironic, carnivalizing, and hermetic lyrics were not even interested in denouncing oppression, in opening the eyes of the oligarchy or referring to it in any way whatsoever. On the contrary, if the oligarchy wanted to understand what was being said and played, it had to learn the secret codes of the street. Cortijo's music was not folkloric; it resisted its placement at the altar, the dawn of nationhood. Cortijo's music was, and still is, the direct offspring of industrialization; a cultural expression of the part-human, part-machine entity of the black, white, and mulatto proletarian. Puerto Rican writer and cultural critic Edgardo Rodriguez Juliá comments:

Entonces llega Cortijo con una nueva presencia, la del mulataje inquieto que la movilidad traída por el desarrollo muñocista posibilitó. La plena proletaria de Canario, la del barrio y el arrabal, se convierte en música de caserío. Para esa nueva música surge un nuevo medio: la televisión se convierte en el foco de luz que destaca no sólo una nueva fisonomía musical, sino también una amenazante presencia social.

[Then came Cortijo with a new presence, the unsettling presence of the mulattos that Muñoz's developmental programs made possible. The proletarian plena, native to the shanty towns and old barrios, transformed into the musical expressions of the housing projects. For this new kind of music came a new media: television highlighted not only a new musical physiognomy, but a threatening social presence.][10]

Juliá's description of the Cortijo phenomenon mentions that which would become even more central to the development of salsa: mass media and their new communication technologies. Since Cortijo, bomba and plena have constructed ties with a larger and more dispersed audience, a largely proletarian community of displaced rural workers migrating to industrialized centers, of housing-project dwellers displaced from their original communities. The very livelihood and vitality of these musical forms (Cortijo's bombas and plenas) depended on whatever technologies would enable them to reach their more remote audiences. Salsa, in turn, needs technologies of an even further reach, as it wants to get to those urban Caribbean centers as well as "first world" cities inhabited by Caribbean workers in exile. Therefore salsa can also be understood as a "nueva manera" of regrouping after uneven development disarticulated rural communities, old proletarian barrios, forcing migration to industrialized cities and metropolitan centers.

As Rondón explains in his book, New York was the place for salsa because it provided musicians with a commercial space that favored experimentation. In the rest of Latin America, clubs were very few and mostly dominated by imported bands. Local bands still depended largely on private family parties for their subsistence. In the case of Puerto Rico and Venezuela, economic conditions permitted more clubs than in the rest of Latin America, with the exception of prerevolutionary Cuba. Therefore, the music scene in the Caribbean was mainly controlled by dominant groups; the only gigs available were weddings, *quinceañeras* (a special birthday party for fifteen-year-old girls), and society parties— that is, minstrel shows for the *blanquitos*.[11] The music was mostly produced for the entertainment of the ruling class. Yet there was another type of music that worked as a kind of chronicle that narrated community events. Bomba, but even more specifically, plena served as social commentary that recorded anecdotes and communal history.

In this setting, experimentation, whether at the level of music or lyrics, was very limited. "Nueva Yor" was a space that freed musicians from oligarchic vigilance and intervention, freed them even from tradition. In economic terms, this freedom resulted in the creation of a larger market demand, constituted in its majority by the Latino working-class community that lived in el barrio. Competition between groups for the control of market shares combined with a larger supply of dance halls had the effect of not only increasing the number of opportunities for musicians to experiment with rhythms, rhymes, and lyric content, but also forcing them, in effect, to continue to experiment in order to become, or stay, "hot." Audiences were more heterogeneous than ever before; thus lyrics could, but also were forced to, deal with a wider variety of themes and issues, leaving aside the anecdote and launching itself into a new level of analysis that narrates or represents not just what happens, but how things happen in the street. A comparison between a traditional plena like "Tragedia en Barrio obrero" by Los Pleneros de Quinto Olivo[12] and Willie Colón's salsa song "Calle Luna, Calle Sol"[13] highlights differences between the range of inclusion developed by anecdote versus the range developed by description and reference to daily life in el barrio.

In the plena song by Los Pleneros del Quinto Olivo are detailed descriptions of the event (a plane crash), including the exact time (6:45 P.M.) and place (Barrio obrero, between Borinquen and Barbosa Avenues). In Colón's salsa song, however, the mention of streets refers to a topos: el barrio de *guapos*,[14] where tough young men hang out. It then proceeds to describe this type of setting and to advise the listener-audience-interlocutor about how life is on the streets and how to deal with it. Thus even though Calle Luna and Calle Sol are two streets that really do exist in Old San Juan, P.R., in this song they could be anywhere; their names (Moon and Sun Streets) manage to evoke a space that is almost mythic. The narrow audience that could be drawn into the participatory exchange of the plena song gets enlarged in salsa as anecdote gives way to a description of prototypical and topical situations.

However, Juliá sees this element as a "lack," arguing that by moving away from anecdote, salseros are not interested in real content:

A nadie le interesa; la clave, o la ausencia de ésta, forma todo el significado, o casi todo; la anécdota ha perdido su valor de crónica, se ha resquebrajado el mundo proletario, ya apunta en esta plena el código de las composiciones salseras niuyorkinas, ese jaleo inseguro entre las evocaciones de un paraíso caribeño que ya no es, que nunca fue y la clave oculta en la picaresca de callejón.

[Nobody was interested; the clave beat or its absence composed all the meaning, or most of it, the anecdote lost all its value as a chronicle, the proletarian world broke into pieces; in these plena compositions one could foresee the code of the New York salsa compositions, those insecure semantic negotiations between evocations of a lost Caribbean paradise that no longer exists, that never existed, and the secret codes of street picaresque.][15]

What this blanquito does not understand is precisely that the codes of the street are a closed signifying system only understandable for those who are "entendidos."[16] It is not self-referential, since the system for deciphering the message lies outside the limits of the song. We are not talking about another manifestation of Jackobson's poetic function. Salsa language sings of street philosophy, prototypes of el barrio, and about music itself as an act of signifying through a code, a clave that is unrecognizable to those who do not inhabit the spaces delimited by salsa music.

Willie Colón's "Calle Luna, Calle Sol" is an example of street philosophy. Rubén Blades's "Pedro Navaja" and "Juan Pachanga"[17] describe prototypes in urban Caribbean worlds: *el mamito jodedor*[18] who spends all he earns on clothes, discos, and picking up *mamis*, and the unrepentant hitman who will rob and probably has robbed his own mother. There are also songs such as Celia Cruz's biggest hit "Quimbara,"[19] which are basically a call to the dance floor, where the purpose of rhyme, rhythm, and lyrics is to bring to consciousness the act of salsa itself, an act of bonding where audience, dancers, musicians, and singers come together as a community of "entendidos."

Marvin Santiago's "Nueve de la noche"[20] is the best example I could find of a salsa song in which most of the elements outlined above are at play within its lyrics and form. It is sung by a *preso*, a prisoner who yearns for the street, to be together again with his barrio people in an informal dance or guaguancó. The song consists of a phrase that serves as an introduction to the central feeling and theme, followed by a long section of improvisation called a soneo. This phrase has two functions in Santiago's salsa; first it introduces an atmosphere of solitude, nostalgia, and yearning. This is done through the stanza sung by a chorus. Then the soloist describes what happens at his old barrio while he is alone in his cell, thus transporting himself in spirit to the *rumba de solar*. After this section the soneo starts. In "Nueve de la noche," the chorus emphasizes simultaneity through the adverb "mientras" (meanwhile). The long soneo is a development of the phrase. Up to this point, "Nueve de la noche" is a traditional salsa song that does not offer more space for interpretation. However, there are certain verses at the very beginning and at the end of the song that offer certain clues to the audience.

After Marvin Santiago's introduction he says before starting to sing:

Cucutín Masacote
Golpe de estado
para tí boricua
[Cucutín Masacote
Coup d'etat
for you Boricua]

These somewhat cryptic verses are easy to dismiss as onomatopoeias or word games, something to fill the time while the band starts playing the theme. However, the fact that they are being said by a presidiario who is singing from inside the jail points at the actual referentiality of these verses. The prisoner is committing a spiritual coup d'état as his voice breaks through the confined walls of the jail to reunite with the barrio community. He is not only defying the state but denying its power to keep him isolated. The guaguancó is the form of music that acts to restore the links that the state has severed. The recorded song becomes the technology that enables isolated people, such as those of the Puerto Rican diaspora, to communicate important messages to one another, and in a way that permits remote participation, not simply passive, vicarious enjoyment. In doing so, it also manages to bring together what the state and other power structures have a vested interest in keeping apart.

At the end of the song there are also several verses that provide another important element for the understanding of the song as well as the intentions of salsa and this *sonero del pueblo*. Marvin, before announcing the end of the song, says:

Mongolache, mongolón
y vamonos

Mongolo, mongolache quiere decir calle
y esto sí que se acabó
óyeme presumete.
[Mongolache, mongolón
And let's go
Mongolo, mongolache, that means street
and now it's really over
Listen up, presumptuous one.]

By revealing one small detail and defining the slang term "mongolache," Santiago reveals the existence of a code that is inaccessible to those who do not live in el barrio, those who have not been in jail or shared with those who have. His final word, "presumete," is a reference to the arrogant, elitist listener who, like the author Rodríguez Juliá, denies the value and "real meaning" of salsa songs.

Yet this reference also points at the existence of outsiders in this participatory musical economy. Two circuits are thus drawn: (1) the insiders' circuit, constituted by the people of el barrio, and (2) the outsiders' circuit, that is, those listeners who are standing around listening and watching without participating *en la rumba* because they do not entirely get it. The participatory exchange system of salsa can thus coexist with a market economy so long as it can use the latter, that is, entrepreneurs who recognize that they can profit from the demand for salsa recordings, in order to reach their most isolated members and *entendidos*. In such a way, salsa reconstitutes a community, one that supersedes the geographic limits of the nation.

The salsa community is not a sedentary one; it never stays in one place for very long and is often on the run. Salsa, not to mention salseros, cannot afford to get stale and formulaic. If they stop moving, improvising, and inventing new ways of carrying on, they become a target. If they stay put, they get towed away. The only way out of the conundrum is to keep moving, keep dancing, but this time to their own beat, their own clave. This is one of the most important messages that salsa transmits to its people, the migrant contract laborers, to the workers in the drug industry, to musicians, students, community activists, to all the inhabitants of an urban Caribbean whose current livelihood depends on international structures such as the music industry, the academy, drug cartels, telecommunications, political alliances, and agrobusiness.

I am not sure if salsa and salsero pragmatism can be applied in the same way to other areas of cultural production. Neither am I sure if this particular Afro-Boricua can dance to any son/beat that the ruling minority plays, and still manage to do it with *sabor boricua*. But then again, I know I have a larger repertoire of options, a greater variety of *sones* I can dance to, than a kid from the Bronx or Villa Palmeras. The straightforward identification of salsa with a particular community of people and their role in the international market economy liberates it from pretentious ambitions, while also buffering it from attempts to trivialize it as just so much musical kitsch. And I guess this is, in effect, what I learned as I was growing up, smuggling salsa and cigarettes into the girls' bathroom of the Catholic school. We were providing ourselves with means for analysis and expression that meant something in the community where we came from and in the larger barrio beyond. And showmanship, the act of displaying dexterity, is part of that endless experimentation, that codified violence needed for the continuous interplay between tradition and innovation.

Notes

1. Music for commoners, for hustlers, for unrepentant blacks.
2. A refined and well-groomed black young lady.
3. Puerto Ricans of African descent.
4. For dark girls like me.
5. Okay, here I go.
6. Angel Guillermo Quintero Rivera, "El soneo salsero," *Claridad,* June 22–28, 1990, 20–21.
7. The cauldron where salsa was cooked.
8. The first salseros proper.
9. César Miguel Rondón, *El libro de la salsa: Crónica de la música del Caribe urbano* (Caracas: Editorial Arte, 1980).
10. Edgardo Rodriguez Juliá, *El entierro de Cortijo* (Rio Piedras: Editorial Huracán, 1985), 31–32.
11. Upper-class whites.
12. "Tragedia en Barrio obrero," *Los Pleneros del Quinto Olivo* TTH 1835.

13. "Calle Luna, Calle Sol," *All-Stars Salsa Party* SO-1182, 1989.

14. Good-looking tough guys.

15. Rodriguez Juliá, 71.

16. "In the know."

17. "Pedro Navaja," *Ruben Blades Greatest Hits* Sony CD7-80718, 1992. "Juan Pa-changa," *Ruben Blades Greatest Hits* Sony CD7-80718, 1992.

18. The womanizing troublemaker.

19. "Celia Cruz, Quimbara," *The Best* Sony Discos CD-80587, 1991.

20. "Nueve de la noche."

Notes toward a Reading of Salsa

Juan Carlos Quintero Herencia   *Translated by Celeste Fraser Delgado*

La islita del corazón—Ramón
La islita de mis amores.
[That little island of my heart—Ramón
the little island of my loves.]
—Marvin Santiago

ANCIENT MAP. In loving, most search for an eternal motherland. Others, a few, for an eternal voyage. These last ones are melancholics that must flee from contact with the land. They search for somebody who can keep at bay the melancholy of the motherland. And they are faithful to them. Medieval treatises about bodily fluids know of the thirst for long voyages of these sort of people.—Walter Benjamin

Que salgan las bestias.
[Unleash the beasts.]
—Bobby Cruz

We must start with the commonplaces, with those clichés dragged through the apparently innocent circulation of salsa. To know how to listen to salsa, how to follow behind, is no easy task. You can't know anything about salsa until you take it in through each and all of the senses—including the self-lubricating body—which make salsa (pre)sense. Take the ear inserted in the stereo system, along with the other senses, playing the part of the conductor of the orchestra in order to facilitate in the listener of the radio or in the dancer the incredible possibility of following the rhythm and the clave. Imagine the scene: the zone cut by the arc swirling from the music perceived in the auditory shell—that drumming c(h)oral; from there we go to the visual simultaneity of a group of dancers in absolute communion with that same music; from there to the next version, essential and simultaneous, of the first synthesized movement, a rehearsal of rhythm: the first step. To

Salsa associates itself with divinities: Celia Cruz, 1975. (Courtesy of the
Miami News Collection of the Historical Museum of Southern Florida)

begin dancing is to believe that you're hearing the music for the very first
time. From here we play by ear.

But before beginning, I will have to say that this essay transverses an
itinerary not yet completed—impossible to complete—as long as recordings and orchestras of salsa exist to be heard. If talking about music (even
in the most specialized cases) is to resign oneself to approximations, to
scant insights playing on the openings upon emotion that music articulates, to talk about salsa assumes a knowledge of the process of constant
inscription upon the body of all types of information: intuitions, stories,
genres, intensities, places, and even the *uncanny*. I'm speaking of the
songs and the productions of salsa which themselves contain specializa-
tions and ways of knowing that I myself can barely master.

I approach the act of *reading* salsa without being able to disassociate
the transcribed lyrics from the music and the rhythm that surround and
transverse the words. To transcribe a salsa song sitting next to the sound
system—the stereo—is the premeditated production of the fossil of a

complex cultural product. The poverty of the graphic sign cedes to the speed and reverberation of Ismael Rivera, to the knowing force of Celia Cruz, to the overlapping delirium of Marvin Santiago. Still, the written version of a salsa song reveals the densities found in the interventions of the sonero or sonera, the repetitions of the chorus, the entrance of the principal instruments, the forces unleashed by the musical arrangements. In the blank spaces, revealed as much horizontally as vertically by a transcription of the voices of salsa, the music appears in its very absence—precisely as the work that sustains and intensifies voices. But, as with a fossil, there are always lacunas and imprecisions left behind, which only the musical piece can fill. And for me, to *read* salsa is always to be humming the music—coming and going. Once you hear the lyrics of salsa set to music they remain, quite literally, recorded; to read salsa without the inflections and the alterations inherent in the recording would be impossible if not parodic. Each instrument is indissolubly interrelated as the trumpet ushers in the refrain; the piano signals the verse; a blast of sound (*descarga*) exclaims our beloved's cries; a trombone marks a date on the calendar; kettledrums resound an epoch, and from there on down. To recite a few of these songs—to *simply* read them—may well seem bad comedy. You find two registers in salsa and in the act of transcription one eventually forces the other to feel out of place, out of synch with the genre, which the pause in the rhythm ultimately dictates. Salsa transcribed—including the soneos and all the other oral interventions in the song—unveils a tapestry of superpositions disguised as a causal succession with a beginning and an end. Still, in fleeting moments this *morcilla*,[1] this exquisite stuffing of voice-lyrics-chorus-arrangement, draws a broken spiral that comes together again when and how it pleases, that articulates and disarticulates itself without aspirations, with unspoken assumptions and misunderstandings vibrating in the memory like bits of bait set out to trap the intuition. To confront salsa exclusively through a transcribed version is indeed the best description of what the judges call the "dead letter." To take on salsa in its entirety requires of necessity an effort that presupposes other knowledges, circuits, and specifications. I cannot cover all of them here. However, I ask myself: Is salsa's seductive danceability a handicap for auditory appreciation? Can salsa as dance and discourse be separated artistically? Under what circumstances, and under what hypotheses can this distinction be made? Whom do such separations serve? Whom does the distinction help or invoke? How would we constitute institutional spaces that speak, make use of, or exclude gestures like those of salsa: in a specialized library, in a university, in a book? Could there be other modes of processing the glorious ensemble of rhythms and experiences in simultaneous moments of delight and scrutiny? Why not take what salsa says "seriously" and not believe it inoffensive in its *pachanga?*[2]

Rather than addressing the simple fact of salsa as an excited sensibility through a well-intentioned folklorism or through the fuss of a musicological expertise I do not possess, I will set out to follow along the political gesticulations and effects present in certain salsa songs. Discarding simplistic polarities such as the "popular" versus the "elite," the "native" versus the "foreign," or the center versus the margin—just a few of the many distinctions so readily at hand, frequently created by and for the convenience of official institutions and reproduced acritically in antagonistic sectors—I believe I can establish with greater accuracy the textuality and strategies these polarized categories presuppose. I do not believe these categories, in any way, to be mere semantic lucubrations without repercussions or localizable practices—such pernicious polarities still enjoy good health in certain institutions and systems of domination. Neither do I claim that such oppositions do not exist or that people do not, for example, use these terms to debate the national or the popular. Put simply, in this text I highlight certain reservations about any polar/binary construction that generally forms a part of the definitions and uses of the above-mentioned concepts by reducing their complexities to a mere series inflected as either good or evil. We would have to observe whether salsa flees from, uses as camouflage, or refutes the very conditions of the attempted reading or confrontation.

As I read and hum these songs—which have constituted both a site for my emotions and a poetics that crosses me through with contamination of every kind—salsa swells with its complexity and carefree moral depredation. I am far from exhausting the thematic—salsa won't let me. To begin with, I could debate with my own cousin. Angel G. Quintero Rivera, in his analysis of Puerto Rican music, amasses a considerable historical bibliography, demonstrates an enviable musical familiarity, and performs a forceful exercise in historiographic contextualization.[3] Nevertheless, we can rethink some of his conceptualizations and critical presuppositions from other places, with other plots and alternative poetics. Thinking principally about the implications of the maroonage (*cimarronaje*) of past centuries, Quintero Rivera poses the following supposition: "In societies, such as Puerto Rico, with a weakly structured plantation system, but with sturdy military bastions, runaway slavery occurred as passive rather than active opposition. The military in the fortresses did not view the rural world of the *cimarrón* as a threat but rather as the habitat of indolent primitives. Thus, the fugitive slaves felt no need to mount organized opposition and their anti-urban nature discouraged the formation of free slave stockades. A kind of counter-plantation developed, characterized by isolated dwellings of familiar nucleii engaged in domestic subsistence production. An essentially 'slash and burn' agricultural process lent this form of life a semi-nomadic character, with little attachment to any particular territorial property" (149). As a "prelude" to his study, Quintero Rivera takes salsa as a movement that would inherit a series of rhythmic and thematic characteristics and values from the maroons and their countercultural formation. The challenge posed by "intimacy" to public norms and to "capitalist alienation between personal life and work" can be seen in the song written by Curet Alonso for Isadora Duncan, with which my cousin opens his text. Salsa retains improvisation from maroonage as an essential device for the bringing together of diverse musical forms. Above all, maroonage bequeaths the call to spontaneity and freedom as surviving traits of the "common, authentic cultural skeleton of the Caribbean"—a skeleton itself produced by the dialectical tension between plantation and counterplantation, slavery and maroonage, throughout the entire Caribbean. The maroon's "world of escape"—the flight to the mountains and hills to evade subjection and brutality—would lay down the "roots" of Puerto Rican popular forms that would timidly avoid direct confrontation with the colonial state. The study and the restructuring of the meaning of the word "cimarrón" (maroon), according to Quintero Rivera, is the product of a historiographical amplification of this term's connotations. Extensive debate has posited the constitution of a sociocultural conglomerate in the Caribbean based on various types of fugitives (including but not limited to indigenous peoples and enslaved Africans who escaped from oppression).[4]

Flight, the diverse methods for avoiding state interference and repression, emerges in Quintero Rivera's work as a result of the framing of two opposed social and political realms. This opposition of worlds—the plantation and the counterplantation—put forth as a premise establishing a reflection on the forms and uses of music in the Caribbean, particularly in Puerto Rico, can run the risk of naturalizing a binary structure from which cultural genres and forms emerge as direct expressions or as "heirs" rooted in opposing traditions. Although Quintero Rivera acknowledges that salsa is not "merely an expression of class but rather a music of class interaction" (164), a remnant of functional polarities still lingers in his text. To claim the interaction of separate entities, or antagonistic classes in this case, requires at least positing as definitive certain traits and cultural elements capable of mutual exchange and interaction. This always presupposes an extremely difficult, if not impossible, process of distillation. There exist specificities of class, gender, sexuality, and race that exceed traditional class categorizations. Perhaps these specificities would, in turn, require being understood as a series of appropriations, situations, or battlefields, each one deployed in determinate spaces with specific agendas. Such shifting acts of appropriation obviate the possibility of assuming a particular poetics and politics as the monolithic dictates of a singular sociocultural lineage.

Gilles Deleuze and Félix Guatarri have pointed out the recurrence of the use of the tree as a cultural metaphor of ample interdisciplinary diffusion in Western systems of knowledge, as a favored emblem believed to be stable, hierarchical, and capable of tracing genealogical zones.[5] The firmly rooted tree has often, though not always, functioned as the ideological synecdoche of a desire for continuity that guarantees and privileges those sociocultural formations that validate the notion of a pure and uncontaminated origin. Although I recognize the evident affiliation of this figure in Quintero Rivera's work, we should not underestimate its diverse uses and functions in specific historical and national contexts. I emphasize this distinction because I think that the genre of salsa as the cultural "expression" of maroonage formally pulverizes any patri/matrilineal affiliation. In short, salsa eradicates all arboreal paradigms.

Two zones: that of maroonage and that of the city or the plantation. Far from antagonistically opposing each other, though by no means nonviolent, these zones intermingle in apparent transactions and fluctuations. We see evidence of such mingling in Quintero Rivera's analysis of the use of the *bombardino* (saxhorn) during the nineteenth-century foundation of the Puerto Rican *danza* in the hands of mulatto and black artisans. Music composed by these artisans *for* the landed class, the danza is considered by some on the island to be the "first national music." In an interesting analysis of the transformations and negotiations performed by the artisans in a quest for "civil acknowledgment," Quintero Rivera indicates how the form and melodic interior of danza, produced by the use of the bombardino, achieves the effect of *camouflage* of the rhythms and percussions of the maroons. This seems to me the most innovative proposal of my cousin's work, and in fact enables some of my own approximations regarding salsa.

But here we might consider flight, like camouflage, not as defining "traits" of a Caribbean sociocountercultural formation, but rather as a ruse. The act of camouflage conceals an act of contestation, an oppositional proposal known to be used by "others" not in order to escape, but instead to merge with their surroundings. I will read the democratic alternative of salsa in the forms through which salsa chooses to invoke its listeners, its interlocuters, its *pana* (kindred). I will work the concept of flight, of voyage, deprived of sociological and ethnographic implications, as a (con)text *interior* to certain salsa songs. This imaginary flight understood as a collocation of converging and divergent rhythms, as a collocation even of the voice of the sonero or sonera, seems to convert itself into a more complex, more cunning poetic. More than offer flight, I would say salsa plays the fool, pretends not to know what it is saying, staging a certain friendly spontaneity, a certain forced *jaibería*. To camouflage resistance and work it constantly does not necessarily signify the evasion of opposition, but perhaps the avoidance of a repressive violence. To sing and thematize this camouflage in the very lyrics is a strategy in the war over the *sabor* (flavor) of the nation, what Josefina Ludmer has called the "weapons of the weak,"[6] *pero no se lo crea mucho compay. Y si se me escapó, disculpe, yo sé que nada se puede hacer.*[7]

Salsa is not countercultural in the aforementioned sense; salsa does not presume stable poles to oppose; on the contrary, salsa plunders, corrodes, articulates, and superimposes without having the undergirding of any master text such as the conscience of one class foreclosed by another, without any zone of monolithic sociocultural production defining less industrious "others" on the other side. Salsa surges through the archipelago, but salsa needs a disguise to survive. Salsa promises not to get you wet, while soaking you through and through. In short, salsa *plays* innocent, *la salsa se hace la pendeja*. Salsa is, above all, a genre. Stopping at this specification provides a key with which to enter the body of salsa— electrified, perhaps, for the first time by the Cuban son. Many musicians, singers, and/or actors have addressed the signifying lack or the mirage of totality contained in the word "salsa." The history of the name, and the polemic regarding its origin, have links to salsa as a genre. Salsa is also a scenario: a space of representations, harmonies, and resonances made for the market.[8] The production of salsa as a spectacle—simultane- ously as a concert, a film, and a recording company—is the multiple assemblage that marks, to the present day, the acceptance of the term "salsa" and its circulation. From the beginning, salsa has been thought through a process of mass reproduction, through the packaging of the genre for the enjoyment of the listening public. As the seasoning and spice of urban space, "salsa" is the sign of the well made, the flavorful, the specialty of the house cooked up by a friend in the intimate space of the kitchen. The culinary reference is the ultimate expression of the sur- vival of the tone of a community in constant migration—the key to a scent that keeps you on track and the point of entrance to a thematic that turns into a genre in both the formal and political sense. Frank Parilla Jr. interviews the salsero Willie Colón:

Q: Willie, for many people, salsa is nothing but Cuban music. What's your opinion?

A: Not true! Sure, Afro-Cuban music and other folkloric forms are Cuban, but Salsa is not Cuban music. A son is Cuban music just like a guaguancó, matancero, or a danzón, but this salsa is neither a guaguancó nor any of the other variations and wonderful manifestations of Cuban folklore. *Salsa is a genre, not a rhythm, collecting elements from Cuban music, from the Caribbean in general, from South Amer- ica, North America, all of which we Puerto Ricans—more than anybody else—began to combine until we came up with salsa.*[9]

In this way, salsa as genre is constituted as an instance of combination, as the site of a transnational amalgamation reworked by a national group. The matrix revealed by Willie crucially establishes a spatial relation, a national musical operation that extends beyond the mere inclusion of rhythms. Josefina Ludmer has suggested that "the nation is found in its tones."[10] The combination of Puerto Rican, Cuban, and U.S. American rhythms, among others, in New York, like any other work consisting of all manner of choral gestures, of the convocations of the sonero, of the exclamations of the sonera, delineates the map of salsa. Such is the genre of salsa: a space for the debate, negotiation, representation, and rehearsal of national forms and identities in the processes of movement and consumption. From this space we can think the contextualization of salsa. Salsa's nomadology is the emotional version of a culture that circles constantly—almost to a point of delirium—around the problems of a nationality interdicted and reaffirmed from diverse angles. In the words of salsero Rubén Blades: "About salsa, I can say that even though people don't want to accept it, these supposedly insignificant musicians and uncouth songsters—which is what a lot of people think about us salseros—are today the ultimate representatives of the Puerto Rican race in the world. And I, speaking as someone originally from Panama, include myself in this group. Rafael Cortijo and Ismael Rivera are two of the greatest monuments music has ever produced."[11]

Without requiring any kind of conspiracy behind closed doors, salsa camouflages and is camouflaged by immediacies and historicities while at the same time celebrating what seems only to talk about food, a dead pal, crime in the city, or the neighborhood. The packaging of salsa is its best alibi, it's best corrosive strategy. Cesar Miguel Rondón remarks on this process: "The opening scene of the movie, *Nuestra Cosa,* depicts a boy kicking an empty can down a solitary alley with overflowing garbage cans. Right away we know we're in el Barrio, that we're in a closed world in which, despite being in the heart of the *Capital of the World,* scarcely participates in the benefits of progress and development . . . I have here the element which will have to be repeated not with a little insistence throughout the film: the maintenance of a tradition in a medium that corrodes and destroys. In a canny way, the movie tells us that salsa is more than this, more than the prolongation of the same tradition always molded and born from the garbage of an alien culture."[12] The barrio as a ship; the barrio as a monad that awaits reformulation and porification—a community made porous like the sponges of the c(h)oral reefs of the Caribbean. Ismael Rivera, in a composition by Tito Curet Alonso, speaks in this way about the outlying barrio, la Perla, in Old

San Juan. This barrio boasts a cemetery where important personages in Puerto Rican history take their final rest:

Y la Perla,
donde sepultan lo(s) patriotas,
Ay tiene un deseo que no se nota,
una amargura de ala rota,
y nunca se la mereció.
[And la Perla,
Where the patriots are buried,
Ay, la Perla has a desire no one notices
The bitterness of a broken wing,
and this she never deserved.][13]

The songwriter works imprecisions to a purpose, juxtaposing resistances that at the same time sell records. Salsa is always in motion even when seemingly against its will. As a genre, salsa is a space where the contamination is so precious that if a musical session awakens opposing sentiments and sensations—made evident in their differences—we accept these sentiments, despite their flight, their polyphony, which would be the only possible sentiments for approaching the experience recently lived. The mixed feelings in salsa, the mixture of tones and notes, of absences and knowledges, have made eternally correct the experience alluded to by the word "misunderstood." Listening to salsa, a "misunderstanding" is inescapable sooner or later; in the best salseros there are always elements—zones—that "don't make sense," things saved, which remain hidden until later. From this instant, our pleasurable efforts make these misunderstandings a part of the recording. The zone of misunderstanding is a place of truth in the strictest sense that occasionally shatters you like a ritual. The salsero Maelo (Ismael Rivera), as always, sums up the whole thing in a gesture: "Esa negrita se hace y sale a gozar [This sweet Black woman plays the fool and goes out for a good time]."

In its modes of affiliation, in its gestures toward the public, in its presupposed tonalities, salsa sets out in the form of an amiable commodity, of an identity in flux. A secret ceremonial character is inscribed in the meeting of a *rumbón* (dance party). However, the history of the genre as a series of strategic spectacles and productions for the circulation and consumption of the images and stories of a community should not be underestimated. Many of the tones and effects of salsa's dense politics can be calculated through the marks of the preparation of the genre for mass marketing at salsa's emergence. Salsa songs are ceremonial centers erected to reign over the mysterious apprenticeship of the bodies and emotions of a mobile nation. We are then on the terrain of surfaces. The neighborhood is a surface; Luis Rafael Sánchez's "Air Bus" is a surface; the vacant lot is a surface; the ghetto is a minor surface—all of which have the smells of roots, gunshots, and cooking spices. Puerto Rico is a mountainous surface measuring "100 miles x 35"; a kind of raised sponge, the mountain stretched out would augment our length but would sink in the sea with a single strike, finalizing her immersion in the luminous fluids. In the city, above the sponge, the porosity of the ancestral ritual and of urbanity cohabitate, as do the porosity of industrialization and of consumption. Two or more circulations competing to dismember everything.

These songs of salsa cannot claim to be the unique or even the best material for a discussion of the tones and textualities of Puerto Rican politics. They are songs, then, that facilitate a discussion over and of the political subjectivities constructed in the soneo, utopic proposals, and vindicating projects detonated from the density of everyday practices. With the *contraseña* (liner notes) in front of me like any good fan—of whom no one demands any c.v. or dossier greater than corporeal attention—I ask myself: What are the essential enigmas of salsa? True, the only prerequisite I believe to be required of me to *belong* is to connect with the feeling, with the flavor, but such a connection assumes a certain mastery: What makes a song a hit beyond the sum of the record's sales? What makes a song a hit in the memory, a hit in the dailiness of the future? A system of coincidence and convocation? You know: those songs that wake up on your lips after years of silence, this sensation of invasion submerged beneath the fortuitous.

A salsa song always presupposes "a friend" to whom the song addresses itself without formalities (*tapujos*). This does not mean that among friends all things are known; rather the intimate address of salsa means only that you share a certain closeness and solidarity as fragile and context bound as emotions themselves. The proximity shared by the sonero or sonera and his or her audience is sometimes thematized in salsa, even when the songs narrate unexpected visitations by gods. Ismael Rivera, in a song written for *el negrito lindo de Portobelo* (the black Christ of Portobelo in Panama),[14] narrates how the voice of Christ spoke to him—like Paul in Damascus—and how God gave him in one gesture—like Moses's tablets of the law: the politics of salsa solidarity. Just before this moment the salsero was in a *vacilón* (party) when he heard the voice of *el nazareno* (the Nazarene) give him this advice:

"házle bien a tus amigos
y ofréceles tu amistad,
y verás que a ti lo malo
nunca se te acercará,
en cambio todo lo bueno,
contigo siempre estará."
Óyelo bien. Suena.
(Coro)
El nazareno me dijo,
que cuidara a mis amigos.
["Treat your friends well,
And offer them your friendship,
And you will see that no evil
will ever come close to you.
Instead, all good things
will be with you forever."
Listen up good. Strike it up.
(Chorus)
The Nazarene told me
to take care of my friends.][15]

Christ told Maelo he should take care of his friends and not cede to any other his place or his pose, whether in his show or in his work. Maelo quotes the words of the Black Christ in a hymn of the solidarity among friends.

In salsa, you encounter hundreds of greetings, interjections, interpellations, and questions: "What?"; "Ah?"; "Eh?" Commands that you listen: "Listen up good"; "Hear this"; "Listen well, my friend"; "Strike it up." These words are spoken to someone who is there. The soneros respond to the instruments; they are allowed to speak so that the listeners can "understand well." To find oneself, then, convocated by salsa is to feel yourself touched, up and "high" within the grain of the music, to be permitted to enter the current like someone trapped by a wave that will take you to the fragile shore and, repentant, hauls you as though it didn't mean to. This friend—the listening public—sometimes also has witnessed the distance of the sonero, his "other world." Maelo dressed now in the eclipse predicting his death; Maelo—the black star—trapped between languages. The sonero speaks in tongues. The eclipse speaks:

(Cuerpo)
Yo yo yo yo creo que voy
solito a estar, cuando me muera,
he sido el incomprendido,
ni tú ni nadie me ha querido
tal como soy
. . .
Incomprendido,
yo soy Maelo el incomprendido,
jáj jáj já,
Ecua, Yemayá [o ¿quema ya?]
[(Verse)
I, I, I, I, I think I'm going
to be alone, when I die,
I have been misunderstood
Not you nor anyone else has loved me
as I am.
. . .
Misunderstood,
I am Maelo, the misunderstood,
hah, hah, ha,
Ecua, Yemayá (or "Burn it now"?)][16]

As a matter of fact, the burial of Ismael Rivera was a national spectacle that drew thousands of people, and the procession carrying his coffin covered with the flag of Puerto Rico sang the song just cited more than one time.[17] That's the way it was with Maelo: the *Sonero mayor* (the best sonero), the equal of Celia Cruz, the *Rumbera mayor* (the best rumbera). Salsa associates itself with divinities. Having already established their career and name before the phenomenon of salsa, both Maelo and Celia integrated themselves into the circulation of the genre effortlessly, with all the honors and recognition of their being masters.

Starting with Maelo's group, El Combo de Cortijo, we can establish a genealogy: El Combo de Cortijo, El Gran Combo de Puerto Rico, Roberto Rohena and His Apollo Sound, Elías Lopez and His Orchestra, Andy Montañez and His Orchestra, Salsa Fever . . . But with the soneo, and with Maelo especially, we sense the problems and implications of the uses and products of the voice to be much more dense than any family album. Like no one else, Maelo gathers together and stuffs, without ever losing the clave, incredible quantities of voices and sounds into a single and resounding morcilla. When he cuts this morcilla, when he opens it with his skillful machete, secret elixirs flow from within, reverberations cause waves within the soneos, within the words, within the very sounds; spaces are opened. All this magic is worked by Maelo—or the hummingbird trapped inside his throat.

Salsa knows that the "intimate" space of the emotions is the enabling site of the most clandestine of complicities, the most ritual of the projects of the mobile community. Salsa does not emerge from its appeal like a refracted reflection of the society that produces its form. On the contrary, salsa is a distinct sphere of Caribbean social action, implicated and intertwined with localizable political and ideological relations of power that flow through the history of the archipelago. By this I don't mean to say that these relations could be empirical and irrefutably concrete or in any way delineable and in opposition, or even that salsa will describe its proposition from within these relations. The response of salsa to these relations of power and domination presupposes a secret in excess of any intentionality or individual "consciousness"; at times salsa does not even respond with anything but the most diaphanous declaration or description: Ismael Rivera, in the middle of a guaguancó, exclaims "componte," a word that can be read as "get yourself together" but that also designates one of the most repressive episodes in nineteenth-century Puerto Rico.[18] Likewise, Celia Cruz shouts "azucá, candela" (sugar, fire) in the middle of her songs. *Candela,* the ritual flame, designates the combustion center of the sugar mill, the weapon, the torch, wielded against the exploitation in the cane fields, the synecdoche of the musical furor that occasions the subject of salsa. Sugar, the commodity that recalls and names par excellence the world of the plantation. Sugar, the subject to which the anthropologist Sidney Mintz has dedicated an entire book.[19]

From the decade of the sixties through the decade of the seventies (a critical decade for the genre) until the uneven (for the genre) decade of the eighties, salsa came together through an itinerary of friendships, confidences, and barbaric rhythms that had as an axis the urban New York experience; today people say that the axis has shifted to Puerto Rico. In the seventies, the sixties went underground until they lost themselves in the alleys, never to escape again. The seventies and salsa came together like a slogan that no one copyrights nor declares property of the state. The seventies were the era of salsa's vinyl hemorrhage: the albums that saved us from the patron saint who accompanied the "holy" wars in Vietnam and Czechoslovakia; the albums that diluted the price of petroleum. The decade that saw how salsa invited the "minor" nationalities to seek refuge on its stage, the seventies for salsa was a *rumba* (dance party) with no cover charge because no one knew where the club of the future would be. Better to follow the *bembé* (party, ritual) because maybe tomorrow we won't be able to sing.

The Caribbean migrations toward New York City are an indispensable framework for thinking about the genre and its machinery of importations, voyages, mixtures, and the international appropriation of emotion. The *solar*, the community lot, is demarcated within and without the Caribbean barrio. In the city too exist materials through which to rethink the mountain. New York is another barrio that once in a while shuts out the sun; friends hear each other in their histories, in their laments, in their desires and atrocities. From time to time, people will enter from other neighborhoods, with other languages and other genres, but not merely to contribute to the closed boundaries of the ghetto. Rather, these others find themselves in the succulence of the stew, of the *sofrito*—in order to reaffirm the lines of escape, other intermittent versions, entering and exiting from the shifting aroma of salsa, to introduce other ingredients. The stewpot is salsa, salsa is the stewpot: the sound presupposes both. The metallic qualities of this flavor are indivisible; no single ingredient serves as antecedent. Here is where the gods live. Remember that a cauldron must be cured to better perform its task. The slow curing of the metal with the ingredients conserve and remake a flavor that always recedes after each new stew.

The anteriority of salsa rests in the ports, in the passages, the barrios, and the streets left behind to be recomposed once again later. Friends see how the memories pale, chilled by nostalgia, while a few decide to come and go like a pendulum bearing gifts and ingredients eaten away in the process of migration. Sometimes opting to return to the homeland is only a trip, in the narcotic sense, in the sense of subsistence and love. But even in the sacred sense of the flight to the mountains set out by "Vámonos pal monte" (Let's go to the mountain) by Eddie Palmieri and Ismael Quintana, the flight is not innocent. The joy is fleeting and the mountain is thought *through* the city. The asphixiating urban "complexity" serves as a double backdrop for the proposition of flight and for reflections on the repressive future that will require vigilance. From here emerges the flavor, the beat, of the mountain—this makes us want salsa more:

Vámonos pal monte,
pal monte pa guarachar,
vámonos pal monte,
que el monte me gusta más,

. . .

Este mundo es tan travieso,
y aunque eso me importe a mí,
yo no puedo controlarlo,
sigo contento y feliz.
[Let's go to the mountain,
To the mountain to get the beat,
let's go to the mountain,
because I like the mountain more.

. . .

This world is so tricky
and even though this gets to me,
there's nothing I can do,
I go on content and happy.]

The sonero does not lose much sleep over his inability to control the world's tricks. Confronted with such an extensive and complex situation, the sonero declares his interest but opts for pleasure as an antidote. His escape is apparent.

Dicen que poquito a poco,
se acerca la represión,
si no se aguzan mi amigos,
nos tumban el vacilón, vacilón.
[They say that little by little,
Repression draws near.
If you don't stay on your toes, my friends,
they'll overthrow our fun, our fun.][20]

This going to the mountains is no solo flight. It is a collective performance that invokes others—"Let's go"—before the worst happens: the end of the party.

It is true, the trip is thematized: "La Maleta" (The suitcase) by Rubén Blades; "Zambúllete" (Plunge in) is an invitation to a trip to Panamá, sung by Celia Cruz; "Plantación adentro" (Plantation within) by Tito Curet Alonso is the textual return to the indigenous exploitation of the plantation of the eighteenth century, among others. However, more than a thematic, the song itself constitutes a trip. In the fabulous song "Vasos en colores" (Colored glasses), the sonero goes to the market where he meets his friend Tingüaro "con tremendo tumbaíto" (in a terrible fix) and staving off his hard luck by selling "colored glasses" on the island. Santiago follows his friend on a journey to the island from which he brings back colored glasses to his listeners:

(Marco)
Pueblo que yo quiero y me quiere,
aquí llevo vasos con sabor.
. . .
(Coro)
Yo me voy a Puerto Rico,
vendiendo vasos en colores,
(Soneo)
La islita del corazón, Ramón,
la islita de mis amores.

[(Frame)
People whom I love and who love me,
I bring you glasses with *sabor,*

. . .

(Chorus)
I'm going to Puerto Rico,
selling colored glasses,
(Soneo)
That little island of my heart, Ramón,
The island of my loves.][21]

Through Marvin Santiago we begin to witness among his neologisms, overlappings, and verbal horseplay not only a mechanism of camouflage but also the very movement of the trip—in whichever sense—working over the national tongue. Marvin tells us: "Pa' que te trepes Mario. Bayamóntate, Bayamóntate, Barranquítate, Vegabájate," turning names of towns in Puerto Rico (Bayamón, Barranquitas, Vega Baja) into verb forms that express movement and command: climbing, descending, getting away; the national geography is displaced by the subject who both articulates and consumes the song. Hearing this displacement, the listener travels through/with the country as both vehicle and destination. The song—salsa as genre—becomes a declaration of the pleasurable voyage into the interior of the national geography, which is appropriated and seasoned through the voice in the middle of the market—through both persistent violence and apparent accident.

The thickness of the sauce/salsa is shaped by the apparent malleability of the container: the immediate filiation of a song on the radio. The segregation of the ghetto, the impoverished barrio, is broken by the salsadian incorporation of the rhythms and the knowledges that exceed the unity of any given language—friendship as sect. There is a sect of initiates posited by the lyrics of salsa that has spread without leaving any trace of the identity of its members. Faced with exploitation and colonization, forced emigration, racism and sexism, salsa has decided to protect its participants by granting them the grand gift of aspiration: the conversion of sound into breath. The aspiration of consonants, the aspiration of whole sentences, the aspiration of all clear referents. Salsa is the ideal genre for the phonetic aspiration of Puerto Rican Spanish. It saves time and grants malleability to the sonero(a). Marvin: "A(h)ve María!" Here the names of the sect gather.

There is a post-ritual silence in certain salsa songs, a certain hypnotic state of mind lingering after the intensity of the rite of death, or the rite of survival, which is barely enunciated but from which a good sonero or sonera intermittently breaks away without putting his or her pals into danger. The oblivion and the expropriations rehearsed in the threshold of silence that follow the song suddenly strike an instant of pleasure and declamation. It is from this space that we can speak of how salsa figures its historicities. The fortuitous as a strategy of salsa. Haphazardness promoted and incited in order to witness the possible combinations. A game played with truths and beyond-truths, which is not always agreeable although always flavorful. You're always arriving at the rumba, a celebration is always in progress, you're always arriving at the right time to say something, to dance a tune. The composition and voice of Ismael Miranda, "Señor sereno" (Mister Serenity or The night watchman), vocalizes an attempt to censor a song dedicated to Puerto Rico. The sonero, a youth—"Now I'm twenty-one"—offended at finding himself interrupted and denied the opportunity to sing to his country after having dedicated songs to all the other nations, curses the messenger of "Mister Serenity" to his face for his unjust intervention.

Empiezo yo por cantar,
una cumbia pa Colombia,
un guagancó a Venezuela,
son montuno a Panamá,
y cuando voy a empezar
a cantarle a mi Borinquén,
viene uno a interrumpir,
dice que el señor sereno,
a mí me manda a dormir.
[I begin to sing,
a cumbia for Colombia,
a guaguancó for Venezuela,
a son montuno for Panama,
and just when I begin
to sing to Borinquén

someone comes to intervene.
He says that Mister Serenity
orders me to bed.][22]

"Someone," an anonymous intermediary, has given him notice of the
mandate of "Mister Serenity": he who regulates the streets and marks
the hours in the neighborhood.[23] The state of siege interdicting the song
dedicated to Puerto Rico makes the sonero defy the order by playing
with the resonances of the vocable *sereno* (serenity) in contrast to the
rhythm and tone of the song. The song is a tense acceleration that makes
the repetition of the word "serenity" the paradoxical index of the non-
conformity and defiance of the subject who sings. The sleep mandated in
the middle of a street celebration of identities by an authority who would
deny homage to the homeland—who sings *an other* song—is defied with
more noise from within the song itself.

Observing how the sonero/as invoke the mobile nation of their listeners, I would next have to emphasize that the fans/initiates address
the soneros and soneras in familiar terms (*tutea*) in order to break the ice
of every traditional institutional vestige and bad ceremony. You do not
call the stars "sir" or "madam" (*no se las trata de usted*). Even though at
times, in appreciation of what the stars have made, the terms of utmost
respect fall from our lips (*usted y tenga*). Returning to the name and the
knowledge of the nearby, there are no administrative or scholastic initia-
tions: you don't learn a name and a title in order to earn the praises of the
institution, you don't constitute the State of the genre. Rather the entrance through the proper name results in a familiarity that can transform itself from song to song, causing a brief period of readjustment that
becomes part of the respiration of the genre. On hearing the nickname,
the alias, we immediately know that we have plugged into a stereo-
phonic apparatus that requires a *connection* in order to begin the functioning of the names the system carries. Once they begin to make themselves present with names, first and last, we're in the formal introduction
of the band, of the group, or in the case of Fania, of the stars on the stage.
This salutation serves to grant the stars the authority and glory won from
dance to dance, from concert to concert, distancing with their work the
flatness of life. The singer only comes to celebrate the true and unique

glory granted to the singing being, to the *being-for-the-music:* the being on the stage. To be applauded by thousands of people, adored, cheered as the one who knows how to do it well, the one who can make it to the moon, the one who speaks in tongues.

Maelo, Celia, Cheo, Héctor, Lavoe, Willie, Rubén, Bobby, Andy, Pellín, Marvin are pseudonyms in the underground resistant to excavation by those committed to the project of Progress. They possess a knowledge that sometimes regrettably coincides and tends to be confused with the name that appears on the birth certificate of each. The name of the so-nero/a is the sign of a guerrilla's identity, whose possible and continuous overthrow do not aspire to be exemplars as understood in any immolatory tradition—where immolation is a kind of fetish for the only means believed available to confront domination. Rather the various faces of violence, like jail, drugs, and exile, form part of the social process through which to discover a language capable of speaking of what is happening in the neighborhood. This process is not idealizable nor can it be touted acritically. To sing, *sonear,* in an effort to detain death, to bear witness to brutality, is part of a gesture of convocation where an open strategy is composed. But also to stop speaking in order to sing, to sing in order not to cry, to speak in order to celebrate the deities, in order to say to death: You'll get your due. "Ni hablar, ni hablar/ni hablar, mejor cantar [Don't speak, don't speak/don't speak, better to sing]."[24] It is a station of the cross that is constantly sabotaged, that leads away from the route to Calvary, that forgets about sacrifice, rehearsing it constantly, degrading it, accelerating it, detaining it in order to hit us over the head with it, forging an alternative route, another surface. At this juncture, the threat and defiance of salsa command their (im)proper space.

Not only do the salseros challenge each other—the songs in salsa are full of barbs that tell us of rumors and rivalries within the "rhythm machine"—but they even defy the public in the form of an invitation that conceals a spectacle, a potential strike. The gesture is "follow me if you can, so you can find your own pleasure." The speed of the sonero constitutes his deployment of arms. The salsero's defiance partakes of a poetics of closeness (*cercanía*), of the immediacy, of that which is just there, at the foot of the stage. Fragments of Hector Lavoe, in "El cantante" (The singer):

(Coro #1)

Hoy te dedico

mis mejores pregones.

(Se repite el Coro #1 dos veces)

Son mejor que los de ayer,

compárenme criticones.

[(Chorus #1)

Today I dedicate to you

my best verses.

(Repeat Chorus #1 two times)

They are better than yesterday's.

Compare them yourself, you big critics.]

In Héctor Lavoe most of all, but also in Ismael Miranda in his "Venceré" (I will overcome), as in certain of Willie Colón's recordings of the 1980s, there is a constant repetition of the defiant tone that presupposes criticism or even betrayal.[25] Speaking with someone nearby, the sonero reaffirms his capacity in the face of adversity; he recognizes his masters; he announces his death; he declares his "manhood"; he opens his ars poetica.

Un saludo a mis contrarios mando yo,

también merecen honores.

. . .

Mi saludo a Celia, Rivera, Feliciano,

esos son grandes cantores,

(Coro #1)

Ellos cantan de verdad,

siempre ponen a gozar a la gente.

(Coro #1)

Escuchen bien su cantar,

aprendan de los mejores.

[I send a salute to my rivals,

they also deserve honors.

. . .

I shout out to Celia, Rivera, Feliciano,

These singers are the big ones,

(Chorus #1)

They really sing,
They always get the people going.
(Chorus #1)
Listen up to their singing,
Learn from the best.][26]

The intergalactic message reaches the streetcorner where the guys hang out, the barrio like a coral laid out in front of El yunque. Amid the old cans of vegetable stew and corned beef, the bros jam on the drums just so you know they can. The neighborhood becomes a minor surface overrun by crabs and fossils, disinterested in Olympian gestures and grand tones of public, if well-intentioned, words. The knowledge of the names marks the return to the cave. Because only in searching do you find, and the most marvelous thing of all is to see yourself as a crab in the middle of the mangrove swamp with a lantern in your hand. But in the mangrove swamp there are also she-crabs, as Celia Cruz reminds us in no uncertain terms. The songs that she chooses and that are written with her in mind speak of (an)other gender and offer a version of the masculine violence that cannot pass unperceived here. Salsa and Celia's *azucá* (sugar) are synonyms for a moment of sweet aftertaste, for reflection on the marvel we have just heard. It's not the same when Celia cooks, even when she uses the same ingredients. But Celia knows how to talk to the boys on the corner. Fragments of Celia Cruz in *"Dos jueyes"* (Two he-crabs) speak to the "sister" (*comay*) as well as to the man:

Dos jueyes en la misma cueva—mira—.
Imposible.
No pueden vivir,
se matan a palancazos
—mira—no pueden vivir.
. . .
Y si son machos comadre,
es un revolú buscao,
la pelea está segura,
y uno de los dos talao
—digo—.
[Look, two crabs can't live in the same cave—
It's impossible.

They can't live,
they beat each other with claw-blows—
look, they can't live.

. . .

And if they're machos, girlfriend,
it's a sure mess,
the fight's guaranteed,
until one of the two is destroyed—
that's what I say—.][27]

The enclosure of the two machos in their obsessive binarism before life and the danger of leaving the cave is unhinged by the tremendous voice of the singer. The devouring of the most macho is the result of his intransigence before the hormonally inspired declaration of proprietary rights: What is mine is mine, no one enters here. This proprietariness makes Celia laugh throughout the song. Celia's soneo ridicules the uses of this delicious protuberance, the "phallic" crab claw—the appendage that helps to distinguish between the male and female crab. As always, Celia has the last bite.

Another of Celia's songs, "Burundanga," sets in motion a chain of resonances that seem to tackle the origin of violence between masculine entities. The repetitions and the apparent monotonous singsong of the arrangement underline the dead end of that desire to take into account the origin of violence; this moment contains only the arbitrariness that launches the automatic reproduction of this chain of violence:

Celia—.¿Por qué fue que Songo le dió a Borondongo?
Coro—.Porque Borondongo le dió a Bernabé.
Celia—.¿Por qué Borondongo le dió a Bernabé?
Coro—.Porque Bernabé le pegó a Muchilanga.
Celia—.¿Y por qué Bernabé le pegó a Muchilanga?
Coro—.Porque Muchilanga le echó a Burundanga.
Celia—.¿Y por qué Muchilanga le echó a Burundanga?
Coro—.Le echó a Burundanga. Le jinchan los pies.

. . .

—Burundanga.
[Celia—.Why was it that Songo hit Borondongo?
Chorus—.Because Borondongo hit Bernabé.

Celia—.Why did Borondongo hit Bernabé?

Chorus—.Because Bernabé slugged Muchilanga.

Celia—.Why did Bernabé slug Muchilanga?

Chorus—.Because Muchilanga slammed Burundanga.

Celia—.Why did Muchilanga slam Burundanga?

Chorus—.He threw Burundanga on him. He's fed up.

. . .

—Burundanga.][28]

We have already run across the name or the word "burundanga" at various times; Ismael Miranda uses it in one of his lines in the soneo "Mister Serenity": "To burundanga, to burundanga, to burundanga/ to burundanga with you."[29] It seems that this little word and Puerto Rico are attracted to each other. Without entering now into the significations and possible connotations of the word, in the case of the name in Celia's song, Burundanga is the one responsible, the one with which Celia's lips close the song. It is Burundanga who is fed up; he is the one with the key to open one of the enigmas of salsa.[30] I have written in my notebook: " 'Burundanga' might be read and heard as the axis of the salsa text, 'my discussion' on the political impossibility of a cultural and historical linearity in the Caribbean (context or utopian writing), which pulls together all of its heterogeneities." Salsa opposes the univocal. The price is anonymity and the perpetual pretense of speechlessness, speaking sometimes like an idiot, almost naming the confusion ("mixup") innocently like a faulty repetition in those games prescribed to children. It is not possible to think for a single moment of abstraction in salsa, like the negative gesture of an entity that does not yet dare to risk confronting otherness and that prefers its own shadows in the cave. Salsa as a Puerto Rican proposition that is not required, that doesn't interest it, that sucks "the essence of things." Salsa cannot think binaries, nor will salsa struggle with parallels that cannot think historical densities without flattening them out into *cuentos de bandos* (tales of the good guys against the bad). Salsa cannot think binaries because it was engendered in the same spatial distemporality as its materials. And this place was already a fiesta—humble, it's true, but what really matters is that this fiesta was not organized by any traveler on safari through the region. No idea of salsa was "abstracted" from the contexts and the political textualities that produce the conditions from which salsa could begin. We could never speak of the origin with any definitive clarity. Salsa neither reclaims nor unifies, rather whatever claims it makes on anterior tones only establishes a precedent that will not make her Immortal. Salsa never dies except in the hearing. The sophistication that accompanies salsa—and does not accompany certain other officialized musical genres with exclusive memberships like those of the tourist clubs—demands not the solidification of a single language, but rather requires the fluid obscurity of a hermeticism that everyone can understand. Puerto Rico: the tonal exception that pivots the genre because there are still things left to be done; the mixup that is capable of anything and still continues to combine flavors (tastes) in order to reclaim a space in the scenario (scene/stage). For this reason, Ismael Miranda curses the watchman who will not let him sing to his country, with the word: "To burundanga, to burundanga, to burundanga, to burundanga with you."

But we were saying that the names coincide with the titles earned in a war for the clave, a war neither easy to follow nor to end: *el sonero del pueblo* (The sonero of the people), *el Sonero mayor* (The best sonero), *el Cantante* (The singer), *la Voz* (The voice), *el Niño de Tras Talleres* (The kid from Tras Talleres), *la Rumbera mayor* (The best rumbera), *el Malo* (The bad guy), *el Niño bonito de la Fania* (The pretty boy of Fania), *el Diferente* (The different one), and so on. These epithets carried by so many soneros refer to a minor system of glory, a makeshift system of cables and cans that assures a gig and an audience. One confers through these names a stature won through song; these titles refer to battles and territories that can only be seen in their obviousness. The baptisms these titles reveal—when they relate how or why a particular name became attached to one musician or another—speak of redundancies, of the place where things began, where I was born, a hierarchy of the evident that nevertheless lends to the obvious a certain degree of immortality, a trace of the imperishable in memory, a guarantee like a letter of introduction to the public. In narrating a baptism one constructs a lineage; the naturalness of the anecdote reveals the specificity and mastery of the initiated with the pertinence and definitive entrance into the family history, into the guild, into the *Combo* of the future.

In a moving recording of "Cúcala" as a duo with the Fania All-Stars,

Celia Cruz and Ismael Rivera not only enact one of the most impressive duels in salsa, but each one cites the other, they baptize one another, they caress one another, they pay mutual homage in reciting their past accomplishments. Celia knows Maelo's lyrics from El Combo de Cortijo: Maelo has heard the *Matancera*. Only out of consideration of the constraints of space, not from any lack of love, will I refrain from quoting the song in its entirety. Here are some of my provisional notations.

This encounter between two "divinities" is a critical point in the history of the genre. Not only do the histories of their careers intertwine, but they salute each other. Following closely the production of Maelo's group, the Cortijo, especially in the doubled shout—"Ay, blessed one, the Puerto Rican" (*¡Ay bendito! puertorriqueño*)—the Master Sonero is flattered and observed by the Guarachera of Cuba. In turn he declares her reign on this earth. Celia addresses Maelo: "You are a natural-born sonero." She continues in his praise: "*Puerto de oro,* this is your sonero/ no one can stop him." Likewise, Maelo addresses the crowd and speaks of Celia—with reverence and in the third person:

Está moderna,
oye mira es un monumento,
esa negrita sabe de todo,
caballero no pierda tiempo.
[She is a modern woman,
listen up, look, she's a monument.
This sweet black woman knows everything.
Gentleman, don't waste any time.][31]

This is an institutional moment for salsa. The modernity of this entity who "plays the fool and goes out to have fun," rests in her ability to enter and exit the cave. To provoke her (*cúcala*) is to invite her to boast, to get out of the cave, to invite her to show off what she's got. This invitation is a challenge issued from the edge of the cave, to which Celia responds: "I am a modern woman, / I swear to you my dear *negrito* that I am a marvel, / I swear to you that I know everything / so if you talk to me don't tell me any stories." The possibility that the Rumba Queen might "go out"—that she might offer her knowledge/flavor (*saber/sabor*)—depends on that modernity of hers that curiously knows "everything" and that demands of the sonero that he be loyal and candid in his speech. Maelo will exceed these demands and the Fania All-Stars will go on to contemplate a piece of wonder.

The soneo is the last of those anachronisms inspired by a divine breath from the tombs of the past that inaugurate the festivity of the present. For this reason, to perform salsa is to search forever for the names and flavors found in and through the histories of violence, happiness, and slavery that the songs have resurrected. The sonero/a sings in a duel that is always already decided beforehand. Whether he or she wins or loses doesn't matter; what counts is doing the best he or she can. The sonero/a always maintains a personal relationship with the cultural masses, with the spectators and the radio listeners. They take part in a homey familiarity that has to pass through the rhythms of the spectacle and the recording studio. "Family," says Cheo Feliciano in his songs. The sonero and the sonera struggle to keep their cool in the middle of the *descarga* (blast of music). If they do, without losing the clave, it's not because they manage to establish a monolithic, unifying meaning, rather because they have converted themselves into glorious vessels capable of processing the voices and the tones that encircle and precede them. Not losing the clave is the sign of a meticulous talent. Both the soneros and the listeners make a nation of nostalgia. They make of the nation nominally known a cardboard Eden, an exalted arrangement, a community in which only Héctor Lavoe dares to set foot and briefly gesture toward the heights of the soneo the gods announce: "Get it! They put it in China"— in other words in the other world, in the beyond. Celia and Maelo have spoken in Chinese, in another tongue, about how to throw yourself into the street where you can do salsa.

The political circulation of salsa has escaped both official and patriotic conjugation simply because salsa doesn't take things too seriously (it doesn't think itself so important as to declare an Empire or a Political Party) and because it is only interested in such "clandestine" action as can be heard on every stereo and on every street corner in the Caribbean. Salsa's capacity for reproduction is so artificial that nothing more than a group of friends is required to cross-dress (*trasvestir*) or disguise salsa's musical and textual complexity. The arcane hooks up with the cheap goods in a pulsating etiquette. The arcane and the slipshod speak through this merchandise, which is hardly sold in the major markets of the world. Salsa cannot aestheticize poverty or violence, because it doesn't have anything to hide; it is dressed, or disguised, as everything, and this vestiture is what salsa carried over the middle passage along with the hunger and chains.

Little by little the soneros and soneras come to stand for leaders without tribunals, without administrative committees. This is the effect of salsa's "healthy" appearance as the everyday. The sonero is an orator without trenches. An intoxicated senator who wants to get away from the desk when he discovers himself to be a sage in the ancient wisdom from the heart of Africa. A convocator with neither caravan nor hired chair. Salsa is a game of borrowed skins. The sonero creates a tangle of voices, which the sonera unravels. The sonera is the sugar (*azúca*), the elaborate product left by the immense effort in the labor of the enslaved, the peon, the "free" wage laborer with his coffee. The sonera devours the heavy, wounded bodies of the bolero, which only she is capable of composing. She sets those bodies against the mustache and growl of the sonero. The two come together in their best key: the conservation among friends. They are always addressing friends, as if here we were to find the real United Nations. There is always a call for movement, for the recognition of the body's capacities to negotiate differences. In the physical recognition of the dancer we find an entrance into the politics of salsa. In the musician's solo, salsa partners up and shows off its skill. The challenge, the defiant gesture in salsa is a digestive process, a steady payment made in lines and explosions. What the serious call the "possibilities of language" in salsa is a voice-activated switch flipped on by song. Moreover, this switch is not a "possibility," but rather the very reason for being behind salsa's precarious pose—behind the cardboard force of the song. The cohabitation of languages, the rubbing together of bodies, the cheek-to-cheek of opposed forces is in salsa a temporal process. This friction forms a musical space in which everything fits; *it is the musical piece*. The contemplation that prepares us for death must be musical.

The sonero and the sonera know that their work is not that of fortune-teller for hire by the establishment. The genre emerges in an attempt to elaborate a configuration of the present before we lose it through urbanization, forced diaspora, deforestation, and debt. The genre appears in order to transcribe a space in the present tense. In the offering of the family circle, salsa cooks up the flavor of its projects. Salsa is a genre ready for battle, decidedly with an attitude; only in this way is it possible to argue with the administrators of the future, with those who wish to have their orchestra seat reserved without knowing what the concert is about, in order to know how it is that "the natives" move: "remember that we are movement and bodies bathed in sweat beneath a palm tree drinking piña coladas."

I'm going now. The ear as the point of access to the commodity of salsa; the primary function: to break through the boundaries of the enclosure and declare an auditory "free territory in the Americas." Extract the nationality of the ghetto, decolonize the land; haul everything out of the closet in order to reformulate and interrogate the rights of possession. To call things by their name has never been easy. With Cheo Feliciano, I'm going:

Bello digo al sol que nace,
porque nace para todos,
aunque no tengo la casa mía
y puedo usar la de otro.
—.Bendito, pero la vida es así,
¿y qué voy a hacer? ¡Ay Dios mío!
[I say the sun is beautiful when it is born,
because it is born for everyone,
even though I don't have a house of my own
I can use the house of another.
—.Blessed be, that's the way life goes.
What am I going to do about it? Ay, my lord!][32]

With Maelo, I'm going, I'm going, I'm gone: "Pero que el mar me tumbó mi casita, / pero como me gusta el ruidito volví a hacerla [But even if the sea topples my little house / since I love the sea's sounds I'll rebuild her again]."[33]

Notes

This text is a preliminary version of one of the essays that will comprise a book in and about salsa. I have been working in this topic since spring of 1989. The present text is a poetic celebration of the incredible perplexity and joy that this music has given me, even if for brief moments. I only aspire to initiate a dialogue with some of the gestures that salsa articulates. This is a critical celebration of salsa's generous intermittance; a salute to salsa's unbridled sharpness, to salsa's instinctive histories. I am grateful for the conversations and suggestions of Ivette Rodríguez, Israel Ruíz Cumba, Celeste Fraser Delgado, and Carlos Cortés during the preparation and translation of this text.

1. *Morcilla* is a pork blood sausage, hot and spicy most of the time, and mainly served during the Christmas season.

2. Jacking off or fooling around.

3. Angel Guillermo Quintero Rivera, "La música puertorriqueña y la contra-cultura democrática; espontaneidad libertaria de la herencia cimarrona," *Folklore Americano* 49 (January–June 1990): 135–167. Future references will be in the text.

4. Quintero Rivera convincingly notes the complexity of this process of amplification in the notion of the Caribbean by recounting the practices of the surveillance and regulation of converts such as Jews and Moors who for diverse reasons adopted the Christian religion in Spain and the Americas from the sixteenth to the eighteenth centuries.

5. See Gilles Deleuze and Félix Guattari, *A Thousand Plateaus: Capitalism and Schizophrenia,* translation and foreword by Brian Massumi (Minnesota: U of Minnesota P, 1987).

6. Josefina Ludmer, "Tretas del débil," in *La sartén por el mango,* ed. Elena González and Eliana Ortega (Rio Piedras: Ediciones Huracán, 1984), 47–54.

7. But don't you believe it all, brother. And if I slipped up and said it, I'm sorry, I know there's nothing that can be done.

8. José Arteaga, in the first chapter of his book *La salsa,* under the headings *La salsa* and *El otro diá fui a bailar a la ruñidera y me encontré la salsa,* narrates a fascinating version of how the term "salsa" came into use as the etiquette that accompanies the production of the salseros. Arteaga proposes that it was the film *Salsa* (1973–1974) that catapulted the name internationally, even though he recognizes that another history could be traced with a duration of more than a century. Arteaga, following in the footsteps of the producers Ralph Mercado (Puerto Rican) and Jerry Massuci (North American Jew) in New York in the 1970s, establishes that, through the preparation and absolute success of the concert of August 21, 1973, in the ballroom El Cheetah, at which performed the best musicians of the Massuci label (Fania Records), both producers saw the musical and commercial possibilities of the genre. According to Arteaga, already in 1973 Ralph Mercado was a "highly valued impressario of Latin music in New York" and Masucci saw the profits from his recording business multiply. Nevertheless, it is the concert episode at Yankee Stadium on August 24, 1973, that detonated the name of the genre. Arteaga mentions some references to a possible origin for the word; for example, recalling the work of Fernando Ortíz he points out the uses of the word during the breaks from work of enslaved people in Cuba, the uses of the word in 1928 by the Cuban Ignacio Piñeiro in his son "Échale salsita," and the immortal exclamations of Beny Moré in the middle of his songs, among others. How-

ever, it is with the production under the Masucci label of two albums and two films, directed by Leon Gast, entitled *Nuestra cosa/Our Latin Thing* and *Salsa,* that the term came to be associated with the genre as a cultural commodity. The two albums and the films took up the concert in El Cheetah. The film *Salsa,* with great pretensions both artistic and commercial, alternates images of the concert of the Fania All-Stars—directed by the Dominican Johnny Pacheco—in Yankee Stadium with everyday-life images of the Hispanic community in the United States. Masucci even borrows from the archives of Hollywood, taking images from the films of Dolores del Río, the Castro sisters, and Desi Arnaz to include in the film. The montage of these images focused a larger public while offering a history that should be included and associated with the product (salsa) and the salsa community. The main course of the movie was, of course, Yankee Stadium, which was planned for this purpose. Still, the public that attended the concert literally broke the barriers that separated them from the musicians during the presentation, resulting in the event's cancellation. Even so, the film *Salsa* was subsequently released under the Fania Records label and surpassed the box office success of *Nuestra cosa.* (See José Arteaga, *La salsa* [Bogotá: Intermedio Editores, 1990]), and Juan Carlos Báez, *El vínculo de la salsa* [Caracas: Dirección de Cultura-UCV, Fondo Editorial Tropykos, Grupo Editor Derrelieve, 1985]).

9. Willie Colón, "Interview with Willie Colón," by Frank Parilla Jr., *La Klave* 1.2 (November–December, 1988): 32; emphasis added. The critical discographic production of Willie Colón, Héctor Lavoe, and Rubén Blades will be discussed in a separate chapter in the book I am preparing. It is impossible to speak of salsa and not touch upon productions such as *Lo Mato, La gran fuga, Maestra Vida, Siembra, Canciones del Solar de los Aburridos.* How could we not talk about the phenomenon of "Pedro Navaja"? I will anticipate myself in saying that Colón and Blades probably changed the direction and form of the genre more than any other salsa combination. The trombone of Colón and his work with Puerto Rican rhythms, the impressive soneos of Lavoe, and the compositions of Blades deserve more study. The genre necessarily changes and becomes affiliated with a new series when lines like these appear: "como en una novela da Kafka el borracho dobló por el callejón [like in the novel by Kafka, the drunk turns into the alley]."

10. Josefina Ludmer, *El género guachesco: Un tratado sobre la patria* (Buenos Aires: Editorial Sudamericana, 1988).

11. See Jorge Meléndez, "Un futurista que no olvida sus raíces," *La Klave* 1.1 (September–October, 1988): 23.

12. César Miguel Rondón, *El libro de la salsa: Crónica de la música del Caribe urbano* (Caracas: Editorial Arte, 1980 [1985]), 63.

13. "La perla," written by T. Curet Alsonso, vocals by Ismael Rivera, *Ismael Rivera y sus cachimbos: Esto sí es lo mío,* 5:26, Tico Records, JMTS 1428, 1978. [For our readers who do not read Spanish, I have approximated as best I can the meaning of the songs. However, that approximation is at times necessarily remote, so I have included the author's original transcription of the songs as well. *Trans.*]

14. The literal translation of *negrito* is "little black man," of *negrita* is "little black woman." But within Puerto Rican culture this word has manifold interpretations. To grasp Maelo's use of the word it will be better if we recall Pedro Pietri's rendering at the end of his well-known poem "Puerto Rican Obituary": "Aquí Qué Pasa Power is what's happening / Aquí to be called negrito / means to be called LOVE" (Pedro Pietri, *Obituario puertorriqueño/Puerto Rican Obituary*, trans. A. Matilla Rivas [San Juan: Instituto de Cultura Puertorriqueña, 1977]).

15. "El nazareno," lyrics by D. R., vocals by Ismael Rivera, *Fania All-Stars Live*, live version, 5:40, Fania, JM CD 00515, 1978; emphasis added. In *Eclipse total*, Tico records, LPS 88606, 1975, Henry Williams appears as the author of "El nazareno."

16. "El incomprendido," lyrics by Bobby Capó, *Eclipse total*, Tico Records, LPS 88606, 1975.

17. A similar "spectacle" took place at Héctor Lavoe's funeral in New York during the summer of 1993.

18. "During the Summer of 1887, as a response to some reports on the activities of Secret Societies operating in the Island, [Spanish Governor Romualdo Palacios] unleashed a wave of repression which principally affected the towns of Juana Díaz and Ponce. During the following weeks, arbitrary arrests, abuses, and torture against the prisoners were numerous, as were threats to the press and free expression. This State's effort to sow panic in the countryside encouraged some members of the Conservative Party to organize their own inquiries and violent acts" (Fernando Picó, *Historia general de Puerto Rico* [Río Piedras: Huracán-Academia, 1986], 213).

19. Sidney Mintz, *Sweetness and Power: The Place of Sugar in Modern History* (New York: Penguin Books, 1985).

20. "Vámonos pal monte," lyrics by Eddie Palmieri and Ismael Quintana, vocals by Ismael Quintana, *Eddie Palmieri and His Orchestra: Vámonos pal monte*, 7:08, Tico Records, T-1225, 1978.

21. "Vasos en colores," lyrics by Hugo González, vocals by Marvin Santiago, *Marvin Santiago: Fuego a la Jicotea*, TH Rodven, THS 2061, 1984.

22. "Señor Sereno," lyrics and vocals by Ismael Miranda, *Jerry Masucci Presents: Super Salsa Singers*, Vol. 3, 5:20, Fania, JM 580, 1980. This album is an anthology of songs.

23. In the *Diccionario de uso del español* (Dictionary of Spanish usage) by María Moliner, (Madrid: Gredos, 1988), we find the following under "sereno": "A man who patrols the street during the night from the hour at which the portals are closed. They have keys to the portals and they open the doors to the homes of neighbors who return home after this hour. They used to sing out the hour, adding afterwards a report on the weather. For example: 'Three o'clock on the dot and clear/calm (*sereno*).' "

24. "Ni hablar," lyrics by Anam Munar, vocals by Celia Cruz, *Celia y Johnny: Tremendo caché*, 3:09, Vaya VSCD-37, 1975.

25. See the songs "Mi gente" in *Héctor Lavoe "La Voz,"* lyrics by Johnny Pacheco, arrangement by Willie Colón, 5:23 Fania, SLP 00461, 1975; and the interpretations by Willie Colón of Bill Seidman/Willie Colón's "Falta de consideración," 5:20, and Willie

Colón's "El diablo," 6:37, Willie Colón, *Tiempo pa' Matar,* Fania, JM 631: 1984. For Ismael Miranda: "Venceré," lyrics and vocals by Ismael Miranda, *Orquesta Harlow & Ismael Miranda: Con mi viejo amigo,* 4:21, Fania, SLP 494, 1976.

26. "El cantante," lyrics by Rubén Blades, vocals by Héctor Lavoe, *Comedia,* 10:17, Fania, JM 00522, 1978. This album was produced by Willie Colón.

27. "Dos jueyes," lyrics by Tito Curet Alonso, vocals by Celia Cruz, *Celia y Willie,* Vaya Records, LPS 99417, 1981. In a homage to the Cuban women of mixed African and European ancestry (*la mulata cubana*), Celia assembles and sings a continental rumba in "Dulce habanera," which calls to and names almost all of the nationalities of Latin America through the feminine gentilic noun. This is the convocation of the rumbera, baptized in the song as a salsera, to a women's *bembé* (party). And as always in the soneo: "La puertorriqueña es la más salsera" (The Puerto Rican woman is the best salsera). The surface of the genre itself has genders, and these are not always in perpetual accord. See "Dulce habanera," lyrics by D.R., vocals by Celia Cruz, *Cruz & Colón: Only They Could Have Made This Album,* 4:03, Vaya Records, JMVS 66, 1977.

28. "Burundanga," lyrics by D.R., vocals by Celia Cruz, *Cruz & Colón: Only They Could Have Made This Album,* 2:56, Vaya Records, 1977. "Burundanga" is one of many songs that, having been recorded previous to the phenomenon of salsa, would be arranged and recorded again by salsa musicians. Recycling, or the actualization of certain songs, is another of the genre's modes of incorporating times and spaces.

29. It's not a bad idea to turn now to poet Luis Palés Matos and to his book, *Tún tún de pasa y grifería* (1925–1937). In his celebrated poem "Canción festiva para ser llorada," we find the following strophe repeated in the manner of a break between series of longer strophes: "Cuba—ñáñigo y bachata— / Haiti—vodú y calabaza— / Puerto Rico—burundanga" (Luis Palés Matos, *Tún tún de pasa y grifería,* ed. Mercedes López-Baralt [San Juan: Instituto de Cultura Puertorriqueña y Editorial de la Universidad de Puerto Rico, 1993]). In the second edition of *Tún tún de pasa y grifería* (1950) burundanga has been defined as the "amorphous mix-up of heterogeneous things (Puerto Rico)."

30. "Le jinchan los pies"—which can be literally translated as "he got his feet swollen"—perhaps hides, as an expression, a double connotation. "To get one's feet swollen" could be a reference to the shackles of slavery; but also it could allude to men's testicles as a way of expressing annoyance to the chain of violence, which ends in "Burundanga" something like: "I'm up to my balls" (*estoy encojonao*).

31. "Cúcala," lyrics by Wilfrido Figueroa, duet version with Celia Cruz and Ismael Rivera, *Fania All-Stars Live,* 6:26, Fania, JMCD00515, 1978. Both have earlier versions of the song. See Cruz with Johnny Pacheco on *Celia y Johnny: Tremendo caché* and Maelo with *Combo de Cortijo: Ismael y Cortijo: Los dos grandes para siempre, sus 16 éxitos,* Armanda y Fernández of Florida, CD 8002.

32. "Desahogo," vocals by Cheo Feliciano, *Estampas,* composed by Juan Antonio Corretjer and José Nogueras, Vaya Records, 4XT-JMVS 86, 1979.

33. "La perla," lyrics by T. Curet Alonso, vocals by Ismael Rivera, *Ismael Rivera y sus cachimbos: Esto sé es lo mío,* 5:26, Tico Records, JMRS 1428, 1978.

Una verdadera crónica del Norte

Una noche con la India

Augusto C. Puleo   *Translated from Spanglish by Celeste Fraser Delgado*

I, myself, was my own route.—Julia de Burgos

The moment has arrived for raising our voices, which have been mute
for so long, in order to prove that—as women and as human beings—we
are strong and we are the nation.—Luisa Capetillo

Here I am . . . if you want to know.—La India

July 12, 1995: Carnegie Hall: The Espectáculo Billed as Two Queens and a
Lion: La India, Celia Cruz and Oscar De Leon.

Nenes, if you weren't there, you missed it! Everyone was there: the
lumpen from the South Bronx, the entire barrio, even Filadelfia was
present. Families from Condado, Santurce, and the capital, "Mi viejo San
Juan," had taken the "air bus" to pay homage to "The Queen of Puerto
Rican Salsa"—as Celia Cruz called her when she crowned her last year.
There were more people there than turned out to meet the newest Puerto
Rican Miss Universe in San Juan two years ago (you know we already
have three, even though we aren't even a country yet). You are probably
wondering qué carajo, what kind of scholarship is this? Well, moments in
my life have shaped who I have become or what I think . . . I guess it
could be called theorizing through autobiography. So let me try to bring
you back with me, using the genre of the chronicle as adapted by Puerto
Rican writers Ana Lydia Vega and Edgardo Rodríguez Juliá.[1] Let me
recapture for you this "noche con la India"—this night with la India.

Here I am seated in the darkness of Carnegie Hall, perfectly seduced
by my aficionado's solitude. Nevertheless, I am not alone, even though
the theater is completely dark. I hear the soft sounds anticipating the
apparition, her appearance. I find myself halfway between dreaming
and observation, indecisive between the genres of the false chronicle and

the true. This is a difficult equation: I should bear witness and at the same time I should rescue myself from this turbulent enemy there outside, the euphoria of seeing and hearing a queen coronated.

At 8:00 on the dot, seconds before the show is going to start, the doors are flung open and in come four Indias—with closer scrutiny aren't they las dragas, the drag queens from La Escuelita, that famous bar close to the Port Authority Bus Station? Which one of the four will win our applause, which is the most India of all, and who did they know to get those front row seats next to the row of "patas" / dykes wearing lipstick and leather vests? At 8:05 on the dot the great impresarial mogul Ralphie Mercado, the Berry Gordy of Salsa, comes out to plug his next two shows: la India and the Barrio Boyz, and la India and Kid Frost. Afterwards, he screams into the microphone ironically: "Señoras y señores! Ladies and gentlemen, the Queen of Puerto Rico, la India!!!" Deafening applause. La India appears on the stage out of nowhere. Fantasy radiates light, while my gaze is hidden in darkness. As the lights shine more brightly, each fan, including me, has erased a little bit more of her/his solitude; as in the cinema, in the darkness, we are all converted into solitary spectators of the film. The illuminated scene is as voracious as she is. Her luminescence illuminates us. Even though the scene disrobes her, her power over us is such that we remain completely absorbed in her, la India, the chimera of desire. The irreality of her show and her music seduces me with each note that she sings and each step that she dances.

Immediately we enter into the substance. From the first note la India sings, she plays the role of the seductress. She plays the schoolgirl who flirts with everyone, women and men. She is the woman who innocently bends over to pick up a book or a piece of paper that a little boy dropped on the floor on purpose. She is the girl in high school that everyone wanted to date. However, she—la India, a woman—is singing salsa. Isn't that odd? At this exact moment, I remember the words of the Puerto Rican musician Jorge Manuel "el Giro" López, who asserts that "Salsa used to have a nasty image, with its sexuality and rough performers. It used to be all about the timbales and bongó, but now it's about sweet and elegant words, and the girls like it much more than the earlier, macho salsa."[2] The sexist, misogynist, and machista ways of thinking and behaving been reflected and glorified in the patriarchy of salsa music.

We have all sung along with the lyrics of the famous Pedro Navaja, who lives in the city of 20 million stories, but who is a player or an assassin. And who can forget that Juan Pachangas is a mamito, or playboy? What these two salsa figures have in common is that they were both done wrong by women: one a prostitute who kills Pedro Navaja and the other a lover who has deceived the supposedly macho Juan Pachangas. As I see and hear la India, I remember the words of the musicologist Jorge Duany, who wrote that salsa is "clearly a male's vision of the world; like most salsa songs, it was conceived and written by a man, and executed mostly by men."[3] For this world of salsa, the female morena (dark woman) is an alien object that is never fully understood, always feared and desired at once. The woman projected in salsa songs is only represented as a source of pain and pleasure, but never as a person in her own right.

So la India is singing now, and next on the bill is Celia Cruz. Can they both be encoded as masculine figures? A man's power is enhanced by singing salsa, but does a female salsera diminish her femininity? Soon my mind starts to wander as I remember the poster at the entrance to Carnegie Hall—a poster of la India with a cigar in her mouth. Can you imagine the commentary the night before when the elite of the Upper East Side came to hear the Philadelphia Symphony Orchestra, and they found this poster of la India with a cigar in the lobby? That image, bold and colorful like that of la Virgen de la Caridad, evokes a sense of promise and possibility, a vision of freedom. Feminist in the sense that she dares to transgress sexist boundaries. With a cigar in her mouth, she reclaims the female body as a site of power and hope. As Yvonne Yarbro-Bejarano states in her essay "Deconstructing the Lesbian Body": "The mouth plays a crucial role in a sexual/textual project, fusing two taboo activities, female speaking and sexuality." La India graphically and symbolically shows how "the mouth and the cunt merge, both represented as organs of speech and sex."[4]

I can't help but remember the closing words of the essay "A Long Line of Vendidas" by Cherríe Moraga: "My mouth cannot be controlled. It will flap in the wind like legs in sex . . . It's as if la boca were centered on el centro del corazón, not in the head at all."[5] La India has reconstructed her body around her mouth and words. Lacan imparted to us his idea of the "symbolic law of the father," which he insists is entrenched in lan-

La India, salsa's new queen.

(CD liner from la India, *Dicen Que Soy,* Sony Tropical)

guage. He argues that language is wrought with symbols that dictate patriarchal power, as Emma Pérez skillfully explains in her reading of Foucault's *History of Sexuality:* "In a single paragraph, Foucault 'thrust,' 'penetrated,' 'rigidified,' and 'extended power.' In his discussion, he, like Freud, dismisses women, and exalts the phallus, again because women do not have 'one.' "[6] Well, la India shows that she has and does not have one, and thereby subverts the law of patriarchy. La India has learned about patriarchy's language and symbols in order to parody them, invert

226

them, and finally subvert masculine power. For she gains access to power and privilege in her reappropriating of words and symbol that had been denied her.

Other artists, such as Frida Kahlo, participated in the same type of subversion. How can one forget that memorable photo taken by her sister in 1942 when she cross-dressed as a man to gain a voice and therefore be taken seriously as an artist? Of course, I remember the famous Kahlo painting *Autorretrato con pelo cortado* (1940)—one of the numerous self-portraits of Kahlo dressed as a man, with scissors in her hands that apparently have been used to cut her own hair. She appears as a man with her cut hair strewn about the floor. Looking closely, one sees that there are verses written at the top of the painting that are just as important as the painted image. The picture in itself is problematic and even more complicated by the words that crown the work: "Mira que si te quise / fue por el pelo / Ahora que estás pelona / ya no te quiero [See that if I loved you / it was for your hair / Now that you're bald / I don't love you anymore]." This declaration is ambiguous, even ironic, since the poetic voice here is masculine. These words seem directed to a woman by a man. As the painter assumes a masculine voice while dressed as a man, she reappropriates the use of dominant rhetoric in order to subvert it. Her short hair and masculine clothing shout out a contradiction of the verse written on the top of the painting. With scissors in hand, Kahlo not only testifies that she has cut her own hair, destroying the myth that long hair represents femininity, but in addition her act of painting is a sign of liberation when she assumes the power and symbols that have traditionally been associated with men.

In the same vein, the great Puerto Rican poet Julia de Burgos in her poem "Pentacromia" (1943) wrote the telling verses: "Hoy, quiero ser hombre. Sería Don Juan. Sería un Quijote. Sería el Alonso Quijano verdad . . . [Today, I want to be a man. I could be Don Juan. I could be Quixote. I could be the real Alonso Quijano . . .]."[7] The vocalization of these sentiments by de Burgos demonstrates her recognition that power in love, art, and creation belongs in the domain of men. Even though de Burgos does not dress like a man, she states in her poem "Quiero ser un hombre [I want to be a man]." As seen by their art, both of these women have symbolically crossed from the world of powerlessness to a world of privilege.

Which leads me to remember a portrait of Luisa Capetillo, taken in Havana in 1915. In the photo, as described by the Puerto Rican critic Julio Ramos, she "is shown with a panama hat, with a broad brim, slightly inclined and shading the left side of her face. She wears a white shirt, with a high collar, firmly buttoned beneath the knot of her tie. The lines of the female body are unrecognizable beneath the loose cloth. The pant-legs do not cover the man's shoes she wears. In effect, Capetillo appears here dressed as a man." However, this strong political statement by Capetillo comes with a price: this photo was taken just before she was arrested "for using clothes meant only for men."[8]

Being known as the "first woman to wear pants in Puerto Rico," as documented by Norma Valle Ferrer in her book *Luisa Capetillo*, Capetillo responds to the dominant culture of her epoch by breaking boundaries and impugning with precision aspects only apparently insignificant in everyday life. Capetillo reappropriates and uses literary discourse to destroy the myth of gender and class.[9] In her writings and speeches, she subverts the idea that working-class women could not participate in the creation of Puerto Rico and its society. The "phallus"/cigar takes on new meanings. The cigar is free-floating in space, not attached to any human body but in the hands of la India, demonstrating her control over her own sexuality. All of us boricuas recognize how a cigar in a woman's mouth often connotes a *curandera* who has special powers to first clean an area with the smoke from a cigar and then to start "diciendo la verdad" (speaking the truth). In addition, the cigar takes on a certain historical significance as I link it with Luisa Capetillo. This great Puerto Rican intellectual was self-taught. She worked as a reader in a cigar factory in Arecibo. At that time, a cigar factory was among other things, a cultural space where many free-thinking socialists and anarchists received an alternative education, an education frequently offered by young people, who often served as readers. Capetillo read aloud to workers as they rolled tobacco. As Bernardo Vega points out in his memoirs: "The institution of factory readings made the *tabaqueros* into the most enlightened sector of the working class."[10] In her provocative essays, Capetillo writes that for centuries women have been considered objects of little value, war booty, slaves, and even "domestic slaves." She affirms that "today we sing of our liberty, which we had acquired by divine right, since men and women are born the same way." As the first "feminist" in Puerto

Rico, Capetillo with her essays attacks old rules of patriarchy, especially those that restrict women in the workplace, the house, and even in the social institution of marriage. She asks: "Why can the man always be at a woman's side at dances, at the theater before marriage, then after he has her for his mate he leaves her alone at home and goes out with other women?" Her answer is universalist as she responds that we should all contribute our energies and will to substituting the restrictive traditional customs that are obstacles in the way of progress. She continues, postulating that "if women were represented, educated and emancipated from routine formalities as fit them, the politics of the people would be different." This reintegration, proposed by Capetillo, with a whole new set of rules allows for the self/selves to grow.[11]

By now, lost in my thoughts, I realize that la India has moved from her first number to a song that I do not recognize from her albums. The transitional minisong is a gospel-like blues hymn sung in English, but with Latin overtones. All of these music-loving Latino/as around me, of course, know that the Cuban *son* and *clave* are the main ingredients in the structural arrangements of Salsa; however, major cultural elements and social realities as well as representative experiences of barrio people have also combined to form the musical foundation of salsa style. From the stage, one hears the distinctive sounds of the *maracas* and *guiro*, two popular instruments in Puerto Rico that reflect the native Taino indigenous culture, which la India and her band have incorporated into the rhythmic instrumental arrangement of her songs. The dance and chants of the Afro–Puerto Rican tradition, embodied in the folkloric bomba and plena, represent another set of traditional Puerto Rican cultural elements. We boricuas know that the bomba was the dance of plantation sugarcane workers and was named after a wooden drum covered with goatskin. The bomba is the blending of both non-Hispanic and Spanish elements, the latter being evident in the rhythmic instruments used. These patterns establish an African beat. The rhythm of the plena, music of the Puerto Rican townspeople, is African but the melodies are Spanish. Thus the fusion of both of these distinctive elements evolved into a combination dance-song, but today it is specifically a song. Rafael Cortijo, who came from the town of Loiza Aldea, known as the center of Afro–Puerto Rican music, is the best example of one performer whose music was embraced by the rhythmic patterns of the popular bomba and plena, and whose distinctive sounds are still heard in the music of salsa musicians and singers such as la India.

The beats and sounds lead me to the words of Frances Aparicio, who has asserted: "Salsa music functions as an ethnic marker for Latinos in the United States."[12] It is our cultural expression, a true artistic product that finds its genesis in the everynight life of el barrio, the South Bronx, Filadelfia. Thus it is analogous to Nuyorican poetry. The music and the poetry are defined by the urban conditions from which they arise, sharing a violent, almost raw language. In poetry, this translates into a refusal to follow the lyrical modes of literature; in salsa, the violence and diction of the lyrics, coupled with the harsh sounds of the brass section, challenge the lyrical sounds of traditional boleros and rumbas. Both salsa and Nuyorican poetry derive from syncretic forms of orality: the everyday speech of working-class communities and of African Americans in the United States. These art forms represent forms of cultural resistance to anglicization, even though the lyrics are often reactionary and retrograde in their depiction of women. The songs reaffirm Latino ethnic identity and the presence of African roots in our community. While Salsa has syncretized jazz, blues, and rock within its repertoire, it has never given up its clave rhythm or its polyrhythmic Afro-Caribbean forms, not to mention the Spanish lyrics. I sat and thought of the indigenous and Afro-Caribbean traditions in the salsa of la India, and how they interweave with black and other Caribbean cultures in the United States since shared and parallel social experiences primarily influence the cultures, the language, and here the music of working people.

However, one cannot escape the definite soulful quality in the minisong of la India. Of course, we all knew her as a house singer who opened acts for rock singers for years. For Americans, the figure of the female blues singer has been reconstructed in poetry, drama, fiction, art, and music and used to mediate upon conventional and unconventional power and sexuality. Many narratives both fictional and biographical have mythologized women blues singers and these same works have become texts about sexuality. These same singers, like la India, appear as liminal figures that play out and explore the various possibilities of sexual experience. In addition, they are representations of women who attempt to manipulate and control their construction as sexual objects. The blues singer often has a strong physical and sensuous presence. Sherley

Anne Williams in a poem about Bessie Smith writes: "Bessie singing / just behind the beat / that sweet sweet / voice throwing / its light on me."[13] In an essay, Williams argues that blues singers and their songs "helped to solidify community values and heighten community morale in the late nineteenth and early twentieth centuries."[14] She reinforces her statement by demonstrating that the female blues singer uses song to create reflection and an atmosphere for analysis to take place. The blues were certainly a communal expression of black experience that had developed out of the call-and-response patterns of work songs from the nineteenth century and that have been described as a "complex interweaving of the general and the specific" and of individual and group experience. John Coltrane has described how the audience heard "we" even if the singer said "I."[15] Of course, singers are entertainers, but the blues are not an entertainment of escape or fantasy, but often address historical or social events. La India's salsa is part of the discourse of human and sexual relations within the Latino community, especially of those boricuas who emigrated, for emigration had distinctively different meanings for men and women.

Celia Cruz, la India, and female blues singers have broken out of the boundaries of the home and taken their sensuality and sexuality out of the private into the public. For these singers were/are overflowing with talent and often stunning in appearance; in fact, their presence has often elevated them to being referred to as the Queen, the Goddess, the Empress, la Reina. This physical presence is a crucial aspect of their power. The visual display of spangled dresses, furs, gold teeth, diamonds, along with all the sumptuous and desirable aspects of their body help to reclaim female sexuality from being an objectification of male desire to a representation of female desire. These women undermine mythologies of phallic power and establish a series of woman-centered demands. La India accuses her lover of betrayal: "me traicionaste."

In the interlude, I glance over to see the ironic presence of the man who epitomizes "Puerto Rican machismo." None other than Hector Macho Camacho, who has strategically placed himself in the corner of the stage facing the audience. In case you don't know who he is: he is the world featherweight champion. How small he stands there with a silk offwhite tropical suit, sporting his signature medallion that is bigger than life (and his chest), with the name Macho Camacho spelled out in 24-carat gold and trying to steal the spotlight. However, la India has complete control. Someone shouts "We love you, India" as she moves onto the next salsa song, "Ese hombre" (This man). In Spanish, she accuses her lover of *traición* (betrayal). She unleashes a volley of insults after describing him as "amable, seguro y aparece ser divino . . . Es un gran necio, un éstupido ingreído, egoista y caprichoso [amiable, confident, and seems a divine being . . . is a big idiot, a stupid X, egotistical and capricious]. The salsa song, like the soulful fragment sung by la India, exercises her power and control over sexuality.

La India threads together the many issues of power and sexuality and seeks possibilities that arise for women on the move who confidently assert their own sexuality and desirability. I can't help hearing the echoes of Bessie Smith and Ida Cox in the song, especially that famous "One Hour Mama": "I don't want no lame excuses, / 'bout my loving being so good, / That you couldn't wait no longer / Now I hope I'm under-stood."[16] Or la India's debt to soul music, especially Aretha's "Think about whatcha trying to do to me / Think and let yourself be free."[17]

For the Puerto Rican salsera, expressions of powerful sexuality are nec-essarily linked to the questions of Puerto Rican national identity. During this song, a woman's voice is heard above the crowd as she shouts "Viva Puerto Rico!" Another voice, a man's this time, continues the scream as he adds "Viva Puelto Rico Libreeeeeeee" (Long live a free Puerto Rico), in the style of Suzie Bermudez de Vega's "Pollito Chicken"! As the literary critic Arcadio Díaz Quiñones has reiterated numerous times: "All Puerto Rican artists and writers have to address and come to terms with the problems of national identity and the status of our territory."[18] Since our magic number is three—three political possibilities, as reflected in our name, Estado Libre Asociado/Free Associated State; three acts in the play *La carreta* (The oxcart)—there is a third segment to this unplanned, unrehearsed drama being written and created spontaneously in Carnegie Hall before our eyes. A young man dressed in hip-hop style—oversized jeans, a shirt, and a baseball cap proudly displaying the location BRONX—salsas to the stage and hands la India a small Puerto Rican flag, which she accepts and continues to hold and wave for the remainder of the show.

As the music embraces me, I fall into thoughts about salsa music and how, at a more sophisticated level, musical intertexts and subtexts sug-gest that listening to music and dancing are ways of acquiring knowledge about the world around us and Latino culture in general. However, it also empowers one to achieve authority and control as a community that has been influenced and exploited by mainstream currents. In other words, the popular salsa de la India reclaims the community identity and authority of Latinos through the symbolic power of ethnicity and control. La banderita puertorriqueña seems to have made a U-turn, like the carreta, as the small lonely flag seems to have lost its direction along the Puerto Rican Parade route on Fifth Avenue and, after passing 58th Street, to get itself set back on the course of real historical and cultural experience.[19] After all, can music written and performed in English, Spanish, and/or a mixture of both be considered contemporary North American music and/or Puerto Rican music? The very groping for a category in which to place a characteristic singer or songs quickly lands us at the center of the assimilation controversy, the problems of multiculturalism, and the problematics of identity construction.

During the song, a voice is heard—"La India is in the house"—which leads us to the name: la India. Born Linda Caballero in the South Bronx, she is the married mother of two nenes. ("No," insists one of my panas upon hearing her songs: tortillera/dyke). Now she is known as "la India," baptized with that name due to her physical resemblance to a person from India. Or really, in Puerto Rico los indios, as named by Colón, were the indigenous Tainos and Caribs. Those who make up the forgotten basement of *El país de cuatro pisos* (The four-Storied house), by José Luis González. This essayist metaphorically constructs Puerto Rican national identity as a house of four floors. The first is the most stable and represents the strong African influence on the island. The second floor is composed mainly of European emigrants from England, France, Holland, and elsewhere. He postulates that in 1898 the North American invasion sparks the building of the third floor, on top of "the second poorly furnished floor." The fourth floor, as he describes it, is cracking and divided since it is built upon North American capitalism and Puerto Rican popular opportunism as found in the 1940s.[20] However, our great contractor forgot the "attic," which are the boricuas who have emigrated and now live in the cities of New York, Philadelphia, Chicago, Miami, Boston, and so on. In addition, his famous essay does not take into account women, gays, lesbians, or others who do not fit easily into his categories. So when la India starts singing and signifying, it is very easy to see now that perhaps she is the symbol or another manifestation of multiple Puerto Rican identity/identities.

As she begins her last song of the set, la India sings the "national anthem": "Dicen que yo" (They say about me). She boldly stands aloof and menacing as she tells everyone that you can talk and say what you want, "estoy aquí" (I'm here). "Dicen que soy" is the chorus of a song that insists that la India is not a traditional *chis mosa* (gossip); however, the unnamed "they" are. In the phrase, the only defined person is the pronoun "yo," since many others anonymously say about me . . . Yes, we have been called "a sick people" and "a wasted body," characterized by "our permanent docility," as Antonio Pedreira writes in *Insularismo* (Insularity).[21] René Marqués echoes the sentiments of Pedreira in an essay entitled "El dócil puertorriqueño" (The docile Puerto Rican), describing us as "orphans of Spain the mother and the United States, the godfather"—children who cannot control our own destiny.[22] Our powerlessness is seen in his creative works. In particular the short story "En la popa hay un cuerpo reclinado" shows a man who castrates himself because of his powerlessness.[23] All of us who have seen *La carreta* have seen how men are nonexistent from the beginning or totally without any power or authority: the son in prison and the *abuelito* in a cave who refuses to participate in modern Puerto Rican history and emigration. In the short story "Osadía," Emilio Díaz Valcárcel represented the hope for our future in the form of a mannish-dressing, unnamed lesbian.[24] With this story, Díaz Valcárcel subverts and rebels against the destructive masculine ideology and patriarchal construction of nationhood. La India takes this idea one step farther.

As I witness and hear the new hit by la India:

Dicen que soy una gata negra . . . que he castrado tu mente, que he devorado tu razón, que te tengo embrujado, soy fruta envenenada. Tambien soy una manzana envenenada, una flor engañosa, poca cosa para ti y una pobre disfrazada.
[They say that I am a black cat . . . that I have castrated your mind, I have devoured your reason, that I have bewitched you, that I am a poisoned fruit. They also say I am a poisoned apple, a deceptive flower, not good enough for you and dressed up trash.][25]

In her lyrics la India reclaims and reappropriates all of these myths, starting with Adam and Eve and continuing with the "Malinche" legend and women being blamed for being coconspirators with the conquistadores for control of the land; the castrating woman; and the mannish lesbian. This sexual, political, social, and psychological violence against la India—"the core" of Latinas, as described by Emma Pérez—is plundered from conquest through colonization. La India reclaims this core as a woman-tempered space and tongue. Again, I make a connection with Moraga's last line of her essay "A Long Line of Vendidas": "And there is a woman coming out of her mouth [Hay una mujer que viene de la boca]."[26] Here, the body of la India is reconstructed and redistributed, as her head and mind are now located in "la boca." This process reveals the constructedness not only of our attitudes about our bodies and lives, but also our identities. We have to consider "positionalities" that shake up the idea that inherently we are anything—when really we *become* who we are. This moment of performance for la India is described well by bell hooks: "where you might step out of the fixed identity in which you were seen, and reveal other aspects of the self . . . as part of an overall project of more fully becoming who you are."[27]

The song raises these issues about women. La India in her rage conveys that women have been spoken about, written about, spoken at but never spoken with or listened to. By her presence and words, distinctive in salsa music, she inverts male power. La India ends her concert in the light, hands on her hips, stating that she is here to stay. The dismantling and reconstructing of the body in this work tries to mirror the splits of the multiple identities of Puerto Ricans. Here one sees the multiplicity of meanings that are attached to the whole body of la India. Yes she represents Puerto Rican identities as her presence and talent intersect the various cultures that make up Puerto Rican experience. A Latina under attack, but a complete figure, now might serve as an example to us to move us as a people toward freedom and empowerment.

Notes

[This text was originally written in Spanglish, a complex mixture of English and Spanish. I have retained here only traces of Spanish within the English, translating these only where critical to understanding the argument.—*Trans.*]

1. *La crónica* or the chronicle is one of the oldest genres in literature. It was first used in the first centuries by Sexto Juliano African and Penodoro to give a detailed history of

an era, a country, or a year from an actual observer's point of view. In Europe from the fifth to the tenth centuries many clerics and nuns wrote chronicles in Latin or in "romance" in order to relate the history of nations. Some of the famous Spanish chronicles are the *General de España* written by Alfonso X and his "school" in the thirteenth century, the famous chronicles of the voyages of Columbus written in the late fifteenth century, and of course, the *crónicas de la conquista* (chronicles of conquest) such as Cortès's conquest of Mexico in the early sixteenth century. In Puerto Rico today the chronicle has been adapted by writers to give a detailed and immediate vision of the nation from an eyewitness point of view of events and historical developments. Contemporary writers such as Ana Lydia Vega and Edgardo Rodríguez Juliá write extensively using this genre.

2. Jorge Manuel López, "El Giro," interview, *El Diario* 24 (September 1993): 32.

3. Jorge Duany, "Popular Music in Puerto Rico: Toward an Anthropology of Salsa," *Latin American Music Review* 5.2 (Fall–Winter 1984): 204.

4. Yvonne Yarbaro-Bejarano, "Deconstructing the Lesbian Body," in *Chicana Lesbians: The Girls Our Mothers Warned Us About,* ed. Carla Trujillo (Berkeley: Third Woman Press, 1991), 165.

5. Cherríe Moraga, *Loving in the War Years: Lo que nunca pasó por sus labios* (Boston: South End Press, 1983), 142.

6. Emma Pérez, "Sexuality and Discourse: Notes from a Chicana Survivor," in *Chicana Lesbians: The Girls Our Mothers Warned Us About,* ed. Carla Trujillo (Berkeley: Third Woman Press, 1991), 165.

7. María M. Solá, ed., *Julia de Burgos: Yo misma fui mi ruta* (Río Piedras: Edición Huracán, 1986), 71.

8. Julio Ramos, ed., *Amor y anarquía: Los escritos de Luisa Capetillo* (Río Piedras: Edición Huracán, 1992), 11; translated here by Celeste Fraser Delgado.

9. Norma Valle Ferrer, *Luisa Capetillo: Historia de una mujer proscrita* (Río Piedras: Editorial Cultural, 1990), 19; "la recordaban como la primera mujer que en Puerto Rico había utilizado pantalones en público."

10. Bernardo Vega, *Memoirs of Bernardo Vega: A Contribution to the History of the Puerto Rican Community in New York,* ed. César Andreu Iglesias and trans. Juan Flores (New York: Monthly Review Press, 1984), 22.

11. Ramos, 190, 191–192, 193–194.

12. Frances Aparicio, "Salsa, Maracas, and Baile: Latin Popular Music in the Poetry of Victor Hernández Cruz," *MELUS* 16.1 (Spring 1989–1990): 44.

13. Sherley Anne Williams, "The House of Desire," in *Black Sister: Poetry by Black American Women 1746–1980* ed. Erline Stetson (Bloomington: Indiana U P, 1981), 46.

14. Sherley Anne Williams, "The Blues Roots of Contemporary Afro-American Poetry," in *Chants of the Saints,* ed. Michael S. Harper and Robert B. Stepto (Chicago: U of Illinois P, 1979), 124.

15. Cited in Williams, "Blues Roots," 130.

16. Ida Cox, "One Hour Mama," *Mean Mothers,* Rosetta Records, RR 1300, 1980.

17. Aretha Franklin, "Think" *Aretha,* Atlantic Records, ARCD-8556, 1968.

18. Arcadio Díaz Quiñones, *Conversación con José Luis González* (Río Piedras: Editorial Huracán, 1977), 133.

19. "La banderita puertorriqueña" or "the sweet Puerto Rican flag" refers to a popular song by that name. The "carreta" or "oxcart" refers at once to the play by René Marqués, *La carreta*, which gives a critical view of the experience of Puerto Ricans migrating to New York City in the 1940s and 1950s, and to the book of poetry by Tato Laviera, *La Carreta Made a U-Turn*, which details Nuyorican life.

20. José Luis González, *El país de cuatro pisos* (Rio Piedras: Huracán, 1980).

21. Antonio Pedreira, *Insularismo* (Río Piedras: Editorial Edil, 1992).

22. René Marqués, "El dócil puertorriqueño," in *El puertorriqueño dócil y otros ensayos 1953–1971* (Río Piedras: Editorial Cultural, 1992), 166.

23. René Marqués, "En la popa hay un cuerpo reclinado," in *Cuentos puertorriqueños de hoy* (San Juan: Club del Libro de Puerto Rico, 1959), 45–61.

24. Emilio Díaz Valcárcel, "Osadía," in *El asedio* (México, P.R.: Editorial Arrecife, 1959), 24–68.

25. La India, *Dicen que soy*, Sony Tropical, RMI-81373, 1995.

26. Moraga, 142.

27. bell hooks, *Outlaw Culture: Resisting Representations* (New York: Routledge, 1994), 210.

Ricky and Lucy rumba. (Video capture from *Babalú Music* [Weird Al Yankovich])

I Came, I Saw, I Conga'd

Contexts for a Cuban-American Culture

Gustavo Pérez Firmat

In the summer of 1990, the cover story of the June 25 issue of *People* magazine was devoted to Gloria Estefan, who, as you know, is the most important moving part of the Miami Sound Machine. At the time Estefan was staging what the magazine termed an "amazing recovery" from a serious traffic accident that had left her partially paralyzed; Estefan herself was upbeat about her prospects, and the point of the story was to reassure all of the rhythm nation that little Gloria would conga again.[1]

I begin with this anecdote for two reasons: first, because it gives fair indication of the prominent role that Cuban Americans play in the increasing and inexorable latinization of this country—by now, few Americans will deny that, for better or for worse, the rhythm is going to get them. My other reason for bringing up the *People* story has to do with the photograph on the cover, which showed Gloria holding two puppies whose names happened to be Lucy and Ricky. Like one of the Miami Sound Machine's last records, the photograph cuts both ways: it suggests not only the prominence but also the pedigree of Latino popular culture. After all, if Gloria Estefan is one of the most popular Hispanic figures in this country today, Ricky Ricardo is certainly her strong precursor. Surprising as it may seem, Desi Arnaz's TV character has been the single most visible Hispanic presence in the United States over the last forty years. Indeed, several generations of Americans have acquired many of their notions of how Hispanics behave, talk, treat or mistreat their wives, by watching Ricky love Lucy. And just last semester I had a Cuban-American student who claimed that he had learned how to be a Cuban male by watching *I Love Lucy* reruns in his home in Hialeah.

But the connection between Estefan and Ricky goes further than this. The Miami Sound Machine's first crossover hit was "Conga"—the song that contained the memorable refrain, "come on, shake your body, baby, do the conga, / I know you can't control yourself any longer"; well, the person who led the first conga ever danced on North American soil was none other than Desi Arnaz, who performed this singular feat in a Miami Beach nightclub in 1937. Alluding to this historic (and quite possibly, hysteric) event, Walter Winchell later said, in a wonderful phrase, that a conga line should be called instead "a Desi-chain." It is well to remember, then, that a few years ago when Gloria Estefan entered the Guinness Book of World Records for having led the longest conga line ever (119,984 people), she was only following in Desi's footsteps, only adding another kinky link to the Desi-chain.

I can summarize the significance of this photograph by saying that it illustrates in a particularly clear manner the two forces that shape ethnic culture, which I will call *traditional* and *translational.* As a work of tradition, the photograph points to the genealogy of Cuban-American culture; it reminds us that Gloria Estefan is only the latest in a fairly long line of Cuban-American artists to have come, seen, and conga'd in the United States. As a work of translation, it reminds us of the sorts of adjustments that have to occur for us to be able to rhyme "conga" and "longer." In this the photograph is typical, for ethnic culture is constantly trying to negotiate between the contradictory imperatives of tradition and translation.

"Tradition," a term that derives from the same root as the Spanish *traer,* to bring, designates convergence and continuity, a gathering together of elements according to underlying affinities or shared concerns. By contrast, translation is not a homing device but a distancing mechanism. In its topographical meaning, translation is displacement, in Spanish, *traslación.* This notion has been codified in the truism that to translate is to traduce (*traduttore, traditore*); inherent in the concept of translation is the sense that to move is to transmute, that any linguistic or cultural displacement necessarily entails some mutilation of the original. In fact, in classical rhetoric *traductio*—which is, of course, the Spanish word for translation—was the term to refer to the repetition of a word with a changed meaning. Translation/*traslación,* traduction/*traducción*—the mere translation of these terms is a powerful reminder of the intricacies of the concept.

What I should like to do here is explore these notions a bit further by discussing *The Mambo Kings Play Songs of Love,* a recent novel by Oscar Hijuelos that has been termed "the best Hispanic book ever published by a commercial press."[2] Although only a couple of years old, *Mambo Kings* is already becoming something of a contemporary classic. Not only is Hijuelos the first Cuban-American writer to receive the Pulitzer prize for fiction; he is the only one of a tiny group of *Latino* writers to be published successfully by a major North American publisher. Just to mention one contrasting example: within a few months of the publication of *Mambo Kings*, William Morrow brought out another novel by a Cuban-American writer, Virgil Suárez's *Latin Jazz*. Yet Suárez's novel elicited only moderate interest and quickly sank from sight. One major difference between the two novels is that, unlike Suárez, Hijuelos writes from what may be termed a "translational" perspective. Like *Latin Jazz, Mambo Kings* divides its attention between Cuba and the United States, as it tells the story of a Cuban family that migrates to this country. Unlike *Latin Jazz*, however, *Mambo Kings* does not pledge allegiance to its Cuban roots, for it is very much a novel written *away* from Spanish and *toward* English; this drift is already visible in the title, which also moves from Spanish to English, from "mambo" to "songs of love." One reason for Hijuelos's success may well be the savvy—and even the *sabor*—with which he translates tradition. In subject matter, intention, and design, *Mambo Kings* places itself in the line of descent of some central works in the canon of contemporary Latin American fiction. At the same time, however, the novel's translational drift distances it from its Hispanic pedigree. Although *Mambo Kings* invites a general reading as a product of Hispanic culture and specifically as part of its literary tradition, it makes such a reading virtually impossible. In rhetorical terms *Mambo Kings* may be regarded as a sustained traduction, that is, a transfigured repetition of certain elements in Spanish American literature and culture.

The novel follows the lives of two Cuban brothers, César and Nestor Castillo, who emigrate to New York in the late forties and form an orchestra called the Mambo Kings, achieving ephemeral fame one night in 1955 when they make an appearance on the *I Love Lucy* show as Ricky's Cuban cousins. In talent as well as temperament, Nestor and César are worlds apart. César, the leader of the band, is a consummate ladies' man with slicked-back hair, a mellifluous voice, and an irrepressible libido. He remarks that he had only three interests in life: rum, rump, and rumba. His brother Nestor is moody and melancholy; his main claim to fame is having written the Mambo King's greatest hit, "Bellísima María de Mi Alma," "Beautiful María of My Soul," a sad ballad about the girl who broke his heart in Cuba. For years Nestor works tirelessly on this tune, coming up with twenty-two different versions of the lyric; only his death in a car accident puts an end to his scriptural obsession. The story of the Castillo brothers is told in flashbacks by the agonizing César, who by 1980 has ended up broke and broken in a New York tenement and who spends his last hours replaying records of *recuerdos*.

The novel's debt to Hispanic literary tradition is evident in two principal ways. Given the episodic plot and the explicitness with which César's sexual exploits are recounted, one cannot read *Mambo Kings* without thinking of the genre of the picaresque, a subgenre that in Cuba includes such texts as Carlos Loveira's *Juan Criollo* (1927) and Guillermo Cabrera Infante's *La Habana para un infante difunto* (1979).[3] Like the protagonist of Loveira's novel, César is a Don Juan *Criollo*, a creole translation of the Spanish literary type. In the classical picaresque, the protagonist is driven by hunger and spends a large part of his life in the service of successive masters. In the erotic picaresque, the moving force is a different kind of appetite, and instead of going from master to master the protagonist goes from mistress to mistress—not *de amo en amo* but rather *de amorío en amorío*.[4]

This is perhaps the aspect of the novel that has elicited the strongest response from its readers, for the narration's attention to the nature of things erotic verges on the pornographic.[5] This is not to say, however, that the text unequivocally endorses its protagonist's phallocentrism, for César's recollections are filtered through his nephew Eugenio, who puts distance between the reader and César's view of himself. Eugenio's mediating presence helps to turn the novel into something other than a celebration of the Castillos' not-so-private members. As César's closest relative and the author of the book's fictional prologue and epilogue, Eugenio occupies a position halfway between the narrating "I" and the narrated "he." In fact, as I will argue a bit later, Eugenio is best seen as César's translator, which means that their two voices are formally separate but often hard to tell apart. In this respect *Mambo Kings* is what one might call a "hetero-autobiography"—a text whose narrator and protagonist are in some ways distinct, in other ways indistinguishable.[6]

Even though César's recollections are given in the third person, Eugenio's presence at the beginning and end makes him the medium for the interior story—so much so that some of his sentences are repeated verbatim in the interior text; thus, for example, his description of the Castillos' cameo on *I Love Lucy* matches word for word the description that the supposedly impersonal narrator had provided earlier (404–405 and 142–143). It's not entirely clear what one should make of this duplication, which is inexplicable unless one posits that the *entire* account is Eugenio's invention—an intriguing possibility that the text insinuates but does not confirm. Without going this far, however, one can at least venture that Eugenio "underwrites" César's memoirs. I use this verb in both of its meanings: to write beneath something and to guarantee. Even if Eugenio is not responsible for the specific verbal shape of César's recollections, he is at least generally responsible for the memoirs as a whole. As the novel begins, Eugenio is watching a rerun of *I Love Lucy*. After the episode is over he remarks, "the miracle had passed, the resurrection of a man" (8). Since the "resurrection of a man" is precisely the novel's own miracle, *Mambo Kings* can be regarded as a type of rerun whose origin is Eugenio. As his name already suggests, Eugenio is the source, the progenitor of the account.

The other token of tradition in the book is music, for Hijuelos's novel also connects with a spate of recent works of Spanish American fiction that derive inspiration from popular music. I am thinking generally of books like Sarduy's *De donde son los cantantes* (1967), Lisandro Otero's *Bolero* (1986), and even Manuel Puig's *El beso de la mujer araña* (1976), with which Hijuelos's novel shares also the practice of providing explanatory footnotes. More concretely I am thinking of two specific novels: Luis Rafael Sánchez's *La guaracha del Macho Camacho* (1980) and Guillermo Cabrera Infante's *Tres tristes tigres* (1965). Like *La guaracha del Macho Camacho*, which centers on a tune by the same name, *Mambo Kings* revolves around one song, "Beautiful María of My Soul," whose lyric is finally transcribed in the last chapter; as in Sánchez's novel, Hijuelos's text establishes a counterpoint between music and text, or *música y letra*. Cabrera Infante's novel, which also gives high visibility to forms of popular music, includes a section entitled "Ella cantaba boleros" (She sang boleros), a phrase that Hijuelos seems to be transposing in his title, since the "songs of love" in the title is a translation of the Spanish *boleros*.

With its juxtaposition of mambo and bolero, Hijuelos's title alerts the reader to the importance of these two musical genres in the novel. The mambo was a mixture of Afro-Cuban rhythms and North American big-

Mad for Mambo at the Hotel Biltmore, June 18, 1957. (*Courtesy of the Various Photographic Collections, Centro de Estudios Puertorriqueños, Hunter College, City University of New York*

band instrumentation popularized by Dámaso Pérez Prado, whose nickname was in fact "el rey del mambo."[7] Championed also by such orchestras as Tito Rodriguez and the Mambo Devils, Tito Puente and the Picadilly Boys, and Eddie Carbia y los mamboleros, the mambo enjoyed a remarkable popularity during the early and mid-fifties, giving rise to such mamboid compositions as "Papa Loves Mambo," with which Perry Como had a number-one hit in 1954; Vaughn Monroe's "They Were Doing the Mambo (But I Just Sat Around)"; Mickey Katz's "My Yiddishe Mambo" (about a woman who's "baking her challes for Noro Morales"); Rosemary Clooney's "Italian Mambo" (sample lyric: "you calbrazi do the mambo like a-crazy"); and Jimmy Boyd's "I Saw Mommy Doing the Mambo (With You Know Who)." This last song is a yuletide ditty about a little boy who catches his mother mamboing with Santa on Christmas eve (and it wasn't the only yuletide mambo—there was also a "Santa

Claus Mambo," a "Jingle Bells Mambo," and a "Rudolph the Red-Nosed Mambo").

By the latter part of 1954, the whole country had fallen under the Afro-Cuban spell of the mambo. That fall, Tico Records organized "Mambo U.S.A.," a fifty-six-city tour that took the mambo to America's heartland and which Hijuelos's recounts; the troupe of forty mambists included Machito, Joe Loco, Facundo Rivero, and many others (as well as César and Nestor Castillo, of course). In December stores were full of mambo gifts: mambo dolls, mambo nighties, and mambo "kits" (a record, maracas, and a plastic sheet with mambo steps to put on the floor.) And that same month Paramount released *Mambo*, with Silvana Mangano in the role of a dancer who has to choose between marriage and mambo. As a headline in the December 1954 issue of *Life* put it, with more than a tinge of racism, "Uncle Sambo, Mad for Mambo."[8]

Pérez Prado himself was enormously successful. He appeared on American television and was booked in the best nightclubs. When he opened at the ritzy Starlight Roof of the Waldorf Astoria in July of 1954, his was only the second Latin orchestra ever to play that venue (the other was Xavier Cugat's).[9] A year later his band was picked as the most popular orchestra in this country; that same year one of his songs, "Cherry Pink and Apple Blossom White," stayed on the Billboard charts for twenty-six weeks; surprisingly, only one other song in the history of U.S. popular music has enjoyed a longer run on the charts—Elvis Presley's "Don't Be Cruel," which became a hit the following year.[10] "Cherry Pink" also became the theme for a highly successful RKO movie, *Underwater!* (1955), in which Jane Russell, accompanied by Pérez Prado, dances a modest mambo—in a bathing suit.

Most of Pérez Prado's mambos are instrumental compositions characterized by Afro-Cuban percussion and dissonant sax and trumpet riffs. (Pérez Prado's favorite composer was Stravinsky.) The laconism of Pérez Prado's mambo was proverbial; typical in this respect is the lyric of the first famous mambo, the *ur*mambo as it were, whose title is "Qué rico el mambo," and which ran in its entirety: "mambo, qué rico el mambo, mambo, mambo, qué rico é é é é." Even the apopé of the "es" to "é" betrays Pérez Prado's penchant for verbal minimalism. It is not accidental, thus, that another of his hits was entitled "Ni hablar." In Pérez

Prado's hands, the mambo was a medium for sound, not sense. Indeed his signature became the guttural grunts with which he punctuated the breaks in the music and which the jazz historian Marshall Stearns has compared to the cries of an "excited muledriver."[11] I mention this because the mambo's lovely inarticulateness makes it an odd choice as a model for literary composition. To the extent that *Mambo Kings* derives inspiration from the mambo, it tends toward a kind of expressiveness whose medium is *not* language. Most literary transpositions of popular songs focus on their lyrics—thus it is, for example, with *La guaracha del Macho Camacho*. But with the mambo, literary transposition is difficult because of the form's instrumental nature.

It is not surprising, for this reason, that what the mambo kings play are not mambos but "songs of love," for in the novel the bolero fills the void left by the mambo. Unlike the mambo, most boleros are sad, even whining ballads whose distinctiveness has less to do with the music than with the words. In the bolero, rhythm and melody take a back seat to verbal elaboration, as is suggested by Nestor's twenty-two versions of the lyrics to "Beautiful María of My Soul." The narrator describes Nestor's bolero as "a song about love so far away it hurts, a song about lost pleasures, a song about youth, a song about love so elusive a man can never know where he stands; a song about wanting a woman so much death does not frighten you, a song about wanting a woman even after she has abandoned you" (405). The repetitive intensity of this description, which echoes Nestor's own obsessive rewriting, gives some idea of the bolero's involvement with language. In the novel, the bolero modulates the narrator's voice, providing him with structures of feeling and forms of expression. This identification is evident in the fact that the title of the book is also the title of one of the mambo king's LPs—the scriptive record merges with the musical recording.

Not only does the bolero's wordiness contrast with the mambo's laconism; the two genres also serve as vehicles for discordant emotions. If the central preoccupation of the bolero is loss, the central impulse of the mambo is conquest. Both as music and as dance, the mambo is aggressive, uninhibited, seductive: wham, bam, thank you, mambo. It is no accident that one of the central numbers in the movie *Dirty Dancing* was a mambo ("Johnny's Mambo"). By contrast, in a bolero the speaker is typically passive and mournful. Like Nestor's "Beautiful María of My Soul," the bolero is a medium for bemoaning unhappiness in love, for questioning the injustice of fate. For this reason, the novel as a whole becomes a musical agon between mambo and bolero, lust and loss, conquest and relinquishment. And the musical question the novels asks is ¿la vida es mambo? ¿o la vida es bolero? Is life a chronicle of conquest—or is life a dirge?

This question is answered, of course, in the lives of the two brothers. César, with his "king-cock strut" (47), is the mambo king; Nestor is the spirit of the *letra* of the bolero. As the narrator puts it succinctly, "César was *un macho grande;* Nestor *un infeliz*" (114). The irony is that, in the end, the great macho turns out to be no less of an *infeliz* than his brother. Indeed, the plot narrates how, after Nestor's death, César gradually takes on his brother's temperament; early in the novel Nestor is described as "the man plagued with memory, the way his brother César Castillo would be twenty-five years later" (44). The gradual merging of the two brothers culminates with César's last act, which is to transcribe the lyrics of his brother's composition, "Beautiful María of My Soul." When he writes down the lyrics as if they were his own, César becomes Nestor, remembrance becomes impersonation. César merges with his brother, becoming another man "plagued by memory."

César's final impersonation summarizes the drift of the book. Like the title itself, the novel moves from mambo to bolero, from conquest to loss. César lives in frenetic mambo time only to discover that life actually follows the languid measures of the bolero. The account of his many conquests is modalized by the reader's awareness that these chronicles of conquest are actually a derelict's last words. If Nestor composes his bolero in order to get María back (44), César reminisces in order to recapture his life as a *macho grande;* and the narration explicitly plays on the punning relationship between "member" and "remember"—at one point César "remembered a whore struggling with a thick rubber on his member" (393). For César, remembering is a way of re-membering himself, a way of sleeping with the past. And like the bolero composed by Nestor, the novel itself is very much "a song about lost pleasures, a song about youth." Not one to avoid extremes, the narrator carries the mourning into the most unlikely places. Loss is so ubiquitous that even penises weep: "By evening they were sitting out on a pier by the sea necking, the head of his penis weeping semen tears" (99–100; see also 187).

My discussion thus far is intended to give some idea of the ways in which *Mambo Kings* incorporates Hispanic literary and musical culture. Having said this much, I should now like to reflect briefly on how the novel distances itself from this same culture. That is to say, I should like to reflect on the text's translational impulse, which is evident, first of all, in the ambivalence that Hijuelos's novel demonstrates toward the Spanish language. In one sense, Spanish is everywhere in the text: in the place and character names, in the characters' hispanicized diction, and in the constant references to Cuban music. In another sense, however, Spanish is nowhere, for Hijuelos has of course rendered in English all of the characters' thoughts and words. Indeed, since César's memories make up most of the novel, and since these memories were almost certainly framed in Spanish, the text we read presupposes an invisible act of translation, somewhat in the manner of *Don Quixote.* The source of this translation must of course be Eugenio, who is both narrator and translator; indeed, Eugenio's genius, his *ingenio,* is to filter César's recollections in such a way that the reader tends to overlook Eugenio's responsibility for the text's language.

Significantly, the only sustained Spanish passage in the book is the lyric of "Beautiful María of My Soul," which appears at the very end. One cannot overlook the overdetermination of its appearance: Nestor's song of love, the book's preeminent statement on loss, is transcribed in a language that itself has been lost. The Spanish lyric is a testament to what is lost in translation. And Nestor's beautiful María may then be the emblem for the maternal language that was left behind in Cuba. Moreover, since César's last act is to transcribe this lyric, this Spanish interpolation is literally a testament. When readers finally come upon these words, they find themselves at a loss. For Anglophone readers, the loss is more acute—since they cannot understand what they read. The bolero, which is one of the novel's principal links to Hispanic culture, is also the novel's figure for the loss of that culture, a loss whose most fundamental manifestation is linguistic.

In a narrow but significant sense, this linguistic loss has been present throughout the novel in the surprisingly large number of misspellings of

Spanish words and names. For example, Antonio Arcaño, who is one of the seminal figures in the early history of the mambo, becomes Antonio Arcana; the famous singer Bola de Nieve is strangely transformed into a Pala de Nieve; the equally famous Beny Moré loses his accent and becomes Beny More—a notable example of how "more" can be "less." These errata and others like them may be evidence of sloppy editing; nonetheless, they also constitute typographical reminders of translation as loss, displacement, as *traduction*.

But perhaps the best example inside and outside of the novel of traductive translation is Desi Arnaz, who is an important secondary character. In fact, the book ends with Eugenio's account of his visit to Desi's house in California, where Desi and Eugenio reminisce about the mambo kings. Think for a moment about the name of the character that Desi played on TV: Ricky Ricardo. The name is a bilingual text that contains both original and translation, since Ricky is a familiar American rendering of the Spanish Ricardo. But it is a translation that distances, a traductive translation: the Germanic Ricardo (which, incidentally, means "king") is not only anglicized but turned into a diminutive: it does not become Richard, or Dick, or Rick, but Ricky—a child's name (much as, one may add, Desiderio became Desi). And of the two given names—Ricky, Ricardo—it is the North American one that comes first. Ricardo—which in Spanish is seldom a last name and at that time was the first name of one of Hollywood's leading Latin lovers, Ricardo Montalbán—becomes the last name.[12] It is as if Ricky has pushed Ricardo into the last-name position, with the consequence that Ricardo's "real" last name, say, "Rodriguez," drops out of the picture entirely. In a sense, Ricky Ricardo is an orphan's name, one that reveals nothing about Ricky's parentage.[13] Still, what matters about Ricky's ancestry is that he is Hispanic, and Ricardo functions well enough as a marker of ethnicity. Ricardo signifies that the subject is Hispanic; Ricky signifies that the Hispanic subject—the "I" in *I Love Lucy*—has been acculturated, domesticated, maybe even emasculated. Ricardo is the Latin lover, Ricky is the American husband.

The contrast between Ricky and Ricardo may well boil down to the different connotations of the final letters in each name, "y" and "o." In English, the suffix "y" is used in forming diminutives, nicknames, and terms of endearment or familiarity. By attaching a "y" to a proper name we establish an affective relation with the name's holder, we make the name contingent or dependent on us—an effect that may have to do with the other function of the suffix "y," which is to turn a noun or a verb into an adjective, as when we turn "touch" into "touchy" or "feel" into "feely." By contrast, the final "o" is a marker not of familiarity but of foreignness, and not of endearment but of distance. Think, for a minute, of the words in English that end in "o." Once we get past the names of some instruments—piano, cello—and a few fruits and vegetables—potato, tomato, avocado, mango—we run into such words as psycho, weirdo, tyro, bimbo, Drano, Oreo, buffo. The fact that in Spanish "o" is a masculine ending probably also acts on our sense of the suffix in words such as macho, mambo, Latino, Gustavo. The story of "o" is a tale of estrangement, for the English language treats o-words like foreign bodies. Thus by replacing the "o" in Ricardo with the "y" in Ricky one removes the unfamiliarity, and perhaps the threat, of the foreign body. (One might recall here that the radical spelling of "women" is "womyn, where the "y" feminizes, takes the "men" out of "women.") Replacing Ricardo with Ricky is, at the very least, an acculturating gesture, a way of turning the resident alien into a naturalized citizen. Ricky is the price that Ricardo pays for sleeping with Lucy—the price he pays for being allowed to enter Lucy's bedroom and America's living rooms. Lucy and Ricky—the "y" that ends their names is not the least significant thing they have in common.

Ricky Ricardo's name alerts us, therefore, to the schisms that bisect what Michael Fisher has called the "ethnic I."[14] For me a handy emblem of the erosion of Ricky's subject position is the transition from the initial "I" of the show's title to the final "y" of his Americanized name (Desi Arnaz once remarked that he wanted to be remembered as the "I" in *I Love Lucy*). This is a transition from agency to contingency, from activity to passivity, from visibility to invisibility. It would be easy to ridicule the stereotypical elements in the portrayal of Ricky, who like Desi himself used to do, ends each rendition of the Afro-Cuban song "Babalú" with an entirely un-African "olé." But it may also be possible to see Ricky Ricardo (name and character) as a moving emblem for what is lost—and perhaps what is gained—in translation. Every time Ricky breaks into his nearly unintelligible Spanish or says "wunt" for "won't" or "splain" for "explain," his words, beyond whatever comedic value they may have, remind us of the risks—and also of the rewards—of loving Lucy.

I propose something similar happens in Hijuelos's novel. At one point in the *Mambo Kings,* during an interview on a radio show, César Castillo praises Desi Arnaz. The emcee replies: "But no one has ever considered him very authentic or original." To which César counters: "*Bueno,* but I think what he did was difficult. For me, he was very Cuban, and the music he played in those days was good and Cuban enough for me" (339). "Good and Cuban enough"—this statement may apply equally well to Hijuelos's novel, a dance to the music of time that, like Desi and Ricky, loses and finds itself in translation. As a Hispanic product re-packaged for North American consumption, *Mambo Kings* clearly illus-trates the predicament of ethnic culture, which is that it must walk a narrow line between the danger of co-optation on the one hand and of unintelligibility on the other. In this also it resembles the mambo, whose big-band sound was similarly criticized for not being Cuban enough, but whose success was due in some measure to its impurities.

In a fine book, *Chicano Narrative: The Dialectics of Difference,* Ramón Saldivar has argued that what distinguishes Chicano narrative is the power to demystify relations between hegemonic and minority cul-tures.[15] I do not think that *Mambo Kings* is demystifying in this sense; rather than dealing with relations between hegemonic and minority cul-tures, *Mambo Kings* focuses on the transactions between two cultures, each of which asserts its own particular kind of hegemony. Even if the novel's very existence in English seems to tilt the balance in favor of Anglo-American culture, the novel's content, suffused as it is with His-panic culture, tends to rectify the scales. Indeed, as we have seen, even the text's English betrays a Spanish accent. Hijuelos's own version of the "dialectics of difference" faces off Spanish American culture on one hand and North American culture on the other, but without treating the for-mer as a subaltern or "minority" culture. Their relation is "appositional" rather than "oppositional." It may be, in fact, that Cuban-American lit-erature differs from Chicano literature in conceiving of culture contact as appositional. Apposition may more accurately reflect the nature and history of Cuban-American participation in the Anglo-American mainstream.

In any event, Hijuelos's considerable achievement is to stage the nego-tiation between cultures in such a way that the novel neither forsakes nor is enslaved by its family resemblance to things and texts Hispanic. Spanish American culture figures in the novel as a distant relation—much as César and Nestor appear on *I Love Lucy* as Ricky's Cuban cousins. The art of the *Mambo Kings* resides in knowing how to cultivate distant relations, which means also knowing how to put them in their place. By taking distance from its ancestry, the novel is able to occupy an eccentric space somewhere between Havana and Harlem, a kind of make-believe border ballroom where North meets South, where Ricky loves Lucy, and where mambo kings play songs of love forever.

The preceding sentences may sound like a conclusion, but they are not. I would like to end on a more personal note. Most Latino writers of my acquaintance have thoroughly detested this novel, considering that it sacrifices genuine Hispanic flavor in order to cater to the tastes of a North American readership. For them, *Mambo Kings* is a sort of literary Taco Bell: inauthentic and even indigestible. For me, however, the issue is whether authenticity, or a certain kind of authenticity, is really worth pursuing. As one who has feasted more than once on a Double Beef Burrito Supreme, I am less quick to dismiss fast food, however hyphenated. Hyphens are curious creatures; they connect, they separate, and above all, they are elastic. *Mambo Kings* is a study in the elasticity of hyphens; the novel distends the hyphen inside "Cuban-American" to the breaking point, but without letting it snap. To my mind, this is Hijuelos's most important lesson: he teaches us to stretch the hyphen, to get lost in translation. Sometimes you can even stretch the hyphen so much that it becomes a conga line.

And how about the phrase "lost in translation?" What does *this* phrase evoke? In what kind of a place does one end up if one gets lost "in translation?" When I try to visualize such a commonplace, I imagine myself, on a given Saturday afternoon, in a shopping center in Miami called the Town and Country Mall. Since I'm thirsty, I go into a store called Love Juices, which specializes in nothing more salacious or salubrious than milk shakes made from tropical fruits; having quenched my thirst, I want to buy some Liz Claiborne jeans, and I head for a boutique called Mr. Trapus, whose name—*trapo*—is actually the Spanish word for an old rag; undaunted by the consumerist frenzy that has possessed me, I then purchase a hand-painted Italian tie in another store nearby called Cachi Bachi—a name that, in spite of its chichi sound, is a Spanish slang word for junk, *cachibache*. And then, for dinner, I go to

Garcia's Caribbean Grill, where I have something called a Tropical Soup, the American version of the traditional Cuban stew, *ajiaco*. In this way, I spend my entire afternoon lost in translation—and loving every minute. Translation takes you to a place where cultures divide to conga. My effort here has been to show you the way to such a place. Now, enter at your own risk. Who knows, you might end up becoming the missing link in the Desi-chain.

Notes

1. Steve Dougherty, "One Step at a Time," *People* (25 June 1990): 78–84.
2. Rev. of *The Mambo Kings Play Songs of Love,* by Oscar Hijuelos, *The American Review* 18.1 (1990): 113. Page numbers from the novel refer to Oscar Hijuelos, *The Mambo Kings Play Songs of Love* (New York: Farrar, Straus & Giroux, 1989).
3. According to Cabrera Infante, *La Habana para un infante difunto* is "una suerte de memoria erótica" (a kind of erotic memory), as quoted in Rosa María Pereda, *Guillermo Cabrera Infante* (Madrid: EDAF, 1979), 141.
4. In fact, César's success with women is so phenomenal that it has even spilled out of the pages of the novel into real life. Some months ago newspapers carried the story that Hijuelos has been sued for libel by a singer named Gloria Parker, who appears briefly in the book and who in the fifties had a band called "Glorious Gloria Parker and Her All-Girl Rumba Orchestra." Parker's suit quotes from the novel, which states that César "made it with three of the musicians who played with Gloria Parker and her All-Girl Rumba Orchestra, among them a Lithuanian trombone player named Gertie whom he made love to against a wall of flour sacks" (198). I cannot resist remarking that this incident is bound to give the notion of "deflouring" a whole new meaning.
5. According to Laura Frost, "Although Hijuelos' narrative is implicitly critical of Castillo machismo and the conditions that contribute to its psychological makeup, this 'criticism' is undermined by a narrowly male domination of the text. Women play their parts in the Castillos' macho duets and return to the background of this over-whelmingly male discourse" (Rev. of *The Mambo Kings Play Songs of Love,* by Oscar Hijuelos, *Review* 42 [January–June 1990]: 65). Hijuelos has said the following: "I intended a little bit of parody of the super-sexual virility that men are obsessed with in macho cultures. I was having fun with it. Also, for me, it's a play on morality, and the body and how one can be hyperphallic—built like the Empire State building—and it won't make any difference to the ultimate issues of love or family or death" (Michael Coffey, "Oscar Hijuelos," *Publishers Weekly* [21 July 1989]: 44).
6. I have discussed a similar phenomenon apropos Loveira's *Juan Criollo* in *The Cuban Condition: Translation and Identity in Modern Cuban Literature* (Cambridge: Cambridge

U P, 1989), 112–126. On third-person autobiography, see also Phillipe Lejeune, "L'autobiographie à la troisième personne," in *Je est une autre* (Paris: Editions du Seuil, 1980).

7. There were actually three *mamboleros* that laid claim to the title of "king of the mambo": Pérez Prado, the New York–born Puerto Rican percussionist Tito Puente, and Merced Gallego, a West Coast bandleader. Of these Pérez Prado was best known.

8. "Uncle Sambo, Mad for Mambo," *Life* (20 December 1954): 14–19.

9. Reviews of Pérez Prado's debut at the Waldorf register puzzlement at his "startling" stage antics and refer to the "variegated clothes" of the "frantic horde" of mamboniks and to the numerous "fems who shrieked in ecstacy" at the first riffs of "Qué rico el mambo" (*Billboard* 7 August 1954). Pérez Prado's may not have been the best band to play the Starlight Roof, but it was certainly the loudest. To an audience used to Xavier Cugat's watered-down rumbas, Pérez Prado's hot mambo must have come as something of a shock.

10. Joel Whitburn, *The Billboard Book of Top 40 Hits* (New York: Billboard Books, 1989), 593.

11. Marshall Stearns, *The Story of Jazz* (New York: New American Library, 1958), 182.

12. In the prehistory of Ricky's name it may be significant that Lucy's TV husband was originally supposed to be played by another Richard, the actor Richard Denning, who played her husband on the radio show *My Favorite Husband,* on which the TV series was based. Only Lucy's refusal to do the show unless Desi played the part of her husband persuaded CBS to allow Desi to play her TV husband. In the episode called "Hollywood Anniversary," Ricky gives his full name as "Ricardo Alberto Fernando Ricardo y Acha." Acha was Arnaz's own matronymic.

13. The motif of orphanhood is present in the novel, as Eugenio himself is an orphan. This may be another link to the picaresque tradition.

14. Michael Fisher, "Ethnicity and the Post-Modern Arts of Memory," in *Writing Culture: The Poetics and Politics of Ethnography,* ed. James Clifford and George E. Marcus (Berkeley: U of California P, 1986), 194–233. See also James Craig Holte, *The Ethnic I: A Sourcebook for Ethnic American Autobiography* (New York: Greenwood Press, 1988), 3–14.

15. Ramón Saldívar, *Chicano Narrative: The Dialectics of Difference* (Madison: U of Wisconsin P, 1990), 5.

Caught in the Web

Latinidad, AIDS, and Allegory in

Kiss of the Spider Woman, the Musical

David Román and Alberto Sandoval

"Con quién te identificás?"—Manuel Puig, *Kiss of the Spider Woman*

It's Wednesday afternoon, 20 October 1993, and I am in New York.
I've taken the train from Philadelphia to meet Alberto for the first
time. We have been exchanging our work this year—both of us write on
performance—and have decided to meet for a show. It's a theater thing. I
am supposed to meet him at the Drama Book Shop on 7th Avenue at 1:00.
The plan is to catch a matinee, share a meal, and then attend another
performance in the evening. We are both promiscuous theatergoers.

It's Wednesday afternoon, 20 October 1993, and I am heading to New
York. The train from Springfield, Massachusetts, is delayed an hour,
and I will not be able to meet David on time. We'll have to skip lunch. If
this happens, I will not be able to take my medication. And in my ner-
vousness over being late, I have confused the time for the matinee, delay-
ing it an hour like the train. When I finally arrive in New York, it is
pouring rain. My lover, John, who lives in New York, has arranged for
David and me to meet at the Drama Book Shop on 7th Avenue at 1:00. I
have no idea what he looks like. I am meeting him for the first time after
exchanging our work by mail and after a series of conversations by
phone. Because of the rain, the taxi ride from John's apartment in the
Village takes forever.

Alberto's late. It's 1:30 and pouring. I am getting anxious because I am
needing a theater fix and don't want to miss the matinee show. I also
don't want to miss Alberto. I have no idea what he looks like. I hope he is
okay and that his lateness is not related to his health. I am cruising

everyone at the bookstore. Are you my theater companion? I decide to look for him on the first-floor lobby.

I finally arrive at the bookstore. I am worried that David will think that I am the stereotypical Latino who's late. But I am also worried about whether or not I will recognize him. How "Latino" will he look? (Whatever that means.)

We bump into each other in the lobby—Alberto? David?—and embrace.

Alberto: I apologize. There's no time for lunch. I want to see a matinee.
David: Then let's get to the theater.

We run to TKTS, which is only a block away, eager to see what shows are on the boards for half-price.

Alberto: What about *Kiss of the Spider Woman, the Musical*? I've already seen it, but I would enjoy seeing it again. Chita is fabulous.
David: *Kiss of the Spider Woman, the Musical*? (I've resisted this production for months. But with only fifteen minutes before curtain, it's too late to negotiate. At this point, I'll even go see *Cats*. At least *Kiss of the Spider Woman, the Musical* has Chita.) Let's do it.

We buy the tickets. We have box seats at the Broadhurst.

Once in my seat and before the show begins, I wonder about my participation in a representation of torture as entertainment. For me, this translates to entertainment as torture. And yet I feel great pleasure being with Alberto at the theater—in our box seats, no less. We share—it's obvious to us both—much more than simply our identities as Latino gay men. He loves the theater, and so do I. I begin to feel the pleasures of anticipation, the rush through my body that makes me available for the erotics of performance and permits me the promiscuity of countless theatrical encounters. Alberto cannot stop talking about Chita Rivera's performance.

I really want to see the show again because I am interested in placing it within an AIDS context. As a person with AIDS, I had the immediate response when I first saw it with John that the musical works culturally as an AIDS allegory. I want to confirm this interpretation with a second viewing. However, I do not tell David this because I don't want to influence his first encounter with the production. Instead, I keep mentioning to him how fabulous Chita's performance is. She is the location of the pleasures and erotics of my viewing. The rhythms of the movement of her body, the unique intonations of her voice, her very presence on stage are what I most admire in this production. To watch Chita perform with such agility and discipline at sixty only confirms my impression of her as a legendary star.

Genealogies and Critical Contexts

Kiss of the Spider Woman, the Musical is, of course, based on Argentine writer Manuel Puig's 1976 novel, *El beso de la mujer araña,* which has been translated into twenty-seven languages. In 1985 the novel was adapted for film by Hector Babenco and for the stage by Puig. In 1988 John Kander and Fred Ebb, the musical collaborators of such Broadway hits as *Cabaret* and *Chicago,* proposed a musical adaptation to director Harold Prince. Terrence McNally joined the artistic team and wrote the musical's book. A workshop production was presented in the spring of 1990 at the New Musicals at Purchase, New York. Puig, who attended this workshop, approved the adaptation and made suggestions that have since been incorporated into the show. The musical's program provides the official history of the production:

After the workshop in the spring of 1990, no producer could be found who was willing to risk financing the additional work the show needed to move on to a full, commercial production. Undaunted, Harold Prince and the creative team continued their collaboration to refine *Kiss of the Spider Woman,* and presented a reworked version to Garth H. Drabinsky, Chairman of the Live Entertainment Corporation of Canada. Impressed with the changes, Mr. Drabinsky agreed to mount a new production in Toronto, Canada. A new choreographer, set designer, lighting designer and cast were enlisted and Mr. Drabinsky worked closely with Harold Prince and the creative team in the tradition of an old-fashioned, "hands-on" Broadway producer.[1]

Kiss of the Spider Woman, the Musical received its world premiere in Toronto in June 1992 and ran until August 1992 at the St. Lawrence

Anthony Crivello watches Chita Rivera and Jeff Hyslop dance in *Kiss of the Spider Woman, the Musical. (Photo Catherine Ashmore; courtesy of the artist)*

Centre for the Arts, Bluma Appel Theatre. The London premiere took place at the Shaftsbury Theatre on 20 October 1992—exactly one year before our joint experience of the musical. It opened on Broadway at the Broadhurst on 3 May 1993 and won the 1993 Tony award for Best Musical.

The main storyline of the novel, preserved through these adaptations, centers on the relationship between two cell mates in a Buenos Aires penitentiary: Molina, a thirty-seven-year-old gay window dresser jailed for alleged sexual relations with minors, and Valentin, a twenty-seven-year-old heterosexual Marxist political revolutionary. Molina entertains himself and Valentin by retelling the plots of old films. Molina identifies with the heroines of these movies. In the musical, a fictional actress named Aurora serves as a muse for Molina. Her roles include the Russian beauty Tatyana Alexandrovna and the haunting filmic portrayal of the Spider Woman. The two men grow to appreciate one another. Toward the end, Molina, who has fallen in love with Valentin, is released.

Once outside of the prison, Molina is killed while trying to contact Valentin's political comrades. The novel ends with Molina's death and Valentin's torture.

Both of us were familiar with the plot and adaptation history of Puig's novel. Our interest, therefore, was not primarily in the unfolding of the story—suspenseful for the uninitiated, no doubt—but rather in how the book would be shaped as a musical. What would be the effects of adapting Puig's graphic novel of political torture and state repression as entertainment for Broadway? Why adapt Puig's novel as a musical now? How would a non–Latin American production team translate the cultural and political context of Puig's original novel? In what ways would gayness and ethnicity be fetishized, occluded, marked, or eradicated by the move to Broadway?

Given the paucity of Latin American and Latino presence and representation on Broadway, *Kiss of the Spider Woman, the Musical* was already overdetermined, much as *Miss Saigon* has been for Asian Americans and Pacific Islanders.[2] Moreover, given its ethnic specificity, it would stand apart from the 1993 wave of gay representations on and off Broadway in such plays as *Angels in America, Falsettos, Jeffrey, The Destiny of Me,* and *Twilight of the Gods.* Unlike these plays, *Kiss* stages both sexual *and* cultural otherness. While it could easily be read as a gay musical—after all, Terrence McNally adapted the book, Puig was gay, and the central hero is gay as well—and therefore readily located within the context of gay male theatrical representations (as various critics have done), it may be more useful to foreground the musical's ethnic representation, which has escaped critical attention. Gay male critics have already begun the necessary historicization of homosexuality in cultural representation, questioning the ubiquity of drag queens, sexual perverts, or social outcasts.[3] And while as gay male theorists we both have contributed to this critical practice, our emphasis here will be on unsettling the comforts of ethnic exoticism—particularly as it relates to sexuality—in the U.S. cultural imaginary.[4]

Cultural exoticism, like gay male sexual otherness, has been so naturalized in U.S. mainstream cultural representation that to call it into question demands a genealogy of representation in popular culture. Such a critical project entails raising a series of related questions specific to the theater. Since Latin Americans and U.S. Latino/as have been represented on Broadway primarily in musicals, in what ways would *Kiss of the Spider Woman, the Musical* continue the trajectory set in 1939 with Carmen Miranda in *The Streets of Paris* and Desi Arnaz in *Too Many Girls*, where Latinidad is signaled by or perceived as tropical rhythms, colorful locales, and exotic costumes?[5] If Latin Americans are imported as ethnic stereotypes, up to what point can a U.S. Latino/a spectator identify with such constructions? Or would *Kiss* follow the paradigms established by Latino/a self-representations in musicals like *A Chorus Line* and *Zoot Suit*, where identity itself becomes the central trope? Since there are now at least two modes of representations of Latino/as on Broadway—the dominant culture's "Latin" as entertainer and exotic other and the U.S. Latino/a self-representation as working-class underdog—and since Latin American and Latino are so often themselves conflated within the dominant U.S. cultural imaginary, in what space of fantasy would *Kiss*'s representation emerge?[6]

We are not interested in setting up or continuing a binarism between sexuality and ethnicity that privileges one category over another; as Latino gay male cultural critics we accept as axiomatic that identity is a dynamic and sometimes contradictory category. We raise the questions above mainly to locate our own project in the juncture of gay studies and Latino studies, a critical location that has been, at best, left unexplored.[7] And while we are interested in contributing to the growing fields that constitute what is now institutionally identified as lesbian and gay studies, we are also interested in participating in the vibrant discipline of Latino studies. Our focus will be on performance; specifically, we hope to begin a much needed contextualization of theatrical representations of Latinidad. The romantic and undertheorized use of this concept to refer to a type of organic understanding and appreciation of all things Latino further complicates the critical project set forth in Latino studies. *Latinidad* was introduced by Latino and Latina critics as a term identifying and codifying various practices within Latino popular culture and also as a tool for social organization. It stands in direct relation to the term "Latino." Just as "Latino" emerged as a term for self-identification to protest the U.S. government-imposed census term "Hispanic," "Latinidad" emerges as a term out to agitate the imposed imperialist notion of *Hispanic* culture (or *Hispanidad*). Chon Noriega explains the complex interplay of social forces constructing the self-designated "Latino" versus the imposed "Hispanic" terminology and provides a useful context for understanding the emergence of the notion of Latinidad: "The fact that 'Hispanic' emerges as a U.S. census category suggests the difficult play between race and ethnicity, as the government seeks institutional control through homogenization ('Hispanic'), and social movements undertake radical change through the formation of a collective identity ('Latino')."[8] Latinidad grows out of this crisis of categorization and this tension between competing political ideologies; it arrives on the scene as a nostalgic reinvocation of the markers of a cultural heritage and homeland—wherever that may be—for the *gente* by the *gente*. It is always understood to imply a certain, although undefined, Latino vernacular. Within Latino studies, Latinidad circulates as a critical shorthand valorizing seemingly authentic cultural practices that challenge both colonial and imperialist U.S. ideologies in North and South America.[9] The basis of its own ideological construction and sustenance, however, is never overtly challenged. No need, then, to belabor the point that Latinidad does not distinguish between the various races, ethnicities, national origins, languages, and cultures housed under its label, or that the term slyly and comfortably homogenizes gender. Like many other terms that appear to irritate and unsettle dominant U.S. mythologies of Latin American and Latino cultures and identities, Latinidad circulates in the Latino imaginary as a galvanizing democratic intervention in racist and imperialist practices. As such, Latinidad remains unchecked.[10]

In our effort to promote an informed dialogue between Latino studies and gay studies, we raise five points central to our project:

1. Both the self-chosen term "Latino/a" and the imposed term "Hispanic" conflate specific Latin American and U.S. identities. We relate the process of conflation in dominant culture to the construction of Latinidad. The term "Hispanic," as sustained by the technologies of official regulatory regimes, sets out to interpellate, discipline, homogenize, and contain the heterogeneous experiences of U.S. Latina/os.

2. When appropriated by dominant U.S. culture, Latinidad takes the form of tropicalization, a process that represents Latin Americans and U.S. Latina/os as stereotypical exotic others, political terrorists, poor peasants, gang members, or illegal aliens.[11]

3. Within dominant constructions of Latinidad, there is virtually no room for

queers that is not already marked as either expendable or assimilationist; within dominant gay culture, there is virtually no room for Latina/os that is not already marked as either expendable or Other.

4. The issues specific to queer Latina/os are never staged or represented within the prevailing cultural practices labeled "Latinidades" or within the prevailing cultural practices labeled "lesbian and gay culture."[12]

5. The relationship between Latinidad, homosexuality, and AIDS—one of the leading causes of death among Latinos and Latinas—remains unarticulated in dominant culture.

These five points inform one another and maintain their currency both in representations of Latina/os in the dominant U.S. cultural imaginary and in the perceptions of Latina/os who internalize popular representations or romanticize new ones. This is the burden of representation inherited by *Kiss of the Spider Woman, the Musical*. For Latina/os—especially queer Latina/os—seeing a production like *Kiss* entails a constant deconstruction of the legacy of Latinidad as imagined by the technologies of dominant culture. At the same time, *Kiss,* like all other representations of Latinidad, offers Latina/o spectators the opportunity to articulate our identities through our reception. This process of articulation is experienced along a continuum of identificatory practices from direct identification to direct rebuttal. Moreover, the process is facilitated by various and often competing signifiers that claim for *Kiss of the Spider Woman, the Musical* cultural and ethnic authenticity. These markers of Latinidad, which include musical styles, dance patterns, regional fashions, tropical locales, and even cultural artifacts as specific as Manuel Puig's novel, signify an ethnic heritage of cultural production from *within* Latin America.[13] All of these elements contribute to the idea of *Kiss* as an authentic Latin American product—*despite* its translation, adaptation, and appropriation by Broadway.

Perhaps more than other signs of ethnicity, the presence of Chita Rivera enables this tenuous recognition of authenticity.[14] Her participation mediates our responses to the musical as both cultural appropriation and authentic Latin American/Latino cultural product. For queer Latina/os already aware of and invested in Puig's gay novel, the process of identification in *Kiss of the Spider Woman, the Musical* is in place before the actual performance.[15] But what can *Kiss* offer Latina/o spectators with queer consciousness and AIDS awareness other than a vexed ethnic and queer identification? And what political efficacy or personal agency does such identification offer the musical's audiences in the age of AIDS?

To begin answering these questions, it is essential to foreground the musical's relationship to both AIDS and Latinidad. We therefore will focus on various components of *Kiss of the Spider Woman, the Musical*: dramaturgy and translation, music and choreography, casting and performance, spectatorship and reception. Manuel Puig's death from AIDS complications, coupled with the general refusal of Latino/as to acknowledge its cause, suggests the necessity of our critical project. The closeting of the cause of Puig's death is symptomatic of the more general and nearly universal repudiation of AIDS and of homosexuality in Latin American and Latino cultural politics and indicates the consequences of divorcing Latinidad from AIDS and from the queer. The fact that *Kiss of the Spider Woman, the Musical* had a long run at the Broadhurst and that Chita Rivera began a national tour in 1995 demonstrates the relevance of unraveling the production's AIDS ideologies, especially as they relate to Latin Americans and Latinos.

We will argue that *Kiss of the Spider Woman, the Musical* can be understood as an AIDS allegory. We support this claim initially with two arguments; the first, a semiotic reading of the referents of AIDS signification in the musical's dramaturgy, directly informs the second, a contextual reading of the musical's closer association with AIDS after its Broadway opening. We will then argue that the choreography of *Kiss* provides spectators one model of resistance that may prove useful in confronting AIDS; the choreography, in particular Chita Rivera's dances, stages a series of identificatory practices that, taken together, instruct spectators how to maintain cultural resistance in the face of seemingly endless tragedy. For this reason, Chita Rivera is one of the organizing principles of our paper. She is the initial screen for the AIDS allegory Alberto had glimpsed but wanted to conceal so as not to influence David's reading, and she serves as the site for projections of our identities as Latinos, queers, and Broadway aficionados. Chita brings us to the production, her participation occasions our collaboration, and our collaboration provides us the opportunity to raise the issue of Latina/os and AIDS.

Latina/os and AIDS

AIDS, like Latinidad, is a cultural construct. As Douglas Crimp argues,

AIDS does not exist apart from the practices that conceptualize it, represent it, and respond to it. We know AIDS only through those practices. This assertion does not contest the existence of viruses, antibodies, infections, or transmission routes. Least of all does it contest the reality of illness, suffering, and death. What it does contest is the notion that there is an underlying reality of AIDS, upon which are constructed the representations, or the culture, or the politics of AIDS. If we recognize that AIDS exists only in and through these constructions, then hopefully we can also recognize the imperative to know them, analyze them, and wrest control of them.[16]

For Latina/os, this imperative to know, analyze, and wrest control of the constructions of AIDS is of primary importance. "Hispanics" are currently the second-fastest-growing AIDS population in the United States. (African Americans are the first.) According to the *HIV/AIDS Surveillance Report*, among "Hispanics" 47,351 men, 8,273 women, and 1,194 children—a total of 56,918—had been diagnosed with AIDS and reported to the Centers for Disease Control as of September 1993.[17] Rates of HIV infection, seroconversion, and fatality among Latina/os will continue to accelerate unless the Latino community directly addresses and intervenes in this crisis. Our project supports the work of Latina/o AIDS activists—straight and queer—who set out to break the silence about AIDS in our communities. "Maintaining the silence is to cede terrain," write Ana Maria Alonso and Maria Teresa Koreck, "is to let dominant discourses define the politics of ethnicity, disease, sexuality and morality."[18] In writing about *Kiss of the Spider Woman, the Musical* we intervene in the unnamed and unexamined convergence of Latinidad and AIDS. *Silencio=muerte*, still.

Once placed in the context of AIDS, *Kiss of the Spider Woman, the Musical* can be read as an allegory of AIDS.[19] The novel, *El beso de la mujer araña*, facilitates such a reading because it already contains the signifying discursive units of AIDS: torture, pain, horror, blood, oppression, endurance, survival, death, state terror, and gay identity. The transference of the signifying referents of horror and oppression from the political situation in Argentina in 1976 to the horror and oppression of AIDS in the 1990s bridges the gap between these discrete historical and social phenomena. The slippage from the cruelties of fascist regimes to the calamities of AIDS is enabled by a process of signification that functions through associations, contiguities, and connections of referents. The interchangeability of signs illuminates both sets of historical experiences. The spectator's awareness of AIDS locates the narrative of torture, pain, and death in a new context. This context does not ignore the novel's original cultural and political reading to impose a new interpretation; for spectators with a critical consciousness of AIDS, the signs for an AIDS allegorical reading are unmistakably present in both the novel and its adaptation. These signs structure the allegorical reading.

Furthermore, the allegory of AIDS functions in relationship to the politics of representation and reception in the contemporary theater. The spectator's allegorical interpretation is not limited to personal awareness of the allegory or to speculation about the author's intentions. In the process of encoding and decoding the allegory of AIDS, the spectator intervenes in the cultural imaginary and its discursive representation of AIDS. Thirteen years into the epidemic, it is no longer possible to stage a gay representation without invoking the experience of AIDS. This is not to say that all contemporary gay theater is about AIDS. And while we recognize that the widespread equation of gay male sexuality and AIDS is usually a homophobic conflation, we want to emphasize that an AIDS-activist-critical consciousness is needed to disentangle this equation. Our point is that gay theater continues to participate in the shaping of our understanding of AIDS in multiple and contradictory ways.[20] And the context of AIDS now informs all productions of gay male representation regardless of the actual content of the representation.

The AIDS Allegory in Kiss of the Spider Woman, the Musical

Kiss of the Spider Woman, the Musical portrays Molina's gay identity and oppression in a series of scenes that evoke the AIDS crisis. The spectator witnesses the continual torture of prisoners and an escape from this pain through Molina's celluloid fantasies. Because death is the only way to end the torture (and AIDS), for Molina and Valentin—as for many people with AIDS—death itself would be the ultimate escape. In the musical, the

Spider Woman embodies death. Molina fears her fatal kiss, which conflates eros and thanatos.

Despite the ravaging of gay men in the Americas by AIDS, the association between sex and death, already present in Puig's novel, is problematically situated in the musical's AIDS allegory through the association of gay male sexuality and AIDS. In the opening scene of the musical Molina is being seduced by the Spider Woman:

Come and find me
Hear my song
Let me hold you here where you belong
Lips are waiting
Pain will cease
Calm your anguish
I can bring you peace.[21]

Only through her kiss will Molina be able to escape pain. As the narrative structure of the musical unfolds, gay male sexuality and AIDS become coterminous. At that moment, the Spider Woman/Death appears at the center of a giant spider web from which there is no escape:

And you're aching to move but you're caught in the web
Of the Spider Woman
In her velvet cape
You can scream
But you cannot escape

. . . .

You can run
You can scream
You can hide
But you cannot escape!

Indeed, being trapped in AIDS is being trapped in the spider web—death itself: there is no available vaccine or foreseeable cure. Cruising men implies cruising death. In these circumstances, the Spider Woman awaits Molina with confidence:

Sooner or later
You're certain to meet
In the bedroom, the parlor or even the street.[22]

The Spider Woman conflates all gay male sexual practices as "unsafe" and positions all gay men as "victims."

The constant portrayal of pain and torture is at the center of the AIDS allegory. Over and over, the signifiers of AIDS can be anticipated in the musical's unfolding, the unfolding of the allegory. Blood, excrement, and lesions, for example, can be read allegorically as the characters experience torture and pain. The sign *blood* is omnipresent throughout the performance, as is AIDS, which is so much about contaminated blood. In the performance, the spider web itself is lit blood red in the torture scene. A huge red web is also projected over the vertical prison bars, suggesting a double imprisonment. In this representational system there is no escape at all. Within our allegorical reading, to be trapped in blood is to be caught in AIDS.[23] A significant moment centered around blood occurs in act 1, when a prisoner screams that he is not afraid of blood and touches the blood of the recently tortured Valentin, who is paraded by the guards as a warning to the others. "Do you think blood frightens me?" he defiantly cries. "But I can't be frightened. Look." For an audience with an AIDS critical consciousness, the emphasis on blood overlays the original narrative with the connotations of AIDS. AIDS is no longer a hidden meaning in the musical; it is the absent presence evoked through the sign *blood*. By supplementarity, *blood* fills the lack: AIDS hemorrhages on the stage.[24] It is the excess of signification registered in the sign *blood*. Stage blood activates the fear of real blood.[25]

If blood is a constitutive signifying unit in the musical, so is excrement. In their first conversation, Molina and Valentin negotiate their space in the cell. Physiological needs are discussed:

Molina: But the pot. How about the pot?

Valentin: What about the pot?

Molina: It's on your side.

Valentin: So what?

Molina: So when I have to use the pot, I intend to use the pot.

Unfortunately, when they are tortured with poisoned food, neither will actually reach the pot. In one such scene, as Molina cleans Valentin after a bout of diarrhea, the spectator is again invited to think of AIDS. The characters' lack of control over bodily functions recalls AIDS. If "AIDS is about shit and blood," as George Whitmore insists, the musical, through its representation of shit and blood, locates the spectator in the discursive web of AIDS.[26] Molina cares for and nurtures Valentin as friends care for people with AIDS. His act of caring alludes to the heroic endurance of those infected and affected.

In act 2, the scene entitled "Morphine Tango" functions metonymically with other hospital scenes in the cultural production of AIDS. The scene gains its significance from the ubiquity of hospital rooms in representations of AIDS on film, television, and the stage. After Molina is poisoned, he is taken to the infirmary, where morphine shots cause him to hallucinate. The male orderlies, dressed in green hospital gowns, stage a campy musical revue featuring Molina pushed around on a gurney. They hold hypodermic needles containing the morphine that will put him to sleep, make him dream, and stop his pain. In Puig's novel the reader is told only that Valentin refuses to go to the infirmary: "Un preso politico no debe caer a la enfermeria nunca, me entiendes, nunca [A political prisoner should never give in to the infirmary, understand me, never]."[27] The scene is central to the musical, however, and to our allegorical reading. When placed within the context of AIDS, this scene evokes the continuous hospitalizations, dementia, and deathbed scenes of people with AIDS.

After "Morphine Tango," the Spider Woman reminds Molina about her kiss:

Some day you will kiss me . . .
Yes, all men kiss me and you will too . . .
When you kiss me
And you will kiss me
But not now!
Not yet! Not now!

Molina resists her vehemently. He is not ready to die; he will not "let go." The orderlies advise a change of scene and mood: "Just change this morbid scene / Take some more morphine." The "Morphine Tango" sequence is not simply a structural unit of the hospital scene; the scene also carnivalizes the torture experience (and the medical torture of AIDS) through Molina's morphine-induced fantasies. In the end, his celluloid fantasies will be his salvation. Much later, in "Only in the Movies," the musical's final scene, Molina welcomes his death. The Spider Woman offers the long-awaited kiss. It is at this moment that Molina plays the leading man who accepts death. Although initially fearful of the Spider Woman, after their kiss Molina can tango with her. In fantasy, he has found his way out of hell.

There is only one moment in *Kiss of the Spider Woman, the Musical* when AIDS is explicitly suggested. In the finale of act 1, Molina tells Valentin a movie plot (*Amazon Love*) set in a jungle. The musical number is titled "Gimme Love." Chita Rivera portrays Aurora, the fictional star of the various films Molina narrates. Aurora, who is Molina's alter ego, sings two lines: "If there's a war on, don't bring me the news" and "If there's a plague don't invite me, my friend." During the song—a catchy fast-paced seduction song that accelerates desperately in rhythm, desire, eroticism, and passion ("Gimme, gimme, gimme, gimme . . . Let's make love . . . Hugs, squeezes, lips, kisses . . . Gimme Love")—Chita Rivera is accompanied by a chorus of scantily dressed hunks, an ironic and campy mention of the epidemic that separates AIDS from its most prevalent associations with sex. In this song, love and sex become the antidote to plague.

In scenes before and after this showstopper, the musical cannot be read as simply escapist; it can also be understood as a cultural, political, and historical commentary on AIDS. "I Do Miracles" is perhaps the most obvious moment in the production when references to torture and pain remind the spectators of AIDS. As Aurora offers escape and relief to Molina and Valentin, the imagery of blood, torn flesh, breathing difficulties, pain, and bruises evokes the repertoire of AIDS representations:

I do miracles
Though the lash of the whip has caused your flesh to tear
I will place my lips on you everywhere
And I'll do miracles
Blood
On your slender hips
Blood
Underneath your eyes
Blood on your firm young thighs
Let me kiss it away
So I can hear you say
I do miracles.

Indeed, the allegorical reading of *Kiss of the Spider Woman, the Musical* is materialized in the references to "each bruise" and "purple stains." Lesions on a disfigured face and debilitated body are the markers of Kaposi's sarcoma and AIDS in stereotypical depictions of people with AIDS:

Though your breath racks your ribs and you throb with pain

. . . .

As I cradle you close and caress each bruise
What I've come here to give you, you must not refuse.[28]

Molina conjures Aurora to help him alleviate Valentin's condition. Marta, Valentin's lover, also appears to help care for Valentin. Valentin imagines Molina as Marta, and Molina imagines himself as Aurora. It is only through these substitutions that Molina is able to "homecare" for Valentin, to nurse him. Molina's kiss—or is it Aurora's or Marta's?—provides relief from Valentin's torture. But what about Molina's pain? Although the musical continually searches for an escape from pain, torture, and death, Molina cannot escape physical and mental suffering even with morphine. The result is a fluctuation between fantasy and agony, between escapist entertainment and politics. The Spider Woman constantly beckons Molina, asking for the fatal kiss, for the final union in fantasy (and in death): "Come up here. Play with me. Play with me."[29] Molina continues to refuse.

For the spectator aware of the militancy and activism surrounding AIDS, "The Day after That," sung by Valentin, seems to call to join the war on AIDS. It expresses the need to mobilize and functions as an anthem, as it enacts the political activism of the families of "los desaparecidos." At this point, *los desaparecidos*—those who were tortured, jailed, mutilated, killed, and buried by Latin American fascist regimes—are linked to people with AIDS through illness, suffering, agony, and death.[30] Their relationship is staged theatrically when the families hold up portraits of *los desaparecidos*: their relatives and friends. The portraits, like the Names Project AIDS Memorial Quilt, function to raise consciousness and memorialize the dead.[31]

As a ritualistic performance and symbolic act, the raising of the portraits of *los desaparecidos* and the display of the quilt panels are monumental reminders that people are dying at the torturing hands of fascist regimes and in the global catastrophe of AIDS. The portraits and quilt panels become floating cemeteries without bodies that help people understand emotionally the loss and suffering caused by military dictatorships and AIDS. Both rituals invite contemplation, collective mourning, and political activism. The links between disappearance and AIDS are manifest not only in their outcomes (blood, bruises, death) but also in their cause. The portraits and quilt panels honor the dead, give meaning to their lives, and provide hope, strength, and courage to those who survive to continue the wars against totalitarian regimes and AIDS:

Someday we'll be free
I promise you, we'll be free
if not tomorrow
then the day after that
And the candles in our hand
will illuminate this land
if not tomorrow
then the day after that.

Our allegorical reading is further supported by the adoption of "The Day after That" as the official anthem of the American Foundation for AIDS Research (AMFAR). On World AIDS Day, 1 December 1993, Liza Minnelli performed the song at the United Nations. She has also recorded it in English, Spanish, and French and donated all proceeds to AMFAR. Minnelli explains that the song is "about a lot more than revolution. It is about hope, about fighting despair."[32] Minnelli intentionally appropriates the song, without music, for an AIDS agenda: "we have no song for the war against AIDS," she told the *Advocate*.[33]

We want to consider Minnelli's comments as they relate specifically to the context of AIDS in *Kiss of the Spider Woman, the Musical*. Although she extracts the song from the musical, her version—along with her public performances and her efforts to raise AIDS awareness—helps confirm the existence of an AIDS allegorical system available to the spectator with an AIDS consciousness. Moreover, Minnelli and AMFAR's appropriation of "The Day after That" shapes the expectations of prospective audiences and invites previous spectators to reconsider the significance of the musical.[34] People who have heard Minnelli's version of the song, seen the video, or are simply aware of their appropriation may now bring to the production of *Kiss of the Spider Woman, the Musical* a heightened sensitivity to its relation to AIDS. Such spectators will fill in the indeterminacy of the pronoun "that" in the title "The Day after That" with the signifieds of AIDS. For them, "that"=AIDS. AIDS becomes the unsaid signifier, the unnamed signified.[35]

Finally, Terrence McNally's authorship of the book for the musical supports a reading of it as an AIDS allegory. McNally also wrote the AIDS telescript *Andre's Mother* and such dramas as *The Lisbon Traviata, Lips Together, Teeth Apart,* and *A Perfect Ganesh*—all plays that, while not necessarily "about" AIDS, acquire much of their cultural meaning in relationship to AIDS. Manuel Puig, who died of AIDS complications, also figures in our reading. The musical discloses perhaps his ultimate secret, allegorically speaking, and makes a statement about AIDS in relation to Latino cultures where AIDS remains taboo. The Colombian American writer Jaime Manrique writes in an article on Puig and AIDS, "Although he officially died of a heart attack . . . I began to hear stories that he had been ill with AIDS. Some of the people close to him reluctantly began to admit it, while others denied it vehemently, as if having the disease would somehow make him a lesser man and tarnish his achievements. After all, if homosexuality is the greatest taboo in Hispanic culture, AIDS is the unspeakable."[36]

Allegory, Performance, and Spectatorial Identification

To claim that *Kiss of the Spider Woman, the Musical* is an AIDS allegory is to risk dehistoricizing the original and adapted narratives in order to re-historicize them in the interests of AIDS. If we understand allegory as a system of referents that combine to achieve a level of meaning outside the narrative structure, the historical and sociopolitical contexts of a work need to be considered in allegorical interpretation. Like all acts of interpretation, allegorical readings can only be rhetorical positions informed by and offered from specific political motivations. Interpretation can never be divorced from political subjectivities and agendas.[37] To argue for an allegorical AIDS reading of *Kiss of the Spider Woman, the Musical* is to claim a specific (albeit unstable) performative interpretation that illuminates not only the object of interpretation but the act of interpretation itself. Allegory is a form of counterdiscourse; it speaks something other (from the Greek *allos* [other] and *agoreuein* [to speak]). The question remains: Why employ allegory in *Kiss of the Spider Woman, the Musical* to speak the something other—in this case, AIDS?

Allegory simultaneously arouses and disavows identification. Recognizing an allegorical structure in *Kiss of the Spider Woman, the Musical* allows the spectator entrance into a new system of meaning. Allegory makes AIDS present—or omnipresent—in the act of interpretation. Our interpretation of the performance of *Kiss* as an AIDS allegory informs the politics of the production as well as the context of its reception. Casting doubt on the structure of meaning in the literal narrative calls into question both the literal and allegorical possibilities of interpretation; this is what Todorov describes as the reader's hesitation about adopting an allegorical interpretation.[38] This hesitation invites identification and its disavowal. The spectator first begins to identify the connotative meaning embedded in the allegorical structure; the pleasure of inscribing meaning onto the narrative suggests the pleasure of discovery. The spectator both discovers and constructs the allegorical meaning embedded in the performance. In the process of identifying the other meanings, the spectator moves toward negotiating the process of identification with what is represented. "Con quién te identificas?" Molina asks Valentin in the novel, after narrating one of his movies. This question of identification is central to allegorical interpretation. In *Kiss of the Spider Woman, the Musical,* the spectator with an AIDS-critical consciousness recognizes the AIDS allegory and begins to negotiate identification with the characters' responses to (the allegorical representation of) AIDS.

If allegory allows for the spectator's identification with the material of allegory, the connotative structure of allegory allows for its simultaneous disavowal. Since AIDS is never explicitly present in *Kiss of the Spider Woman, the Musical,* and since it is made present in the performance only through the spectator's allegorical interpretation, the spectator may also disavow or deny that the musical is a representation of AIDS. Allegory—functionally and inevitably—enacts distancing. Allegory layers meanings in narrative; it insists upon the always possible other connotative meanings in representation and interpretation. It suggests, as Maureen

Quilligan has demonstrated, a pretext or "the source that always stands outside the narrative."[39] In *Kiss of the Spider Woman, the Musical,* this pretext is cultural and ideological: AIDS.

And yet it remains problematic to assume that the pretext of AIDS no longer needs overt articulation. The distancing process characteristic of allegory may reinforce the cultural denial of AIDS. *Kiss of the Spider Woman, the Musical* is especially vulnerable to the cultural denial of AIDS, since as entertainment—in particular as a Broadway musical—the production is placed within the realm of escapism and fantasy.[40]

Citationality and Performativity, Actors and Audiences

Escapism and fantasy are, of course, basic survival tactics for Molina. Molina's investment in popular films, especially his identification with their heroines and the star who plays them, is what keeps him alive in prison. Molina offers Valentin this tactic, but Valentin at first resists. In time Valentin asks for more fantasy, more Molina. Molina in turn identifies with Aurora's beauty and courage; she is the phantasmatic force that compels him to construct himself as a subject not already and always abject.[41] Molina's attempts to materialize this fantasy become the driving force of his performance. Valentin, Molina's cell mate, is his spectator.

Molina's performance participates in a complex web of citational practices endemic to the musical and the Puig novel. Citational practices are performative reiterations of prior performances introduced to either affirm or resist (depending on the political allegiance of the actor) a dominant ideological system. Molina's efforts to perform Aurora for Valentin are citational insofar as they refer to previous performances—performances, it must be understood, that were precisely that. Aurora acts scripted roles. Her performances are singular and deliberate occasions. She is an actor in the conventional sense. Molina, too, "performs"; however, his reiteration of Aurora's acting, while arguably an act, is a site of citationality, the inevitable and deliberate declaration of a legacy of referentiality that for him includes his own abjection. Despite their seemingly analogous relationship to the disciplining power of a script, performativity as citationality is not the same as acting. "Reiterations," as Judith Butler reminds us, "are never simply replicas of the same."[42]

A citational politics of resistance deliberately sets out to refer to previous historical and cultural practices not authorized within the law. Puig sets the force of referentiality into motion in the novel, which includes verbatim sections of films and footnotes. In citing old films, Puig foregrounds the processes of identification and offers his own homage to the cinema. And yet in creating his own scripts and in forging footnotes, Puig both unsettles the authenticity of the originals and calls attention to his own authorial presence. Of course, the process of adapting the novel into *Kiss of the Spider Woman, the Musical* is an obvious and deliberate citation of Puig.

In the actors' performances in *Kiss of the Spider Woman, the Musical,* the practice of citation becomes a foundational structure of the production.[43] The actor who plays Molina quotes Puig's character from the novel; he also quotes Aurora, a fictional star in the musical. It needs to be stressed that in the narrative of the musical Molina creates Aurora, insofar as it is the gay man who makes her a legend. In other words, Aurora remains fictional throughout. Only through Molina does she become iconic, legendary. This idea is reinforced by the production history of the musical; it is gay men who have formed and shaped the role of Aurora. Chita Rivera performs this role, which in "The Russian Movie / Good Times" scene requires her to perform Aurora performing the role of Tatyana Alexandrovna in *The Flame of St. Petersburg*. Harold Prince's direction has Rivera "overact" to help the audience distinguish between the various layers of Rivera's performance. Her campy, melodramatic performance, while wonderfully entertaining, serves also to comment indirectly on the limited kinds of roles available to women actors in popular theater. One could argue that the musical rehearses the appropriation of female actors and their roles for the fantasies of gay men. Both the novel and the musical *stage* diva identification. Indeed, the roles for women in *Kiss of the Spider Woman, the Musical*—muse, mother, and loyal lover—do nothing to expand the representational possibilities for women in mainstream production. So on top of the layered role Rivera must play in this scene, she is also citing some of her own previous stage performances.[44] This is true throughout *Kiss*. It is impossible to watch Rivera's splendid performance without being aware of Rivera. The choreography, the direction, and musical numbers all suggestively cite her past performances. To some extent, this is the inescapable consequence of long-standing success, for popular performers, although performing different roles, must employ the same body in performance.

In the case of Chita Rivera, whose theatrical career spans decades, the body itself enacts a type of citation. Her high kicks and extensions, for example, are glorious not simply because she is over sixty; rather, her performance is a revelation because her previous performances survive through choreographic citation. The very concept of survival is staged continuously in her every performance. Her body becomes, then, not only the sign of ethnic "authenticity" but the site of citation and endurance as well. Since Chita Rivera is the only recognizable star in the production—the other parts were all cast with "unknowns"—the idea of endurance is marked by her presence. In this sense, Molina's investment in Aurora is cited in the history of the production. The legendary Chita Rivera corresponds to Aurora in the very process of production. For this reason, Vincent Patterson's choreography throughout and Rob Marshall's choreography of the "Aurora" movie sequences deserve special mention. Patterson's and Marshall's work calls attention to the dynamic of citation and performativity in a manner the music does not. While the music at times suggests earlier popular styles and, more obviously, attempts to invoke certain exotic motifs, it does not participate in the citationality that characterizes the choreography and direction.

The director Harold Prince exposes the relationship between Chita Rivera and Aurora in his staging of "Gimme Love." It is in this scene that the politics of citation begin to converge with the process of identification embedded in the production. Molina is telling Valentin one of his movies. As he begins to describe Aurora's performance, she appears. Rivera makes her entrance in a huge elevated birdcage and begins the musical number accompanied by "Aurora's men": four male actors from the ensemble. At one point she breaks into dance front stage center. The actor playing Molina replaces Rivera in the cage, which remains downstage center, and begins to mime her performance. He studies her performance, quotes her gestures, and performs his identification. Within the plot of the musical, Molina is quoting Aurora; within the performance of the musical, the actor cast as Molina is quoting Chita Rivera, the actor cast as Aurora.

The conflation of actor and role, when seen in this light, suggests that the actor who plays Molina is directed to identify with Rivera. Rivera's performance has been studied and learned by the actor who plays Molina. He is her understudy, so to speak. His staged rehearsal of her role—as Aurora, as Chita, as legend—calls attention to the power of citational practices to preserve these specific performances. Through the actor's study of Rivera's role, the performance will continue to exist in the memory of the actor directed in the practice of reiteration, quotation, citation. His future citational performances invite memory to historicize the original signifier and transfer that meaning to its current context. In this scene, Molina, the gay window dresser who loves the movies and especially their heroines and the actresses who play them, underscores his identificatory and citational practices through dance. Molina—and the actor hired to play him—invite audiences to participate in this process of recontextualization.

In the end, *Kiss of the Spider Woman, the Musical* is a production that highlights the relationship between the spectator and the performer. As such, identificatory and citational practices—when read in collaboration with an interpretation of the production as an allegory of AIDS—position the spectator to appropriate both the text and the performance. The spectator is shown the steps of this appropriation in the rehearsed movements of the production's musical numbers. The musical's choreography thus positions dance as a type of pedagogy. In *Kiss of the Spider Woman, the Musical,* identifications are learned through movement. In regimes sustaining disappearance and AIDS, bodies are strictly policed; bodies are continually and forcefully disciplined into socially sanctioned movements and punished for socially transgressive ones. The movements and motions of the resisting body are rehearsed, performed, and learned through choreography. Choreography emerges as a vehicle for cultural memory, for passing on undocumented cultural resistance, which thereby remains vibrantly available for generations informed by and engaged in the citational politics of motion. It is in these liberatory subversive moments—undocumented but not lost—that the collaborative motions of bodies in resistance rupture the psychic hegemony of resignation and despair. With AIDS as its pretext and Latinidad as its *urtext, Kiss of the Spider Woman, the Musical* inevitably participates in the ideological formations surrounding each of these constructions. Our task as spectators must always be to locate our position around these constructions, to unleash the power of interpretation and counterinter-

pretation in order to destabilize them, and to identify the possible pleasures still available in their production.

Performance and Collaboration

It's Wednesday evening, 20 October 1993, and we are in New York. We
are with John at a gay bar in the West Village recounting to him our day.
We tell him (and rehearse for ourselves) the day's events: our nearly
missed meeting at the Drama Book Shop, the fabulous matinee performance of *Kiss of the Spider Woman, the Musical,* which now even David
loves, our—at last!—shared meal after the performance, and our impressions of yet another AIDS play, Nicky Silver's *Pterodactyls,* we have just
seen this evening. But if we tell John anything of substance at all, we tell
him of our pleasure in the discovery that we have established a foundation for friendship. David and I part secure in our affection but unclear as
to how our friendship will develop over time.

I don't remember the specific steps that have led us to this collaboration.
I do remember this: Alberto and I are on the phone and he is telling me
the status of his various projects. He wants to write an essay on *Kiss of
the Spider Woman, the Musical* as an AIDS allegory but feels reluctant to
start something he may not be able to complete. We start a series of conversations that flesh out his ideas, and I realize through these conversations that I also have some things I want to say. I am interested in
addressing the citational practices of the production, especially the relationship between actors and roles. (Weeks later, Alberto tells me that he
really wanted to write something in tribute to Manuel Puig.) Through
these conversations, our correspondence, and our memories of 20 October 1993, we began exploring the possibility of working together on an
article on *Kiss of the Spider Woman, the Musical.*

It's 20 January 1994. Three months after seeing the show, David has come
to Massachusetts so we can write our piece on *Kiss of the Spider Woman,
the Musical.* Our time together involves getting to know each other and
long hours of work. Because of my AIDS condition, we have to slow
down at times and take breaks. David is concerned about the effect on

my health of the stress of writing. Frankly, so am I. And yet I am delighted to be working in such a way that I can share my ideas without carrying the burden of isolated academic labor. I am stimulated by this collaborative effort: I don't have to type, edit, or organize the structure of the paper. I feel relief that I can keep on working. The paradox of invigoration and fatigue is a familiar feeling for me as I continue to live with AIDS. Our intellectual exchanges and intense conversations on critical methodologies and theoretical approaches shape our writing process. They allow us the freedom to explore creatively our writing styles. David worries that he is disciplining me into his writing style and voice. Those are his words, not mine. I remind him that my voice is here, present on the page. (*Estoy aquí, todavía existo* [I am here. I still exist].) I tell him that he thinks this because he is the typist, the one who places the words into the computer—his computer. While he types, we continuously negotiate ideas, approaches, and ways of reading. This is how the article takes shape.

I haven't left Alberto's apartment in days; just as well—it's now below zero here. Each night, before he goes to sleep, Alberto announces to me the temperature—one night it's two degrees, the next night it's down to zero—even though I don't ask. For me, cold is cold. His proclamations of degrees remind me of T-cell counts. We want to keep these degrees above zero—we want those numbers high.

The academic profession disciplines the scholar into the fallacy of intellectual scholarship as an isolated activity. We are trained to work alone. (Sometimes, if we are lucky, we have mentors or colleagues who contribute to the development of our ideas, read and comment on our work, and make suggestions for overall improvement.) Nevertheless, thinking and writing are imagined primarily as exercises of the self, of the "individual."[45] To collaborate suggests the scholar's inability to work alone. For us it is more complicated than that. We enter into collaboration in the spirit of feminism—as academics—where collaboration yields innovative scholarship and an intervention in the myth of the intellectual as sole contributor to the construction of knowledge. We enter into collaboration in the spirit of our discipline—as theorists of theater and performance studies—where collaboration enhances both performance and production. We enter into collaboration in the spirit of identification—as Latino gay men—where collaboration unsettles the myth of our uniqueness in the profession and in our social lives. We enter into collaboration in the spirit of political affinity—as AIDS activists—where collaboration is a tactic for empowerment and survival.

For me, as a person with AIDS, there is an urgency in writing. This urgency is related to living day by day with the reality of elusive energy and health. Writing is a process that materializes at the moment of the act of writing. As a person who lives day by day and always in the moment, I don't have time to postpone the act of writing. And yet I don't always have the energy to write. I have many ideas and essays germinating in my head, and I carry these prospective writings into my day. I fear that I will not be able to get these ideas out in time. Through collaboration I can counter this fear, experience the pleasure of accomplishment, and feel relief that my work achieved materialization. I have shared my ideas with David so much that, should I collapse, I am confident that he will be able to complete the work. Ultimately, this collaboration is for me a strategy for survival and an opportunity to continue producing scholarship. I have learned through AIDS how to restructure creatively the means by which I express my identity, experience my pleasures, maintain my health, and make the best of the here and now. All of this has been confirmed for me through the process of our collaboration.

Sharing this experience provides me the pleasure of being alive. Although I have my limitations because of AIDS, I am dying to write. I am not dying to be published. It is a popular misconception that to be published is to achieve immortality. For me, immortality is in the moment of writing that confirms I am alive.

Writing is a type of performance and collaboration always a dance. I am participating in a performance that no one other than Alberto and me will experience or witness. This is the intimacy we offer each other in collaboration. Alberto and I may be promiscuous theatergoers—we will go to the theater at any time and with just about anyone to see nearly anything—but we get picky when it comes to collaboration. Three months ago we met in New York and shared the experience of *Kiss of the Spider Woman, the Musical*. Now we are here in his Massachusetts home writing—collaborating—on our impressions of the performance, our collaboration a performance in and of itself. (We return again and again to the space of performance.) But you know what, Alberto? If AIDS is the pretext for *Kiss of the Spider Woman, the Musical,* as we have argued, then maybe we can say that *Kiss of the Spider Woman, the Musical* is the pretext for our friendship, "the source that always stands outside [our] narrative." Like Molina and like you, I am now caught in the web. At first, I worried that I was disciplining you into my writing style and voice, not to mention writing habits. But now I wonder how it came to be that I am here with you writing about this musical. I wonder if, in part, I am here—like the actor playing Molina—to understudy your role, to observe and learn the intricate choreographies of your discourse, your style, and your way of thinking. Who's rehearsing whom? Who's leading in this, our dance? And while I am not comfortable surrendering to the narrative trajectory of *Kiss of the Spider Woman,* which ends, after all, in death, in writing about these *Kisses* (Puig's, Broadway's, our own), I keep returning to the pleasures of these contacts: the pleasures of spectatorship, of writing about performance, and of our friendship. Each of these performances is a temporal instance of intimacy and presence, of shared pleasure and identification. I wonder, too—since I am now caught in the web—if this collaboration is primarily our effort to draw more people into the entanglements of identifications and affinities necessary to resist the despair of AIDS.

Performances are always ephemeral.[46] Publication of our essay can only be a documentation of our own performances, a record that we have lived these shared moments. I know that for you publication is not the issue. A part of me supports this, but there is another part of me that still wants to have a record of our encounters. It's an impossible demand, I know. Publication confirms the completion of the collaboration, the transference of the act of performance into a documentation of the performance. Once outside the performative, our performance becomes vulnerable to resignification and appropriation by others in the performative act of reading. I know that what matters most is the experience of performance and not its documentation. (And so it is that I return again and again to the space of performance.) But I still want a souvenir that confirms to us that this is real. So let this be that for me, okay? Let the record show that we are together here—wherever this here may be—

c/siting ourselves and speaking out about AIDS, collaborating in the various performances that constitute our lives.

Notes

This chapter first appeared in *American Literature*, volume 67, number 3 (September 1995). The original version was presented at the conference "Screening Latinidad: A Project on Media, Performance, and Visual Culture" at Duke University on 5 February 1994. We would like to thank José Muñoz, Tiffany Ana López, Carmelita Tropicana, and Ela Troyano for their encouragement and support. We are also indebted to Susana Chavez-Silverman, Celeste Fraser Delgado, Jaime Manrique, and Karen Remmler for their critical engagement through the revision process.

1. Official production program of *Kiss of the Spider Woman, the Musical.*

2. See Yoko Yoshikawa, "The Heat Is on *Miss Saigon* Coalition: Organizing across Race and Sexuality," in *The State of Asian American Activism and Resistance in the 1990s,* ed. Karin Aguilar-San Juan (Boston: South End Press, 1993), 275–294.

3. See *Out Front: Contemporary Gay and Lesbian Plays,* ed. Don Shewey (New York: Grove Press, 1988); and John M. Clum, *Acting Gay: Male Homosexuality in Modern Drama,* rev. ed. (New York: Columbia U P, 1994).

4. Most of our individual work on gay theater specifically addresses AIDS and/or Latino issues. See David Román, " 'It's My Party and I'll Die If I Want To!': Gay Men, AIDS, and the Circulation of Camp in U.S. Theatre," *Theatre Journal* 44 (1992): 305–327; "Performing All Our Lives: AIDS, Performance, Community," in *Critical Theory and Performance,* ed. Janelle Reinelt and Joseph Roach (Ann Arbor: U of Michigan P, 1993); " 'Teatro Viva!': Latino Performance and the Politics of AIDS in Los Angeles," in *Entiendes?: Hispanic Writings/Queer Readings,* ed. Emilie Bergmann and Paul Julian Smith (Durham: Duke U P, 1995); Alberto Sandoval, "Staging AIDS: What's Latino Got to Do with It?" in *Negotiating Performance: Gender, Sexuality, and Theatricality in Latin/o America,* ed. Diana Taylor and Juan Villegas (Durham: Duke U P, 1994); "*A Chorus Line:* Not Such a 'One Singular Sensation' for Puerto Rican Crossovers," *Ollantay Theatre* 1 (1993): 46–61.

5. Carmen Miranda and Desi Arnaz are among the foundational images of this Latinidad, beneficiaries of Franklin D. Roosevelt's "good neighbor" policy of expanding business with Latin America during World War II. The cultural importation of Latin American entertainers helps set into motion a trajectory that fetishizes Latin America and constructs Latinidad primarily as tropical other—the beautiful señorita and the Latin lover—and then shifts locales from the tropics to the now ubiquitous representation of the Latino ghetto. See the essays and introduction in *Tropicalizations: Transforming Latinidad beyond Self and Other,* ed. Frances Aparicio and Susana Chavez-Silverman (Berkeley: U of California P, forthcoming).

6. See Sandoval's "*A Chorus Line*," and "A Puerto Rican Reading of the 'America' in *West Side Story*," *Jump Cut* 39 (1994): 59–66, for explanations of these modes.

7. Recent work by Latino gay male academics has begun to respond to the lack of scholarship in this area. Chicana and Latina lesbians have been more consistent and prolific. In theater and performance studies, the writings of Yvonne Yarbro-Bejarano are indispensable. For a bibliography, see her essay "The Female Subject in Chicano Theatre: Sexuality, 'Race,' and Class," in *Performing Feminisms: Feminist Critical Theory and Theatre*, ed. Sue-Ellen Case (Baltimore: Johns Hopkins U P, 1990).

8. Chon Noriega, "El Hilo Latino: Representation, Identity, and National Culture," *Jump Cut* 38 (1993): 46. See also the indispensable essay by Juan Flores and George Yúdice, "Living Borders / Buscando America: Languages of Latino Self-formation," *Social Text* 24 (1990): 57–84.

9. In *Megalopolis: Contemporary Cultural Sensibilities* (Minneapolis: U of Minnesota P, 1992), Celeste Olalquiaga identifies three distinct types of what she calls "cultural recycling," the complex process by which Latino/as and Latin Americans effect cultural change: "The matter of direct, unmediated adaptation aside, the processes of cultural transformation that involve Latin America as an object, subject, or both are: the Latinization of urban culture in the United States, the formation of hybrid cultures such as the Chicano or Nuyorican, and what I call the pop recycling of U.S. icons of both Latin American and U.S. culture itself at the moment of postindustrialization" (76). Although Olalquiaga never uses the term "Latinidad," she offers the best contextualization and critique of what this "contemporary cultural sensibility" provocatively suggests for other Latino/a critics.

10. In this sense, we are reminded of the way the idea and practice of "camp" in gay culture was until recently historically undertheorized by gay scholars, although continuously evoked. On this idea, see David Bergman's introduction to *Camp Grounds: Style and Homosexuality* (Amherst: U of Massachusetts P, 1993) as well as the essays in the anthology by Jack Babuscio, Esther Newton, and Andrew Ross.

11. See especially *Chicanos and Film: Representation and Resistance*, ed. Chon Noriega (Minneapolis: U of Minnesota P, 1992); *Jump Cut* 38 (1993), a special issue on U.S. Latino media; and *Centro de Estudios Puertorriqueños Bulletin* 2:8 / 3:1 (1990–1991), a special issue on Latinos and the media. Also of interest are Allen Woll, "How Hollywood Has Portrayed Hispanics," *New York Times*, 1 March 1981, D17, 22; Enrique Fernández, "Spitfires, Latin Lovers, Mambo Kings," *New York Times*, 19 April 1992, H1, 30; George Hadley-Garcia, *Hispanic Hollywood: The Latins in Motion Pictures* (New York: Citadel Press, 1990); Arthur G. Pettit, *Images of the Mexican American in Fiction and Film* (College Station: Texas A & M P, 1980); *Chicano Cinema: Research, Reviews, and Resources*, ed. Gary D. Keller (Binghamton, NY: Bilingual Review Press, 1985).

12. Recently, however, queer Latino/as have entered into self-representation in national and regional theater and performance venues. Playwrights and performers such as Cherríe Moraga, Luis Alfaro, Monica Palacios, and Beto Araiza now have a cultural currency unimagined only a few years ago. The crossover success of

Marga Gomez suggests some of the more immediate possibilities within mainstream venues.

13. The irony, of course, is that Puig's novel is set in the cosmopolitan city of Buenos Aires.

14. And yet it needs to be noted that the musical also includes an unfortunate racist and homophobic stereotype of gay Latinos. In the scene where Molina, just released from prison, returns to visit his former coworkers in the window-dressing department, the actors who play these roles are directed to speak in heavy "Spanish" accents and to act with "effeminate" mannerisms. Since Molina rejects these former coworkers and friends in this scene, the production seems to suggest that we should reject these "types" as well. The scene is the only moment in the production where "Spanish" accents are employed to remind the spectator of its Latin source. *Kiss of the Spider Woman, the Musical* practices, for the most part, colorblind casting. This is true even for the actor hired to play Aurora/the Spider Woman. Chita Rivera originated the role and was replaced by Vanessa Williams, the popular and talented African American singer.

15. For this reason, John Clum's curt and unsubstantiated dismissal of *Kiss of the Spider Woman, the Musical* in *Acting Gay* (356) is especially unfortunate, an annoying reminder of the almost total lack of identificatory possibilities available to queers of color in the few products of popular culture that (attempt to) represent some of our issues in mainstream venues.

16. Douglas Crimp, "AIDS: Cultural Analysis/Cultural Activism," *October* 43 (1987): 3–16.

17. AIDS statistics were provided by the AIDS Information Network in Philadelphia. These statistics reflect the number of AIDS cases reported to the Centers for Disease Control in Atlanta up to the time of our viewing of the musical in October of 1993.

18. Q by Ana Maria Alonso and Maria Teresa Koreck, in "Silences: 'Hispanics,' AIDS, and Sexual Practices," *differences* 1.1 (1989): 118.

19. As a definition of allegory, we use the following: "We have allegory when the events of the narrative obviously and continuously refer to another simultaneous structure of events or ideas, whether historical events, moral or philosophical ideas, or natural phenomena . . . Hence there are two main types of allegory: historical or political allegory, referring to characters or events beyond those purportedly described in the fiction; and moral, philosophical, religious, or scientific allegories, referring to an additional set of ideas. If the allegorical reference is continuous throughout the narrative, the fiction is an allegory" (*Princeton Encyclopedia of Poetry and Poetics*, ed. Alex Preminger [Princeton: Princeton U P, 1974], 12).

20. Román, "It's My Party," 326–327.

21. All quotations from the lyrics of the musical are drawn from the album notes for the 1992 original Broadway cast soundtrack (music by John Kander and lyrics by Fred Ebb), available from RCA/Victor.

22. The Spider Woman keeps a diary where she enters her sexual encounters or "tricks": "She's a woman / A perfume by Lanvin / To dab across her wrist / A secret, ribboned diary / Of all the men she's kissed / So many men she's kissed." Given that

Molina projects himself onto Aurora, her role as the Spider Woman is an incarnation of himself. Consequently, the lyrics refer to Molina's sexual life. Within our allegorical reading of the musical, cruising and sex offer more than pleasure, because sex can become a "kiss of death" with AIDS; as the song "Kiss of the Spider Woman" states, "Sooner or later / You're certain to meet . . . There's no place on earth / You're likely to miss / Her kiss."

23. Consider the anxieties around blood as it concerns AIDS: transfusions, blood test results, T-cell counts.

24. Jacques Derrida defines the "supplement" as follows: "The supplement adds itself, it is a surplus, a plenitude enriching another plenitude, the fullest measure of presence. It cumulates and accumulates presence . . . it adds only to replace. It intervenes or insinuates itself in-the-place-of, if it fills, it is as if one fills a void . . . The supplement has not only the power of procuring an absent presence through its image; procuring it for us through the proxy (procuration) of the sign, it holds at a distance and masters it. For this presence is at the same time desired and feared" (*Of Grammatology*, trans. Gayatri Chakravorty Spivak [Baltimore: Johns Hopkins U P, 1976], 144–145).

25. "Red blood" appears in other forms in the production, always working within a metonymical relationship with AIDS. For example, Aurora as Tatyana wears a red satin gown; the scarf Molina gives Valentin at the moment of departure is red. The red gown foreshadows Tatyana's bloody death, which Molina describes as follows: "Red blood stains the snowy street." The scarf could be a symbol of the blood/semen exchange between the two cell mates. Blood is most graphically present when the tortured bodies of Molina and Valentin are made visible at the end of act 2.

26. George Whitmore, *Someone Was Here: Profiles in the AIDS Epidemic* (New York: New American Library, 1988), 24.

27. Manuel Puig, *El beso de la mujer araña* (Barcelona: Seix Barral, 1976), 117.

28. "Breathing" is also a sign in the song "Kiss of the Spider Woman": "And your breath comes faster and you are aching to move."

29. Tatyana's song reverberates with the need for escape: "There's going to be good times / Nothing but good times / They are going to be scatterin those clouds of grey / And all those bad times / Those terrible bad times / Are going to be packing up and leaving town today / So put on a smile."

30. Tatyana's final words ("Viva la guerra, viva la revolucíon, viva—") echo the revolutionary consciousness of the protesters. In the final scene, Molina cites the lines in his performance: "Viva la guerra, viva la revolucíon, viva whatever it is." The indeterminacy of "whatever," as in the pronoun "that" in "The Day after That," is a gap of signification in the musical. Within our allegorical reading, both can be filled with the signifieds of AIDS.

31. To further clarify the political context and social meaning of "los desaparacidos," it is useful to quote here Renato Martínez's semiotic reading of "los desaparecidos" in Chile: "The body of the disappeared is a ghostly sign that lives on in the heart of the disappeared's family. However, the absence of the disappeared is also full of meaning

for the rest of the repressed (?) community. It is what Jurij Lotman calls a 'minus device,' a meaningful absence that justifies itself in the structure of the whole text. The body is the ultimate sign in a symbolic system that looked for the representation of presence; it is also the quintessence of social essentialism. For that reason, the disappeared is also the absolute threat. Seen as a social text in the authoritarian episteme, the body is restricted to only a small set of meanings and removed from a pluralistic society's wider semiotic process. This larger universe to which the body is now inscribed is the very real world of the Chilean socioeconomic situation and its dictatorial vigilantes" (100). See also Michael Taussig's excellent discussion of the disappeared in *The Nervous System* (New York: Routledge, 1992). For photographic documentation and a sociocultural reading of the AIDS quilt, see Peter Hawkins, "Naming Names: The Art of Memory and the Names Project AIDS Quilt," *Critical Inquiry* 19 (1993): 752–779; and Marita Sturken, "Conversations with the Dead: Bearing Witness in the AIDS Memorial Quilt," *Socialist Review* 2 (1992): 65–95.

32. Quoted by Glenn Collins in "On Stage and Off," *New York Times,* 2 July 1993, C2.

33. "Liza with an Anthem," *Advocate,* 14 December 1993, 79. We feel obliged to contest the truth of Minnelli's claim that "we have no song for the war against AIDS." Her comment ignores the history of AIDS awareness in popular songs commissioned and composed as "songs for the war on AIDS"—from mainstream efforts such as the 1985 collaboration "That's What Friends Are For" to Madonna's 1993 "In This Lifetime." Disco and dance music's response to AIDS includes the hits of Jimmy Somerville, Diamanda Galas's AIDS songs (admittedly not easily available for sing-alongs or public dancing), and, especially, the music of Michael Callen. Callen's "Love Don't Need a Reason," perhaps the most recognizable "song for the war on AIDS," is performed frequently at AIDS benefits, walk-a-thons, and lesbian and gay events. Furthermore, "The Day after That" is not even the first Broadway song to invoke AIDS. One need only recall some of the musical numbers from William Finn's 1990 *Falsettoland,* which became the second act of his 1992 Broadway production *Falsettos.* Moreover, music for AIDS is not an exclusively U.S./British enterprise. See, for example, the discussion of AIDS and music in Africa in the unsigned "Rockbeat" column of the *Village Voice,* 18 January 1994, 74.

34. Minnelli's performance at the United Nations was televised nationally and reported in mainstream print media, her video continues to play in gay bars across the country, and the CD single has received widespread distribution. An official spokeswoman for *Kiss of the Spider Woman, the Musical* has said, "we're all hoping this song is successful in doing as much as possible for the cause" (*Advocate,* 12 December 1993, 79).

35. It cannot be forgotten that AIDS has been deliberately compared to the Holocaust, especially by Larry Kramer; see his *Reports from the Holocaust: The Making of an AIDS Activist* (New York: St. Martin's Press, 1989). Both historical experiences are human tragedies. In *Kiss of the Spider Woman, the Musical,* AIDS can only be read through allegory; AIDS is the referent "beyond" those described explicitly in the narrative of the musical; in Kramer's writings, the comparisons are explicit and literal.

36. Jaime Manrique, "Manuel Puig: The Writer as Diva," *Christopher Street* (July 1993): 26.

37. This is by now a commonplace. See Steven Mailloux, "Interpretation," in *Critical Terms for Literary Study*, ed. Frank Lentricchia and Thomas McLaughlin (Chicago: U of Chicago P, 1990), 121–134, for a more complete articulation of this idea.

38. See Tzvetan Todorov, *The Fantastic: A Structural Approach to a Literary Genre*, trans. Richard Howard (Ithaca: Cornell U P, 1973).

39. Maureen Quilligan, *The Language of Allegory: Defining the Genre* (Ithaca: Cornell U P, 1979), 97.

40. The glitz of the Broadway musical—sets, lighting, design, costumes, and stars—contributes to its fantasy. We never anticipate a direct representation of reality in Broadway musicals. The technological apparatus distances Broadway productions from the material lives of its spectators. An exciting exception to this genre is William Finn's *Falsettos*, a musical explicitly about AIDS. *Falsettos* resists the technological apparatus of the big Broadway musical; in fact, its success stems from its extremely low budget. On the politics of entertainment, see Richard Dyer, *Only Entertainment* (New York: Routledge, 1992). On the politics of mass culture, see Tania Modleski's discussion of Puig's novel, "Femininity as Mas(s)querade: A Feminist Approach to Mass Culture," in *High Theory/Low Culture: Analysing Popular Television and Film*, ed. Colin MacCabe (New York: St. Martin's Press, 1985), 37–52.

41. On the idea of the phantasmatic, see Judith Butler, "Force of Fantasy: Feminism, Mapplethorpe, and Discursive Excess," *differences* 2.2 (Summer 1990): 105–126. See Modleski on the possible agency in this system of identification.

42. Judith Butler, *Bodies That Matter: On the Discursive Limits of "Sex"* (New York: Routledge, 1993), 226.

43. See also D. A. Miller's *Place for Us: Essay on the Broadway Musical* (Harvard U P, forthcoming). Miller argues that *Kiss of the Spider Woman, the Musical* allegorizes the relation of gay men to musical theater. While we agree with this idea, it is not a topic that we will pursue in this paper. Our thanks to David Miller for sharing with us his ideas on *Kiss of the Spider Woman, the Musical*.

44. Given the limited range of roles available to women on Broadway, Rivera's triumph is all the more spectacular. That she is able to make complex an ultimately clichéd role is a testimony to her talents. Her role also raises the question of the possible identifications for women spectators in *Kiss of the Spider Woman, the Musical*. The allegorical structure of the musical fails to account for women's experience of AIDS. In all the male world of the prison, women figure only as outside fantasies.

45. Jeff Masten explains: "The authorial paradigm with which we are more familiar, of course, depends upon the construction and policing of the borders of personhood, an identification of the textual parent" ("My Two Dads: Collaboration and the Reproduction of Beaumont and Fletcher," in *Queering the Renaissance*, ed. Jonathan Goldberg [Durham: Duke U P, 1993], 298).

46. On this issue, see Peggy Phelan, *Unmarked: The Politics of Performance* (New York: Routledge, 1993).

Against Easy Listening

Audiotopic Readings and Transnational Soundings

Josh Kun

Music is a "spatial practice." Moving across multiple locations—both before and especially after the age of mechanical reproduction—music follows a "spatial trajectory." Understanding music spatially, we can track sonic movements, witnessing and listening for its migrations and travels. Music might be considered "delinquent," in Michel de Certeau's seductive terminology, in that music presents a "challenging mobility that does not respect places." This is not to say that music is located in no place. Music does not respect places precisely because it is capable of inhabiting a particular place while at the same time moving across several places—of arriving while leaving. Through music, space is constructed and deconstructed, shaped and shattered, filled up and hollowed out. Music creates spaces where cultures can be both contested and consolidated, both sounded and silenced. Moving through space, music performs a double act of delinquency that unsettles both the geopolitical boundaries of the modern nation-state and the disciplinary boundaries that govern the study of music in the academy.[1]

Through these acts of delinquency, music builds what Edward Soja has called "the lifeworld of being creatively located not only in the making of history but also in the construction of human geographies, the social production of space and the restless formation and reformation of geographical landscapes."[2] I believe that a consideration of the role of music in the mapping of these "postmodern geographies" across the Americas will be helpful in the development of a critical theory that is both historical and spatial, moving not only through timescapes and landscapes, but through soundscapes as well.[3] These soundscapes constitute what I will call "audiotopias." The extranational musical territory of the African diaspora of the black Atlantic and of the borderland between the United States and Mexico provide two exemplary soundings of audiotopia. Surveying these soundscapes through the audiotopic readings of Paul Gilroy and Rubén Martínez, I will demonstrate how music acts as a network of connection among the geographies of the black Atlantic and of Latin/o America, unsettling the assumptions of territorially fixed notions of blackness and of *Latinidad*.

I derive my motion of "audiotopia" from Michel Foucault's concept of the "heterotopia." Foucault argues that while the nineteenth century was obsessed with history, the grand obsession of the twentieth century is space: "We are in the epoch of simultaneity: we are in the epoch of juxtaposition, the epoch of the near and the far, of the side-by-side, of the dispersed. We are at a moment, I believe, when our experience of the world is less that of a long life developing through time than that of a network that connects points and intersects with its own skein."[4] I am concerned with the role music plays in this twentieth-century spatial obsession: the ways in which, transported by the technologies of transnational capital, music becomes an experiential network of connection and intersection that enables global simultaneity by juxtaposing the same with the different, bridging the near with the far, and confusing the local with the global. By tracking music as a system of dispersal across the human geographies and geographical landscapes of the Americas, we can understand precisely how music creates and reflects social spaces and mediates between distant and dissimilar ones.

Foucault contrasts the concept of the "heterotopias" to that of "utopias," which he dismisses as "sites with no real place." By contrast, heterotopia represents "a kind of effectively enacted utopia" characterized by the juxtaposition "in a single real place of several spaces, several sites that are themselves incompatible."[5] Because of music's ability to act *effectively* as an agent of intense utopian longing[6] and its uncanny ability to absorb and meld heterogeneous national, cultural, and historical styles and traditions across space and within place, we might consider "audiotopias" as specific instances of "heterotopias": sonic spaces of effective utopian longings where several sites normally deemed incompatible are brought together not only in the space of a particular piece of music itself, but in the production of social space and mapping of geographical space that music makes possible.[7] Listening for audiotopias has a dual function: first, to focus on the space of music itself, including the different spaces music juxtaposes within itself; second, to focus on the social spaces, geographies, and landscapes that music can enable, reflect, and prophecy. In this sense, audiotopias are "contact zones"—both sonic and social spaces. Here disparate cultures and geographies historically mapped and maintained separately interact with each other and enter into relationships whose consequences for cultural identification are never predetermined.

My aim is to highlight the audiotopias of music as ideal sites for the study of the creation of geographical homeplaces within border and diasporic cultural formations. By asking precisely how music creates and reflects social spaces and mediates between distant and dissimilar ones, we can track music as a system of dispersal across the human geographies and geographical landscapes of the Americas. Understanding music's potential to create and live through audiotopias helps us to better track migrations and travels across the borders and throughout the diasporas that disrupt conventional mappings of the Americas.[8]

Diaspora Soundings

Throughout his groundbreaking analysis of the place of the black Atlantic in the history of modernity, Paul Gilroy is unable to stop hearing music. Wherever his analysis leads him, Gilroy keeps his ears tuned: He thinks not only *about* music, but *through* music as well. In his discussion of the black diaspora as a counterculture of modernity, Gilroy recognizes music as an ideal site from which to begin a critical examination of nationalism and of the limits and limitations of theories of racial particularity. He focuses on the popular music of the black diaspora precisely because it makes ethnocentric and nationalist theories of culture incredibly difficult to shape. Music becomes part of an "expressive counterculture"—one of the "arts of darkness"—that fuses art with life, culture with politics, the aesthetic with the social, and allows a space for the fashioning of both subject positions and the various strategies necessary for collective liberation and emancipation. By working through the music of the black Atlantic world, Gilroy enters into a series of audiotopic spaces that disrupt the dominant discourse of modernity by sounding a "syncopated pulse of non-European philosophical and aesthetic outlooks." Gilroy continually hears this syncopated pulse, "this unexpected time signature," which supplies "the accents, rests, breaks, and tones that make the performance of racial identity possible" while at the same time providing the tools necessary for "a different rhythm of living and being."[9]

Gilroy's argument suggests a method for mapping both geographical and cultural space. Tracking the migrations of different versions of the song "I'm So Proud," originally written by African (U.S.) American Curtis Mayfield and performed by his trio The Impressions in the mid-1960s,[10] over a thirty-year period from Chicago to Jamaica to Britain, Gilroy argues that the song "brings Africa, America, Europe, and the Caribbean together."[11] Reading music as map, Gilroy does not propose any static representations of racial, cultural, and national essence. Rather, he argues for a sounding within the musics of the black Atlantic, a process of identification that takes place through a shifting series of convergences and borrowings.

While Gilroy astutely traces the spatial dimensions and coordinates of the black Atlantic through music, his geographical emphasis on former British colonies constrains his study.[12] Furthermore, in his discussion of the role of "America" in the cultural formation of the black Atlantic, Gilroy frequently conflates the United States with the hemisphere as a whole. This emphasis foregrounds the influence of African (U.S.) American musics on the formation of black Atlantic cultural and sonic cartographies, while neglecting mutual soundings and re-soundings of blackness throughout Latin/o America. Tracking the musics of the black Atlantic across nonanglophone island routes from Haiti to the Dominican Republic, Puerto Rico, and Cuba begins to reveal the geographical and binary racial limits of Gilroy's study. A multilingual mapping would extend the black Atlantic audiotopia through the sonic sites of the popular musics of Latin/o America.

The "sounds of blackness" played in African (U.S.) American rhythm and blues, soul, funk, and hip-hop and in Jamaican reggae and dancehall mix on a different register with the African sonic traditions of Haiti. Drawing from these traditions, the group Vodu 155 extend the hip-hop idiom to play what they call "vodou funkadelic." This form combines the anglophone influences Gilroy analyzes with Haitian vodou and rara rhythms, and with dub poetry in both English and Haitian Creole. In another location, the New York–based rap trio Fugees self-identify as Haitian immigrants or "re-fugees" who use the rap medium to address their deterritorialized experience as displaced Haitians. On the entirely acoustic rap song "Vocab" (consisting only of vocals and acoustic guitar it is perhaps the first of its kind), they speak of radio and music industry anti-Haitian racism and their determination to overcome it: "He looked at me and laughed / and said my music would never make FM / Station / You're Haitian / You'll never get nowhere / But I sweared on my grandmother's grave / we'd be here." Fugees speak most directly to the Haitian immigrant experience on "Fugees on the Mic," a call for unity and visibility among Haitian immigrants and refugees as a means of overcoming anti-Haitian biases from *within* the black diaspora; a critique of any view of coherence and consensus based solely on racial particularity. In fact, the song is preceded by an introductory dialogue in which two African American women refuse to speak to one of the band members because he is a Haitian who "stinks" and they "just can't be talkin' to no fuckin' Haitian." The song offers an explosive and impassioned response: "I want all the refugees out there to just put up your mother-fuckin' hands. You know you're a fuckin' immigrant. Put up your hands, you know what I'm sayin'. I'm gonna start this shit off like this, this time around. H to the A to the I to the T to the I, live or die!" Fugees use rap to create dynamic immigrant soundings of deterritorialized, migratory, and transnational black diasporic experience, as well as to call attention to intraracial prejudice and disunity.

The long and vexed tradition of the sounding of blackness or African-ness in Latin America has critical significance for any understanding of a "black" Atlantic. Take, for example, the extremely popular bachata music of the Dominican Republic's reigning musical superstar Juan Luis Guerra. Deborah Pacini Hernández has argued that in accord with the Dominican Republic's notoriety for being "afro-phobic," Guerra's music has tended to draw heavily upon African styles and influences (not to mention entire songs by contemporary African songwriters) without acknowledging them. The result has been the construction of bachata as an exclusively "Latin American" music, a construction meant to gloss over African presence.[13] Yet it should be pointed out that while this may have been true in the past, Guerra's latest album, *Fogaraté*, suggests that this afrophobia may be receding. Guerra performs two songs written by African guitarist Diblo Dibala and one by Ivory Coast singer and songwriter

Papa Wemba. Wemba's "Viví" becomes Guerra's hit single "Viviré," and one of Dibala's compositions, "Amour et Souvenir," becomes "Fogaraté," the album's title track. But what makes *Fogaraté* perhaps one of Guerra's most exuberant and well-crafted releases to date is that Dibala actually plays on the recording, lending his wonderfully distinctive guitarwork to a number of the album's songs. The result is a series of Dominican bachatas and merengues that have never sounded, and never before confessed to being, so rooted in African musical style.[14]

The last alternative audiotopic cartography of the black diaspora that I wish to consider is one that Gilroy himself has written on only to omit it later. I am referring to his discussion of Kid Frost, one of East Los Angeles's leading Chicano rappers, in his essay "Sounds Authentic: Black Music, Ethnicity, and the Challenge of the Changing Same," which is actually an earlier version of the chapter dedicated exclusively to music that appears in *The Black Atlantic*. While it is a welcome sign that Gilroy addresses Latino participation in black diasporic musical conversations, it is equally unfortunate that his discussion of Kid Frost and the emergence of Latino hip-hop drops out of the book version.[15]

Gilroy's brief reading of Kid Frost as representing "the construction of a Mexican-American equivalent"[16] to black nationalist rap fails to follow his own advice of not relying on strictly textual critiques. If we go beyond the level of text and lyric with Kid Frost and listen to the music he raps over, a much different and much more enabling critique results in which music manages to connect the East Los Angeles Borderlands with the black diaspora via both 1990s rap and 1960s jazz. Rapidly becoming an urban Chicano anthem, Kid Frost's "La raza" is built around a looped break from a 1970 Billboard Top 40 recording of "Viva Tirado" by East Los Angeles Latin/jazz/rock group El Chicano, who offer their own sounding of "Viva Tirado" as originally written and performed by African American jazz artist Gerard Wilson.

"Viva Tirado" was not the only jazz composition El Chicano covered. Only two months after recording their version of "Viva Tirado," they recorded African American jazz pianist Herbie Hancock's classic "Cantalope Island." But in both cases, El Chicano took a strictly jazz sound and fused it with elements of sixties rock and various hybrid Afro-Latin rhythms, most notably salsa, to create what some have called the "East-side sound." By the end of 1970, El Chicano had become the first Chicano band to play Harlem's legendary Apollo Theater. They also went on to play the Ohio Jazz Festival on bills with the diverse likes of Michael Jackson, Olivia Newton John, Chaka Khan, Rod Stewart, and Earth, Wind, & Fire, and on tours that traveled to Canada, Nicaragua, and Korea. El Chicano also went on to cover "Ahora sí," a song by legendary Afro-Cuban salsero Ray Barretto.[17] The connections and interactions at work in this transoceanic and transnational sonic network draw an overtly Afro-Latin musical map that charts travels from Africa to New York City to East L.A. to Cuba, undermining assumptions of racial particularity and ethnic absolutism that attempt to elide black and Latino intercultural identification and performance.[18]

Using the example of Nelson Mandela listening to Marvin Gaye while in a South African jail, Gilroy argues against a view of the global flow of black music as unidirectional. The audiotopic juxtaposition of Mandela and Gaye, South Africa and Detroit, Africa and the United States, highlights how "the purist ideas of one-way flow of African culture from east to west was instantly revealed to be absurd." It makes visible both "the global dimensions of diaspora dialogue" as well as the simultaneous confirmation and challenge of "music as the principal symbol of racial authenticity."[19] The routes were returning to the roots; the direction of the cultural winds was changing.

This is, of course, just one of many examples of such a migratory inversion. In 1990, Cameroon superstar Manu Dibango (who had become internationally famous for his Afro-European approach to jazz fusion and R&B on songs like "Soul Makossa") collaborated with black British rapper MC Mello to record "Senga Abele." Just this year African American jazz saxophone legend Pharaoh Sanders, who has used a variety of African instruments and styles on numerous previous recordings, traveled to the medina of Morocco under the auspices of producer Bill Laswell to record a live free improvisation with Maleem Mohmud Ghania and an entire cast of Gnawa musicians.[20] Or there is the case of the African rappers known as Zimbabwe Legit who perform a very standard U.S. brand of rap music while addressing the role of Africa in the construction of the U.S. hip-hop imagination. Rapping predominantly in English with occasional bits of Shona, Zimbabwe Legit attempt to perform what they call "doin' damage in my native language." They bring rap back to where it is usually thought of as coming from and use it to create an "African jam session" of their own, completing a transnational musical circuit of return. In one song, they assemble a short series of samples to ask the question, seemingly directed to Afrocentric U.S. rappers who imagine an authentic, antiquated, and overly romantic version of Africa as Motherland: "Africa? Do you know what it means?" They question what Manthia Diawara has similarly identified as "afrokitsch," the commodification and consumption of museumized African symbols and icons in order to forge an African American identity.[21] Zimbabwe Legit rap of "people wearin' beads, some are hypocritical / Cash in on the fashion / Africa is an attraction / . . . Africa's a continent but they don't know the area." As Africans questioning the representation of Africa in an African-derived musical art form such as rap, Zimbabwe Legit challenge claims to racial essence and racial origin.

While a great deal of critical attention has been paid to the African roots of, for instance, Cuban music, considerably less has been paid on the reverse direction of flow: the Latin American roots of much of contemporary African popular or Afro-pop musics, specifically the Afro-pop recontextualizations of various forms of Puerto Rican and Cuban salsa. Everyone from the Trio Matamoros in the 1930s to Ray Barretto in the 1950s and Orquesta Aragon and Johnny Pacheco in the 1960s have achieved considerable popularity throughout Africa. The influence is so strong in fact that Zairean soukous was originally known as rumba congolaise, and Senagelese mbalax, which once even featured lyrics sung in Spanish, continues to draw heavily upon Afro-Cuban styles. The two-volume 1993 *Africando* project highlights the Africa–Latin America musical circuit through music, with some of New York's top salsa and Afro-Cuban jazz performers providing the musical backdrop for three of Senegal's top singers. On a song like "Trovador," for example, salsero Ronnie Baro, brother-in-law of Malian flautist Boncana Maiga, pays tribute to great singers of both Africa and the Americas, a list that includes Beny Moré, Tabu Ley Rochereau, Joseito Fernández, and Salif Keita.[22] Lyrics are sung in both *wolof* and Spanish, and what "began" in Africa (roots), traveled and continues to travel to Cuba and Latin America (routes), now makes its way back (routes to roots) to Africa.

Border Soundings

In his journalistic explorations along and across the multiple borderlines and borderlands between Los Angeles, Havana, Tijuana, San Salvador, and Mexico City in *The Other Side*, Rubén Martínez, like Gilroy, hears music wherever he wanders.[23] *The Other Side* combines poems, auto-biographical journal entries, and chronicles of emergent Latin/o American youth culture that take Martínez from the performance art of Tijuana to the graffiti of Los Angeles to the New Latin American Cinema of Havana. His movement back and forth across the borders between the first and third worlds is used to critically mirror his own biography as a Latino raised in Los Angeles born of Mexican and Salvadoran parents. *The Other Side* is a Pan-American vision of destruction and rebirth, of the collapse of old paradigms, structures, and orders (a Salvadoran earthquake, the Cuban revolution) and the struggles to develop new ways of seeing, new ways of surviving. Ultimately, though, *The Other Side* is about Martínez and what this series of cultural and political transformations across national borders means for the construction of his own identity.

In his frustrated quest for a cultural home that is both North and South, both on *el otro lado* and *este lado,* Martínez proves to be not only an incredibly astute cultural observer, but an incredibly astute cultural listener as well. It is no matter of mere coincidence that the "travel stories" of music play such a central role in these pieces of "travel writing." Nor is it mere coincidence that music can be found at the heart of Martínez's critique of the unified subject and his realization that his own "I" is riddled with difference, an unstable set of multiple selves that forces him to "be much more than two" and hope that "the many selves can find some kind of form together without annihilating one another." Music becomes an integral part of Martínez's attempt to be "South in the South, North in the North, South in the North, and North in the South," an audiotopic condition in which musical, national, and cultural spaces exist in both harmony and dissonant contradiction.[24]

Music is never where Martínez expects to find it. It is the perennial child who misbehaves, never doing what it is told and never staying in one place. While in Havana, Martínez hears a musical cosmopolitanism of disco, salsa, jazz, and nueva canción that he doesn't expect to find anywhere outside of Mexico City. He also comes across Chicano graffiti artists in Los Angeles who listen to not only "lowrider" oldies from the fifties but to hip-hop as well. And the New Age folklórico band he hears plays "garish renditions of spacey *indígena* music" at an official dinner for the late Father Luis Olivares at La Placita. In his poem "Manifesto," Martínez uses the metaphor of earthquake, of a shuddering and shaking ground, to describe the contemporary political and cultural climate, a generation "dancing a San Andreas cumbia!" Yet it is also a generation in which *guatamaltecos* and African American youth in Los Angeles "all together now dance to Eazy-E and BDP, crossing every border ever held sacred."[25]

Martínez's essay on emergent Tijuana performance artists also renders interesting musical conclusions. Driving down Tijuana's Avenida Revolución, Martínez finds himself surrounded by a heavy, booming bass beat that is a "familiar sound, as though a lowered Toyota pickup truck has just pulled up next to me at the height of cruising night on Hollywood Boulevard." Tijuana is a double place, both North and South, and the music Martínez hears is understood as indicative of this dual geography: "The North is here—the disco music. The South is here—the *norteñas* and *cumbias.*"[26]

One evening he accompanies a group of artists to a favorite local hangout, La Estrella, and goes out of his way to point out that this is no "strobe-lit disco bar" and that "everyone is dancing to a cumbia, not a disco beat." In this particular *Tijuanese* semiotic system, music signifies place and culture, with disco as North and cumbia as South, with all of the accompanying cultural baggage each signification entails. But even these signifiers get rendered unstable when Martínez notes the juxtaposition of the assumed-to-be-incompatible cumbia—a "*campesino* tradition from the South of Mexico"—and the urban life of Tijuana in the audiotopic space of a Tijuana nightclub. The presence of cumbia on la Avenida Revolución tells its own "travel story" of "the millions of southerners who have come north seeking work."[27]

On a similar evening, Martínez and performance artist Hugo Sánchez travel up and down la Avenida Revolución searching for signs of some authentic "Tijuananess," of "the real Tijuana." But again expectations are disappointed. Within the single space of this one urban main drag, multiple sounds compete for audibility: Irish rock group U2, the pop salsa of

Miami Sound Machine, and the ever-present cumbias. They try one bar only to find a place "where the disco pulses and a naked woman writhes under the red spotlight on stage," and yet another where "a young long-hair croons pop songs in English to the Americanized Tijuana bourgeoisie."[28] The juxtaposition of all these "incompatible" musical places along la Avenida of course frustrates the search for cultural authenticity and ends up rendering U2, Miami Sound Machine, disco, and cumbia as much "the real Tijuana" as anything else.

But it is perhaps in Martínez's chapter on the Mexico City rock scene that the relationship between music and national geography on both sides of the U.S.-Mexico border gets most effectively played out. Rock and roll has always been a field of cultural contestation and disputed cultural ownership,[29] and its recontextualization in Latin America as *rock en español* proves no exception. Rock en español refers to the development of a musical movement across Latin America that blends conventional U.S. rock and roll tropes with significant regional and national Latin American stylistic interruptions, revisions, and alterations.

The history of rock en español in Mexico is the history both of what Cuban sociologist Fernando Ortiz has called "transculturation" and what is known in Mexico as *naco*. Transculturation is a condition of the U.S.-Mexico "contact zone," what Mary Louise Pratt has described in the context of colonial encounters as a social and geopolitical space "where disparate cultures meet, clash, and grapple with each other" and establish "ongoing relations."[30] A neologism coined by Ortiz in 1940, *transculturación* is meant to replace the more conventional sociological couplet of acculturation and deculturation and signify "el proceso de tránsito de una cultura a otra y sus repercusiones sociales de todo género [the process of transition from one culture to another and its social repercussions on every level.]"[31] Pratt understands it as the process by which "subordinated or marginal groups select and invent from materials transmitted to them by dominant or metropolitan culture."[32] Somewhere between transculturation and appropriation is the Mexican concept of naco. Meant to refer to the invasion of Western spaces by Mexican cultural forms, naco—the Toltec definition of which is "with or of two hearts"—signals "the insertion of elements clearly associated with traditional Mexican culture in spaces regarded and respected as Western [American]."[33]

A version of naco transculturation is alluded to by George Yúdice in his discussion of Latin American liberation theology's emphasis on *conscientización,* by which the Christian Gospels are rewritten and reconceptualized through the lens of everyday experience. Transculturation becomes an active form of cultural resistance that can thus be linked to what Yúdice calls "struggles for interpretive power."[34] Like the "postcolonial mimicry" outlined by Homi Bhabha, rock en español is "at once resemblance and menace," capable of problematizing "the signs of racial and cultural priority, so that the 'national' is no longer naturalizable." By transculturating or mimicking U.S. rock sensibilities using Mexican traditions, styles, and worldviews, rock en español bands suggest that "what emerges between mimesis and mimicry" is not a "writing" but a sounding, or re-sounding, of music from across the Americas.[35] Through the performance and production of popular music, they forge a new interpretive space for the re-imagining of culture that transcends the boundaries of frozen folkloric authenticity and the geopolitical limits of the modern nation-state.

Martínez traces the origins of contemporary rock en español in Mexico to the fifties, when U.S. hits would be translated and rerecorded in Spanish with "a shifting toward Mexicaness that, many years later, would come to exemplify the best of the country's rock." The sixties and seventies saw the birth of *la onda,* a musical response to the hippie culture of peace, love, and psychedelia, that while on the one hand may have been little more than unthinking cultural imitation did manage to challenge "institutionalized concepts [of culture]" and signal the possible "extinction of cultural hegemony." But it was in the eighties, with the arrival of *guacarock* and Sergio Arau and his band Botellita de Jerez, that rock en español began to gain speed and strength as a musical movement in Mexico.[36]

The emergence and popularity of guacarock was naco culture at work, in that it fused the cultural heritage of Mexico with the sounds of rock and roll, proving "they didn't have to go north to take back rock and roll."[37] In fact, they probably only had to go as far as Rockotitlán, the first venue in Mexico City reserved for Spanish-language rock, known as "the place where Aztecs heard rock."[38] The 1985 opening of the club and the subsequent proliferation of Mexican rock bands led the radio and recording industry to coin the term *rock en tu idioma.* The late eighties and early nineties witnessed increasing record industry attention and sign-ings by such labels as BMG, Ariola, and Warner Brothers Mexico. This unique history of the transculturation of rock and roll into the rock en español of Mexico's naco culture is not missed by Maldita Vecindad y Los Hijos del Quinto Patio lead singer Roco when he proclaims, "It might be true that rock began in the north. But now it's all ours."[39]

As Gilroy reminds us in his discussion of black diasporic music travel-ing both east to west and west to east, so is it important to remember that the flow of rock and roll between north and south is not unidirectional. Consider Maldita Vecindad's appearance as opening act for Los Angeles hometown heroes Jane's Addiction and the appropriations of Mexican culture and religion that dominate the packaging of Jane's Addiction's *Ritual De Lo Habitual*. While rock en español may be creating the biggest stir in Mexico, Argentina, and Chile, most recently the music has itself made a particularly noisy journey al otro lado, gaining immense popu-larity with Latino audiences in cities and towns throughout California: in San Francisco, Café Tacuba recently played a sold-out club date; in Berkeley, the nightclub Berkeley Square, which usually reserves its stage for alternative rock and punk acts, hosts a weekly rock en español night featuring videos and performances by bands from across Latin America as well as bands like La Bohemia and Orixa from the East Bay's own burgeoning rock en español scene. And both a salsa club in Mountain View and the legendary Whiskey-a-Go-Go in Los Angeles, one of the central sites of sixties rock mythmaking, also host weekly rock en es-pañol events. Rock en español becomes a floating, migrating musical audiotopia that creates new Borderland regions with coordinates like Mexico City/Los Angeles and Mexico City/Berkeley.[40]

While some critics have chosen to view rock en español as overly derivative and as just another instance of U.S. cultural imperialism at work,[41] I prefer to understand it as signaling the birth of a truly hybrid-ized cultural and interpretive space produced by the meeting of cultures that challenges the binary logic of assimilation/resistance and local/ global that so much of contemporary mass culture theory relies on. Within Mexico, rock en español offers a new musical language of expres-sion that simultaneously resists the monologism of the institutionalized *cultura nacional* as well as the "Americanization of the Mexican middle class." It is this new naco aesthetic of what Sergio Arau has called "culture-in-the-making"[42] that helps explain a live performance by Maldita where Roco splays his legs "like Elvis being chased by la migra" and uses rap to address the police abuse of Mexico City barrio youth as the band moves through free jazz, mambo, danzón, R&B, reggae, ska, and hip-hop, while always "possessed by the most sacred of rock demons."[43]

Of all the rock en español bands, Maldita Vecindad has undoubtedly received the most critical attention. Songs like "Pachuco" and "Mojado" deal directly with the cultural and human traffic within and across the U.S.-Mexico borderlands. "Mojado" tells the story of a Mexican national who leaves home to cross the border as an undocumented *mojado* and work in the United States. The song is dedicated to "los que se ven forzados a separarse de sus costumbres, seres queridos, raíces y objetos cotidianos [all those who have been forced to separate themselves from their customs, loved ones, roots, and everyday things],"[44] and during a recent live performance the song was dedicated to "todos los hermanos en todo el mundo que andan dispersos y especialmente para los Chicanos [all those *hermanos* dispersed all over the world and especially for the Chicanos.]" Narrating the experience of human migration northward, Maldita uses music as a transnational sonic circuit to both figuratively and literally cross the U.S.-Mexico border and speak to Chilangos and Chicanos alike.[45]

This musical aesthetic of national and cultural crossings resonates strongly in the sounds of Café Tacuba, whose latest album, *Re,* covers a diverse musical ground that spans the entire hemisphere and ranges from Amerindian folk strains to speed metal to ska to *mariachismos* to fifties U.S. rock to salsa and back again. Their music more explicitly addresses the relationship between contemporary Mexican cultural politics and those of the United States. Their song "El borrego" is a musical embodiment of Martínez's struggles with his multiple selves and his constant straddling of national and cultural geographies, as well as the often contradictory aspects of Mexican cultural identity he finds in Tijuana and Mexico City. They sing:

Soy anarquista, soy neonazista, soy un esquinjed y soy ecologista. Soy peronista, soy terrorista, capitalista y también soy pacifista
Soy activista, sindicalista, soy agresivo y muy alternativo . . .
Me gusta el jevimetal, me gusta el jarcor, me gusta Patric Miler y también me

gusta el gronch. Me gusta la Maldita, me gusta la Lupita y escucho a los Magneto
cuando está mi novicita
Me gusta andar de negro con los labios pintados, pero guapo en la oficina
siempre ando bien trajeado. Me gusta aventar piedras, me gusta recogerlas . . .
[I am anarchist, I am neo-Nazi, I am skinhead, and I am ecologist. I am Peronist, I
am terrorist, capitalist, and I am also pacifist
I am activist, syndicalist, I am aggressive and very alternative . . .
I like heavy metal, I like hardcore, I like Patrick Miller and I also like grunge. I
like Maldita, I like Lupita and I listen to Magneto when I'm with my noviecita.
I like to wear black with my lips painted, but I am always well-dressed and
handsome at the office. I like to throw stones, I like to pick them up . . .]

The Mexican subject of "El borrego" occupies multiple subject positions
and speaks from a multiple and often contradictory set of enunciative
modalities—less a unified subject primed for interpellation by a monologic national ideology and more of what Norma Alarcón calls a "geopolitical subject-in-process" characterized by "irreducible difference"
and "nonequivalency."[46]

Café Tacuba also adds to the complexities Martínez writes about by
openly playing with heterosexist assumptions of sexuality. "El baile y el
salon" beautifully and cleverly tells the story of two men falling in love
while dancing together and kissing in the middle of a crowded dance
floor. The narrator assures his lover that "hay muchas parejas bailando a
nuestro alrededor [there are many couples dancing at our side]," and
later tells him, "Así bailando quiero que me hagas el amor, de hombre a
hombre *voulez-vous coucher avec moi*? [I want you to make love to me
dancing like this, from man to man *voulez-vous coucher avec moi*?]." The
dance floor becomes a performative locus of queer desire and the dance
its seductive modality, as teasing flirtation gives way to physical passion
and romantic love. This musically and lyrically elegant foregrounding of
queer subjectivity and male homosexual desire challenges the heteronor-
mativity that predominates in the discussion of diaspora and border
subjects offered by Gilroy and Martínez, respectively.

But it is on "El fin de la infancia" that Café Tacuba asks the question
central to Martínez's analysis and to the critiques of rock en español as
merely imperialist residue: "When will I stop being afraid of becoming
part of the vanguard? without having to go to New York in order to see

what's going on there?" This leads to even further questions: When will being "part of the vanguard" mean being Mexican? When will the music of Mexico stop being compared with the music of the United States? When is it time to stop looking to New York and Los Angeles for answers that can be found right here in Mexico City? When, to echo Néstor García Canclini, will Latin America's heterogeneous entrances and exits in and out of its own condition of modernity stop being read as part of the grand narratives of Western modernity and postmodernity? The song concludes by extending this litany of interrogation to a deeper level, asking: "Will we be able to dance by ourselves? Will we be able to think for ourselves? Will we be able to think?" Café Tacuba put to rest all suspicions of their music as uncritical imitation as they use music to reveal a set of political, cultural, and sexual differences that questions any notion of contemporary Mexican culture as an unchanging same.

The music of a band like Café Tacuba begs the same question of national and cultural borders that Michel de Certeau has asked in his important theorization of frontiers, rivers, and bridges: "to whom does it belong?"[47] Blending various manifestations of U.S. rock and disco, Mexican and Colombian cumbia, Amerindian folk traditions, Tex-Mex conjunto, and a whole array of traditional Mexican folklórico musics, including traces of mariachi and huapango, Café Tacuba exposes music as an undocumented border-crosser that questions the national ownership of cultural expression. A heterotopic space of emergent artistic creativity is heard loudly in Café Tacuba's rich soundings of a musical, middle birthing space built upon interactions, exchanges, and encounters. The travel story of music transforms the frontera space that constantly overflows into and between the national containers of Mexico and the United States into a "crossing" that reveals "inversions and displacements" and "welds together and opposes insularities." Their music represents "a transgression of the limit, a disobedience of the law of the place"; it betrays the dominant logic of fixed, stable, and self-contained cultural and national hegemonies. Or, as Certeau puts it, "What the map cuts up, the story cuts across." Café Tacuba's music is therefore transgressive in that it recognizes the place of the local while also traveling within the space of the global—a transnational musical movement that begins to blur the very distinction itself and exposes the local as constituted by the global and, what is often forgotten in such analyses, the global as also constituted by the local. I see music operating here as both "topological," in that it deforms figures and disrupts orders, as well as "topical," in that it participates in the generation of local creativity and resistance and the articulation of place. Music operates here in a double movement between local place and transnational space, acting as a sonic *metaphorai* that moves between and maps places along spatial trajectories.[48]

I propose that we consider to what extent the nationally transgressive and culturally delinquent border-conscious and border-crossing music of bands like Café Tacuba and Maldita Vecindad can be theorized and understood within the larger process of what George Yúdice has described as Latin America's attempt at (re)constructing hegemony in the context of transnational capitalism and the theoretical and universalizing dominance of postmodern discourse. Rock en español represents just one attempt within Latin America to negotiate cultural capital and rearticulate tradition. Café Tacuba's music evidences how local and regional traditions can be "recycled" and re-formed as they become cultural commodities in both the national and international marketplaces that are intended for consumption on both sides of the border.

On songs like "El aparato" and "El tlatoani del barrio" where the sounds of tradition, of the "premodern," meet the sounds of the post-industrial, the sounds of the machine, and the sounds of (post)modern technology, new relationships with tradition are forged. Traditional soundings are neither silenced nor overemphasized but reconfigured and reimagined in new relationships and new settings. The pastiche that occurs in Café Tacuba's music is best understood not strictly along the theoretical lines of European postmodernism but rather in the context of Latin America's *culturas híbridas* of modernity, in which pastiche neither refuses the past through mockery and parody nor museumizes it through reverence, but "assumes it";[49] in which cultural articulations construed as "avant-garde" (or "la vanguardia") coexist with traditional and contemporary elements from multiple cultural and national locations. Thus, according to a framework outlined by Yúdice, their musical strategy of cultural rearticulation is both old and new; "old because they draw from their tradition; new because they no longer operate solely within the framework of class or nation."[50]

Café Tacuba's music loudly participates in what Néstor García Canclini has termed "cultural reconversion," by which cultural capital is placed in new settings, relationships, and circuits of exchange and imbued with new systems of meaning and interpretation such that it becomes reconverted. Such cultural conversion can be heard when in one song an electronic drum machine provides the synthesized beat for a lilting mariachi melody, Amerindian chants compete with the beeps and bleeps of postmodern communications technologies, cumbias erupt into disco infernos, and sweaty ska workouts transform into an accordion-driven conjunto. "Instead of the death of traditional cultural forms," argues García Canclini, "we now discover that tradition is in transition, and articulated to modern processes." Café Tacuba's music and its participation in the global capitalist commodity flow of the transnational recording industry reconverts musical capital by transferring "one symbolic patrimony from one site to another in order to conserve it, increase its yield, and better the position of those who practice it."[51] At work in Tacuba's sound and vision is a multiplicity of symbolic systems that suspends the one-to-one equivalency of cultural identity and inherited national belonging to reveal a "culture-in-the-making" that is a site of conflict and contact "between traditional symbolic systems and international information networks, culture industries, and migrant populations."[52] Bands like Maldita and Tacuba re-sound U.S. rock and roll through multiple and heterogeneous musical rearticulations and reconversions of cultural enunciation, capital, and formation. Because rock en español is simultaneously local and global, simultaneously national and transnational, it becomes an effective site for witnessing the failure of monocultural and monologic national paradigms to understand emergent cultural expression on both sides of the border.

As the structures and meanings within contemporary global culture continue to undergo massive transformations and realignments, and as issues of (im)migration, displacement, and exile continue to move toward the foreground of everyday experience, the development of a well-tuned critical listening to music along spatial trajectories becomes of paramount importance, enabling a rich critique of national and cultural unities: in this case, a critique of the unity of a strictly African American and/or Afro-European blackness in the context of the black diaspora and the unity of "America" as both geography and discourse in the context of Mexican rock en español. Ultimately, it allows us to witness the unique power of popular music to overflow the national boundaries that pretend to contain it, creating audiotopias across transnational geographies that sound both through and against the hegemonic properties of the multinational capitalist recording industry.

Notes

1. Michel de Certeau, *The Practice of Everyday Life* (Berkeley: U of California P, 1984), 115, 130. For Certeau, "space is composed of intersections of mobile elements. It is in a sense actuated by the ensemble of movements deployed within it. Space occurs as the effect produced by the operations that orient it, situate it, temporalize it, and make it function in a polyvalent unity of conflictual programs or contractual proximities" (117).

2. Edward Soja, *Postmodern Geographies* (New York: Verso, 1989), 11.

3. Michel Foucault, "Of Other Spaces" *diacritics* 16.1 (Spring 1986): 22.

4. Foucault, "Of Other Spaces," 22.

5. Foucault, "Of Other Spaces," 24–25.

6. In *The Black Atlantic: Modernity and Double Consciousness* (Cambridge: Harvard U P, 1993), Paul Gilroy has argued that music enables a "resolutely utopian politics of transfiguration" (37).

7. My definition of audiotopia is admittedly very much a definition-in-progress, and I have yet to fully realize the scope of its implications and meanings. I offer it as a starting point for further discussion and analysis and use it here more along the lines of what Clifford has called a "translation term," a word "of apparently general application used for comparison in a strategic and contingent way" (cited in Mark Slobin, *Subcultural Sounds: Micromusics of the West* [Hanover: Wesleyan U P, 1993], 12).

8. As Vera Kutzinski reminds us in the context of literary practice, such migrations "are hardly a recent phenomenon. What has changed, it seems, is our willingness to acknowledge that traffic's existence and imagine actively its consequences" ("American Literary History as Spatial Practice," *American Literary History* 4.3 [Fall 1992]: 552.

9. Gilroy, *Black Atlantic*, 58, 202.

10. Gilroy notes how The Impressions were an important influence on Jamaican vocal trios like The Wailers and how "I'm So Proud" went on to be covered by, among others, U.S. R&B pop singer Deniece Williams in 1983 and versioned as "Proud of Mandela" on Britain's reggae charts in 1990 by toaster Macka B and Lovers' Rock singer Kofi.

11. Gilroy, *Black Atlantic*, 95.

12. Alternatively, an argument could be made for the racial, as opposed to colonial, limits to Gilroy's study given his brief treatment of the rise of Bhangra music in Britain's immigrant South Asian communities with its incredible fusion of traditional Punjabi and Bengali musics, languages, and themes with both Jamaican and British

ska, reggae, raggamuffin, dancehall, and sound system culture and U.S. house, soul, and hip-hop.

13. Deborah Pacini Hernández, "Crossing Over: Dominican Bachata in the 1990s," paper presented at International Association for the Study of Popular Music conference, Havana, Cuba, October 1994.

14. For a more specific illustration of what I refer to as "African musical style," see Peter Manuel, *Popular Musics of the Non-Western World* (Oxford: Oxford U P, 1988), 84–114. I am thinking generally of what Manuel describes as "complex polyrhythms and layered syncopations" and the predominance of simplified rhythmic structures.

15. From Puerto Rican rapper Lisa M to the Cuban-born Mellow Man Ace to Chicano rappers Aztlan Nation to a growing list that includes Afro-Rican, Cypress Hill, Funkdoobiest, Lighter Shade of Brown, Tha Mexikanz, Funky Aztecs, The Beatnuts, Proper Dos, and Shootyz Groove, studies of the role of a Pan-American Latinidad in the construction of U.S. blackness through hip-hop and rap music remain too few and far between. Indeed, hip-hop is rarely understood as the hemispheric American music that it is. Critical discourse around hip-hop never takes very seriously the claim that rap is not the sounding of a fixed racial, national self, but rather a diaspora music born out of the immigrant movement of both Latino and non-Latino Caribbean populations and sound systems into African American and Latino New York City neighborhoods. See, for example, Juan Flores, "Puerto Rican and Proud, Boyee!: Rap Roots and Amnesia," in *Microphone Fiends,* ed. Andrew Ross and Tricia Rose (New York: Routledge, 1994).

16. Paul Gilroy, "Sounds Authentic: Black Music, Ethnicity, and the Challenge of the Changing Same," *Black Music Research Journal* 11.2 (Fall 1991): 115.

17. Ruben Guevara, liner notes to *Viva! El Chicano: Their Very Best*, MCA 1988.

18. I am not trying to suggest here that these examples are anomalies. I realize that the interaction between U.S. blacks and Latinos/Afro-Latinos from Mexico, Puerto Rico, Cuba, and the Dominican Republic is a much longer and historically intricate story. See, for example, John Storm Roberts, *Black Music of Two Worlds* (New York: Praeger, 1972), or listen to Duke Ellington's *Latin American Suite,* the "latin tinge" of Jelly Roll Morton's music, any Afro-Cuban jazz, or even consider Langston Hughes's boyhood in Mexico and his travels in Cuba. The examples are, of course, too numerous to cover here.

19. Gilroy, "Sounds Authentic," 96.

20. Ghania is Morocco's most respected performer of Gnawa music, ceremonial trance music used to purify and heal the dancers. African American musicians traveling to Africa to record with African musicians is nothing new. Artists such as Randy Weston, Dizzy Gillespie, Duke Ellington, Art Blakey, and many others have done so.

21. Manthia Diawara, "Afro-Kitsch," in *Black Popular Culture*, ed. Gina Dent (Seattle: Bay Press, 1992).

22. Larry Birnbaum, liner notes to *Africando, Volume 1: Trovador*, Stern's Africa, STCD-1045, 1993.

23. Rubén Martínez, *The Other Side* (New York: Verso, 1992).

24. Martínez, *Other Side*, 2, 1.

25. Martínez, *Other Side,* 135, 133–134.

26. Martínez, *Other Side,* 83.

27. Martínez, *Other Side,* 94–95. While cumbia has its origins in mulatto and African populations of nineteenth-century Colombia, its popularity has spread throughout Central and South America.

29. Historical accounts of the emergence of rock and roll abound. For an entertaining introductory look into this rich and complex history, see Michael Ventura, "The DNA of Pop," *Pulse!* (November 1994), 55.

30. Mary Louise Pratt, *Imperial Eyes: Travel Writing and Transculturation* (New York: Routledge, 1992), 4–6.

31. Fernando Ortiz, *Contrapunteo cubano del tabaco y el azucar* (Caracas: Biblioteca Ayacucho, 1978), 93.

32. Pratt, *Imperial Eyes,* 6.

33. Alvaro Enrique, quoted in Yareli Arizmendi, "Whatever Happened to the Sleepy Mexican?" *TDR* 38.1 (Spring 1994): 107.

34. George Yúdice, "Postmodernity and Transnational Capital in Latin America," in *On Edge:* (Minneapolis: U of Minnesota P, 1992), 23.

35. Homi K. Bhabha, *The Location of Culture* (New York: Routledge, 1994), 86–87.

36. Martínez, *Other Side,* 156.

37. Martínez, *Other Side,* 158.

38. Arizmendi, "Whatever Happened," 117.

39. Cited in Martínez, *Other Side,* 149.

40. Such transnational musical mappings coincide with what Hamid Naficy, *The Making of Exile Cultures: Iranian Television in Los Angeles* (Minneapolis: U of Minnesota P, 1993) might refer to as exilic media systems, in which, for example, Mexican news services and television programming are readily available in the United States, including the launching of MTV Latino into over 3 million homes in twenty different countries including the United States (Leila Cobo-Hanlon, "Heating Up the MTV Latino Connection," *Los Angeles Times,* 22 November 1994, F11) and the very recent creation of CineLatino, a twenty-four-hour cable service featuring uncut Spanish-language films from around the world that will additionally sponsor the production of fifty-two new cable films each year. CineLatino is currently being offered in California, Arizona, Nevada, New Mexico, Texas, Florida, and Puerto Rico (Shauna Snow, "The Morning Report: 'Se Habla Español,'" *Los Angeles Times,* 2 December 1994, F1). There is also the case of Televideo, a videotaping service in Northern California that tapes personal messages from Mexican nationals working and living in the United States and sends them to their families in Mexico. Media have become essential components of what Roger Rouse has called "transnational migrant circuitry" and the construction of new identities and the maintenance of family ties across national borders that they enable ("Mexican Migration and the Social Space of Postmodernism," *Diaspora* [Spring 1991]: 271).

41. See Enrique Fernández, "El Norte: Worlds Collide," *Village Voice,* 10 November 1992, 28.

42. Sergio Arau in Arizmendi, "Whatever Happened," 108.

43. Martínez, *Other Side,* 154–155.

44. From the liner notes to Maldita Vecindad y Los Hijos del Quinto Patio, *Gira pata de perro,* BMG Ariola, 1993.

45. "Pachuco" is a tribute to the "hybrid, contradictory, and vital" pachuco culture that emerged in both U.S. and Mexican barrios after World War II. They laud the pachuco's ability to juggle multiple cultures: speaking Spanglish, wearing zoot suits, and dancing swing, mambo, and "boogie."

46. I borrow this concept from her important discussion of Chicana subjectivity, the development of oppositional hegemonies, and the strategic uses of theory in Norma Alarcón, "Conjugating Subjects: The Heteroglossia of Essence and Resistance," *An Other Tongue,* ed. Alfred Arteaga (Durham: Duke U P, 1994), 137.

47. Certeau, 127.

48. Certeau, 128–129.

49. Silviano Santiago, quoted in Yúdice, 22.

50. Yúdice, 24.

51. Néstor García Canclini, "Cultural Reconversion," in *On Edge,* ed. George Yúdice, Jean Franco, and Juan Flores (Minneapolis: U of Minnesota P, 1993), 31–33.

52. García Canclini, 42. It is important to note here Café Tacuba's participation in a transnational U.S.-Latin America recording industry best exemplified by Warner Brothers and Warner Music Mexico, Argentina, and Chile and BMG/RCA and BMG Ariola. They have played concerts in Los Angeles and San Francisco, work with U.S. producers, musicians (Café Tacuba and Jane's Addiction, as well as Caifanes's work with Greg Ladanyi, Stuart Hamm, and Graham Nash), and other players in the culture industry, such as agents and publicists (both Maldita and Caifanes are represented by the L.A. office of the William Morris Agency).

Of Rhythms and Borders

Ana M. López

Music has no borders.—Amparo in *Break of Dawn*

We Got Rhythm?

Halfway through Isaac Artenstein's independently produced *Break of Dawn* (1990), the principal character, the Mexican singer and radio show host Pedro González, is at a fancy 1930s Los Angeles party in honor of a newly elected politician. He is introduced to an up-and-coming tango singer, a woman named Amparo, who sings a tango at his request. His newly instituted early-morning Spanish-language radio show (the first in the L.A. area) is a great success, and her performance is meant to serve as an informal audition. Afterwards, while sharing glasses of champagne in a quiet corner, he asks her, "How does a girl from Nogales end up singing tangos?" To which she responds flirtatiously, "Music has no borders."

Despite Amparo's remark, Latin American music and dance have been perfect markers of the instability of borders and have served as indices of the imaginary demarcations that constitute the process whereby Self/Nation defines itself (and is defined) in relationship to Others. If communities, as Benedict Anderson argues, "are to be distinguished not by their falsity/genuineness, but by the style in which they are imagined,"[1] it is not surprising that the boundaries of the Latin American nation or Latino community have often been closely associated with music, dance, and their performance and representation as stylistic markers of (imagined) national essences: Argentine tangos, Brazilian sambas, Mexican mariachis and rancheras, the merengues of the Dominican Republic, the Cuban danzón, son, rhumba, mambo, and cha cha cha, the urban Latino salsa. In fact, we could argue that in addition to being "narrated"—a fictional or enunciated construct—the nation (and some more so than others) is also insistently sung and danced. Latin American nations have foundational literary romances,[2] but they also have foundational rhythms which are fought over—and crossed—with as much regularity as their painfully real cartographical borders. Rhythms have been an integral part of the complicated process of establishing and maintaining Latin American nations (creating the different "feeling" or style of the imaginary community), but Latin American music and dance have also been used by "others" to collapse such markers of national differences. Thus "Latin music" in the United States has often existed in a colonialist vacuum as a catchall category that collapses all the carefully nurtured (though often imagined) nationalistic origins of specific rhythms. By the same token, however, that colonial vacuum has also been the space where different notions of (an often gendered) *Latinidad* have emerged that realign the idea of "Latino" rhythms with a contestational Pan–Latin American/Latino community and/or identity.

The position of music and dance as privileged signs of imagined Latin American nations/communities highlights what Homi Bhabha has so well characterized as the temporal split between the pedagogical and the performative in discourses of nationness.[3] According to Bhabha, such discourses must simultaneously sediment the nation's historical past—the pedagogical that signifies the people as an a priori historical presence—and provide the means for cultural identification in the present—the performative. This double inscription, as pedagogical objects and performative subjects, produces a double time, a profound and ambivalent instability disavowed in historicist discourses. When music and dance are invoked as national discursive units of gestures, rhythms, and sounds, Bhabha's double-time becomes only too apparent. The rhythm must stand in as that which has *always* been part of the national imaginary, but it must also serve as that which can *performatively* interpellate social actors into a community in the present. Much more so than with narration, through music and dance "the nation reveals in its ambivalent and vacillating representation, the ethnography of its own historicity and opens up the possibility of other narratives of the people and their difference."[4] Thus we cannot ignore the fact that Latin American national "rhythms" also have complicated histories marked by multiple attempts to erase/inscribe class, racial, and gendered differences in the service of the idea of nationness.[5] This is not the place to lay out this complicated history—the African roots of most Cuban rhythms, the French Creole roots of danzón, the African *and* working-class-lunfardo genesis of the Argentine tango, the Afro-Brazilian–urban favela context for the development of samba. Nevertheless, one must stress that the idea of these specific rhythms as emblems of the nation already involves the process of appropriation and assimilation of differences that comes into play when we talk about the circulation of such rhythms outside the nation-state in question. These are, indeed, ambivalent signs of nationness.

Yet music and dance also invoke another kind of troublesome splitting. Although by definition always evocative of the performative, music and dance can assume markedly different forms: they are vernacular forms of self-bodily expression as well as explicit performances for audiences which may acquire a representational half-life (or double life) through the mass media. First of all, then, beyond the national paradigm, music and dance operate in "other" spaces—domestic and semipublic spheres—where they serve as vehicles for different forms of transgressions and crossings linked to desire and other processes of identity-formation and contestation. After all, Amparo's remark in *Break of Dawn* that "music has no borders" is not only meant to elide national boundaries, but the domestic and social barriers that stand between her and the ostensibly happily married male protagonist who will become her lover that same evening. Preceding this scene of mutual seduction, Amparo's passionate public performance of the famous tango "Cuesta abajo" (the first lyrical lines of which already invoke the border-crossing scenario: "Si arrastré por este mundo la vergüenza de haber sido y el dolor de ya no ser")[6] is an act that may transgress national borders/identities, but which narratively initiates an ultimately very dangerous series of domestic and sexual transgressions that erupt onto the film's public sphere. Furthermore, just as in the film, I have not (immediately—see note 6) translated the lyrics of the tango "Downhill"; that they are untranslated in the film complicates processes of reception and the analyses of any such textual givens, for the bicultural spectator may identify with Amparo's transgression, while the monolingual Anglo audience may perhaps relegate her performance to the space of undecipherable and therefore safely meaningless local color of the gendered kind.

Second, as a bodily vernacular we can think of Latin American music and dance as forms of "signifying," as José Piedra argues in his suggestive essay about rumba, "Poetics for the Hip," and its companion piece about the Cuban *son*, "Through Blues."[7] For Piedra, the rumba is a concentric form of signifying, "a questionably ethical and superficial means of compliance aimed at yielding a profound and aesthetic means of defiance."[8] But when this vernacular travels and crosses borders to become a musical fad or dance craze, it is also the means whereby others can sexily—yet safely—indulge in difference as a masquerade by performing the other and, as Jane Desmond argues in this volume, "inoculating" themselves against their potential danger. Even then the masquerade takes different forms: the colonizer slums by appropriating the subaltern's rhythms, but the subaltern also masquerades when she/he performs them for the other. As in all masquerade scenarios, the crucial point is not the masquerade itself, but what it conceals. Here it reveals, not some genuine or authentic national or other essence, but the means by which nationality, ethnicity, sexuality, and the contests over their authenticity are linked, reproduced, and marketed.

The third dimension of this problematic deals with the question of the re-presentation and circulation of Latin American music and dance in the mass media, for this is the terrain where we can most clearly trace the processes whereby "performances" are inserted into the social imaginary to assume the emblematic power with which I began this essay.

In summary, then, my project involves a two-tiered, somewhat syncopated analysis. On the one hand, I am questioning the special "signifying" of Latin American music and dance and their ability to cross and be crossed by borders and, on the other, I am concerned with analyzing how music and dance have effected such troublesome crossings in one specific mass medium, the cinema. Of course, "the cinema" as such—in the abstract—is a film theorist's fantasy. My analysis derives its rhythm from a multiple historical focus that compares the crossings of Latin American music and dance in the classic Hollywood cinema, in the classic (or "golden") Latin American cinema, in the New Latin American Cinema, and in the contemporary Latin American and U.S. Latino cinemas. Despite the linear history invoked in this chronological approach, I shall endeavor to demonstrate not a history of the overcoming of difference but the complex mediations effected by Latin American rhythms *as* markers of difference and identity, a process crystallized in the Mexican film *Danzón* (Maria Novaro, 1991), which I analyze in some detail in the last section of this essay.

The Movies Say We Got Rhythm?

Latin American rhythms and the cinema have had a long historical association. Certainly, even before the coming of sound, Hollywood films identified Latin Americans and Chicanos with rhythm, as witnessed by the early Edison kinetoscope *Carmencita Spanish Dancer*, featuring the vaguely "Spanish" turns of a dance that was all the rage at Koster and Bial's Music Hall in New York City in 1895 and 1896.[9] Latin American rhythms were also already linked with an eroticized exoticism in the silent cinema. Even Rudolf Valentino's Latin lover, usually not associated with Latin Americanness, portrayed a stylized Argentine gaucho and danced a passionate and aggressive tango in *Four Horsemen of the Apocalypse* (Rex Ingram, 1921).[10] It is safe to assume, furthermore, that the many "fiesta" and "Latin"-inspired dance scenes common in Hollywood silent films were accompanied by appropriately "Latin"-inspired musical passages in theaters and nickelodeons.[11] But sound unquestionably opened the floodgates in Hollywood, and Latin American rhythms poured in.

The affinity between the new technology and Latin rhythms was most consistently exploited in the western and musical genres (although "Latin" sounds often surfaced in any genre film that included cabaret or party scenes and often served to invoke excessive or forbidden sexuality[12] or to economically identify characters or settings as Latin).[13] In the western, Latin-inspired music and dance became an easy way to provide local color and to exploit the possibilities of sound. As early as 1928, the first "talkie" western, *In Old Arizona* (Raoul Walsh), featured Warren Baxter as the Cisco Kid singing a Mexican-inspired song entitled "My Toña." Throughout the 1930s and 1940s, the singing cowboys of the serials—Gene Autry, Roy Rogers, Tex Ritter, and others—would regularly be "inspired" by Mexican and/or Southwestern locales, inhabitants (especially the pretty señoritas), rhythms, and fiestas. Although the singing cowboys have been heralded as the principal agents for the subsequent popularity of Country (and Western) music,[14] they in turn also utilized and exploited Mexican themes and music: think only of the famous Gene Autry song "Down Mexico Way" in the 1940 film of the same title. But the "A" and almost "A" westerns also used Mexican- and Latin-inspired music and dances to good advantage throughout the

1940s and 1950s. In *Stagecoach* (John Ford, 1939), for example, the Mexican singer Elvira Ríos (although portraying an Indian "squaw") sings a nostalgic ballad in Spanish linking a lost love with the distant nation and lamenting the loss of boundaries. However, here, as in most other instances of the Hollywood appropriation of Latin American music, the failure to translate the lyrics for the Anglo audience positions the song as a vague marker of a generalized Latin otherness, empty of specificity and indexing only the romanticized sexuality of the exotic.

The association of Latin American music and dance with female characters, usually but not necessarily of Mexican descent, is thus quite common in the classic Hollywood western. That Pearl Chavez in *Duel in the Sun* (King Vidor, 1946) is to be identified as Chicana is clear not because of her ancestors (upper-class, Spanish-speaking father and Indian mother is all the film tells us), but because her unbridled sexuality is rhythmically prefigured: when she is first introduced she is passionately dancing an unmistakably Latin number. In another western of the same year, *My Darling Clementine* (John Ford, 1946), Linda Darnell plays Chihuahua, a cantina girl who sings and dances in the Tombstone saloon where Wyatt Earp and Doc Holliday battle with the Clanton clan. Like other Mexican/Chicana women in Hollywood films, Chihuahua pays dearly for a sensuality that is graphically linked to her "profession" as a musical performer and to her ethnicity: pushed into the arms of a bad character by Doc Holliday's inattentions, she dies of a tragic gunshot wound. Pam Cook has argued that as the third term between the civilized schoolteacher Clementine and the uneasy taming of the Westerner Wyatt Earp, Chihuahua's "memory lurks in the shadows as a reminder of what civilization represses."[15] But that this "memory" is ethnically other is also no mere accident in a film suffused with the romanticism of paradises lost and regained.[16]

Despite its significant presence in westerns, Latin American rhythms would be most consistently exploited by the musical genre. Obviously based on a generic affinity, the Hollywood musical's attention to Latin America also paralleled the rise of the Latin music boom in the United States in the 1930s and 1940s. The cinematic musical genre and the popularity of Latin rhythms developed simultaneously, each feeding off the other to maximize their market potential. For example, as early as 1929 RKO made a most successful entry into the "all-talking, all-singing" genre with *Rio Rita* (Luther Reed), a musical western comedy set on the Texas-Mexico border. Based on a Ziegfeld show of 1927, *Rio Rita*'s combination of "colorful" characters (especially Bebe Daniels as a Mexican señorita fully equipped with mantillas, peinetas, and giant hoop earrings), sweeping action (the Texas Rangers riding horseback across the screen while singing in unison), and catchy and appropriately ethnified music set the stage for a decade's worth of Hollywood Latinisms in the musical.

Publicly enshrined at the same historical moment, the cinematic functions of the Latin American musical craze and the generic conventions of the Hollywood musical developed partly through each other's agency. Most early musicals followed the pattern of 1920s urban musical theater and motivated the genre's problematic combination of narrative and musical performances professionally, by featuring performers as characters and situating the action in theaters or nightclubs.[17] But another solution was introduced as early as 1929 in Paramount's *Wolf Song* (Victor Fleming, with Lupe Vélez and Gary Cooper), where the awkward transitions between narrative action and singing/performance were naturalized through the veil of ethnicity. As the *Variety* reviewer explained, it was "an old Spanish custom for the characters to sing at each other with guitar accompaniment at the slightest provocation."[18] Thus that "normal" people could break into song to express the joys of youthful coupling—when Lupe Vélez as Lola, the daughter of a California *hacendado*, sings "Mi amado" and "Yo te amo Means I Love You" to Gary Cooper, for example—was justified by claiming a mimetic realism based on the belief that musicality was an intrinsic Hispanic characteristic. The ethnic character—and apparently also those involved with her, since Gary Cooper carries a guitar throughout most of the film—is by necessity a *performative* subject that must enact and reenact his or her cultural identity. Shortly thereafter, once the musical's conventions were more formally established, the ethic "cover" was hardly ever used; on the contrary, Latino/as and Latin Americans appeared most often as exotic performers rather than "regular" citizens driven by love to sing and dance their passions.[19] Such marks of citizenship would rarely be accorded to the Hollywood Latino/as–Latin Americans who were regularly called upon to perform their ethnicities.[20]

Besides lackluster efforts to invoke a (not necessarily appropriate) sense of Latin rhythms in films such as *The Kid from Spain* (Leo McCarey, 1932), Latin settings, music, and talent became de rigueur in at least one major musical film per year throughout the 1930s.[21] From *Cuban Love Song* (Willard S. Van Dyke, 1931) and *Flying Down to Rio* (Thorton Freeland, 1933) to *Under the Pampas Moon* (B. G. De Sylva, 1935), *Rose of the Rancho* (William Le Baron, 1935), and *Tropic Holiday* (Arthur Hornblow, 1938), the Hollywood musical traveled far and wide throughout Latin and Central America in search of "other" forms of musicality. The "South of the Border" musical peaked in the 1940s, when the combination of wartime interests, the popularity of Latin music (embodied in the figure of Xavier Cugat, the Catalan bandleader who epitomized the syrupy Latin big-band sound, and in Desi Arnaz, the conga king), the Good Neighbor Policy, and the box office success of "imported" performers (especially Carmen Miranda, the "Brazilian Bombshell") coalesced into a national obsession with things Latin American.[22] Despite some efforts to deal with national specificities with sensitivity,[23] overall these films participated in the general project of subsuming national rhythmic and other differences under the sign of Latinidad: all Latins and Latin Americans were from South of the Border and *that* border was the only one that mattered as far as Hollywood was concerned. Thus Carmen Miranda is incongruously "Brazilian" in a studio-produced Argentina (*Down Argentine Way*, Irving Cummings, 1940) and Cuba (*Weekend in Havana*, Walter Lang, 1941); Desi Arnaz an Argentine conga-playing student in a New Mexico college in *Too Many Girls* (George Abbott, 1940); Ricardo Montalbán a Mexican classical composer that dances Spanish flamenco in *Fiesta* (Jack Cummings, 1947); and Gene Kelly an Anglo sailor on leave who happens upon a stage version of Olvera Street in the Los Angeles of *Anchors Aweigh* (Stanley Donen, 1945) and dances a "Mexican Hat Dance" to the Argentine tango "La cumparsita." Although a self-declared top priority, national specificity was nearly impossible to represent by the terms of the Hollywood musical.

That Hollywood's interest in all types of "Latin" musicality waned in the postwar period (*Nancy Goes to Rio* [1950] is considered the last "South of the Border" musical) has not, however, been convincingly explained by either musical or ethnic representation scholars. For example, Rick Altman argues that the fifties musical shift from South of the Border to Continental/Parisian settings and themes can be explained as part of the

Carmen Miranda as an incongruous Brazilian in *Down Argentine Way,* 1940.
(*Courtesy of the Kobal Collection*)

general evolution of "American utopian thought." During the war, "the characteristic Latin fiesta appeared to North Americans as a perpetual feast, a symbol of life in what seemed like an unhurried utopia," but postwar Paris seemed "to satisfy peace time pressures for a new utopia."[24] The Mexican scholar Emilio García Riera (the most thorough chronicler of the Latin presence in the Hollywood cinema) presents a similar argument: Hollywood's excessive use of Latin sounds during the war years satiated the public. After the war, Latin America and Latin music were simply passé.[25] As Betty Grable sings in the song "South America, Take It Away," featured in *Call Me Mister* (Lloyd Bacon, 1951): "Take back the rhumba, mambo and samba [because] my back is aching from all that shaking."

Nevertheless, it seems that Hollywood's fascination with Latin music may also have cooled as a result of the increased *public* visibility of Latino/as in U.S. urban centers (growing waves of immigration in the late 1940s, 1950s, and 1960s, especially from Puerto Rico and Cuba) and in

Hollywood (exemplified by the nonmusical "social consciousness" genre of the 1940s and 1950s).[26] Musically, the institutionalization of Latin rhythms as dance music (among others, the mambo in the 1950s) is also accompanied by a growing *mestizaje* between Latin and Anglo sounds. In Latin America, especially in the Caribbean, the influence of "foreign" musical signifiers would generate its own syncretic products such as the mambo, the cha cha cha, and the bossa nova.[27] In the United States, Latin musicians based in New York—like the Cubans Machito and Chano Pozo—would fuse rhythms to popularize dance music and "Latin jazz." In Los Angeles, the success of the Don Tosti's Band's "Pachuco Boogie" (1948)—a mixture of *calo* lyrics, scat singing, and blues harmonies—and, somewhat later, the eclectic musical synthesizing of Ritchie Valens signaled yet a different kind of ethnic mestizaje. Even later, others would produce the syncretic mix called salsa, which has been associated almost exclusively with urban U.S. Latinidad. Thus the formerly exotic rhythms—syncretized, assimilated, transformed in and out of the United States—no longer invoke some pure exotic essence of otherness, but rather the visible seams of U.S. penetration abroad and ethnicity at home, where by 1951 Desi Arnaz already appeared every week as a conga-wielding Cuban bandleader married to the United States' favorite redhead in *I Love Lucy*.

Nevertheless, the reasons for Hollywood's original general interest in Latin American rhythms in the 1930s and 1940s as markers of otherness must be placed in a still broader context: besides the desire for "difference" with which to exploit the new technology in the 1930s and the stirrings of the Good Neighbor Policy in the 1940s, the Hollywood studios were quick to notice that "down South," dance and music had become important commercial markers for the nascent national cinemas that were beginning to successfully compete with Hollywood products for sectors of the Latin American market.[28] These early Latin American sound films exploited "national" talent (popularized through the also booming radio technology) in revue-type films; soon they would incorporate more narrative and assume specific national "forms" (while, alongside them, dance and musical performances would regularly appear in all genres, especially in the melodrama).

Argentina was the first Latin American nation to take advantage of the transition to sound by banking on the popularity of national rhythms.

Argentine silent films had already used tango-inspired themes and iconography to good advantage,[29] but in addition, since 1924 in Buenos
Aires, the exhibition of most films (national or imported) was usually
accompanied by musical groups featuring the best tango musicians. At
a time when the (developing) national radio industry denigrated the
tango, the cinemas were the best and least expensive place to hear tangos
and often the musicians were the principal attraction of the Calle Lavalle
theaters in Buenos Aires. As Paulo Antonio Paranaguá has argued,
sound came to the movies at the right time for Argentina, for by the late
1920s the tango was a mature and expanding form and the nation itself
was ready to accept this quintessential porteño sound as the national
rhythm.[30]

It is therefore not surprising that the first Argentine experiment with
optical sound, a series of ten shorts in 1929–1930, featured the popular
tango singer Carlos Gardel. Gardel's growing national and international
reputation, and the Latin American success of his films for Paramount at
Joinville—especially *Luces de Buenos Aires* (Lights of Buenos Aires, Adel-
qui Millar, 1931) and *Melodia del arrabal* (Melody of the arrabal, Louis
Gasnier, 1932)—and later at the Astoria Studios in New York, stimulated
the interest of national producers in the formerly denigrated musical
form.[31] When Angel Mentasti established Argentina Sono Films, the
company's first production was appropriately entitled *Tango!* (Luis Mog-
lia Barth, 1933). Although little more than a revue-type film with a never-
ending parade of singers and musicians, the success of the film conse-
crated the place of the tango in the Argentine sound cinema and its
popularity engendered a number of sequels, some of them produced by
a rival newcomer producer financed by Argentine radio entrepreneurs
(Lumiton). But the affinity between the melodramatic nature of tango
lyrics and musical narrative was most fully developed by silent-cinema
veteran José Agustín "el Negro" Ferreyra, who had already brought to
national screens the urban iconography and popular stock characters of
the tango and, with sound, would integrate them fully into a "new"
national cinematic form: the "opera tanguera"[32] or tango melodrama. In
Ayúdame a vivir (Help me to live, 1936), Ferreyra fully integrated tangos
into the melodramatic diegesis using music for narrative development
and punctuation and transforming the tango singer Libertad Lamarque

into an internationally known movie star. Beginning in the mid-1930s the Argentine cinema was nationally successful, exported widely throughout Latin America, and synonymous with the tango. As Jorge Miguel Couselo explains it, "the tango was the magic formula that opened all the doors" for the national industry.[33]

In Brazil, the "musical" genre would eventually become known as the *chanchada*, a carnivalesque combination of popular music—especially sambas—dance, and parodic comedy. The chanchada was preceded by "carnival films" that featured each year's most popular sambas, marches, and performers. Unlike the tango in Argentina, the samba was not yet considered a "national" rhythm and was socially and regionally segregated: as Paranaguá has argued, "samba era coisa de negro" and of national interest primarily during carnival.[34] At first simple reports of carnival festivities, the carnival films quickly evolved into narratives around which were interwoven the performances of the most popular radio and record personalities (often playing themselves). The success of *Alo, Alo, Brasil!* (Hello, hello Brazil!, Wallace Downey, 1935) and *Alo, Alo, Carnaval!* (Hello, hello, carnival!, Wallace Downey, 1936), released to coincide with the euphoria of carnival festivities and clearly alluding to their radiophonic allegiances, demonstrated that national music and dance, liberally combined with parodic comedy and performed by popular stars (like Carmen Miranda), were a popular draw for the nascent national sound cinema. The principal production companies of the era—Adhemar Gonzaga's Cinédia, Wallace Downey's Downey Filmes and Sono-Filmes, and, in the 1940s, Moacyr Fenelon's Atlantida—devoted themselves quite successfully to the task of putting Brazilian music, dance, and its own stars on the national screens. Although often critically reviled, the Brazilian chanchadas perhaps represent the most sustained popular response to Hollywood's dominance of the Latin American film market: a popular, low-budget, and often quite biting national cinema for national consumption (linguistic and cultural barriers prevented Brazilian films from successfully exploiting the Latin American export market).

Although the Mexican sound cinema did not begin with musical revue-type films, music was always present and diegetically central in the films of the 1930s. The plot of the first sound feature—*Más fuerte que el deber* (Stronger than duty, 1930)—for example, revolves around a young novice priest who prefers singing popular music to the Church. And *Santa* (1931) prominently features a blind piano-playing singer and the music of Mexico's premier balladeer, Agustín Lara. Most early 1930s Mexican films invoke the musical, either as an explicit causal agent for the diegesis or as an essential part of the ambience. Nevertheless, the national cinema would not find its commercial footings until the 1936 release of *Allá en el rancho grande* (Over there in the big ranch) and the establishment of the *comedia ranchera* genre—a peculiar combination of period/country nostalgia, comedy, and lots of ranchera music and dancing. As Carlos Monsiváis has argued, "After *Rancho,* the Mexican cinema could no longer do without one of its basic connotations—the songs. *Rancho grande* became our Paradise Lost, the image of a kind and idyllic Mexico destroyed by corrupt city life."[35]

The comedias rancheras, like the Brazilian chanchadas and the Argentine tango melodramas, were not musicals in the style of Hollywood. Perhaps with the exception of "el Negro" Ferreyra's films, Latin American films of this period do not weave music and dance into a dual-focus narrative focused on heterosexual romance and the joy of coupling. Instead, rhythms and performance are used as one signifying element in hybrid forms that defy generic definition according to Hollywood. In the rancheras, for example, music and performance often signal the genre's nostalgia for an idyllic past (in "old" Mexico everyone was happy, even when unhappy, thus they sang and danced), while in the more melodramatic films, music is used to mark moral opposites.[36] In melodramas, especially the *cabaretera* subgenre of the 1950s, the Mexican cinema made great use of another great national musical icon: the bolero composer and singer Agustín Lara. A former brothel pianist, Lara specialized in soulful songs exalting prostitutes and fallen women that perfectly matched the needs of the melodramatic genre. Already world-famous by 1944—Walt Disney had used his song "Solamente una vez" (One time only) in *The Three Caballeros* (Norman Ferguson, 1944) and more than nineteen Mexican films had featured his music—by the late 1940s[37] the Mexican melodrama had completely assumed Lara's vision of the prostitute as an object of self-serving worship, and his songs became the central dramatic impulse propelling the action of many cabaretera films. *Aventurera* (Adventuress, Alberto Gout, 1950), for example, is clearly inspired by the song of the same title (sung by Pedro Vargas in the film):[38]

Sell your love expensively, adventuress
Put the price of grief on your past
And he who wants the honey from your mouth
Must pay with diamonds for your sin
Since the infamy of your destiny
Withered your admirable spring
Make your road less difficult,
Sell your love dearly, adventuress

Although difficult to conceive of as nationalistic icons, Lara's boleros and their cinematic renderings also participated in the complex process of Mexican nation-building. As I've argued elsewhere, musically and cinematically they served to inscribe the prostitute and the cabaret life with which she is associated as an anti-utopian paradigm for a so-called modern Mexican life.[39]

Overall there is very little singing and dancing in the classic Latin American cinema that is not diegetically motivated: characters are or have been performers or they go to places of performance. Nevertheless, rhythms are systematically invoked as markers of specific nationalities and as sites for national identification. The national rhythms are the rhythms of the "people" (rather than of individual characters) and simultaneously serve to unify the nation by providing an identity and to market the nation abroad. This is most apparent in those cinemas struggling to define themselves as "national" cinemas in relation to Hollywood and other imports. In the Cuban cinema of the 1930s, 1940s, and 1950s, for example, it is rare to find a film that does not feature the performance of a "typical" Cuban rhythm specifically advertised as such. As early as *El romance del Palmar* (Ramón Peón, 1938), typical *guajiro* music and Rita Montaner's rendition of the popular song "El maniscero" (The peanut vendor) are used to illustrate the nature and authenticity of the Cuban countryside. And even significantly later the melodramatic thriller *Siete muertes a plazo fijo (Seven deaths on the installment plan,* Manolo Alonso, 1950) climaxes with a long musical performance of the history of Cuba through its rhythms, from the slaves' drums to the urban comparsa and the contemporary mambo. However, despite various attempts to promote Cuba as a multiracial and multiethnic rhythmic landscape, prerevolutionary Cuban films consistently invoke musicality as a national trait—to be seductively performed—and an aberration resulting from the also performative process of syncretism. As Blanquita Amaro sings in *Bella, la salvaje* (Bella, the savage, Raúl Medina, 1952), "Lo mismo yo bailo el mambo / Que el son guaracha o la rumba / Pues todas tienen sandunga / Igual que el ritmo africano."[40] Within musical performance, the creation of a national space simultaneously invokes and elides the differences that constitute it, thus also laying bare the traces of its production.

Although we can argue that Latin American national cinemas were literally empowered by the popular appeal and identifiability of "national" rhythms and performers, such rhythms regularly crossed cinematic and other borders throughout the 1930s, 1940s, and 1950s. Historically, Cuban musical performers and dancers had the greatest intercontinental cinematic mobility. The lack of sufficient local cinematic opportunities made Cuban performers a particularly attractive "export" item for other national cinemas. As early as 1933, for example, the Cuban singer Rita Montaner appeared in the Mexican film *La noche del pecado* (The night of sin, Miguel Contrera Torres) with her "Conjunto tropical." Even the often insular Brazilian cinema imported Cuban talent for the chanchada genre: *Carnaval atlantida* (José Carlos Burle, 1952), a film considered a "practical manifesto for a realistic Brazilian cinematic practice" dealing with the (im)possibility of sustaining studio-type "quality" cinema in Brazil,[41] features the dancer María Antonieta Pons (aka "the Cuban Hurricane"), who intones the memorable line "El pueblo quer cantar, bailar, divertirse, tío! [The people want to sing, dance, and have fun, uncle!]."

However, the intercontinental traffic in rhythms was most often ordered by the shifting balance of power among the various national cinemas (and overseen by Hollywood, often with first bidding rights on performers). While early on Argentina and even Cuba regularly imported talent, by the late 1940s the direction of rhythmic exchanges had been reversed and the now hegemonic Mexican cinema became the great musical equalizer, regularly featuring and absorbing popular Latin American rhythms and performers: Argentine tangos (via Libertad Lamarque), Cuban rumbas (Ninón Sevilla, María Antonieta Pons, Blanquita Amaro), sones (Rita Montaner), and later mambos, cha cha chas, and even sambas. Thus, perhaps on a smaller scale but no less pervasively than in Hollywood, the Mexican cinema outside the ranchera genre posited Latin American music and dance as general markers of a "Latinness" increasingly dissociated from any national specificity and greatly invested with sexuality. Other national differences could be assimilated into a broadened, cosmopolitan vision of a "Mexico" that could absorb all the Latinidad of Latin America—and most often displace it onto the cabaret and its female denizens.

The comedy *Calabacitas tiernas* (Tender pumpkins, Gilberto Martínez Solares, 1948)[42] starring the Pachuco-inspired comedian Tin Tán, perfectly illustrates this homogenizing tendency. Tin Tán plays a frustrated and unemployed musician who assumes the identity of a cabaret impresario and orchestrates a show structured like a Pan-Americanist smorgasbord. Working for him are a beautiful Mexican maid (Rosita Quintana) who specializes in the latest rock and roll rhythms, a Cuban rumbera (Amalia Aguilar) and her entourage of bongoceros, a refined Mexican bolero singer (Nelly Montiel), a Brazilian samba-cantora (Rosina Pagan) modeled on Carmen Miranda, and even an Argentine impresario (Jorge Reyes). With boundless energy (and some of the best comedic moments of his career), Tin Tán at will crosses all the borders that surround him: speaking and singing to the rumbera with a distinct Cuban accent and expressions, to the cantora in pidgin Portuguese, and in Spanglish to the maid. Above all, however, he dances smoothly and exuberantly to all the rhythms they embody and perform. Tin Tán energizes all the exchanges, arrivals, and departures and rehearses the performers to get their moves "right" (the rumbera is told to put more hip in her moves, the cantora instructed in how to use her hands more expressively). In his absence, the performers do not cohere as a group. But when rearticulated under his supranational rhythmic and spectacular tutelage, the show is a success, all the comedic mistaken identities are resolved, and the multicultural mosaic is dissolved into a new—and very Mexican—family unit: Tin Tán, the maid, and their five children. As in the Hollywood cinema, other national and exotic rhythmic differences are exploited and spectacularly figured by "others" (women, Afro-Cuban men) only to be subsumed by the greater force of *the* national paradigm of family life.

Aventurera is perhaps the most excessive example of the Mexican cinema's tendency to homogenize Latin rhythms and to identify them with the threat of excessive sexuality. In this cabaretera film, the Cuban rumbera Ninón Sevilla plays a Mexican girl who adapts with great relish to a life of prostitution and violence.[43] With more than ten musical production numbers, the film exalts the cosmopolitanism of Mexicanness by subsuming other national differences under the spell of Sevilla's virulent sexuality. The arrangements by Dámaso Pérez Prado, numbers by Pedro Vargas and the Trio los Panchos, and the suggestive and excessive performances of Ninón in every conceivable "South of the Border" cabaret landscape—including a Banana-land where she sings the sambas "Sigui-Sigui" and "Chiquita Banana" dressed à la Carmen Miranda—almost serve to dispel the myth of cosmopolitanism to reveal its inherently colonizing impulse.

Which Is My Rhythm?

By the 1950s the Mexican industry had thorough distribution networks in Latin America and a well-consolidated hold on the Latin American cinematic imaginary often exercised through rhythms. But growing state intervention and the producers' tendency to rely on formulas—especially melodramas and rancheras with lots of music and films capitalizing on dance fads—began to loosen that hold. Most importantly, the sociopolitical and cinematic climate of the continent was also radically changing. In the late 1950s and early 1960s, a significant nonindustrial cinematic current begins to emerge in Latin America: the cinema of the new Cuban Revolution, a Cine Joven in Argentina, a Cinema Novo in Brazil.[44] Seeking different definitions of the nation and markers of national authenticity in other sectors, these new Latin American cinemas avoided the popular music canonized by the "old" cinemas. Such music was identified with the Hollywood (and, to some degree, Mexican) "tropicalizing" effect—with cultural colonization and alienation—and was, like the melodrama that often featured it, categorically rejected. However, in both Cuba and Brazil, films that are considered precursors of the "new" cinemas dealt specifically with the place of popular music and dance in national and individual life and explicitly used music to articulate a class analysis of the nation: Nelson Pereira dos Santos's *Rio, quarenta graus* (Rio, forty degrees, 1956) and *Rio zona norte* (Rio, north zone, 1957) and Julio García Espinosa's *Cuba baila* (Cuba dances, 1960).

Rio, quarenta graus is a loving, albeit critical, homage to Rio de Janeiro, its people, and the spirit of samba. The film's first images are already indelibly identified with music: the magnificent aerial shots of the city—illustrating the beaches, the chic Zona Sul, and the tourist attractions as well as the Zona Norte and the *favelas* (shanty towns) on the hills—are accompanied by the popular samba "Voz do morro" (Voice of the hill). But rather than serve as a nationalistic paradigm, music is invoked as a marker of class (and race) belongingness.

The narrative is structured around five young favela boys who sell peanuts around Rio's tourist attractions and, without explicit syntagmatic breaks, flows with the casual rhythm of a samba. *Rio, quarenta graus* presents a somewhat sentimentalist critique of the callousness of the *carioca* bourgeoisie, but its analysis of the plight of the favelado is powerful precisely because the film is intoxicated with the image and sounds of the favela and represents them as a form of cultural capital. This fascination is most explicit in the last scenes of the film, shot on location in the rehearsal hall of the Unidos do Cabuçu samba school and featuring the special appearance of the samba school Portela. When the "samba-enredo" for that year's carnival—the one time of the year when the favelado takes over the city by right—is introduced, the plaintive voice of the *puxador* accompanying himself with a box of matches, the chorus joining in, and the dancing feet mark the end of the film with a joy that exceeds by leaps and bounds the doses of daily suffering it has recorded. As the music of the samba school wafts over the *morro*, the camera soars also, in a long crane shot that discovers the mother of an accidentally dead peanut seller, still waiting by the window for his return, and, beyond her, the majestic beauty of Sugar Loaf and Guanabara Bay at night. Pereira's accomplishment in *Rio, quarenta graus*, to produce a social critique based on the contrast between the *photogenie* and musicality of a popular class and the moral ugliness and inauthenticity of the bourgeoisie, would be an important precedent for the Cinema Novo, even though its practitioners would not return to the urban favela or to the samba for many years.[45]

Rio zona norte (the second film of a never-completed trilogy about the city) also deals with samba, but in a more conventional, psychologically realist narrative mode. Structured by a series of flashbacks, the film tells the story of a samba composer of the northern suburbs of Rio, beginning with the accident that, at the end of the film, leads to his death. Once again intent upon contrasting popular and bourgeois universes and upon describing the exploitation and marginalization of one class by another, Pereira uses samba as the narrative motor that drives the popular hero—Espirito da Luz Cardoso (played by Grande Otelo, a well-known and extremely popular black chanchada actor)—against forces that alternately flatter him, cheat him of his chances, and ignore his pleas for help: the *malandro* (Jece Valadão) who steals his samba and refuses him credit and the concert violinist, Moacyr (Paulo Goulart), who admires his spontaneity, flatters him, offers help, and then systematically ignores him. Samba is simultaneously Espirito's gift and his problem—but it is above all a marker of his class and race and the only secure identity he has left.

Espirito's last encounter with Moacyr crystallizes the relationship of samba to the bourgeois nation. After convincing the famous singer Angela Maria (playing herself) to sing one of his sambas on the radio, Espirito needs to have his music transcribed. This opportunity is his last hope. He is well received by Moacyr and his intellectual friends, who politely listen to his samba and look upon Espirito as an exotic example of otherness. But soon their interest shifts and, ironically, they begin a heated aesthetic discussion about the place of popular culture and folklore in the theater. Ignored, Espirito sits by himself on the edge of a sofa, picks up the lyrics to his samba that a hand carelessly dropped on the center table, and gets up to leave. Too self-involved, the group fails to notice that a real representative of the *povo* is sitting in front of them. At the door, Moacyr thanks him for dropping by and casually says: "Oh, and about that music you wanted me to transcribe, why don't you come by next week sometime?" The question remains in the air as the dejected Espirito walks away, once again defeated.

With a somewhat heavy dose of self-flagellation, Pereira dos Santos here inaugurates a strategy that would be developed even further by the Cinema Novo: the bourgeoisie—the self, the audience—is severely criticized while simultaneously (and subsequently) allowed to feel exalted by its sentiment/compassion toward the povo. The political significance of the text resides precisely in the evocation of such sentiment and its association with popular music.

After his visit to Moacyr, Espirito heads toward the train station and home. On a crowded train he overhears two boys debating the merits of various sambas and he comes up with a fortuitous combination of words—"Samba meu / que e do Brasil tambem [My samba / Which is also Brazil's]"—and the rhythm for a new samba. No longer dejected, he changes trains amongst a milling throng and, barely on board and holding on to the open door for support, he begins to tap the rhythm on the edge of the door, humming, and then finally singing out loud. In his excitement and happy concentration he loosens his hold and falls. The film ends after his death in a hospital, where Moacyr, profoundly moved and ashamed, goes to Espirito's neighborhood to listen to and learn at least "two or three" of Espirito's sambas. "My samba / Which is also Brazil's" has obviously disappeared, yet another victim of class inequities. In Espirito's world, you may have your samba, but the nation—fractured, finally, rather than united by differential access to the circulation of rhythm—does not necessarily sing with you.

Although Cuban filmmaker Julio García Espinosa was also concerned with exposing the falsely established dichotomy between elite and popular rhythms and the private and public spaces in which they ambiguously (co)exist, his *Cuba baila* presents a much more complicated map of the interaction between class, rhythm, and pleasure. As the affirmation of the title indicates, the film does not question that the nation dances; what is at stake is rhythm itself and how the pleasure of the dance can be manipulated, if not corrupted, by dishonest political and social forces.

The narrative of *Cuba baila* recounts the problems faced by the family of a minor functionary, Ramón, as they plan a big celebration for the daughter's *quince* (coming-out party celebrating a girl's fifteenth birthday). Flora (Raquel Revueltas), the mother, is determined to give her daughter Marcia a properly bourgeois party with the socially correct music—Viennese waltzes and North American music—even though the cost of such a band is well beyond the family's means. Ramón's efforts to ingratiate himself with his boss and local politicians to get a loan fail and, much to Flora's chagrin, the party can only take place in an open-air popular entertainment garden. What is most interesting about the film is not, however, this somewhat conventional plot, but the degree to which music defines the social spaces where it is played, heard, and danced to. The film begins with a popular dance at the same open-air garden where Marcia's party will eventually take place. In a seamless classical style, with measured tracking shots and few cuts, the camera captures both the pleasure of the crowd and the expertise and fluidity of individual couples focused upon for the pleasure of their performance. As the camera tracks among the swirling crowd, however, it also captures a curiously still figure on the margins: Flora, unmoved by the rhythm, looking disapprovingly at the gyrating bodies. Having identified itself with this popular act—this popular pleasure—the film also quickly sets up its opposite. The family attends the quince party of the daughter of Ramón's boss. Held at a swank club and attended by the very North Americanized upper bourgeoisie, the music here is exactly what Flora wants for Marcia's party, but there is little pleasure among the stiff waltzing bodies, and the principal energy emanates not from the dance floor but from the political and financial connections being established among the guests. In this space, Marcia dances, but robotically and unsmiling. As Flora unwittingly discloses when she tries to compliment the hostess on the waltz with the statement "Su esposo y hija están como de película [Your husband and daughter are like movie stars]," the scene is patently artificial and its performance rehearsed rather than pleasurable.

However, the apparent simplicity of this crude opposition between popular and elite rhythms is quickly dispelled. Ramón attends a political rally to ingratiate himself to his boss and the film records how the pleasure of music and dance can be manipulated. When the politicians hire a band to pull in the crowd (since the turn of the century a common strategy in Cuban political rallies that was popularly called a "chambelona" or lollypop), the people seem unable to resist the rhythm and they abandon their errands and leave their homes to follow it. Like a mad pied piper, the band seduces the people with the pleasure of rhythm and deposits them at the feet of the politician. But when the band stops, the seduction is also abruptly cut short: the crowd does not forget its interests, boos the lies of the politician, and breaks out into a raucous fight.

Thus *Cuba baila* uses music and dance to articulate a keen critique of the prerevolutionary bourgeoisie and its conventions, but it also presents a subtle topography of how rhythm suffuses the nation by capitalizing on previously circulated stereotypes of Cuban musicality. As in the political rally scene, where rhythmic seduction is revealed as a potentially corruptible practice, that Cubans "dance" (or, as Benitez Rojo would say, that they move "in a certain way") is taken for granted. What counts is how the pleasure is inserted into national life. In this prerevolutionary universe, "official" public spaces—the rally, the cabaret where Ramón goes to drown his sorrows—are sites for the corruption of popular pleasure by political greed, ideological manipulation, and Americanization. These are the spaces of the rumberas and bongoceros that peopled the Mexican cinema of the 1940s and 1950s and even the Cuban cinema itself. The domestic sphere is similarly infiltrated: Flora dreams of how her humble apartment could be transformed into a grand salon for the party (the answer: knocking down all the walls) and even holds rehearsals for the waltzing couples within its cramped quarters.

The rhythm of the popular only emerges in the interstices between these official public and domestic spaces where the distance between onlookers and participants literally disappears. The pleasure of rhythm is spontaneously expressed in places like the jukebox-equipped *cafetín* (bar, coffee shop) on the corner of Ramón's house, where a black, female, and well-endowed patron languorously demonstrates the "poetics" of her hips to the admiring eyes of a friend (and the camera), positioned precisely at the crossroads of the inside of the bar and the street beyond it. And this curiously outdoor/indoor, private/public rhythm also reverberates within Marcia's bedroom. When Flora wakes her the morning of her birthday, Marcia is depressed by the uncertain status of the party. Flora tries to cheer her up by describing how the press will report on her party ("Do you realize the importance of a newspaper, daughter? Here on the same page, people will read 'Atomic Bomb Trials' and they will see your picture alongside it"), but Marcia stirs from her bed only when some music and singing, clearly Afro-Cuban and improvisational, rise up from the street. "Can you hear them? They are happy because today is your birthday," says Flora, as she uncharacteristically lets her body sway to the contagious rhythm. This unregulated and almost undefinable infiltration of rhythm effects a transformation of space—the private occurs in public (the pseudo-seduction in the cafetín), the public invades the private—into peculiar places at the crossroads of national life. These impossible narrative places demonstrate most clearly the ambiguity of rhythm as a national marker. Once again, rhythmic "Cubanness" is gendered and "colored"—the cinematic paradigm—but these scenes demonstrate how the stereotype is at once true and a stand-in for a much broader problematic.

García Espinosa's film, with its emphasis on a prerevolutionary world and popular music, was not exactly what the newly instituted Cuban film institute (ICAIC) was looking to celebrate in 1960. Although *Cuba baila* was in fact the first feature-length fiction film produced under the auspices of ICAIC (and in coproduction with the Mexican producer Barbachano Ponce), it was only released after Tomas Gutierrez Alea's more properly celebratory *Historias de la revolución* (Stories of the revolution).[46] Although rhythm (and the representation of musical and dance performance) would rarely be absent from subsequent ICAIC productions, the Cuban cinema would not focus on the place of popular rhythms in national life for more than two decades.

The new cinemas of the 1960s, in Cuba and elsewhere throughout the continent, looked for more "authentic," non-mass-mediated, purer "folk" musical forms. Glauber Rocha and others in Brazil found the harsh rhythms of the northeastern *sertão* a more authentic symbol than the urban samba, the ICAIC cinema in Cuba innovated with orchestral scoring and *la nueva trova* or new (protest) song movement rather than feature guarachas or rumbas. With few exceptions, the New Latin American Cinema simply did not address the nation through popular rhythms.[47]

In the late 1970s and early 1980s, however, several films took on the challenge of popular music and the musical film directly. For example, both *Quilombo* (Carlos Diegues, 1984, Brazil) and *Patakín* (Manuel Octavio Gómez, 1982, Cuba) use the form of the integrated Hollywood musical to reactivate the place of African myths/history in relation to specific social critiques. And Román Chalbaud's *Carmen, la que contaba 16 años* (Carmen, who was sixteen, 1978) relocates the Bizet opera in the world of boleros and melodrama. But by the late 1980s and early 1990s, after decades of almost ignoring mass-market popular music and dance, Latin American filmmakers seem to have returned en masse to popular rhythms. Years after the first and last blushes of populist/socialist revolutions had long faded from the continent and in the context of contemporary international marketing practices and the ever more pressing need to secure international production and distribution deals, this is hardly surprising. As in the 1930s and 1940s, the need to secure local and Latin American—and preferably U.S. and European—audiences is a top priority and often addressed through rhythm. Thus a number of recent Latin American and U.S. Latino films, many of them coproductions among Latin American producers or between Latin American and European financiers, or both, have attempted to recapture the popularity of often archaic but deeply ingrained forms of music and dance as emblems of a national/ethnic unity and sensibility felt to be under siege.

In the United States, Latino filmmakers have regularly sought music and dance as emblems of their beleaguered specificity. The aforementioned *Break of Dawn*, but also *Zoot Suit* (Luis Valdez, 1981), *The Ballad of Gregorio Cortez* (Robert Young, 1982), *Crossover Dreams* (León Ichaso, 1985), and *La Bamba* (Luis Valdez, 1987) rework Hollywood's love affair with Latin American rhythms (most recently evidenced in *Salsa: The Motion Picture* (1989), *Mambo Kings* (1992), and the lambada cycle). Whereas Hollywood's fascination with Latin American sounds continues to be superficial, the Latino films rework rhythms historically: they lay bare the contingent processes from which rhythms emerge and the uneven patterns of ethnic and class formations to which they, in turn, contribute.

In Latin America, perhaps the most famous example of this trend is the French-Argentine coproduction *Tangos: El exilio de Gardel* (Tangos: Gardel's exile, Fernando Solanas, 1985), an invocation of the tango as the national essence par excellence, resistant even to the dirty war and exile.[48] But almost every nation with consistent cinematic production seems to have participated in this recent trend. Cuba, for example, produced *La bella del Alhambra* (The beauty of the Alhambra, Enrique Pineda Barnet, 1989), a re-creation of the rowdy spirit of a now-extinct Cuban burlesque tradition. The most remarkable, among the many Brazilian titles, are *A opera do malandro* (The scoundrel's opera, Ruy Guerra, 1986), a freewheeling French-Brazilian coproduction adapting *The Threepenny Opera* to the *carioca* underworld, and *Stelinha* (Miguel Farias Jr., 1989), a nostalgic encounter between rock and radio-style balladry. The Chilean Valeria Sarmiento (*Amelia Lopes O'Neill*, 1990) and the Venezuelan Marilda Vera (*Señora Bolero*, 1990) explore the relationship between sentimentality, melodrama, and music. Finally, in Mexico, "musical" production has ranged from the extraordinarily experimental *Barroco* (Paul Leduc, 1988), a Spanish-Cuban-Mexican coproduction that eschews dialogue to present the history of musical exchanges between Spain, Mex-

Julia and her partner Carmelo in *Danzón*. (*Courtesy of the Kobal Collection*)

ico, and Cuba chronicled in Alejo Carpentier's *Concierto barroco*, to *Danzón* (María Novaro, 1991), a touching yet cinematically sophisticated homage to the empowering force of an old-fashioned dance.

In many of these films (especially the Latin American ones), the narrative focuses on a female protagonist who dances and/or sings and around whom national dramas are either explicitly or inadvertently played out. Thus music, dance, and gender once again intersect with the need to define and/or invoke the "nation" in terms that exceed the narrowly defined political. In crisis, the contemporary Latin American nation/community is once again (and with variations) represented primarily through the figure of woman as entertainer—dancer, singer, or both—whose nostalgic links with the past bridge the distance between once popular cultural forms and an uncertain present where their position is more problematic.

Danzón sets itself apart from these other films in various ways: directed by newcomer María Novaro (*Danzón* is her second feature film), its female protagonist is *not* a professional entertainer, but a simple working-class woman whose passion for an old-fashioned dance empowers her to live, to make difficult choices, and, ultimately, to work out an independence rarely seen on Latin American screens. The music and her dancing pleasure are neither used for a large-scale invocation of the nation nor for gratuitous spectacle: deeply enmeshed with her identity as a contemporary Mexican woman, they curiously provide her with the backbone necessary to situate herself in a conflictual modern world.

Danzón is a film of deceptively simple pleasures. Julia (María Rojo), a quite capable thirty-something Mexico City telephone operator and single mother of a teenage daughter, indulges her passionate love of dancing, and especially of the measured elegance of the danzón, by frequenting a local dance hall with friends. There she always dances with the same man, the elegant Carmelo, whom she knows only through the dance. When he fails to show up several nights in a row, Julia realizes that perhaps she cares about him more than she had suspected and attempts to find him. She is unsuccessful, but upon hearing rumors that he has returned to his hometown to avoid a false burglary accusation, she travels to Veracruz to find him. Under the spell of the city's colonial and coastal charms, she befriends an odd assortment of characters who help her with her search—the hotel proprietress, a prostitute who lives in the hotel, two transvestite performers, and finally a very young and very handsome tugboat operator. She doesn't find Carmelo, but while looking for him she discovers much more than she had bargained for. Back in Mexico City, no longer anxious or depressed, Julia returns with her daughter and girlfriends to the usual dance hall. The band strikes up a danzón in her honor and, as she prepares to dance, Carmelo appears—as always enigmatically smiling—to resume a place, of sorts, in her life.

As this plot summary makes clear, *Danzón* is a melodrama that, faithful to the genre's development in the Mexican cinema, uses music and dance as a central register for excess. It depicts a resolutely feminine world shaped by romantic ideals and fantasies of the kind circulated by boleros, romantic ballads, and the cinema itself. All the women in this world—even the transvestites—live their romantic fantasies through music and song. Nevertheless, *Danzón* also depicts a world of modern displacements in which the traditional anchors of Mexican society seem to have gone slightly awry: the city is the site for alienated labor and urban anomie; the "interior" (Veracruz), albeit still freeing, is no longer bucolic; the traditional family has all but disappeared; and, in the figure of the transvestites, gendered identity is revealed as radically unstable. Thus the film invokes the spirit and iconography of the classic Mexican melo-drama while turning its traditional referents inside out.

Similarly, the title's insistence on dance and the film's first image—a freeze-frame close-up of a woman's feet wearing dancing shoes—also ask us to consider the film's relationship to the Hollywood musical genre and its Latin American variants. This frozen image of a woman's shoes recalls the iconography of the Hollywood musical, especially the sub-genre Rick Altman calls the fairy tale musical. But, whereas Fred Astaire's top hat and cane in *Top Hat* (Mark Sandrich, 1935) stand in for a world of sophistication and a universe of cinematic conventions, these shoes recall those conventions with a difference. First of all, we have a woman's shoes rather than a man's hat; the focus is on the feet, not on the head; and the image ultimately looks silly—or kitsch—rather than elegant and sophisticated. Not frozen icons, the feet "come alive" when the space of the image is invaded by the aggressive thrust of a man's shoes. Although the pleasure of the pose has been disrupted, the woman parries in response and the dance, a danzón cerrado, begins. As is always the case in danzón, the male dancer leads and the woman follows. The camera, possibly anticipating but miscalculating their next move, pans left and reveals other dancing feet, a community of dancing feet. This is not the rarefied world of the Hollywood fairy tale musical, but the world of working-class ballroom dancing; more precisely, the world where the myths of the Hollywood musical are simultaneously lived and displaced. The characters are neither professional performers who make a living by dancing nor members of a community that spontane-ously break into song and dance to express emotions, but rather simple working-class people attempting to sweeten their lives and performing for the pleasure of the dance.

The title of the film and the music that accompanies the credit sequence also establish how the film will use the idiosyncracies of rhythm as a marker of nationness to complicate questions of national and gendered identity. Danzón is a Cuban rhythm, often called the national dance of Cuba, that emerged—like most Cuban music—out of a complex process of transculturation at the turn of the century: Creole popular musicians who played in aristocratic salons transformed the French contradanza, brought to Cuba by French settlers escaping from Haiti in the mid 1800s, by adding elements of Spanish and African rhythmic modalities.[49] Popularized in the 1910s and 1920s, the danzón and its successor, the even more popular danzonete, traveled quickly throughout Latin America and found a surprisingly receptive audience in Mexico, especially in Veracruz, a city that has, more than other parts of Mexico, a colonial legacy similar to Cuba's. To this day, the danzón endures in Veracruz as a viable form of popular entertainment, long after its popular appeal waned in Cuba (where it is now considered an almost folkloric dance), for this is a crucible city, where the colonial past visibly lives alongside the present. Thus as a marker of multiple processes of cultural repression, the danzón signals the always ambivalent relationship of rhythm to the task of imagining and sustaining communities and nationness.

And as a form of ballroom dancing—a performance that is simultaneously individual, couple, and group—danzón also signals to other processes of identity-formation worked through the film in conjunction with the melodramatic. In *Danzón,* the swelling of surface signification typical of the melodrama affects the multiple registers of music, dance, mise-en-scène, and cinematography equally. The textual work of the credit sequence—where the image and sound-image relations are sites for complex intertextual and contextual referencing—continues throughout the film and is most consistently articulated in relation to questions of gender and identification.

One of the clearest examples of the thoroughness of this melodramatic work occurs halfway through the film, when Julia, already somewhat doubtful that she will ever find Carmelo, first sees Rubén, the handsome tugboat operator. Immediately preceding this scene, Julia has undergone a makeover under the tutelage of her transvestite friend, who claims that she is either afraid of "being taken for a whore" or of "looking good to men" and outfits her with a flirtatious red dress, full makeup, and a red flower behind her ear. Thus masquerading as the sexy woman of innumerable golden-age films, she goes to the docks, looking for the Greek ship where Carmelo is said to have found work as a cook. Her walk is accompanied not only by the appreciative glances of the men she encounters but by a bolero with the telling refrain "amor es una angustia [love is an anguish]." During a series of point-of-view shots that narrate her search for the Greek ship (ironically called *Papanicolau*), the bolero ends with the lyrics "that to love is to become inconsequential," and turns into a danzón as the names of the ships are highlighted by canted close-ups: *L'Amour Fou* (Crazy love), Puras Ilusiones (Pure illusions), *Lágrimas Negras* (Black tears), *Amor Perdido* (Lost love), *Isla Verde* (Green Isle), *Mexican Azalea, Golden Empire,* and *African Azalea.* As if cued by this impossible list of names inspired by bolero titles and exoticism, Julia sees another ship passing by, a tugboat helmed by a handsome man. After an exchange of apparently flirtatious glances with the sailor, she sees the name on the boat: *Me Ves y Sufres* (See me and suffer). This exchange of glances is, however, complex, for she is the instigator of the look. Hers is the active, sexualized gaze, as evidenced by the closeness of the shot of her face, her expression of desire, her voyeurism, the emphasis on *his* physique, naked torso, and prowess. He looks back, but the exchange of glances is actually an illusion. Obviously the tugboat is too far away for him to be smiling at her directly, or even for their eyes to meet. Thus suprafictionalized via this impossible series of shot-reverse shots, *Danzón* offers a beautiful example of the representation of a woman's desire. And a clear patriarchal warning on his boat: See me and suffer.

Julia's response to this warning is, not surprisingly, enacted on the margins of the dance floor, in a semiprivate space, and through the hip. On their first date, Julia and Rubén go to a popular open-air dance place, where all sorts of people, from little kids to old couples, dance effortlessly to the live music. On the dance floor, however, Rubén swings his hips like a salsero and is no match for Julia's danzón elegance. During a *descanso* (dance break built into the structure of danzón), Julia tries to explain the ethos and rules of danzón. We can't hear her words—the orchestra continues playing—but soon she herself gives up on them and uses her body, slowly twirling around Rubén's appreciative glance. Julia transforms what José Piedra calls a "meaningless" body part into a "signifying" bodily attitude: her hips become an icon of femininity activated in offense and defense. He can't dance, this is her dance. But her moves are not those of a danzonera, despite the fact that they are orchestrated to a danzón. These are rumba hips, exaggerated, marked, voyeuristic, exhibitionistic, deified; an acceptance of the bodily and a defiant desiring that, as we see in his visibly appreciative response, is clearly communicated.

Julia, an unlikely melodramatic heroine, does not suffer for appropriating desire, the gaze, the hip. She packs up and leaves Veracruz without even saying goodbye to her young lover. Denied pathos by a relentless, albeit subtle reflexivity, it is the spectator who suffers most. But the film, like Julia and the female feet in the credit sequence, parries gracefully, for there is a "happy" ending.

Back in Mexico City, following the rhythm of her defiance and on the dance floor of their usual ballroom, Julia and Carmelo are reunited. But the victory is Pyrrhic for the spectator. Despite Julia's obsession, we know too little about Carmelo to really care about him as a character. Throughout the film he has simply served as an excuse to motivate Julia's development and her interpersonal encounters and he offers us none of the visual pleasure of Rubén's classic and fetishized beauty.

When Carmelo approaches Julia she is empowered by the very dance that would subjugate her and ready to dance a danzón number that has been publicly dedicated to her. Her dance would celebrate her return to the ordered and familiar world of the ballroom. But when the elegantly poised and silent Carmelo takes her in his arms and they begin the dance, things have obviously changed. Although Julia had demonstrated several times throughout the film the importance of the ritualized codes of the dance while attempting to teach others (her daughter, Suzy the transvestite), here she aggressively ignores them. She looks into Carmelo's eyes unwaveringly until, acknowledging defeat by a nod of the head, he breaks down, smiles, and returns her gaze. Thus the film ends with Julia and Carmelo, dancing and looking at each other, amidst a community of dancing couples. Carmelo may still "lead" the dance, but Julia has discovered a way to assert her own position, her "certain way" of doing things.

Empowered by rhythm, through rhythm, and in rhythm, Julia has redesigned the stage of her performance and desire. Constituted through music and challenged through rhythm, her identity is reworked on the dance floor, where her performance produces a "different" space. Although physically the same, for Julia this ballroom is no longer the same place where the film began. Rather than a microcosm of the Mexican urban working class and its performative pleasures (a national public space) and patriarchal rigidity, the Salon Baile Colonial is now a place where her individual (gendered) identity is affirmed, contested, and reproduced. The danzón is a "cage," a social grid, but it is *her* grid and she can transform its pleasures and risk breaking its rules. As the Veracruz hotel proprietress tells her when she is getting ready to abandon her young lover to return to Mexico City, "Ya lo bailao nadie te lo quita [No one can take away what you've already danced]."

To Have a Rhythm . . .

Unlike Julia in *Danzón,* Amparo in *Break of Dawn* cannot unsettle the codes of her life through border-crossing/rule-breaking rhythms. Her "transgression"—the appropriation of an "other" rhythm and of an "other's" husband—comes to naught. Pedro remains married to his decidedly nonmusical wife, although ultimately "rhythm" lies at the root of the false accusations that land him in jail for most of his life. Nevertheless, even in *Break of Dawn,* music and dance are figured as privileged spaces for the construction and contestation of ethnic/national *and* sexual/gendered identity.

As I hope my survey analysis of the history of cinematic uses of Latin American music and dance has begun to demonstrate, a multinational focus on music and dance opens up an unusual analytical space. Rhythm has been—and continues to be—used as a significant marker of national/ethnic difference: the cinema locates and placates Latino/as and Latin Americans rhythmically. But this placing has also served to provide a curiously unfettered space for ethnic and other nationals: a place for performance and a space of multiple identifications. Here we can perhaps begin to think about a different rhythmic cartography, not tied to borders to be crossed or transgressed, but where spaces become lived-in and dancing places in which the body—reclaimed from its subservience to work—can be a locus of resistance and desire and enjoyed on that basis. If at one level—that of supranational/colonialist appropriation—rhythm can be used to collapse the very differences it embodies, at another level—individual, subnational, contestational—rhythm has also served to posit spaces for rewriting and resisting the homogeneity of the generalizing force of nationness.

Notes

Para Gervasio, que me enseñó a bailar.
My thanks to José Muñoz and Celeste Fraser Delgado, who encouraged me to write—and finish—this essay; and to Chon Noriega, for helpful critiques of earlier versions. The research for this article was, in part, funded by travel grants from the Mellon Foundation through the Roger Thayer Stone Center for Latin American Studies at Tulane University.

1. Benedict Anderson, *Imagined Communities*, 2d ed. (London: Verso, 1991), 6.

2. See Doris Sommer, *Foundational Fictions: The National Romances of Latin America* (Berkeley: U of California P, 1991).

3. Homi K. Bhabha, "DissemiNation: Time, Narrative, and the Margins of the Modern Nation," in *Nation and Narration* (New York: Routledge, 1990), 291–322.

4. Bhabha, "DissemiNation," 300.

5. For an interesting discussion centered on Cuban music, see Leonardo Acosta, "From the Drum to the Synthesizer: Study of a Process," *Latin American Perspectives* 16.2 (1989): 29–46.

6. "If I dragged through this world the shame of having been and the pain of no longer being." Unless otherwise noted, all translations from foreign-language sources are my own.

7. José Piedra, "Poetics for the Hip," *New Literary History* 22 (1991): 633–675 and also included in this volume; and "Through Blues," in *Do the Americas Have a Common Literature?* ed. Gustavo Pérez Firmat (Durham: Duke U P, 1990), 107–129.

8. Piedra, "Poetics for the Hip," 634.

9. See Terry Ramsaye, *A Million and One Nights* (New York: Simon and Schuster, 1926), 117.

10. As Roberto Guidi has argued, the Valentino version of the tango, "a fantastic combination of rumba, paso doble, cueca and apache dance," became *the* international stereotype of the tango as dance (cited by Jorge Miguel Couselo in *El tango en el cine*, vol. 8 of *La historia del tango* [Buenos Aires: Corregidor, 1976], 129).

11. See Emilio García Riera, *México visto por el cine extranjero* (Guadalajara: Ediciones Era/Universidad de Guadalajara, 1987), 1:149–151.

12. The list of potential examples is vast and spans all genres, although the Hollywood melodrama seems to have been especially attracted to Latin sounds. For example, in the inappropriately titled *Bolero* (Wesley Ruggles, 1934), Carlos Gardel lookalike George Raft ravishes Carole Lombard on the dance floor to the tango "El choclo"; Jean Arthur and Charles Boyer consummate their love to the tune of "La cumparsita" in *History Is Made at Night* (Frank Borzage, 1937); and Joan Bennett sings "Chula Chihuahua" in *House across the Bay* (Archie Mayo, 1940) while dressed like Carmen Miranda.

13. Thus Desi Arnaz as the Chicano marine Felix Martínez in *Bataan* (Tay Garnett, 1943) is also known as "the Jitterbug Kid."

14. See the entry for "Music" in Ed Buscombe, ed., *The BFI Companion to the Western* (London: Andre Deutsch Publishing/BFI, 1988), 193–195.

15. Pam Cook, "Women," in Buscombe, *The Western*, 241.

16. Both Chihuahua and Pearl Chavez are heirs to the erotic mestiza legacy of Jane Russell's Rio in *The Outlaw* (Howard Hughes, 1940). Functioning as another narrative "third term," Rio is also an emblem of the indeterminacy of the Hollywood mestiza.

17. Rick Altman, *The American Film Musical* (Bloomington: Indiana U P, 1987), 119.

18. Abel, *Variety*, 27 February 1929, cited in Alfred Charles Richard Jr., *The Hispanic Image on the Silver Screen: An Interpretative Filmography from Silents into Sound, 1895–*

1935 (New York: Greenwood, 1992), 395; and in García Riera, *Mexico visto por el cine extranjero*, 1:155.

19. It seems appropriate to note that the association of pure musical performativity with ethnically and racially differentiated rhythms was only encouraged by those musicals where Anglo principal characters engaged in "ethnic" dance. For example, as Rick Altman points out, in the Astaire and Rogers films ethnic rhythms are always used for the specialty numbers that stress the dancing itself rather than the narrative romance (*Flying Down to Rio, Swing Time*) and in the "new" dances introduced at the end of their films together until *Top Hat* (1935). See Altman, 165.

20. An important exception to this rule is the aristocratic Brazilian character who only dances socially, played by the Mexican actress Dolores del Rio in *Flying Down to Rio* (Thorton Vreeland, 1933).

21. One should also account for the production of musical multilinguals, especially for the Paramount-Joinville series begun in 1930 (with *Luces de Buenos Aires*), featuring the great Argentine tango star Carlos Gardel.

22. For more details, see my "Are All Latins from Manhattan: Ethnicity and Colonialism in the Hollywood Cinema," in *Unspeakable Images*, ed. Lester Friedman (Champaign: U of Illinois P, 1991), 404–424.

23. See Allen Woll, *The Latin Image in American Film* (Los Angeles: UCLA Latin American Center Publications, 1980), 53–75.

24. Altman, 186, 193.

25. García Riera, *México visto por el cine extranjero*, 3:104.

26. See Chon Noriega, "Internal Others: Hollywood Narratives 'about' Mexican Americans," in *Mediating Two Worlds*, ed. John King, Ana López, and Manuel Alvarado (London: British Film Institute, 1993), 52–66.

27. As Antonio Benítez-Rojo argues: "What happens when there arrives, or there is imposed commercially a 'foreign' signifier, let's say the big band music of the 1940s or the rock music of the past thirty years? Well, among other things, the mambo, the cha-cha-cha, the bossa novas, the bolero, salsa, and reggae happen . . . Caribbean music did not become Anglo Saxon, but rather the latter became Caribbean within a play of differences" (*The Repeating Island*, trans. James E. Maraniss [Durham: Duke U P, 1992], 21).

28. Ever mindful of its capitalist prerogatives, Hollywood studios began to invest in Mexican productions as early as 1937–1938, attracting talent and using Mexican locations but also capitalizing on the success of Mexican films throughout Latin America. See Emilio García Riera, *Historia documental del cine mexicano,* vol. 1 (Mexico City: Ediciones Era, 1969).

29. For example, in *La vendedora de Harrod's* (Defilippis Novoa, 1921), *Buenos Aires tenebroso* (Juan Glize, 1917), *El guapo del arrabal* (Julio Irigoyen, 1923), and in most of José Agustín "el Negro" Ferreyra's silent film productions, especially *El tango de la muerte* (1917), *Mientras Buenos Aires duerme* (1921), and *La costurerita que dio aquel mal paso* (1926).

30. Paulo Antonio Paranaguá, *Cinema na América Latina: Longe de deus e perto de Hollywood* (Porto Alegre: L&PM Editores, 1984), 44.

31. See Simon Collier, "Carlos Gardel and the Cinema," in *The Garden of Forking Paths: Argentine Cinema,* ed. John King and Nissa Torrents (London: National Film Theater/ BFI, 1988), 15–26.

32. This is the term used by Domingo Di Núbila in *Historia del cine Argentino* (Buenos Aires: Cruz de Malta, 1959), 1:81.

33. According to Couselo, Latin American distributors often valued Argentine films according to the number of tangos included: the more tangos, the higher the receipts. See his *El tango en el cine,* 8:1314.

34. Paranaguá, 42.

35. Cited in García Riera, *Historia documental del cine mexicano,* 1:132.

36. Thus, for example, in Miguel Zacarías's *La cuna vacía* (The empty cradle, 1937), the Manichean split between the virgin and the whore is inscribed in the musical difference between Ana, who sings pure and spiritual operatic airs, and Elena, who suggestively enjoys her danzón performances.

37. As Jorge Ayala Blanco indicates, in a few months between 1947 and 1948, precisely coinciding with the beginning of the Mario Rodríguez Alemán *sexenio,* over twelve *cabaretera* films were produced. See *La aventura del cine mexicano* (Mexico: Ediciones Era, 1968), 137.

38. The Lara song "Aventurera" had already been featured in the 1946 María Félix film *La devoradora* (Fernando de Fuentes). At the time, Lara and Félix were enjoying a much publicized, albeit short-lived, marriage.

39. See my "Celluloid Tears: Melodrama in the Classic Mexican Cinema," *Iris* 13 (Summer 1991): 29–52.

40. "I dance the mambo, son, guaracha, or rumba, for all of them have sandunga, just like the African rhythm." For a detailed analysis of this and other Cuban films of the period, see Laura Podalsky, "Negotiating Differences: National Cinema and Co-Productions in Pre-Revolutionary Cuba," in *Cuban Cinemas and Imperfect Subjects,* ed. Ambrosio Fornet and Ana Lopez, forthcoming.

41. João Luiz Vieira, "A chanchada e o cinema Carioca (1930–1955)," in *História do cinema brasileiro,* ed. Fernão Ramos (São Paulo: Art Editora, 1987), 166.

42. The film was also released with the title *¡Ay que bonitas piernas!* (Oh what beautiful legs!).

43. For a detailed analysis of this fascinating film, see Ayala Blanco, *La aventura del cine mexicano,* and my "Tears and Desire: Women and Melodrama in the Old Mexican Cinema," in Mediating Two Worlds: Cinematic Encounters in the Americas, ed. John King, Ana M. López, and Manuel Alvarado (London: British Film Institute, 1993), 147–163.

44. For more information, see my *The New Latin American Cinema* (U of Illinois P, forthcoming).

45. With the exception of Carlos Diegues's *Escola de samba, alegria de viver* (Samba

school, joy of life), one of the episodes of the compilation film *Cinco vezes favela* (Five times favela, 1962). However, despite its title, this film does not position samba as a popular form of cultural capital. It argues, instead, that samba is one of the instruments that blocks class consciousness in the urban favelado and is thus vastly different from Pereira dos Santos's films.

46. For more details and an astute analysis, see Michael Chanan, *The Cuban Image* (London: British Film Institute, 1985).

47. For the sake of this argument, I am excluding the emphasis upon Andean indigenous music in the films of the region such as *La tierra prometida* (Miguel Littin, 1973, Chile), with music by Inti-Illimani, or the films of Jorge Sanjinés in Bolivia and Peru.

48. For an insightful analysis of this film and Fernando Solanas's *Sur*, see Kathleen Newman, "National Cinema after Globalization: Fernando Solanas' *Sur* and the Exiled Nation," in *Mediating Two Worlds*, ed. John King, Ana López, and Manuel Alvarado (London: British Film Institute, 1993), 242–257.

49. See Angel Vázquez Millares, ed., *Danzón* (Havana: Coordinación Provincial de la Habana, 1970).

Bibliography

Acosta, Leonardo. "From the Drum to the Synthesizer: Study of a Process." *Latin American Perspectives* 16.2 (1989): 29–46.

Alarcón, Norma. "Conjugating Subjects: The Heteroglossia of Essence and Resistance." In *An Other Tongue*. Ed. Alfred Arteaga, 125–138. Durham: Duke U P, 1994.

Almeida, Bira. *Capoeira, a Brazilian Art Form*. Palo Alto: Sun Wave, 1981.

Alonso, Ana Maria, and Maria Teresa Koreck. "Silences: 'Hispanics,' AIDS, and Sexual Practices." *differences* 1.1 (1989): 101–124.

Altamirano, Carlos, and Beatriz Sarlo. "La Argentina del centenario." *Hispamérica* 25–26 (1980): 35–48.

Altman, Rick. *The American Film Musical*. Bloomington: Indiana U P, 1987.

Alves de Almeida, Raimundo Cesar. *Bimba: Perfil do mestre*. Salvador: UFBA, 1982.

Amado, Jorge. *Bahia de todos os santos*. Rio de Janeiro: Record, 1980.

Anderson, Benedict. *Imagined Communities*. 2d ed. London: Verso, 1991.

Aparicio, Frances. "Salsa, Maracas, and Baile: Latin Popular Music in the Poetry of Victor Hernández Cruz." *MELUS* 16.1 (Spring 1989–1990): 43–58.

Aparicio, Frances, and Susana Chavez-Silverman, eds. *Tropicalizations: Transforming Latinidad beyond Self and Other*. Berkeley: U of California P, forthcoming.

Arizmendi, Yareli. "Whatever Happened to the Sleepy Mexican?" *TDR* 38.1 (Spring 1994): 106–118.

Arteaga, Alfred, ed. *An Other Tongue: Nation and Ethnicity in the Linguistic Borderlands*. Durham: Duke U P, 1994.

Arteaga, José. *La salsa*. Bogotá: Intermedio Editores, 1990.

Assunçao, Fernando. *El tango y sus circunstancias*. Buenos Aires: Ateneo, 1984.

Ayala Blanco, Jorge. *La aventura del cine mexicano*. Mexico: Ediciones Era, 1968.

Babcock, Barbara. *The Reversible World: Symbolic Inversion in Art and Society*. Ithaca: Cornell U P, 1978.

Báez, Juan Carlos. *El víncalo de la salsa*. Caracas: Dirección de Cultura-UCV, Fondo Editorial Tropykos, Grupo Editor Derrelieve, 1985.

Baily, Samuel. *Movimiento obrero, nacionalismo y política argentina*. Buenos Aires: Hispamérica, 1985.

Baker, Houston, Jr. *Modernism and the Harlem Renaissance*. Chicago: U of Chicago P, 1987.

Bartenieff, Irmgard. *Body Movement: Coping with the Environment*. New York: Gordon and Breach Science Publishers, 1980.

Bátiz, Adolfo. *Buenos Aires, la rivera y los prostíbulos en 1880*. Buenos Aires: Aga Taura, n.d.

Bejarano, Manuel. "Inmigración y estructurale tradicionale en Buenos Aires (1854–1930)." In *Los fragmentos del poder*. Ed. Tulio Halperín Donghi, 75–150. Buenos Aires: Sudamericana, 1987.

Benítez-Rojo, Antonio. *The Repeating Island: The Caribbean and the Postmodern Perspective*. Trans. James E. Maraniss. Durham: Duke U P, 1992.

Benjamin, Walter. *Dirección única*. Trans. Juan J. del Solar and Mercedes Allendesalazar. Madrid: Ediciones Alfaguara, 1987 [Frankfurt am Main: Suhrkamp Verlag, 1955].

Bergman, David. *Camp Grounds: Style and Homosexuality*. Amherst: U of Massachusetts P, 1993.

Bhabha, Homi. "Of Mimicry and Man: the Ambivalence of Colonial Discourse." *October* 28 (Spring 1984): 125–133.

——. "DissemiNation: Time, Narrative, and the Margins of the Modern Nation." In *Nation and Narration*. Ed. Homi K. Bhabha. New York: Routledge, 1990.

——. *The Location of Culture*. New York: Routledge, 1994.

——, ed. *Nation and Narration*. New York: Routledge, 1990.

Bialet-Massé, Juan. *El estado de las clases obreras argentinas a comienzos de siglo*. Córdoba: Universidad Nacional de Córdoba, 1968.

Birnbaum, Larry. Liner notes. *Africando, Volume 1: Trovador*. Stern's Africa, STCD-1045, 1993.

Borges, Jorge Luis. *Evaristo Carriego*. Buenos Aires: Emece, 1985.

Borrows, Frank. *Theory and Technique of Latin-American Dancing*. London: Frederick Muller Limited, 1961 [1948].

Bourdieu, Pierre. *Outline of a Theory of Practice*. Trans. Richard Nice. Cambridge: Cambridge U P, 1977.

——. *Distinction: A Social Critique of the Judgement of Taste*. Trans. Richard Nice. Cambridge: Harvard U P, 1984.

Brindis de Salas, Virginia. "Tango numero dos." In Pregon de Marimorena. Montevideo: Sociedad Cultural Editora Indo-Americana, 1953.

Browning, Barbara. *Samba: Resistance in Motion*. Bloomington: Indiana U P, 1995.

Buck-Morss, Susan. *The Dialectic of Seeing: Walter Benjamin and the Arcades Project*. Cambridge: MIT P, 1989.

Bullough, Vern, and Bonnie Bullough. *Women and Prostitution*. Buffalo: Prometheus, 1987.

Buscombe, Edward, ed. *The British Film Institute Companion to the Western*. London: Andre Deutsch Publishing/British Film Institute, 1988.

Butler, Judith. "Force of Fantasy: Feminism, Mapplethorpe, and Discursive Excess." *differences* 2.2 (Summer 1990): 105–126.

——. *Bodies That Matter: On the Discursive Limits of "Sex."* New York: Routledge, 1993.

Cabrera, Lydia. *La sociedad secreta Abakuá narrado por viejos adeptos*. Miami: Ediciones CR, 1970.

——. *Cuentos negros e Cuba*. Madrid: Ediciones Erre, 1972.

——. *Porqué . . . : Cuentos negros de Cuba*. 2d ed. Madrid: Ramos, 1972.

——. *Anaforuana: Ritual y símbolos de la iniciación en la sociedad secreta Abakuá*. Madrid: Ediciones Erre, 1975.

——. *Yemayá y Ochún: Kariocha, Iyalorichas y Olorichas*. Eastchester, NY: E. Torres, 1980.

——. *Vocabulario congo: El Bantu que se habla en Cuba.* Miami: Ediciones CR, 1984.

——. "How the Monkey Lost the Fruit of His Labor." Trans. Mary Caldwell and Suzanne Jill Levine. In *Other Fires: Short Fiction by Latin American Women.* Ed. Alberto Manguel. New York: C. N. Potter, 1986.

——. *La lengua sagrada de los ñáñigos.* Miami: Ediciones CR, 1988.

Cabrera Infante, Guillermo. *Tres tristes tigres.* Barcelona: Seix Barral, 1968 [*Three Trapped Tigers.* Trans. Donald Gardner and Suzanne Jill Levine, in collaboration with Cabrera Infante. 1971. New York: Harper & Row (1971), 1985].

Campion, Chris. "Rise of the Dog Tribe." *URB Magazine* 39 (November 1994).

Carneiro, Edison. *Capoeira.* Rio de Janeiro: Ministerio da Educacao e Cultura, 1975.

Carpentier, Alejo. *La música en Cuba.* Mexico: Fondo de Cultura Economica, 1972.

——. "Tale of Moons." Trans. José Piedra. *Latin American Literary Review* 8 (1980): 67–68.

——. *¡Ecue-Yamba-O!* In *Obras Completas* 1: 21–193. Mexico: Siglo Veintiuno, 1983.

Carriego, Evaristo. *Misas herejes: La canción del barrio.* Buenos Aires: J. Rosso, 1927.

Castillo, Cátulo. *Danzas Argentinas.* Buenos Aires: Ediciones Penser, 1947.

"Celebración del 1 de Mayo: Cientos de heridos y contusos en la Plaza Mazzini." *La Prensa* (Buenos Aires), 2 May 1904, 11.

Centro de Estudios Puertorriquenos Bulletin [special issue on Latinos and the media]. 2.8–3.1 (1990–1991).

Certeau, Michel de. *The Practice of Everyday Life.* Berkeley: U of California P, 1984.

Cham, Mbye, ed. *Ex-Iles: Essays on Caribbean Cinema.* Trenton: Africa World Press, 1992.

Chanan, Michael. *The Cuban Image.* London: British Film Institute, 1985.

Chauncey, George, Jr. "From Sexual Inversion to Homosexuality: Medicine and the Changing Conceptualization of Sexual Deviance." *Salmagundi* 58–59 (Fall 1982–Winter 1983): 114–145.

Chinarro, Andrés. *El tango y su rebeldía.* Buenos Aires: Continental, 1965.

Clifford, James, and George E. Marcus, eds. *Writing Culture: The Poetics and Politics of Ethnography.* Berkeley: U of California P, 1986.

Clum, John M. *Out Front: Contemporary Gay and Lesbian Plays.* New York: Grove 1988.

——. *Acting Gay: Male Homosexuality in Modern Drama.* New York: Columbia U P, 1992.

Cobo-Hanlon, Leila. "Heating Up the MTV Latino Connection." *Los Angeles Times,* 22 November 1994, F11.

Coffey, Michael. "Oscar Hijuelos." *Publishers Weekly,* 21 July 1989, 44.

"El cólera: Informe de la Oficina Sanitaria." *Anales del Departamento Nacional de Higiene* 5 (Buenos Aires, 1895): 85–116.

Collier, Simon. "Carlos Gardel and the Cinema." In *The Garden of Forking Paths: Argentine Cinema.* Ed. John King and Nissa Torrents, 15–26. London: National Film Theater/BFI, 1988.

Colón, Willie. "Interview with Willie Colón," by Frank Parilla Jr. *La Klave* 1.2 (November–December 1988): 32.

Cook, Pam. "Women." In *The British Film Institute Companion to the Western.* Ed. Edward Buscombe, 240–243. London: Andre Deutsch Publishing/BFI, 1988.

Cooper, Carolyn. " 'Something Ancestral Recaptured': Spirit Possession as Trope in Selected Feminist Fictions of the African Diaspora." In *Motherlands: Black Women's Writing from Africa, the Caribbean and South Asia.* Ed. Shusheila Nasta, 64–87. New Brunswick: Rutgers U P, 1992.

Cordero, Carmen. "Negra rumbera." In *Poesía afroantiallana y negrista: Puerto Rico—Republica Dominicana—Cuba.* Ed. Jorge Luis Morales, 428. Rio Piedras: Editorial Universitaria, U Puerto Rico, 1981.

Couselo, Jorge Miguel. *El tango en el cine.* Vol. 8 of *La historia del tango.* Buenos Aires: Corregidor, 1976.

Cox, Ida. "One Hour Mama." *Mean Mothers,* Rosetta Records, RR 1300, 1980.

Crimp, Douglas. "AIDS: Cultural Analysis/Cultural Activism." *October* 43 (1987): 3–16.

Cunard, Nancy, ed. *Negro, an Anthology.* New York: F. Unger, 1970.

"Defensa sanitaria marítima contra las enfermedades exóticas viajeras." In *Anales del Departamento Nacional de Higiene* 8 (Buenos Aires, 1898): 307–324.

del Cabral, Manuel. "Aire negro." In *Obra poética completa.* Santo Domingo: Editora Alfa y Omega, 1976.

Deleuze, Gilles, and Félix Guattari. *A Thousand Plateaus: Capitalism and Schizophrenia.* Trans. and foreword by Brian Massumi. Minnesota: U of Minnesota P, 1987.

Dent, Gina, ed. *Black Popular Culture.* Seattle: Bay, 1992.

Derrida, Jacques. *Of Grammatology.* Trans. Gayatri Chakravorty Spivak. Baltimore: Johns Hopkins U P, 1976.

Diawara, Manthia. "Afro-Kitsch." In *Black Popular Culture.* Ed. Gina Dent, 285–291. Seattle: Bay, 1992.

Díaz Quiñones, Arcadio. *Conversación con José Luis González.* Río Piedras: Editorial Huracán, 1977.

Díaz Valcárcel, Emilio. "Osadía." In *El asedio.* México, P.R.: Editorial Arrecife, 1959: 24–68.

Dibbell, Julian. "Notes on Carmen: Carmen Miranda, Seriously." *Village Voice* 36.44 (29 October 1991): 43–45.

Di Núbila, Domingo. *Historia del cine Argentino.* Vol. 1. Buenos Aires: Cruz de Malta, 1959.

Dixon-Gottschild, Brenda. "Some Thoughts on Choreographing History." Talk delivered at the conference "Choreographing History." University of California at Riverside, February 1992.

D'Lugo, Marvin. "The Time of the Nation: Review of Homi K. Bhabha's *Nation and Narration.*" *Quarterly Review of Film and Video* 14.3 (April 1993): 109–113.

Dossar, Kenneth. "Capoeira Angola: An Ancestral Connection?" *American Visions* 3.4 (1988): 38–42.

——. "Capoeira Angola: Dancing between Two Worlds." *Afro-Hispanic Review* 11.1–3 (1992): 5–10.

Dougherty, Steve. "One Step at a Time." *People,* 25 June 1990, 78–84.

Douglass, Mary. *Purity and Danger: An Analysis of the Concepts of Purity and Taboo.* London: ARK, 1989.

Duany, Jorge. "Popular Music in Puerto Rico: Toward an Anthropology of Salsa." *Latin American Music Review* 2 (Fall–Winter 1984): 204.

Dyer, Richard. *Only Entertainment.* New York: Routledge, 1992.

Enloe, Cynthia. *Making Feminist Sense of International Politics: Bananas, Beaches, and Bases.* Berkeley: U of California P, 1989.

Erenberg, Lewis. *Steppin' Out: New York Nightlife 1890–1930.* Westport, CT: Greenwood, 1981.

Fab Five Freddy. Liner notes. MC Solaar, *Prose Combat.* Island Records, Col-1-697124013-1, 1994.

Fanon, Frantz. *Black Skin, White Masks.* Trans. Charles Lam Markmann. New York: Grove, 1967.

Feijóo, Samuel. *El negro en la literatura folklórica cubana.* Havana: Editorial Letras Cubanas, 1980.

Fernández, Enrique. "Spitfires, Latin Lovers, Mambo Kings." *New York Times,* 19 April 1992, H1, 30.

——. "El Norte: Worlds Collide." *Village Voice,* 10 November 1992, 28.

Ferré, Rosario. *Papeles de Pandora.* Mexico: J. Mortiz, 1976.

Fisher, Michael. "Ethnicity and the Post-Modern Arts of Memory." In *Writing Culture: The Poetics and Politics of Ethnography.* Ed. James Clifford and George E. Marcus, 194–233. Berkeley: U of California P, 1986.

Flores, Juan. *Divided Borders: Essays on Puerto Rican Identity.* Houston: Arte Público Press, 1993.

——. "Puerto Rican and Proud, Boyee!: Rap Roots and Amnesia." In *Microphone Fiends.* Ed. Andrew Ross and Tricia Rose, 89–98. New York: Routledge, 1994.

Flores, Juan, and George Yúdice. "Living Borders/Buscando America: Languages of Latino Self-formation." *Social Text* 24 (1990): 57–84.

Fornet, Ambrosio, and Ana M. López, eds. *Cuban Cinemas and Imperfect Subjects.* Forthcoming.

Foster, Susan. *Reading Dancing: Bodies and Subjects in Contemporary American Dance.* Berkeley: U of California P, 1986.

Foucault, Michel. "What Is an Author?" In *Textual Strategies.* Ed. Josué V. Harari, 141–160. Ithaca: Cornell U P, 1979.

——. "Of Other Spaces." *diacritics* 16.1 (Spring 1986): 22–28.

——. *History of Sexuality: An Introduction.* Vol. 1. New York: Vintage Books, 1990.

Franklin, Aretha. "Think." *Aretha.* Atlantic Records, ARCD-8556, 1968.

Franko, Mark. *Dance as Text: Ideologies of the Baroque Body.* Cambridge: Cambridge U P, 1993.

Freitas, Decio. *Palmares, a guerra dos escravos.* Rio de Janeiro: Graal, 1982.

Frost, Laura. Rev. of *The Mambo Kings Play Songs of Love,* by Oscar Hijuelos. *Review* 42 (January–June 1990): 65.

Gálvez, Manuel. *El diario de Gabriel Quiroga: Opiniones sobre la vida argentina.* Buenos Aires: Arnold Moen, 1910.

Garber, Marjorie. "The Occidental Tourist." In *Nationalisms and Sexualities.* Ed. Andrew Parker, Mary Russo, Doris Sommer, and Patricia Yaeger, 121–146. New York: Routledge, 1992.

García Canclini, Néstor. "Cultural Reconversion." In *On Edge: The Crisis of Contemporary Latin American Culture.* Ed. George Yúdice, Jean Franco, and Juan Flores, 29–44. Minneapolis: U of Minnesota P, 1993.

García Riera, Emilio. *Historia documental del cine mexicano.* Vol. 1. Mexico City: Ediciones Era, 1969.

——. *México visto por el cine extranjero.* Vol. 1. Guadalajara: Ediciones Era/Universidad de Guadalajara, 1987.

Gates, Henry Louis, Jr., ed. *"Race," Writing and Difference.* Chicago: U of Chicago P, 1986.

Gilroy, Paul. "Sounds Authentic: Black Music, Ethnicity, and the Challenge of the Changing Same." *Black Music Research Journal* 11.2 (Fall 1991): 111–136.

——. "Ethnic Absolutism." In *Cultural Studies.* Ed. Lawrence Grossberg, Cary Nelson, and Paula Treichler, 187–198. New York: Routledge, 1992.

——. "It's a Family Affair." In *Black Popular Culture.* Ed. Gina Dent, 303–316. Seattle: Bay, 1992.

——. *The Black Atlantic: Modernity and Double Consciousness.* Cambridge: Harvard U P, 1993.

Gleason, Judith. *Oya: In Praise of the Goddess.* Boston: Shambhala, 1987.

Gobello, José. *Crónica general del tango.* Buenos Aires: Fraterna, 1980.

Goldar, Ernesto. *La mala vida: Historia popular.* Buenos Aires: Centro Editor, 1971.

Gómez, Eusebio. *La mala vida en Buenos Aires.* Buenos Aires: Juan Roldan, 1908.

González, Elena, and Eliana Ortega, eds. *La sartén por el mango.* Rio Piedras: Ediciones Huracán, 1984.

González, José Luis. *El país de cuatro pisos.* Rio Piedras: Huracán, 1980.

González Castillo, José. *Los invertidos.* Buenos Aires: Argentores, 1957.

González Echeverría, Roberto. *The Voice of the Masters: Writing and Authority in Modern Latin American Literature.* Austin: U of Texas P, 1985.

Grossberg, Lawrence, Cary Nelson, and Paula Treichler, eds. *Cultural Studies.* New York: Routledge, 1992.

Guevara, Ruben. Liner notes. *Viva! El Chicano: Their Very Best.* MCA, MCAD-25197, 1988.

Guillén, Nicolás. "Mujer Nueva." In *Obra poetica* 1. Ed. Angel Augier, 120. Havana: Editorial de Arte y Literatura, 1974. Translated as "New Woman," by Langston Hughes and Ben Frederic Carruthers. In *Cuba Libre,* 63. Los Angeles: Anderson & Ritchie, 1948.

Guillermoprieto, Alma. *Samba.* New York: Knopf, 1990.

Guillory, John. "Canon, Syllabus, List: A Note on the Pedagogic Imaginary." *Transition* 52 (1991): 36–54.

Guy, Donna. *Sex and Danger in Buenos Aires: Prostitution, Family and Nation in Argentina.* Lincoln: U of Nebraska P, 1991.

Hadley-García, George. *Hispanic Hollywood: The Latins in Motion Pictures.* New York: Citadel Press, 1990.

Hall, Stuart. "Cultural Identity and Diaspora." In *Identity: Community, Culture, Difference.* Ed. J. Rutherford, 222–237. London: Lawrence & Wishart, 1990.

———. "Cultural Identity and Cinematic Representation." In *Ex-Iles: Essays on Caribbean Cinema.* Ed. Mbye Cham, 220–236. Trenton: Africa World Press, 1992.

———. "Cultural Studies and Its Theoretical Legacies." In *Cultural Studies.* Ed. Lawrence Grossberg, Cary Nelson, and Paula Treichler, 277–286. New York: Routledge, 1992.

Halperín Donghi, Tulio. *El espejo de la historia.* Buenos Aires: Sudamericana, 1987.

———. *Los fragmentos del poder.* Buenos Aires: Sudamericana, 1987.

Harari, Josué V., ed. *Textual Strategies.* Ithaca: Cornell U P, 1979.

Hardy, Phil. "Music." In *The British Film Institute Companion to the Western.* Ed. Ed Buscombe, 193–195. London: Andre Deutsch Publishing/British Film Institute, 1988.

Harlow, Barbara. *Resistance Literature.* New York: Methuen, 1987.

Hawkins, Peter. "Naming Names: The Art of Memory and the Names Project AIDS Quilt." *Critical Inquiry* 19 (1993): 752–779.

Hazzard-Gordon, Katrina. *Jookin': The Rise of Social Dance Formations in African-American Culture.* Philadelphia: Temple U P, 1990.

Hebdige, Dick. *Subculture: The Meaning of Style.* London: Methuen, 1979.

Hijuelos, Oscar. *The Mambo Kings Play Songs of Love.* New York: Harper & Row, 1989.

Holloway, Thomas H. "'A Healthy Terror': Police Repression of Capoeiras in Nineteenth-Century Rio de Janeiro." *Hispanic American Historical Review* 69 (1989): 637–676.

Holte, James Craig. *The Ethnic I: A Sourcebook for Ethnic American Autobiography.* New York: Greenwood Press, 1988.

hooks, bell. *Outlaw Culture: Resisting Representations.* New York: Routledge, 1994.

Jahn, Janheinz. *Muntu: The New African Culture.* Trans. Marjorie Greene. New York: Grove Weidenfeld, 1961.

Jakubs, Deborah. "The History of the Tango." Talk delivered at the conference "Politics in Motion: Dance and Culture in Latin America." Duke University, Durham, NC, January 1991.

Jáuregui, Carlos. *La homosexualidad en la Argentina.* Buenos Aires: Tarso, 1987.

Johnson, Richard. "What Is Cultural Studies Anyway?" *Social Text* 16 (Winter 1986–1987): 38–80.

Jordan, A. C. "Sikhamba-Nge-Nyanga, a Tale from Southern Africa." In *Talk That Talk: An Anthology of African American Storytelling.* Ed. Linda Goss and Marian E. Barnes, 236–243. New York: Simon and Schuster, 1989.

Keller, Gary D. *Chicano Cinema: Research, Reviews, and Resources.* Binghamton, NY: Bilingual Review Press, 1985.

King, John, Ana M. López, and Manuel Alvarado, eds. *Mediating Two Worlds: Cinematic Encounters in the Americas.* London: British Film Institute, 1993.

King, John, and Nissa Torrents, eds. *The Garden of Forking Paths: Argentine Cinema.* London: National Film Theater/BFI, 1988.

Kramer, Larry. *Reports from the Holocaust: The Making of an AIDS Activist.* New York: St. Martin's Press, 1989.

Kubik, Gerhard. "Angolan Traits in Black Music, Games and Dances of Brazil: A Study of African Cultural Extensions Overseas." *Estudos de Anthropologia Cultural* 10 (Lisbon, 1979): 7–55.

Kutzinski, Vera. "American Literary History as Spatial Practice." *American Literary History* 4.3 (Fall 1992): 550–557.

Laman, K. E. *Dictionnaire Kikongo-Français.* Ridgewood, NJ: Gregg, [1936, reproduction] 1985.

Laqueur, Thomas. *Making Sex: Body and Gender from the Greeks to Freud.* Cambridge: Harvard U P, 1990.

Lejeune, Phillipe. *Je est une autre.* Paris: Editions du Seuil, 1980.

Lewis, John Lowell. *Ring of Liberation: Deceptive Discourse in Brazilian Capoeira.* Chicago: U of Chicago P, 1992.

Lipsitz, George. *Dangerous Crossroads: Popular Music, Postmodernism, and the Poetics of Place.* New York: Verso, 1994.

López, Ana M. "Celluloid Tears: Melodrama in the Classic Mexican Cinema." *Iris* 13 (Summer 1991): 29–52.

——. "Are All Latins from Manhattan: Ethnicity and Colonialism in the Hollywood Cinema." In *Unspeakable Images.* Ed. Lester Friedman, 404–424. Champaign: U of Illinois P, 1991.

——. "Tears and Desire: Women and Melodrama in the Old Mexican Cinema." In *Mediating Two Worlds: Cinematic Encounters in the Americas.* Ed. John King, Ana M. López, and Manuel Alvarado, 147–163. London: British Film Institute, 1993.

——. *The New Latin American Cinema.* Urbana: U of Illinois P. Forthcoming.

López, Jorge Manuel. "El Giro." Interview. *El Diario* 24 (September 1993): 32.

Ludmer, Josefina. "Tretas del débil." In *La sartén por el mango.* Ed. Elena González and Eliana Ortega, 47–54. Rio Piedras: Ediciones Huracán, 1984.

——. *El género guachesco: Un tratado sobre la patria.* Buenos Aires: Editorial Sudamericana, 1988.

Mailloux, Steven. "Interpretation." In *Critical Terms for Literary Study.* Ed. Frank Lentricchia and Thomas McLaughlin, 121–134. Chicago: U of Chicago P, 1990.

Maldita Vecindad y Los Hijos del Quinto Patio. *Gira Pata de Perro.* BMG Ariola, 74321-177771-2, 1993.

Manrique, Jamie. "Manuel Puig: The Writer as Diva." *Christopher Street* (July 1993): 26.

Manuel, Peter. *Popular Musics of the Non-Western World.* Oxford: Oxford U P, 1988.

Marqués, René. "En la popa hay un cuerpo reclinado." In *Cuentos puertorriqueños de hoy,* 45–61. San Juan: Club del Libro de Puerto Rico, 1959.

——. *El puertorriqueño dócil y otros ensayos 1953–1971.* Río Piedras: Editorial Cultural, 1992.

Martel, Julián. *La bolsa.* Buenos Aires: Plus Ultra, 1975.

Martin, Emily. *The Woman in the Body: A Cultural Analysis of Reproduction.* Boston: Beacon, 1987.

Martínez, Rubén. *The Other Side.* New York: Verso, 1992.

Masten, Jeff. "My Two Dads: Collaboration and the Reproduction of Beaumont and Fletcher." In *Queering the Renaissance.* Ed. Jonathan Goldberg. Durham: Duke U P, 1993.

Matamoro, Blas. *Historia del tango.* Buenos Aires: Centro Editor, 1971.

Meléndez, Jorge. "Un futurista que no olvida sur raíces." *La Klave* 1.1 (September–October, 1988): 23.

Mercante, Victor. "El fetiquismo y uranismo femenino en los internados educativos." *Archivos de Psiquiatría y Criminología* 4 (Buenos Aires, 1905): 22–31.

Miller, D. A. *Place for Us: Essay on the Broadway Musical.* Cambridge: Harvard U P, forthcoming.

Mintz, Sidney. *Sweetness and Power: The Place of Sugar in Modern History.* New York: Penguin, 1985.

Mintz, Sidney W., and Richard Price. *An Anthropological Approach to the Afro-American Past.* ISHI Occasional Papers in Social Change 2. Philadelphia: Institute for the Study of Human Issues, 1976.

Modleski, Tania. "Femininity as Mas(s)querade: A Feminist Approach to Mass Culture." In *High Theory/Low Culture: Analysing Popular Television and Film.* Ed. Colin MacCabe, 37–52. New York: St. Martin's Press, 1985.

Mohanty, Chandra Talpade. "Cartographies of Struggle: Third World Women and the Politics of Feminism." In *Third World Women and the Politics of Feminism.* Ed. Chandra Talpade Mohanty, Ann Russo, and Lourdes Torres, 1–50. Bloomington: U of Indiana P, 1991.

Mohanty, Chandra Talpade, Ann Russo, and Lourdes Torres, eds. *Third World Women and the Politics of Feminism.* Bloomington: U of Indiana P, 1991.

Moliner, María. *Diccionario de uso del español.* Vol. H–Z. Madrid: Gredos, 1988.

Montalvo del Valle, Julio V. *Estudio psico-etnográfico de la música salsa en Puerto Rico.* San Juan: U of Puerto Rico P, 1978.

Moraga, Cherríe. *Loving in the War Years: Lo que nunca pasó por sus labios.* Boston: South End, 1983.

Mosse, George. *Nationalism and Sexuality: Middle-Class Morality and Sexual Norms in Modern Europe.* Madison: U of Wisconsin Press, 1988.

Moura, Jair. "Capoeiragem: Arte e malandragem." *Cadernos de Cultura* 2 (Salvador, 1980).

Naficy, Hamid. *The Making of Exile Cultures: Iranian Television in Los Angeles.* Minneapolis: U of Minnesota P, 1993.

Nasta, Shusheila, ed. *Motherlands: Black Women's Writing from Africa, the Caribbean and South Asia.* New Brunswick, NJ: Rutgers U P, 1992.

Navarro Gerassi, Marysa. *Los nacionalistas.* Buenos Aires: J. Alvarez, 1967.

Ness, Sally. *Body, Movement, and Culture: Kinesthetic and Visual Symbolism in a Philippine Community.* Philadelphia: U of Pennsylvania P, 1992.

Névarez, Angie. "Subversión, transformación, y rescritura: Acercamiento a la obra narrativa y poética de Rosario Ferré." Master's thesis. Emory U, 1989.

Newman, Kathleen. "National Cinema after Globalization: Fernando Solanas' *Sur* and the Exiled Nation." In *Mediating Two Worlds*. Ed. John King, Ana López, and Manuel Alvarado, 242–257. London: British Film Institute, 1993.

Noriega, Chon. *Chicanos and Film: Representation and Resistance*. Minneapolis: U of Minnesota P, 1992.

——. "Internal Others: Hollywood Narratives 'about' Mexican Americans." In *Mediating Two Worlds*. Ed. John King, Ana López, and Manuel Alvarado, 52–66. London: British Film Institute, 1993.

——. "El Hilo Latino: Representation, Identity, and National Culture." *Jump Cut* 38 (1993): 45–50.

Novak, Cynthia. *Sharing the Dance: Contact Improvisation and American Culture*. Madison: U of Wisconsin P, 1990.

Olalquiaga, Celeste. *Megalopolis: Contemporary Cultural Sensibilities*. Minneapolis: U of Minnesota P, 1992.

Ortiz, Adalberto. *Juyungo*. Trans. Susan F. Hill and Jonathan Tittler. Washington: Three Continents, [1943. Barcelona: Seix Barral, 1976] 1982.

Ortiz, Fernando. *Glosario de afronegrismos*. Havana: Siglo Veinte, 1924.

——. *Contrapunteo cubano del tabaco y el azucar*. Caracas: Biblioteca Ayacucho, 1978.

——. "Los cabildos afrocubanos." In *Ensayos etnograficos*. Ed. Miguel Barnet and Angel L. Fernandez. Havana: Editorial de Ciencias Sociales, 1984.

Pacini Hernández, Deborah. "Crossing Over: Dominican Bachata in the 1990s." Paper presented at International Association for the Study of Popular Music conference, Havana, Cuba, October 1994.

——. *Bachata: A Social History of a Dominican Popular Music*. Philadelphia: Temple U P, 1995.

Palés Matos, Luis. "Majestad negra." In *Tuntún de pasa y grifería*. In *Poesia*. Vol. 1 of *Obras (1914–1959)*. Ed. Margot Arve de Vazquez. San Juan: Instituto de Cultural Puertorriqueña y Editorial de la Universidad de Puerto Rico, [1937] 1984.

——. *Tún tún de pasa y grifería*, 2d ed. Ed. Mercedes López-Baralt. San Juan: Instituto de Cultura Puertorriqueña y Editorial de la Universidad de Puerto Rico, [1950] 1993.

Paranaguá, Paulo Antonio. *Cinema na América Latina: Longe de Deus e Perto de Hollywood*. Porto Alegre: L&PM Editores, 1984.

Parker, Andrew, Mary Russo, Doris Sommer, and Patricia Yaeger, eds. *Nationalisms and Sexualities*. New York: Routledge, 1992.

Pastinha, Mestre Vicente Ferreira. *Capoeira Angola*.

Patton, Cindy. "Embodying Subaltern Memory: Kinesthesia and the Problematics of Gender and Race." In *The Madonna Connection: Representational Politics, Subcultural Identities, and Cultural Theory*. Ed. Cathy Schwichtenberg, 81–106. Boulder: Westview, 1993.

Pedreira, Antonio. *Insularismo*. Río Piedras: Editorial Edil, 1992.

Peiss, Kathy. *Cheap Amusements: Working Women and Leisure in Turn of the Century New York.* Philadelphia: Temple U P, 1986.

Pereda, Rosa María. *Guillermo Cabrera Infante.* Madrid: EDAF, 1979.

Pérez, Emma. "Sexuality and Discourse: Notes from a Chicana Survivor." In *Chicana Lesbians: The Girls Our Mothers Warned Us About.* Ed. Carla Trujillo. Berkeley: Third Woman Press, 1991.

Pérez Firmat, Gustavo. *The Cuban Condition: Translation and Identity in Modern Cuban Literature.* Cambridge: Cambridge U P, 1989.

——. *Life on the Hyphen: The Cuban-American Way.* Austin: U of Texas P, 1994.

——, ed. *Do the Americas Have a Common Literature?* Durham: Duke U P, 1990.

Pérez Perazzo, Alberto. *Ritmo afrohispano antillano: 1865–1965.* Caracas: Publicaciones Almacenadoras, 1988.

Pesce, Rubén. *La historia del tango.* Buenos Aires: Corregidor, 1977.

Pettit, Arthur G. *Images of the Mexican American in Fiction and Film.* College Station: Texas A & M P, 1980.

Phelan, Peggy. *Unmarked: The Politics of Performance.* New York: Routledge, 1993.

Picó, Fernando. *Historia general de Puerto Rico.* Río Piedras: Huracán-Academia, 1986.

Piedra, José. "Through Blues." In *Do the Americas Have a Common Literature?* Ed. Gustavo Pérez-Firmat, 107–129. Durham: Duke U P, 1990.

Pietri, Pedro. *Obituario puertorriqueño/Puerto Rican Obituary.* Trans. A. Matilla Rivas. San Juan: Instituto de Cultura Puertorriqueña, 1977.

Podalsky, Laura. "Negotiating Differences: National Cinema and Co-Productions in Pre-Revolutionary Cuba." In *Cuban Cinemas and Imperfect Subjects.* Ed. Ambrosio Fornet and Ana M. López. Forthcoming.

Pratt, Mary Louise. *Imperial Eyes: Travel Writing and Transculturation.* New York: Routledge, 1992.

Preminger, Alex. *Princeton Encyclopedia of Poetry and Poetics.* Princeton: Princeton U P, 1974.

Primer censo de la república argentina. Buenos Aires: Imprenta del Porvenir, 1872.

Puig, Manuel. *El beso de la mujer araña.* Barcelona: Seix Barral, 1976.

Quilligan, Maureen. *The Language of Allegory: Defining the Genre.* Ithaca: Cornell U P, 1979.

Quintero Rivera, Angel Guillermo. "La música puertorriqueña y la contra-cultura democrática: Espontaneidad libertaria de la herencia cimarrona." *Folklore Americano* 49 (January–June 1990): 135–167.

——. "El soneo salsero." *Claridad,* 22–28 June 1990, 20–21.

Ramos, Julio, ed. *Amor y anarquía: Los escritos de Luisa Capetillo.* Río Piedras: Edición Huracán, 1992.

Ramos Mejía, José María. *Las multitudes argentinas.* Buenos Aires: Felix Lajouane, 1898.

——. *Los simuladores del talento en las luchas por la personalidad y la vida.* Buenos Aires: Felix Lajouane, 1904.

Ramsaye, Terry. *A Million and One Nights.* New York: Simon and Schuster, 1926.

Random House Dictionary of the English Language, unabridged ed., 1967.

Rego, Waldeloir. *Capoeira angola.* Salvador: Editora Itapua, 1968.

Reighley, Kurt B. "Rainbow Rock." *Paper* (September 1994): 27.

Rev. of *The Mambo Kings Play Songs of Love,* by Oscar Hijuelos. *The American Review* 18.1 (1990): 113.

Richard, Alfred Charles, Jr. *The Hispanic Image on the Silver Screen: An Interpretative Filmography from Silents into Sound, 1895–1935.* New York: Greenwood, 1992.

Roberts, John Storm. *Black Music of Two Worlds.* New York: Praeger, 1972.

Rodriguez Juliá, Edgardo. *El entierro de Cortijo.* Rio Piedras: Editorial Huracán, 1985.

Román, David. " 'It's My Party and I'll Die If I Want To!': Gay Men, AIDS, and the Circulation of Camp in U.S. Theatre." *Theatre Journal* 44 (1992): 305–327.

——. "Performing All Our Lives: AIDS, Performance, Community." In *Critical Theory and Performance.* Ed. Janelle Reinelt and Joseph Roach. Ann Arbor: U of Michigan P, 1993.

——. "Teatro Viva!': Latino Performance and the Politics of AIDS in Los Angeles." In *Entiendes?: Hispanic Writings/Queer Readings.* Ed. Emilie Bergmann and Paul Julian Smith, 346–369. Durham: Duke U P, 1995.

Rondón, César Miguel. *El libro de la salsa: Crónica de la música del Caribe urbano.* Caracas: Editorial Arte, 1980 [1985].

Rose, Phyllis. *Jazz Cleopatra: Josephine Baker in Her Time.* New York: Doubleday, 1989.

Ross, Andrew, and Tricia Rose, eds. *Microphone Fiends.* New York: Routledge, 1994.

Rouse, Roger. "Mexican Migration and the Social Space of Postmodernism." *Diaspora* (Spring 1991): 272.

Rowe, William, and Vivian Schelling. *Memory and Modernity: Popular Culture in Latin America.* London: Verso, 1991.

Sábato, Ernesto. "Estudio preliminar." In *El tango.* Ed. Horacio Salas, 11–19. Buenos Aires: Planeta, 1986.

Salas, Horacio, ed. *El tango.* Buenos Aires: Planeta, 1986.

Saldívar, Ramón. *Chicano Narrative: The Dialectics of Difference.* Madison: U of Wisconsin P, 1990.

"¡Salsa!." *Claridad,* 22–28 June 1990, 20–21.

"¡Salsa!" *Avance,* 20 August 1973, 10–17.

Sandoval, Alberto. "*A Chorus Line:* Not Such a 'One Singular Sensation' for Puerto Rican Crossovers." *Ollantay Theatre* 1.1 (1993): 46–61.

——. "Staging AIDS: What's Latino Got to Do with It?" In *Negotiating Performance: Gender, Sexuality, and Theatricality in Latin/o America.* Ed. Diana Taylor and Juan Villegas, 49–66. Durham: Duke U P, 1994.

——. "A Puerto Rican Reading of the 'America' in *West Side Story.*" *Jump Cut* 39 (1994): 59–66.

Schwichtenberg, Cathy, ed. *The Madonna Connection: Representational Politics, Subcultural Identities, and Cultural Theory.* Boulder: Westview, 1993.

Sedgwick, Eve Kosofsky. *Between Men: English Literature and Male Homosocial Desire.* New York: Columbia U P, 1985.

——. *Epistemology of the Closet.* Berkeley: U of California P, 1990.

Segundo censo de la republica argentina. Buenos Aires: Imprenta del Porvenir, 1873.

Shewey, Don, ed. *Out Front: Contemporary Gay and Lesbian Plays.* New York: Grove, 1988.

Slobin, Mark. *Subcultural Sounds: Micromusics of the West.* Hanover: Wesleyan U P, 1993.

Smith-Rosenberg, Carroll. *Disorderly Conduct: Visions of Gender in Victorian America.* New York: Knopf, 1985.

Snow, Shauna. "The Morning Report: 'Se Habla Español.' " *Los Angeles Times,* 2 December 1994, 1F.

Soja, Edward. *Postmodern Geographies.* New York: Verso, 1989.

Solá, María M., ed. *Julia de Burgos: Yo misma fui mi ruta.* Río Piedras: Edición Huracán, 1986.

Solberg, Carl. *Immigration and Nationalism: Argentina and Chile. 1890–1914.* Austin: U of Texas P, 1970.

Sommer, Doris. "Foundational Fictions: When History Was Romance in Latin America." *Salmagundi* 82–83 (Spring–Summer 1989): 111–141.

——. *Foundational Fictions: The National Romances of Latin America.* Berkeley: U of California P, 1991.

Sosa Rodríguez, Enrique. *Los ñañigos.* Havana: Casa de las Americas, 1982.

Stallybrass, Peter, and Allon White. *The Politics & Poetics of Transgression.* Ithaca: Cornell U P, 1986.

Stearns, Marshall. *The Story of Jazz.* New York: New American Library, 1958.

Stilman, Eduardo. *Historia del tango.* Buenos Aires: Brújald, 1965.

Strauss, Gloria B. "Dance and Ideology in China, Past and Present: A Study of Ballet in the People's Republic." In *Dance Research Annual 8, Asian and Pacific Dance: Selected Papers from the 1974 CORD-SEM Conference.* Ed. Adrienne L. Kaeppler, Judy Van Zile, and Carl Wolz, 19–54. New York: CORD, 1974.

Sturken, Marita. "Conversations with the Dead: Bearing Witness in the AIDS Memorial Quilt." *Socialist Review* 2 (1992): 65–95.

Tallon, José Sebastián. *El tango en sus etapas de música prohibida.* Buenos Aires: Instituto Amigos del Libro, 1964.

Taussig, Michael. *The Nervous System.* New York: Routledge, 1992.

Thompson, Robert Farris. *Flash of the Spirit: African and Afro-American Art and Philosophy.* New York: Vintage Books, 1984.

——. *Capoeira.* New York: The Capoeira Foundation, 1988.

Todorov, Tzvetan. *The Fantastic: A Structural Approach to a Literary Genre.* Trans. Richard Howard. Ithaca: Cornell U P, 1973.

Tutuola, Amos. *The Palm-Wine Drinkard.* New York: Grove, 1984.

"Uncle Sambo, Mad for Mambo." *Life,* 20 December 1954, 14–19.

Valle Ferrer, Norma. *Luisa Capetillo: Historia de una mujer proscrita.* Río Piedras: Editorial Cultural, 1990.

Valverde, Umberto. *Celia Cruz: Reina rumba.* Mexico: Editorial Universo, 1982.

Vázquez Millares, Angel, ed. *Danzón.* Havana: Coordinación Provincial de la Habana, 1970.

Vega, Bernardo. *Memoirs of Bernardo Vega: A Contribution to the History of the Puerto Rican Community in New York.* Ed. César Andreu Iglesias. Trans. Juan Flores. New York: Monthly Review Press, 1984.

Ventura, Michael. "The DNA of Pop." *Pulse!* November 1994, 55.

Veyga, Francisco de. "La inversión sexual adquirida." *Archivos de Criminología y Psiquiatría* 2 (Buenos Aires, 1903): 193–208.

——. "El sentido moral y la conducta de los invertidos." *Archivos de Psiquiatría Criminología* 3 (Buenos Aires, 1904): 22–30.

Vezzetti, Hugo. *La locura en la argentina.* Buenos Aires: Paidós, 1985.

Vieira, João Luiz. "A chanchada e o cinema Carioca (1930–1955)." In *História do cinema brasileiro.* Ed. Fernão Ramos. São Paulo: Art Editora, 1987.

Welsch, Janice, Linda Dittmar, and Diane Carson, eds. *Feminist Film Criticism.* U of Minnesota P, 1993.

Whitburn, Joel. *The Billboard Book of Top 40 Hits.* New York: Billboard Books, 1989.

Whitmore, George. *Someone Was Here: Profiles in the AIDS Epidemic.* New York: New American Library, 1988.

Williams, Sherley Anne. "The Blues Roots of Contemporary Afro-American Poetry." In *Chants of the Saints.* Ed. Michael S. Harper and Robert B. Stepto, 124. Chicago: U of Illinois P, 1979.

——. "The House of Desire." In *Black Sister: Poetry by Black American Women 1746–1980.* Ed. Erline Stetson, 46. Bloomington: Indiana U P, 1981.

Woll, Allen. *The Latin Image in American Film.* Los Angeles: UCLA Latin American Center Publications, 1980.

——. "How Hollywood Has Portrayed Hispanics." *New York Times,* 1 March 1981, D17, 22.

Yarbro-Bejarano, Yvonne. "The Female Subject in Chicano Theatre: Sexuality, 'Race,' and Class." In *Performing Feminisms: Feminist Critical Theory and Theatre.* Ed. Sue-Ellen Case, 131–149. Baltimore: Johns Hopkins U P, 1990.

——. "Deconstructing the Lesbian Body." In *Chicana Lesbians: The Girls Our Mothers Warned Us About.* Ed. Carla Trujillo. Berkeley: Third Woman Press, 1991.

Yoshikawa, Yoko. "The Heat Is on *Miss Saigon* Coalition: Organizing across Race and Sexuality." In *The State of Asian American Activism and Resistance in the 1990s.* Ed. Karin Aguilar-San Juan, 275–294. Boston: South End, 1993.

Yúdice, George. "Postmodernity and Transnational Capital in Latin America." In *On Edge: The Crisis of Contemporary Latin American Culture.* Ed. George Yúdice, Jean Franco, and Juan Flores, 1–28. Minneapolis: U of Minnesota P, 1992.

Yúdice, George, Jean Franco, and Juan Flores, eds. *On Edge: The Crisis of Contemporary Latin American Culture.* Minneapolis: U of Minnesota P, 1992.

Index

Contributors

Barbara Browning is an associate professor of performance studies at New York University. She has studied, taught, and performed Brazilian dance in the United States, Brazil, and Europe, and is the author of *Samba: Resistance in Motion* (Indiana U P, 1995).

Celeste Fraser Delgado is an assistant professor of English at Penn State University. Her work on transnational cultural studies has appeared in *Cultural Critique* and in the *Latin American Literary Review.*

Jane C. Desmond teaches American studies and women's studies at the University of Iowa. She has also worked as a professional choreographer and performer. Her work on media and performance has appeared in *Signs, Cultural Studies, Visual Anthropology,* and *East/West Film Journal,* among others. She is the editor of a collection of new dance criticism called *Meaning in Motion* (1997).

José Esteban Muñoz is an assistant professor in performance studies at Tisch School of the Arts, New York University. He has published articles on race and sexuality in *Screen, TDR,* and *GCQ,* and in several critical anthologies. He is coeditor of *Pop Out: Queer Warhol* (1996) and author of *Disidentifications* (forthcoming).

Josh Kun is a graduate student in ethnic studies in the English Department at the University of California, Berkeley.

Ana M. López is an associate professor in communications at Tulane University. Her writings on Latin American film have appeared in *Wide Angle, Cinema Journal,* and *Studies in Latin American Popular Culture.* She is the co-editor of *The Ethnic Eye: Latino Media Arts* (1996), and *Mediating Two Worlds: Cinematic Encounters in the Americas* (1993).

Gustavo Pérez Firmat is a poet and professor in romance studies at Duke University. His work includes *Next Year in Cuba: A Cuban Emigre Comes of Age in America* (1995); *Bilingual Blues* (1995); *Life on the Hyphen: The Cuban-American Way* (1994); *Do the Americas Have a Common Literature?* (1990); and *The Cuban Condition* (1989).

José Piedra is a professor of Spanish at Cornell University. His writings on Afro-Hispanic literature and culture have appeared in *New Literary History* and *American Literature.*

Augusto C. Puleo is an assistant professor of Spanish at Columbia University.

Juan Carlos Quintero Herencia is a poet and assistant professor at the University of Puerto Rico. His work has appeared in *Nómada* and *Híspamerica.*

David Román is an assistant professor at the University of California, Los Angeles. He has published on queer and Latino theater in *American Literature, Ollantay, Theatre-Journal, Women and Performance,* and *Camp Grounds: Style and Homosexuality.*

Jorge Salessi is an associate professor in Spanish at the University of Pennsylvania.

Alberto Sandoval teaches theater and Latino literature. His work on Latinidad, AIDS, and theater has appeared in *American Literature, Ollantay, Revista Iberoamericana,* and *Women and Performance.*

Mayra Santos Febres is a poet and assistant professor in Spanish at the University of Puerto Rico. Her work has appeared in *Cupey,* and her poetry appears in anthologies of Caribbean literature.